Sketches Of Hackett
The Steve Hackett Biography

Sketches Of Hackett
The Steve Hackett Biography

Alan Hewitt

WYMER PUBLISHING
Bedford, England

First published in Great Britain in 2009
by Wymer Publishing
PO Box 155, Bedford, MK40 2YX
www.wymerpublishing.co.uk
Tel: 01234 326691

Copyright © 2009 Alan Hewitt / Wymer Publishing.
This edition published 2011.

ISBN 978-1-908724-01-4

Edited by Jerry Bloom with assistance by Sarah Dean.

The Author hereby asserts his rights to be identified
as the author of this work in accordance with sections
77 to 78 of the Copyright, Designs & Patents Act 1988.

All rights reserved. No part of this publication may be
reproduced or transmitted in any form or by any means,
electronic or mechanical, including photocopying, or any
information storage and retrieval system, without written
permission from the publisher.

This publication is sold subject to the condition that it shall not,
by way of trade or otherwise, be lent, re-sold, hired out or
otherwise circulated without the publisher's prior consent in any
form of binding or cover other than that in which it is published
and without a similar condition including this condition
being imposed on the subsequent purchaser.

Every effort has been made to trace the copyright holders of the
photographs in this book but some were unreachable. We would
be grateful if the photographers concerned would contact us.

Typesetting, layout and design by Richard Nagy.
www.myspace.com/richardnagy
Printed and bound by Lightning Source

A catalogue record for this book is available from the British Library.

Cover design by Richard Nagy.
Front over photograph © Alan Perry. www.concertphotos.uk.com

CONTENTS

vi	Foreword by Steve Hackett
vii	Introduction
1	Chapter 1: A Bed, A Chair & A Guitar
11	Chapter 2: On The Road To A Less Than Quiet World
16	Chapter 3: The Genesis Of A Guitarist
40	Chapter 4: The Acolyte Steps Out
47	Chapter 5: Ripples Never Come Back
61	Chapter 6: What A Carry On!
70	Chapter 7: Towards The Spectral Morning
79	Chapter 8: The Defector Speaks Out
84	Chapter 9: Taking The Cure
90	Chapter 10: Taking The Long Way To The Camino Royale Via The Bay Of Kings
101	Chapter 11: Tuning The GTR
109	Chapter 12: Gaining Momentum
116	Chapter 13: There Are Many Sides To Steve Hackett
122	Chapter 14: Revisiting The Past
128	Chapter 15: A Midsummer's Nightmare In Darktown
135	Chapter 16: Impressionistic Feedback
144	Chapter 17: Sunshine After The Rain
149	Chapter 18: This Vast Life
164	Chapter 19: Paying Tribute
167	Chapter 20: Out Of The Tunnel's Mouth
176	Chapter 21: Squackett And Other Tales Of Mythology
179	Chapter 22: Exploring The Shrouded Horizon
184	Appendix 1: Encounters With Hackett
190	Appendix 2: Album By Album
212	Appendix 3: Collecting Hackett
217	Appendix 4: Discography
226	Appendix 5: Filmography
236	Appendix 6: Unofficial Recordings
260	Appendix 7: Genesis Gigs 1971-77
278	Appendix 8: Solo Gigs 1978-2012
306	Appendix 9: Chronology
310	Appendix 10: Bibliography And Other Source Material
314	Acknowledgements
318	About The Author
320	Index

Foreword

Alan and I first met at a backstage interview almost a hundred years ago. I had the impression that something akin to Beatles humour was alive and well in this irrepressible Liverpudlian. In fact if you closed your eyes you could swear you were talking to one of them.

I was obviously encountering a fan, sage and dry wit, all rolled into one. Many moons later, like all the villages that joined together to eventually become London, a host of separate interviews organically coalesced into the central idea of a book. I think Alan may have been writing this book by stealth, plying the unwary interviewee on numerous occasions with doughnuts and copious quantities of uncontrolled substances such as tea and biscuits.

It's a testament to Alan's staying power that throughout all the changes of musical style I've inflicted upon him over the years, he's remained an avid listener and more importantly a close friend. I figured if Alan could handle the occasional anomaly, then it was highly likely other listeners might also be able to understand my enthusiasm for the odd archaic classical tunesmith. Good music lasts. It also haunts you even when you try to forget… I've found you just have to honour it.

Nostalgia isn't what it used to be. Recollections may be hazy. One interview led to my mother and many other parties who may have been insufficiently bribed. Or if you prefer, two mates talking unguardedly about life's ups and downs, featuring many demented characters, often mistaken for deities (it's an easy mistake to make in the music business). Elvis has definitely left the building, but our applause, like his truth, rings on and on.

Thanks Alan, I know you had to keep your helmet on from time to time during the process, but you ought to be commended for bravery in undertaking the task of making sense of my verbal ramblings. The pen is often mightier than the plectrum… Well done, Alan, and thanks for all your energy and honesty.

Captain's log Stardate 12 January 2009 "Now where did I put that Alan key? And what exactly is the status on that Mutron By-Phaser… Spock where are you?"

Introduction

Steve Hackett... The very name conjures up a myriad of different images. To many, it is the picture (often grainy and in black and white) of an earnest young man, face obscured by thick rimmed glasses and a heavy growth of face fungus (that's a beard and moustache to the uninitiated!) sat in a chair hunched over his guitar in an almost protective manner. To others it is the creator of ethereal soundscapes dressed as a peripatetic gypsy, clad in flowing shirt and knee length boots a-la Ritchie Blackmore - although certainly more modest!

To many others the name is synonymous with the "Classic" line-up of the English rock band Genesis with whom he carved a formidable reputation for studio creativity and live excellence during the period 1971 to 1977, which many still see as Genesis' "Golden Age". In August of that year, Steve bravely walked out of the Genesis "machinery" in favour of a solo career, which was seen at the time as a suicidal decision. Genesis was on the verge of the Big Time and here was Steve turning his back on it all.

His career, both before and during his time with Genesis will be examined in this book, along with the rest of his incredible solo career, which has now spanned over thirty years and almost as many albums. This is the first book that Steve has authorised to chronicle his career as a performing artist and creator of some of the most original music ever to be penned and performed, which is amazing in itself.

What does the name "Steve Hackett" conjure up for me, the author? Well... I have followed Steve's performing career since he first went solo on stage in 1978 although by then I was already aware of the legacy of his Genesis years but sadly had never seen him with that band. Since then however, I have seen just about every live incarnation that Steve has gone under and his dedication to his craft and his determination to "struggle beyond existing stagnant musical forms" has been an inspiration to me as a non musician obsessed with music and also to a host of other musicians Steve's friendship to me personally has also been a great source of encouragement and this is my attempt at a thank you for that from one friend to another.

Biographies are that most difficult of beasts to write, especially when, like me, you are not a professional writer! I would therefore, prefer to think of this not as your traditional biography, more as a series of thumbnail sketches of parts of the life of our hero - maybe that is why this project has been called "Sketches Of Hackett"? It will take someone with far more perspicacity and talent than I have to unravel the essential contradictions that are: Mr Stephen Richard Hackett.

If you are expecting a rattling good selection of salacious tittle-tattle and scuttlebutt, then this book is not for you. This is Steve's story told in his own words and those of many of the people closest to him. The opinions expressed here may not always tally with received wisdom, nor indeed will they always make comfortable reading. Nonetheless they reflect the opinions and knowledge of people who know what they are talking about because they were "there" so to speak.

If you are expecting a musicologist's analysis of Steve's finest chord progressions, then look elsewhere too. I hope that what is contained here will serve as a useful beginning and guide and will give some insight into the man whose work has inspired such admiration among his peers and such fierce and loyal devotion among his fans; the "Hacketteers" of whom I am proud to count myself as one.

Alan Hewitt
Liverpool, January 2009

CHAPTER ONE
A Bed, A Chair, And A Guitar

The Britain of 1950 was a particularly austere place. A mere five years had passed since the end of the most dreadful conflict mankind had ever witnessed which saw many things go down to irretrievable ruin. The British Empire, on which the sun never set, had finally and irrevocably begun to break up.

Britain herself was a pale shadow, financially broken by the wartime efforts and now facing an uncertain future on the world stage. Although the war was over, rationing was still in force and most people struggled to make a decent living. It was into this uncertain world that Stephen Richard Hackett was born in University Hospital London on 12th February 1950. His parents; Peter and June had, like so many other couples at that time, married young and were to strive to bring up their young son in a world altogether more uncertain than the one they had grown up in.

It is a strange irony that within a twelve-month period between February 1950 and December 1951 all of the key players in a drama, in which Steve was to play a large part later in life, were all born. A mere day separates his birthday and that of Peter Gabriel. Tony Banks was born on 27th March that year while Mike Rutherford was born in October 1950. Phil Collins and Anthony Phillips were born in January and December of 1951 respectively. Fate was to play a large part in the "Genesis" of that group of individuals and it will figure largely, later in our story.

There was already a legacy of musical and other talent in Steve's family. Steve's father Peter was always knocking out a tune on the guitar or harmonica and would always experiment with instruments as Steve recalls: "My dad was musical... he played the bugle in the Boy's Brigade and he played the clarinet... my mum always said he was 'learning' the clarinet (laughs). He could certainly in later years play a few chords on the guitar.

The thing I picked up from him was the mouth organ; harmonica and he played both. My mother's father played harmonica as well and it seems that previous generations, my grandmother's family, her father was a bugler as well".

There was also talent on his mother's side with a Comedienne called Saxon Davis, a well-known act on the British Music Hall circuit as Steve's mother recalls: "On both my mother's side and my father's side. My mother's father was a drummer and bugler in the regular army so that's that side. My father's people were minor showbiz people. Music Hall people: "Saxon" Davis - her name was Rose but she had long blonde hair, so she was called "Saxon" Davis. We used to go and see her; I was about six and we would go back stage. I thought it was wonderful with the stage and the makeup. All my father's family including Uncle Ron who played guitar and Cecil who was always known as "Titch", he was a natural performer; he was always telling jokes and they always used to stage their own pantomimes at Christmas. My grandmother was one of those wonderful ladies who were always in the kitchen always cooking up scones and stuff. When I look back at it, it was a very small house but it was always full of people. My dad loved music; he liked people such as Richard Tauber and played the harmonica, which of course was where Steve learned it. He used to play the spoons as well so we grew up appreciating music.

I remember Steve telling me once that when he heard a beautiful piece of music when he was a little boy he couldn't look at people because it was like looking into his soul and I understood that, because I felt the same. If I heard a piece of music on the radio I wanted to go away and listen to it on my own. So that was our beginnings; my sister had a very pretty singing voice and she won a talent contest at Butlins!" (Laughs).

Into this atmosphere of talent Steve would be nurtured. This was still the pre-television era where radio was king and where you made your own entertainment, so anyone with a musical gift was encouraged to "do a turn" to entertain family and friends. The 1950's were a very different musical environment to today, the era of the Crooner and musicals. Artists such as Mario Lanza were the staples of the day and the advent of what we now call rock 'n' roll was still several years away. Steve's mother June also recalls how she met his father: "We used to go to the dances in Lower Regent Street. The Harriers dances were always the best. I was seventeen and there was this very good looking paratrooper and the friends who he was with, one of the girls excused the guy I was dancing with and then Peter came and asked me (laughs). Whether it was a pre-arranged thing I don't know. He was so good looking; he was gorgeous and so gentle. We had no money but we got by and then Steve came along."

Steve's early years were spent in the shadow of a then still fully functional Battersea Power Station, not then the artistic image on a record sleeve that it later became,* but an almost sentient beast which he vividly recalls: "We moved to a housing estate called Churchill Gardens which is absolutely opposite the Battersea Power Station and that was the view from my bedroom window. I spent a lot of time; especially at night gazing at that thing and seeing the neon lights snaking across the water of the Thames. I found it a fascinating view."

The musical influences which were to shape Steve's later development were nothing if not varied and eclectic: The Blues, orchestral and Classical music, Country and Western all played their part in shaping the young Hackett and of course, like any self-respecting toddler; he was soon trying to emulate his parents. "My mother says I was already playing the harmonica at two years old and I think what she meant was that I was going suck-blow, but she says I was playing the same thing over and over again. She said; 'I can sing the tune' so she sang me this tune that she says I used to play but which I don't remember... but I do remember at the age of three or four one day being able to play three or four tunes and suddenly I had a repertoire (laughs). I think it was Oh Susannah; Scotland The Brave and it might have been God Save The Queen... I seem to remember that my dad and my grandfather tended to vamp quite a lot. There was a little bit of chords thrown into it and I think from a very early age I was trying to isolate single notes. It took me many years to figure out what it was that gave notes direction. What made them seem to go up or down; I realised many years later that thing was called 'chords' (laughs). I was a self-taught muso and it took me a long time for the penny to drop!" (Laughs).

Steve's mother, also recalls his early interest in music: "He was a very bright little baby even from a few weeks and in those days you stayed in hospital for two weeks after you gave birth and I had gone off to have a wash or something. When I came back they put him on my pillow ready for feeding and he was only a few days old but his eyes were everywhere. He was a very difficult baby, he hardly slept and there was me a young nineteen year old who didn't know what to do with a baby but we bought him a little upright piano. I think it was blue and he used to sit there and go plink, plink; he loved it. Then later on, as I said, my dad played harmonica and we bought Steve

---

*Battersea Power Station was used for the cover of Pink Floyd's 1977 album 'Animals'.

one of these little tiny harmonicas. I suppose he would have been about eighteen months old and he would stand in front of my dad fascinated while he played the harmonica. Then he would play a tune himself, now it was the same tune, so it was a tune, no big deal sort of thing (laughs). I was always working and my mum used to look after him during the week and she told a story of how he had this harmonica in a case and he took it out, did his little tune and then put it back! (laughs). Later on when he was five, he played Scotland The Brave on a bigger harmonica at a school concert. We always knew that he would be musical."

Much has been made of the sufferings of Steve's erstwhile compatriots in Genesis during their time at Charterhouse. Steve's schooldays were no bed of roses either and in many respects he has been just as much a "victim" of the British school system as any person "privileged" enough to inhabit a Public School. Always a quiet and to some extent, inward looking individual, school was not the pleasantest experience as he recalls: "School years, that was more difficult. No, they weren't the happiest days of my life. I remember school as being this terrible thing that we all had to put up with. I went to a school called St Gabriel's first of all and I still get a shudder when I think of it. Even now it is as if I might be invited to Dracula's castle again any minute! I think I had learnt to read before I went to school; or despite of school or whatever. It seemed to happen. There was a strange thing where as a kid I seemed to have a prodigious memory, and part of it was memorising things, part of it was reading... Luckily my mother realised that it would be better for me if I changed schools and I moved to another school within the same housing estate called Churchill Gardens School. I believe she has got two photos of me as a child; one while I was at the first school and one a year later. They are basically the same apart from the fact that in the first one my face is frowning; and the other one is a big smile."

Steve's introduction to the world of Classical music came from a quite unexpected source. Incapacity, physical or mental was still very much something that was frowned upon, hushed up and hidden in the Britain of the 1950's and Steve not only encountered this directly but also something that was to have a long lasting effect on his musical outlook: "There was this kid who lived on the Tatchbrook Estate where my grandmother lived. He had polio and he had really thin legs. The first time I was invited to his house was by a couple of other friends who said; 'he has got this really great piece of music'. He had this very dark room he was in and he showed me his legs, which were as thin as matchsticks. I had never seen anything like that. Then he put this thing on the wind up gramophone; it was Tchaikovsky's Piano

Concerto in B Flat Minor. I just remember the effect of that, everyone loving the music... You have got to imagine this boy in this room which was very, very dark and this was the only time I had been invited into his world which seemed very dark in the Fifties, drawn curtains and you seemed to be kept apart as if he might contaminate everybody."

The disparate sides of this period in Steve's life were to be examined much later in some of his most recent work even down to the influence of the artistic side of his own family as he admits, " My dad is very quiet but you can't forget my mum! She is a character and a tremendous extrovert. I have covered a few of the non-musical things but in a way this all colours everything for me because I look back on those things now and I think... 'But for this and but for that... perhaps that wouldn't have happened...' perhaps I wouldn't have been musical if I hadn't had the example of my father playing this..."

Aged five, Steve gained the extra fascination of a younger brother, John. " He was such a lovely brother to John," recalls June. "I had been in hospital for a while because I wasn't very well after John was born and when he first saw him I said; 'This is your brother' and Steve said; 'Oh mum, his little hands!' When John first started walking and Stephen would be sitting with his friends John would toddle in to the group and he would launch himself and Stephen would catch him! (Laughs). So Stephen always kind of looked out for him."

As for Steve's fascination with the guitar perhaps it can be attributed to the instrument, which his father brought back with him from Canada. The family, like so many others had opted to try their hand in another country, and when Steve was seven and his brother a mere two years of age; the family emigrated to Vancouver. Their sojourn there was to be a brief one. June did not take to life in Canada although for the older Hackett brother at least, it was quite an adventure: " Canada turned out to be a big mistake. My parents were in search of adventure (laughs) and a lot of their friends decided that they were going to emigrate to Canada. My father went ahead and got himself a job and got us a place. Then my mother, brother and myself went to Vancouver to meet him and we stayed there for four months. I even went to school there and that was fascinating for me as a child because I was seven at the time.

I loved Vancouver; it had a couple of beaches; a place called Jericho Beach and a place called Kitsano Drive... it had a shoreline and mountains ... it was extraordinary; kids had air rifles and they played Cowboys and Indians out the back. It seemed like we were in Cowboy and Indian Territory so it was great for a kid. My mother hated it and wanted to come back so we came back to England and my father stayed for an extra year paying off debts and he borrowed money to get back. That made quite a dent on the family."

June explains the idea behind the family's brief Canadian sojourn: "I was twenty seven years old and we had this very nice flat in Churchill Gardens. I was working and Peter was earning a bit more and we had quite a nice life I suppose. We had two friends and we got all caught up in this Canadian thing. The Suez Crisis (1956-57) worried me and also I wanted a bit of adventure, I had never even been abroad but suddenly life seemed to be… I was twenty-seven and I was thinking 'Is that it?' So we used to get together with these two friends; Peter and Betty Foxhall and we would say; 'We don't care if we live in a wigwam!' So off we went to Canada without giving a thought to both sides' grandparents taking their grandchildren away.

So Peter went first and got a job and eventually found a place to live. It was a basic thing called a Duplex, and we had left a really nice flat overlooking the Thames. On the ship I never saw Steve, he was seven years old and what a terrible mother I was! (Laughs) I was quite seasick; John was seasick, and Steve was off playing his harmonica to the crew! (Laughs) He used to come back with money and I suppose that was his first professional gig (laughs).

We had eight days on the ship before the Saint Lawrence Seaway and then we docked at Quebec and we got the train. We were five days on that and again Steve was always away because they had this observatory car with a dome on it and it was great, especially when you were going through the Rockies. He thoroughly enjoyed himself really. So, thirteen days of travel and then we got off at Vancouver Station and I thought;' I'm not going to like it here'. I knew straight away and I mustn't even think it. We had sold everything and we had nothing to come back to. So, as the days went on it became more and more obvious that I wasn't going to settle there. I suppose Peter might have done if I hadn't… but in those days I used to call the shots (laughs). I was very unhappy and I missed London and I think Londoners make the worst emigrants.

Then the lady whom we had met on the ship invited us to her home. She had taken cine film of London and when we saw the red buses we burst into tears (laughs). My sister came as well because we had never been apart and she'd had a strange romance really with the guy never making his mind up. The moment we got to Canada he started writing letters to her saying 'come back and let's get engaged' so she was kind of wanting to go back. We made plans to come back but it was very difficult because we didn't have any money to come back together. So I came back with the children and lived with Peter's mother and father who were very kind to me and very nice people.

It was very kind of them to put us up and then Peter came back and that was how I came to go to Liverpool because I went up and met him just two days before my sister got married. We had great difficulty finding anywhere to live because we had given up a council flat and the council didn't want to know about re-housing us. So we lived in a basement in Winchester Street and it was very difficult."

June also recalls another unlikely and amusing incident, which happened at their new home once they moved back to England: " That was where the rubbish bins were downstairs in the sort of courtyard and so anybody that came to visit was given a bag of rubbish to… on your way out… So, if I tell you that Peter Gabriel and Phil Collins took my bags of rubbish out (laughs) and a friend of mine who I worked with said; 'I wouldn't call them dustbins if I were you; call them poubelles (laughs). That's the honest truth whenever they used to come and rehearse in the flat I used to cook pans of chips and soup and stuff, and when they had finished and said they were going over to the pub, or sometimes they would call me in and ask 'what do you think?' so I like to think I have put my own two bits in…"

One good thing that emerged from their time in Canada was Steve's father's return with an instrument, which both Steve and John found extremely interesting as John recalls: "He (Steve) took up guitar because our dad brought one back from Canada, this huge guitar in this enormous case. Looking back on it now it was one of those guitars with strings a mile high (laughs) and a fret board… just about the most difficult thing to play. Steve took rather to that and then he bought an electric guitar or rather my parents got an electric guitar for him."

"It was far too big for me; I couldn't play the thing," concurs Steve. "By the time I was twelve I could just about do things on the two bass strings. I daren't venture forth on the other strings, far too confusing! (Laughs)"

Perhaps it is this early fascination with the instrument which later led to Steve's dad remarking that "You would be happy in life if all you had was a bed, a chair; and a guitar". He certainly realised that there was a certain degree of monetary gain to be had from performance at an early age as Steve remembers from his shipboard experiences: "I used to play harmonica all the time to people, whether they wanted it or not and then somebody said, 'why don't you take your cap and go round asking people for money while you're doing that'. And so I did, and people gave me their change. The funny thing was of course, arriving in Canada, you couldn't spend any of it! So I think somewhere in all that the idea dawned on me. The other thing is, at primary school I used to bet the kids that I could play God Save The Queen through my nose (laughs) on the mouth organ. They would say; 'bet you can't' and I used to bet them money and win! (Laughs) I think there were complaints from parents after a while and I had to stop because I was making too much money at it (laughs)".

There was a certain amount of chicanery, which young Master Hackett employed to get his musical way in those formative stages. Having cut his teeth figuratively and not literally on the basic harmonica model; it was not long before he realised, thanks to the theme of then TV favourite Dixon Of Dock Green* that something more was needed if he were to emulate the sounds he was hearing from the TV and on the radio. "I realised that in order to play stuff like that I needed an upgraded harmonica so I told my dad; I feel guilty about it even now. I said I wanted a push-button harmonica; a chromatic one, and he said to me; 'Do you think you will be able to handle that?' I said 'Oh yeah, so-and-so's dad has got one'. I lied but luckily for one Christmas; I think I was six; I got a chromatic one and all the extra notes I couldn't get before. It was a Hohner; it was red and silver I remember. I can still see it now. Some kids dream of shiny cars and engines and all that but this thing was my pride and joy. I remember waking up in the middle of the night on Christmas Eve and at three in the morning trying not to wake everyone up! (Laughs). I had to put it down and get off to sleep. God knows how, I was so excited!"

Steve struggled to cope with the return to life in England after his brief stay in the freer atmosphere of Canada. Returning with a slight Canadian accent and also already plagued with short-sightedness; life for a child wearing spectacles was no easier then than it is nowadays and life was tough for the young Hackett. He was however extremely fortunate to have the support not only of his mother and father, but also his grandparents from whom he received plenty of encouragement. Learning in a classroom full of noisy children was never going to be an easy option for any child and Steve struggled to cope. "In later years I got into a grammar school thanks to my father getting me through the Eleven Plus with his extra tuition, because I didn't really understand what was being taught. I found it very, very difficult being taught en-masse. I tend to have to ask a question a lot of times before it dawns on me... I started to think I was quite slow but at one point I was top of the class with this, that and the other."

One thing that he did excel at during his time at school was gymnastics. "I remember being at Grammar School and I suppose I was average at most

---

*Dixon of Dock Green was a popular BBC television series, which ran from 1955 to 1976, set in a suburban police station in the East End of London and concerned uniformed police engaged with routine tasks and low-level crime.

things and then I started getting interested in gymnastics. There was a young PE teacher whose name was John Bolland, he was almost like a Captain Kirk type; he was a young; fit good looking guy and he was able to do a handspring and a headspring so I thought…'That looks good!' (Laughs) I learned to do first a thing, which he called a backspring, which I doubt I can do anymore! I learned how to do all of them and I was quickly put into the school team and I absolutely loved doing that. I didn't weigh much; I didn't like school dinners and I used to sneak out and get a box of Cheeselets. I existed on starvation rations at the time but that didn't hinder my gymnastic career… That was a lot of fun and I did hours and hours of that."

Even if school in general wasn't holding much appeal for him, Steve was at least opening his eyes up to the events of the moment: "Somewhere in the consciousness while they were grooming us for jobs in the Civil Service, which I found terribly boring, bands like The Shadows appeared, pre-Beatles. I was aware that something was going on which was very exciting".

Fortunately for Steve, not only were his parents supportive but his grandparents were equally so. "I spent a lot of time with both sets of grandparents and they worked very hard to make things possible for my mother and me and my brother. My mother's mother re-married and her husband; Charles Dawson was a big music fan. He used to tell me stories as he came in from his late shift at Fords (then one of the UK's leading car manufacturers). He had all these stories about his childhood and I found it fascinating especially how tough it was, how they had to go without any shoes. It sounded as terrifying as anything in a Dickens novel. It was extraordinary hearing about his early life and experiences in the army and he told me about Dunkirk and how he had been involved with that; clearing a munitions dump and how a bomb had gone off … I think he had a very tough war by all accounts and he managed to get away from Dunkirk unscathed but I think it was a very close call. He was a fascinating character and in many was a big kid himself. I have such a picture of that previous time as told to me through his eyes. He was my connection to history."

Both sets of grand parents had their fair share of experiences from both the First and Second World Wars. In fact Steve's grandfather on his father's side had been mentioned in despatches in the Great War and as an ARP warden had been commended for bravery in the Blitz in the Second World War. Steve's father also served with the Paratroop forces in Palestine at the end of the British Mandate prior to the creation of the State of Israel in 1948 (sharing something in common with the author's father who also served as a soldier in that theatre of operations). All of these individuals contributed to shaping the character of the young Hackett and to providing him with a vast wellspring of ideas to draw upon later in life.

Steve eventually left school and undertook a series of menial desk-bound office jobs mainly because he wanted to get away from school and into the real world. Ironically, his first proper job was with the Local Government Examination Board; hardly an auspicious start for an aspiring rock star. "I left school at sixteen. I didn't want to go on to university, I wanted to get out into the world and get into a band. Meanwhile, I had nearly five years of mainly desk jobs. The first job I joined as a Junior Officer or some such title. You were basically a dog's body. They ran three types of examination for the Armed Services; the police; and ambulance service and the Examinations Board was concerned mainly I think with cataloguing papers from those three services. Most of it was just parcelling things up and counting "Fs" and "Ps" "Fails" and "Passes". It was a fairly grim sort of filing clerk's job. The first of many grim jobs like that."

Not everything was quite so depressing though, as he recalls: "With the day jobs, I had a little pal who was a real entrepreneur and when he couldn't make certain jobs he used to have me depping for him so that included flower selling, working at the fun fair; carrying cases for people between Victoria coach and railway station and it felt great to be out there doing these kind of open air jobs. Then when I left school at sixteen yes they were crashingly boring and there were moments when I would sit down and try to write out a riff or a short story, anything to keep the creative spark going in case I got incarcerated forever within those walls! (Laughs)

CHAPTER TWO

On The Road To A Less Than Quiet World

Growing up in an artistic and musical family, it was only to be expected that Steve would soon begin exploring the world of gigs. The period of Steve's teenage years coincided with the explosion of musical experimentation that groups such as The Beatles, The Byrds, The Beach Boys, Pink Floyd and The Rolling Stones spearheaded. Alongside that, was the burgeoning British Blues boom driven by John Mayall and the fledgling Fleetwood Mac. It was these bands that Steve cut his gigging teeth with. "I started to see a succession of Blues bands and used to like to see John Mayall. In 1966 I saw John Mayall and the Paul Butterfield Blues band, which was knockout. Paul Butterfield was, and still is to my mind, the finest of all Blues harmonica players. He had a band that was half white and half black. I have no doubt that the candle was handed on to him for that single fact. It seems to me that something smiled down on him from on high and he just had the most amazing harmonica style and harmonica tone".

Suitably inspired by seeing performances by such alumni as these; it was not long before Steve began to aspire to performance himself as an escape from the tedium of working life. Like so many before him and indeed since; he soon discovered that the path to fame and fortune in the music business was not going to be an easy one. "I was trying to get stuff off the ground for a very long time and we would do the occasional gig at the odd cricket ground or on a pleasure boat going up the Thames. They were the kind of gigs where two or three people might turn up and sometimes it would be a hundred and none of them had bothered to check out what the band was like! (Laughs) I guess we were pretty rough and there was a lot of enthusiasm and cutting our teeth on it.

We would have included a fair amount of Paul Butterfield material and most of that was covers of other people's material; stuff like Spoonful and something called Loving Cup. We did numbers by The Byrds; probably Mr Tambourine Man and there was this track called Feel A Whole Lot Better which had the same guitar riff in it as Needles And Pins. I had a solid body twelve string and so I could do my Roger McGuinn bit in those days. I seem to recall that I got talked into doing Nights In White Satin quite a lot (laughs). There was a singer called Dave Thompson who was very good and had a really great voice. Funnily enough I was doing a lot of Country stuff and a mate of mine was into that although he was more into Elvis and he was a bit older than me and we recorded quite a bit of stuff."

It was during this period that Steve's first romantic adventure went wrong. Very much a case of puppy love, Steve's first girlfriend; Barbara became a casualty of the Sixties' drug culture and an addict and later suffered from schizophrenia as a result of her addiction. Even to this day, Steve regrets that he didn't do more to help her although what he could have done beyond the support he gave her at the time; is anyone's guess. The Sixties were an incredibly liberated period but also an incredibly naïve one too. Drug culture may well have "freed" the mind but in many cases that same freedom inevitably led to destruction. Freedom without responsibility is nothing more than dictatorship under a different guise; as many of the casualties of this period; Peter Green and Syd Barrett among them, were to discover as the Sixties gave way to the Seventies, and their "experiments" were paid for with interest.*

"My first girlfriend; Barbara lived on a housing estate called Churchill Gardens in Pimlico. It was sort of like puppy love if you like; the break up, you go your separate ways and in her case she became involved with drugs and became schizophrenic. I always had the feeling that there was something more I could have done to prevent that happening… nobody really read the early warning signals. I went to visit her when she was undergoing a drug cure. I went once a week and she was thrilled at the attention and I thought; 'Oh, that went quite well, I'll come along the following week', and the next week she was having a conversation with the therapist and she turned to me and said; 'I was having a really good conversation, why did you do that and why did you cut your hair?' I stayed for about ten seconds and left. As I was getting the Tube at Turnham Green to get back to Pimlico, I said to myself I

---

*Green quit Fleetwood Mac in 1970. He was later diagnosed with schizophrenia, and spent time in psychiatric hospitals undergoing electroconvulsive therapy. Barrett's behaviour during shows with Pink Floyd became increasingly unpredictable, partly as a consequence of frequent experimentation with LSD. The other band members soon tired of his antics and, in January 1968, on the way to a show at Southampton University, elected not to pick him up. Barrett's behaviour masked the fact that he was starting to show the first, as then, undiagnosed signs of the schizophrenia that was to dominate his reclusive life until his death aged 60 in 2007.

am not going to contact her again because I had got to that point where it just doesn't work whatever you do".

Frustrated by the situation that he found himself in, Steve resolved to persevere with his music, becoming quite ruthless in his determination to succeed and prove to himself, and to Barbara that he had been seriously underestimated. As a result, there were many casualties of his determination along the way: "I decided at that moment to try my damnedest to become famous. I'm going to try and make her see that this is someone who she has passed up on here, someone who she has totally underestimated. So, anyway, in the great upward thrust to do all that; there were various friends along the way that I neglected at my time of being most focussed and single minded and I went through a period of about two years of not being the person I would wish to be. I didn't let musicians I auditioned down gently - I sounded more like the Alan Sugar* School of charm! (Laughs) I look back on that time with shame and I think I shouldn't have done that".

Steve's own personal experience of rejection also played its part in his drive to succeed, as he explains: "It's funny isn't it? It can be highly motivating when people say to you; 'your harmonica playing is really good but your guitar playing is crap'. Or, 'your guitar playing is really good but your singing is crap! (Laughs). Whenever people say to me 'you shouldn't really do that' I have always used it as a spur to prove them wrong".

Steve's dogged determination to succeed, saw him enlist the aid of the music press and he soon started advertising in the hallowed back pages of the music papers for like minded musicians, a frequently thankless task but one which he persevered with for almost five years. "I used to advertise in Melody Maker when that was a powerful paper. The thing is there were some weeks when I didn't do it and that was because I didn't have the money to do it because I was mad keen, so five years of ads that were differently worded… Essentially my first bands Sarabande and Steel Pier were the same line up, which usually featured me and a good friend of mine called John Ager** and there was another singer as well. There were a number of people who came through the band most of whom I have lost touch with. We used to just rehearse in an old schoolroom. It was called The Warwick Institute and that was the earliest kind of rehearsal room that we had. I started writing tunes but I didn't realise I had started writing them if that makes sense? When I began I would try and play harmonica and guitar at the same time even before the days of harmonica holders (laughs) and there were two things I wrote;

*Successful British businessman/entrepreneur and central character of real-life TV show The Apprentice.
**Ager later went on to manage Steve during the late 1970s

there was a little tune I used to play on the harmonica called Bats In The Belfry that was really a kind of dissonant tune like music for a horror film. And there was another one, which I had, and the melody was something I had around quite literally when I was twelve years old. It was a theme that I have never been able to develop until now with the song Wolf Work which is on my Wild Orchids album." Steve's early work as a jobbing muso has recently resurfaced with the release - some thirty-nine years late, of the album by Canterbury Glass: Sacred Scenes And Characters which appeared in 2007. Rescued from oblivion, this album is even more a product of the late 1960's than Quiet World's album. Steve only appears on one track; Prologue in which he can be heard playing a typically bluesy styled riff overlaid by a much more typically esoteric track. Not an auspicious beginning but hey, everyone has to start somewhere, don't they?

Eventually, though his persistence paid off as a result of his advertisements when he was invited to join Quiet World; a quasi-Christian outfit who had been signed up by Pye Records' subsidiary; Dawn. Listening to the resulting album: The Road now, there is little evidence of Steve's presence on it; even less of his fifteen year old brother John who was drafted in to play on a couple of tracks. "They used to come round and sings songs and rehearse and then they used to go round to the drummer's house and rehearse," explains John. But yeah... it really was working towards an album. I think it was a real turning point for Steve because it was a pro thing and being in a recording studio, he very kindly hoiked me along; his younger brother (laughs) to come and strum rhythm guitar which was amazing".

Steve remembers the album quite fondly: "It was three South African brothers; the Heathers, who wrote the stuff. Their father was a medium; they had lived in England and then moved back to South Africa only to return to England later. Their father stayed behind in Africa and he used to send them tapes of various characters speaking through him. It was very strange as we used to sit down and listen to these tapes. One of the characters was called Koothume; who claimed to be the 'Spirit Of Music'. He described the way in which music could be written and he described it in very visual terms. He said what was going to happen; there was going to be a kind of hybrid and modern music would include sounds of the street. I still use that as an influence; some of the things he said. It was a heavy Christian message; they were what you would now call a Christian Rock Band.

The reason I joined was not that I was particularly religious or anything but it was just that my attempts at forming bands had really gone nowhere and they used the all important word: 'Contract' - a contract with Pye. So I was ready at that stage to join anybody who was further up the ladder than I was. I would have even joined The Sex Pistols had it been the time (laughs). I was so desperate to get involved and I just happened to be involved with them. It depends on whether you like that album. I think of it more as a product of its time rather than a great album".

June Hackett also remembers the boys in the band: "I remember the Heather brothers, they were very good looking and before that Steve had tried to put bands together and there was Canterbury Glass. We were always trying to think of a title for a band and I came up with Renaissance which I thought was a good title until somebody pointed out there was already a band with that name".

Indeed, listening to the Quiet World album now too, it is very much a product of its time. An evangelical cast surrounds the album and it is hard to imagine the band grabbing the attention of the hard-bitten rock audience with such an album, although valuable studio experience was gained from his brief stints with both Canterbury Glass and Quiet World: One thing that has stayed with Steve since that album is the influence of the spiritual world, which has coloured much of his musical output ever since.

From being influenced by others, Steve was also by this time becoming an influence on his younger brother who shared in Steve's musical adventures when they shared a flat together. "We were living in Victoria," recalls John. "We were in a Council flat overlooking Victoria railway station. It always makes me laugh when I hear the Genesis stories of their early days at Charterhouse and we had a slightly different start. We used to share a bedroom overlooking the railway lines (laughs) playing our blues guitars right by the railway tracks (laughs). I would have been fifteen and we went to see King Crimson; that was the big turning point for me. Steve took me along to the Marquee Club and I remember it as if it were yesterday… just pinned at the back of the Marquee (laughs) when they went into 21st Century Schizoid Man and it was just jaw dropping. Of course, they had Ian MacDonald who was playing flute and sax and when he started playing I Talk To The Wind that was it really; I just loved the sound of the flute and I thought…'Yeah; I'll try that' and so that was the turning point for me."

Ironically enough, Steve told a story on one of his recent acoustic tours of one particularly disgruntled neighbour knocking on the door to their flat to ask how long the budding flautist was going to be practising, to which Steve rather sarcastically, but extremely prophetically answered: "About twenty years". Both brothers have certainly come on a lot since then, haven't they?

CHAPTER THREE
The Genesis Of A Guitarist

Another band who were also heavily influenced by the formative King Crimson were also about to have a defining influence on both the Hackett brothers. Genesis had emerged out of two school bands at Charterhouse Public School in the late 1960's and by 1970 had already experienced the thrill of writing and recording their own material with their debut album; From Genesis To Revelation, released to public indifference in March 1969. Persevering, by the summer of 1970, they had recorded a second album, Trespass; their first for Charisma Records and it was through the back pages of Melody Maker that Steve noticed their increasing cycle of gigs. Continuing with his dogged determination, it was one of his advertisements that caught the eye of Genesis' lead singer; Peter Gabriel:

"Imaginative guitarist/writer seeks involvement with receptive musicians, determined to strive beyond existing stagnant music forms".

How pretentious that advert looks now eh? This was the 1970's though (just), that was the way things were done, and it had the desired effect.

"Peter phoned me up and said they were looking for someone and I had not seen Genesis before I joined. There was another band around at the same time: Quintessence and I wasn't sure who Genesis was and who Quintessence was. I suspect that both the lead singers had long hair and played the flute at one point and seemed to do weird things with the flute (laughs). I remember thinking 'this is gonna be very cosmic' and I wasn't sure if this was the band. Peter said to me, 'We have got an album out called Trespass; it's our second album but it is better that you listen to this one because it is more of the direction and in particular a song called Stagnation.' Perhaps there was something synchronous in the fact that we had both used that word... 'stagnant music forms' and they had done a song called Stagnation. John and I went and listened to the album and he said, 'they sound interesting, don't they?' I said; 'Yeah do you think that is a harpsichord or is it a twelve string?' We weren't really sure what it was; it was this sort of cross between a keyboard and a guitar. This sound that the band already had with the twelve string guitars and I had already been working with twelve strings".

That fateful meeting is recalled clearly by both Steve and John: (Steve)…" Peter and Tony came to see me at my flat when I was living with my parents. At that time my brother and I were playing things together so we were doing guitar/flute duet things. One of the guitar/flute things eventually ended up being recorded on Voyage Of The Acolyte. Tony didn't really say anything; he was very quiet and he sat there and you have to remember in those days everybody had these overcoats (laughs)".

(John)… "A couple of the guys from Genesis came to our flat in Victoria. I suppose it was a mini audition really (laughs) and I played a bit of flute just to flesh things out a bit. I think we played a bit from what became The Hermit which was this tune that Steve had kicking around."

Phil Collins' recollections of his first impressions of Steve make interesting reading: "I remember meeting him for the first time, probably after the audition and I imagine that Mike sat with him first then we all met him. Then this guy clothed totally in black with beard and you know; very intense King Crimson fan, and he came by and he was very intense; very meticulous and anyway he got the job". It seems that some things haven't really changed in all the years since. Steve still dresses predominantly in black and he is, if anything even more meticulous these days!

It is equally interesting to hear Steve's first impressions of his new band mates: "They definitely spoke their own language, somewhere between Venusian and Vulcan and Charterhousisms. I didn't know what they were talking about; all I knew was that I felt that the music was very interesting, texturally. The twelve string forays largely motivated, I think, by Anthony Phillips, my predecessor, between him and Mike, and Tony of course, who also played twelve string. So when you had all these things tinkling away it made a very interesting sound, like a bunch of mad harpsichordists (laughs). It was impossible to pin down how the sound was generated. So that was something of the early mystique of the band and I think it paralleled everything I was interested in; the idea of two instruments sounding like a third; like an unidentified flying guitar".

June has vivid memories of her first impressions of encountering Genesis: "I said to Steve who's that funny figure in the fur coat. You know they all used to wear these fur coats that they got from Portobello Road. Steve said;

'that's the drummer' and I said; 'Yeah, that figures! (Laughs) I thought they were very nice and they were obviously musicians to their fingertips. Of course, I only heard them practising but you know when something is good. The first knowledge I had of the band was when Steve brought the Trespass album home. Of course we had never heard any music by the band and he put the album on and said; 'listen to this mum; see what you think'. Stagnation came on and I said; 'oh, Steve I like that because it is almost classical' and Steve said; I've auditioned with them'. I think he told me he'd put this advert in Melody Maker as you know, and I said to him; 'Stephen, that's so pretentious!' (Laughs). Then Peter Gabriel rang up and Steve went for the audition".

It was Steve's willingness and indeed keenness to experiment with sounds and atmospheres that got him the job with Genesis. His introduction to the band was anything but gentle though. The intensity of the Genesis format was to be as much of a culture shock to him as the difference in backgrounds that had formed and shaped the band and their ethos. Steve's first gigs included London's University College on 14th January 1971 and the Lyceum Theatre a few days later, both of which were memorable for many things, not least being one of the famous after gig fights between Tony and Mike or Peter, which were just as quickly forgotten in the white heat of writing, recording and performance. Despite the veneer of respectability that a public school upbringing gave them, it could not disguise the fact that Tony, Mike and Peter had a steely determination to succeed. To add to these problems, the technical gremlins which dogged early Genesis gigs, were present at Steve's first public outing too, as he recalls: "It was a very shaky concert - not a pleasant experience. There were lots of mistakes. I had a fuzz box that I had been rehearsing with all week; but suddenly on the night they gave me a different one. The fuzz box started to feed back; I played bum notes all night long and I thought; 'That's it; the game's up - I haven't got the gig!' This was followed a few days later by the gig at the Lyceum in London. There wasn't a bigger London gig at the time and although it was well received; when it was finished I was still sitting there on my stool. Finally, roadie Richard MacPhail came onstage; took my arm and said: 'It's finished now, Steve' (laughs) I was that nervous after it!"

His mum admits to having some nerves of her own at this gig: "The first time we ever went to see them was at the Lyceum and I don't know how I got through that evening because my stomach was so tight. I knew that Steve was so nervous because the music was very, very difficult. He sat on the stool and he had the hair, and being his mum... Then we started going to gigs and the

Fairfield Hall in Croydon I particularly remember because the headliners were Van Der Graaf Generator and then Lindisfarne and Genesis, and that was nice for us because my sister lived in Croydon and that was a good gig as I remember. I remember meeting Sonja Kristina from Curved Air and talking with the Lindisfarne guys; I never met the Van Der Graaf people. Gradually... they were nice, there was a guy from Lindisfarne called Jacka (Alan Hull) as I remember and they were very nice and I loved the music and then the fans began to become Genesis fans."

It didn't help that during this gig, Phil Collins was more than slightly inebriated on his favourite tipple at the time; Newcastle Brown Ale; a potent brew and one, which doesn't mix well with the need to concentrate. It must have been bizarre for Steve, trying to concentrate on getting his licks right; watching Phil do complex drum fills around the drum kit without once actually hitting a single drum, even Phil admits it was an unusual happening: "His first gig was University College where I had tried to test the rule about how many pints of Newcastle Brown Ale you could drink and still play the drums (laughs). I proved that night that you shouldn't really drink Newcastle Brown in great quantities and then try and play the set. I was playing and all the strobes were going. All the drum fills were slightly to the left of the drum each time and the tempos were probably all over the place. Steve came off and was so nervous that he thought he had blown it. I don't think anyone was man enough to say: 'You're pissed!' and that was the only time and I remember it because it was Steve's first gig".

Steve was not given time to ease himself into the guitarists' position and was shortly thrown in at the deep end with the first of the now famous Charisma "Six Bob" tours* with label mates Lindisfarne and Van Der Graaf Generator. It must have been quite a shock for the budding guitar hero to be and Steve readily admits that the first few months were quite a struggle, "It was my first professional situation. I had made an album a year earlier but I was not able to make a living and so it looked easy at a distance but when I joined and was playing live gigs; I found it more difficult. For instance, if you have been playing at home for three years or pottering about recording the thing that it doesn't school you for is the volume a live band makes just in rehearsal. I needed to get a new amp straight away because nothing I had could cut through the wall of thunder (laughs). I had seen the band before live once in a club and they seemed quite loud and then at the Lyceum they didn't seem very loud at all. The equipment side of things was not that easy to deal with. There was some very dodgy technology; we used to break down a lot; we all

---

*So called because all the tickets were priced at "six bob" (shillings, or 30 pence in decimal currency).

used to tune up to the organ; the organ would sometimes vary pitch during the concert.* (Laughs) Great when you had eight twelve strings all tuned up perfectly beforehand!"

Technical difficulties aside, Steve rates his contribution to the album very highly: "Spiritually and in terms of trying to cheer people on as a sort of in-house cheerleader/frustrated producer/ frustrated guitarist, frustrated everything (laughs) I would say from the very first album after I joined the band; Nursery Cryme. I was always trying to wring a bit more passion out of everybody. I wasn't very diplomatic and was very critical or so I thought. I was pushing everyone... 'we've got to get a Mellotron, we've got to get a synth' or 'we've got to do that.' So my contributions weren't always musical, they were aimed at the live show and the light show".

The band had already started work on their follow up to Trespass and it was here that Steve immediately gave himself over fully to the creative process. Several of the songs on this album were very much hangovers from the days of Anthony Phillips. None more so than the album's centrepieces: Fountain Of Salmacis and The Musical Box, which had begun its gestation back in 1969. Even so, as the piece evolved, Steve was able to bring the missing element to it. "The Musical Box was the only song that I think was written before I joined and at that point I felt that nobody was... although the song was written there was still a lot more room to make improvements. No one was making the sound of a musical box for a start. So I felt well here's me for a start! I threw myself into it completely. I wracked my brain to come up with the most interesting things and I tried to sound like a keyboard player so I think you got this enlarged keyboard picture. I was trying to be the icing on a very fully formed cake as it were".

One other thing that emerged from Steve's constant noodling and practising was the technique now known as "tapping". "One day I was doing this thing... I was trying to play part of Bach's Toccata and Fugue and I realised that the only way I could do something like that was to use the plucking hand on the fretboard as well, and that was what became known as tapping, centuries later the term was coined! It's worth noodling away, most of the time you bore yourself to tears but once in a a while something interesting will happen and you have to keep noodling away long enough for that".

Tony Banks agrees that Steve brought a harder edge to the band's sound at that vitally important stage of their development: "Steve was more of an electric guitarist and also more into sound actually and I think listening back

*The Mellotron, recognisable for its distinctive sound, was particularly renowned for regularly going out of tune.

to the albums he made a great contribution in that sense. Steve and I also used to play a lot listening to each other, often playing in unison and in harmony and stuff but also when he did a funny sound I would try and do a funny sound too and you got little interplays like that. I think he had a slightly different style from what the original Genesis thing was but nevertheless it was very imaginative and I think it took us into different directions. He was probably a bit more into true classical style perhaps than anybody else and that rubbed off I think on some of the songs".

Musically, Nursery Cryme, drew on the already established elements of Genesis' music; lyrically imaginative and musically developed from a disparate range of influences; Gospel, Classical Soul etc... woven into a unique fabric that was the quintessential Genesis sound. However, a cursory listen to the BBC Sounds Of The Seventies recording from May 1971, shows that Steve was prepared not only to imbue the material which the band were working on with his own stamp, but also to sharpen existing tracks. His playing on Stagnation from this session more than emphasises his talent and ear for melody, as well as striving for new sounds. Gigging continued over the next few months both in the UK and in Europe, which had embraced the band far more readily than in their home base, especially in Italy where the operatic tradition was perhaps more in keeping with such opuses as Harold The Barrel and Fountain Of Salmacis, both of which owe more than a passing nod to librettists Gilbert and Sullivan.

Upon its release in November 1971, the album was well received but that reception did not readily transfer into sales and Charisma soon shifted their promotional efforts to Lindisfarne who were topping the charts with Fog On The Tyne. Charisma persevered with the idea of the package tour however, promoting their stable of acts, and a second tour was organised in October / November 1971. "Charisma were doing this thing where they were basically presenting the whole label: Genesis, Lindisfarne; Van Der Graaf Generator," explains Steve. "Ironically in terms of popularity it ended up being in completely reverse order at the end of the day although Lindisfarne had and still do have their own following. Genesis were like the new boys; the juniors really and Lindisfarne relaxed the audience more; the sing-along and join in. Van Der Graaf were reckoned to be much more cerebral".

In fact, the period between Steve joining the band in January 1971 and the end of the following year was to be the band's most gruelling with over 300 gigs performed. In between this it is still difficult to believe that they found time to write, rehearse and record both Nursery Cryme and its follow-up, the album which broke Genesis into the mainstream both here and abroad:

Foxtrot. Nursery Cryme had not been the success that both the band and Charisma had hoped for. Perhaps this was due to the legacy of the previous guitarist's contribution to the proceedings and a band that was still coming to terms with his departure?

A departure brought on by stage fright and the intensity of the 'gigging' routine causing chronic illness. Phillips was a tremendous influence on the band and his departure was huge as he was considered almost to be the bands leader, massive also in his musical quality and input.

Now, with both Steve and Phil Collins ensconced in the set up, their new album could finally blow away those cobwebs and exorcise the ghosts of that formative period. Creatively, Foxtrot was a massive step up for the band. Exploring new ideas both visually and aurally, it was extremely adventurous especially for Steve, who was still finding his feet and experiencing doubts about his position in the band and whether he was really up to the job; doubts which he expressed to the band at the time: "I had this with Genesis before Foxtrot came out. I didn't think I had contributed sufficiently to the songs on that album. I felt they were very strong without me and I felt, you know … 'I think I ought to leave; you guys are strong enough without me'. And they said, Tony and Mike said… 'Oh, no Steve, we really like your guitar playing and we really want you to stay with the band.' This was day one of recording at Island Studios and at that point I hadn't really understood that they liked my playing; I didn't really understand that and so; suddenly, the pressure was off- 'they think what I do is good' and my confidence was at a very low ebb at this point. I didn't know if I was up to the job. They had much more experience as songwriters and they seemed able to come up with wonderful melodies and I felt very much like the new boy. All these things came out and I thought I was going to get the sack at any minute. I felt that I was just filling in until this professional guitarist was going to come along. Gradually I began to realise that it was a job for life if I wanted it."

Steve's skill was to augment the sound that the band were creating rather than be the flash axeman at the front riffing like crazy. As such, his contribution to this album cannot be understated, although, like most of his contributions to the band; it has frequently been overlooked in the headlong rush to credit the flamboyance of Peter Gabriel with being the true creative heart of the band; an observation which can easily be refuted when you actually listen to tracks such as the wonderful tale of skulduggery in the world of Real Estate; Get 'Em Out By Friday, and the combative guitar playing which coloured the more dramatic moments of the apocalyptic epic Supper's Ready. Steve's contributions are already there for anyone to see, hear and admire - especially if you listen to the recently re-mastered versions of some of these classic tracks.

Nonetheless, being in such a tight and focussed band did sometimes present its problems for a guitarist not used to the composing methods used by the rest of the band: "It was an insight into the way that Genesis used to write," explains Steve. "Some of the guys could read music and some couldn't, and a score sheet was never used. It was always a musical conversation if we were building up something from scratch together it was like: 'You've got that bit and I've got this but…' we jam along and it is a jam that becomes refined. The other way is if someone comes along with a whole song and they are saying: 'And the chords are…' and that is the most that anyone gets; chord shapes and so you might say 'this is a G chord and it is over a D bass' but in those days the bass wasn't considered to be… it was flexible because Mike was underpinning it with whatever bass notes he thought were best.

So it was just; 'This is G… F… it's a major or a minor diminished' and that was it, the most we ever did and the rest was committed to memory - even stuff like the very complex rhythm of Watcher Of The Skies; which I didn't get at all at first. Phil came up with that rhythm and the others clocked it almost immediately and I played what I thought it was and they all laughed and said; 'No, Steve it goes…' And until Phil kind of took time out with me to get that- it took a while".

In fact it was Steve who pointed out the need to go all out to grab the audience's attention by investing in the new technology. Genesis' earnings were already stretched but as Steve had realised, speculation to accumulate was definitely the order of the day, especially with audiences whose attention spans needed something more than mere tales of giant hogweeds to keep them from visiting the bar!

"I remember being the one who said; 'We've got to get a Mellotron; we've got to get a light show' and later on… 'We've got to get a synthesiser'… We had to be in the frontline of all this technology because we had to control our environment with lights; we had to sound as big and broad as an orchestra if we were going to do all this allegorical stuff. I remember being against doing Supper's Ready live before we had all these things because I felt it wouldn't work and I remember it was me and Pete, the two of us saying; 'We shouldn't do it unless we have got all the sound effects of the train door slamming and Uncle Tom Cobley and all' because we had performed a number of these type of things live and people just wandered off to the bar and we wondered why?"

Steve's most lasting contribution to the album was the acoustic prelude (Horizons) to the aural mayhem that was to comprise Supper's Ready. It was his only solo contribution to any of the Genesis albums he was involved with and over a year in the making. He wasn't initially sure that the band wouldn't like it: "I played that piece to them on an electric guitar although I had written it on an acoustic steel guitar and really it should have inhabited neither of those regions (laughs) but the nylon. So, I played it to them a little nervously, thinking they won't like this; they'll reject this... and it was Phil who said; 'It sounds like there should be applause at the end of that' and they sort of clapped, so I was elected to perform this piece on my own on the album... I was very surprised to the reaction to it; after all it is a very short and very reflective piece, for a start".

Underpinning the rest of the album by augmenting the rest of the band where necessary, Steve did make substantial contributions both musically and lyrically to the song Can-Utility And The Coastliners. Even so, he admitted that is was sometimes difficult to shoehorn his playing into a piece already replete with musical ideas: "As was so often the case with Genesis songs I felt that my job was to provide a little bit of shading in one corner of the big picture and I was content with that because so many times Tony was so self sufficient or the trio were so self sufficient that the areas that were left for the guitar to inhabit were either orchestral or synthesiser and so I would try and do impersonations of other instruments and it went into the area of pastiche such as on The Musical Box. I had that approach with so many Genesis things... its crammed full of chords; they don't really want a lead line so what the bloody hell can the guitar do here? (Laughs)."

Steve's doubts were expressed on occasions to his brother John with whom he occasionally still collaborated musically during this period and with whom he still shared a flat, also visited by other members of the band who sometimes were asked to take the rubbish bags downstairs - there's a title for a book in there somewhere! Although John himself, as an observer of the band from a distance, had no doubts about either their talents or Steve's part in it: "I thought they were fantastic, and I mean it. I really did and I put those albums on now and I still think they sound fantastic. They were musically absolutely brilliant; they had fantastic song writing ability and wonderful instrumental playing; great singing; they had the lot. I think most creative people have an element of self-doubt at times and when you look back at it; the other guys were all such strong writers as well. If you were in a band where only one or two of you are the main writers then you are calling the shots but when you are in a group where everybody is such a strong writer; then you are always going to be questioning what you do".

Watching Steve's performances on the Belgian TV Pop Deux show from early 1972, and even a year later on the now famous footage of the band's gig at the Bataclan Club in Paris, he looks frighteningly vulnerable; hunched protectively over his guitar. But listen to the guitar parts on Musical Box and Fountain Of Salmacis and it is obvious that he has brought sharpness and attack to the music which added to Peter Gabriel's increasingly bizarre on stage antics and the frighteningly powerful rhythm section of Collins and Rutherford. This was no longer a pastoral band; more The Texas Chain Saw Massacre meets Hammer House Of Horrors! While Steve and the rest of the band were happy for Peter to front the band in terms of projecting their music, the music itself was always written as an ensemble effort.

Not all of the gigs in this period were massively attended, and Steve vividly remembers playing one in the grounds of a sanatorium where the patients watched in stony silence and another in a fairground where the roustabouts watched and applauded from the carousels! By April 1972 however, when the band finally crossed to Italy for their first gigs there, audiences were prepared to sit and listen; cheering the bits of the performance which they thought merited applause rather than waiting for the end of individual songs. Applause such as that must have been greatly heartening to a man still struggling with his own self-doubts at the time.

By the time that Foxtrot was finally released in October 1972; most of the new album had been well and truly road-tested and Genesis' profile in the UK and in Europe had grown commensurately, aided no doubt by Peter's decision to bring the theatre into the show by clever and inspired use of costumes, first attempted at the band's inaugural gig in Dublin in September 1972, when to the amazement (and perhaps horror?) of the audience he emerged onstage during Musical Box wearing his wife's red dress and a fox's head! The reaction at the time isn't known but Steve certainly remembers the first time Peter brought the rest of the costumes to a gig: "He sprang that on us the night we were doing the Rainbow gig* and I was very happy that he did that.

He just brought them along and they were just standing there backstage before the show. He didn't rehearse with them and then he just put them on during the numbers. I thought it was ... in a way he didn't say, 'What do you think, everybody?' He just did it. Otherwise there might have been a school of thought within the band that went...'I don't know; I'm not sure about that gold lame number!' (Laughs). So, I think he had the right steamrollering approach if he wanted to do it; he just did it.

*9th February 1973

I felt the same musically, it was sometimes better to steamroller things than to try and do them by committee. Composition by committee is something that is very hard to employ in practice. There comes a point when you have to be sufficiently bloody minded to get your own way and you are not going to get everybody to agree with every idea and sometimes even the best players sometimes underestimate each other's great ideas".

Steve's mother also has vivid memories of the band's first Rainbow appearance: "We were in the bar hearing Watcher Of The Skies with the Mellotron and we came out and it was something else because the stage was to my mind, like white silk curtains, and there was Peter in the batwings and then I thought this is a show! This is showbiz! It was brilliant. At that gig was Susan Hampshire and we just had a ball and it really just went on from there... wonderful, wonderful times and I have been so very lucky."

By the end of 1972, the band was playing its last ever gigs on the University/Club circuit between engagements at most of the larger scale city halls and major theatres up and down the UK. It was also starting to gain attention in mainland Europe outside of Italy, where the band was already an established success.

The year culminated with the band's first ever trip to the USA for a show case gig at the prestigious Philharmonic Hall in New York, preceded by a warm-up gig at a university in Boston a couple of days before. Any excitement that the band might have had for their inaugural trip to the US was soon doused by the recurrence of technical problems: differences in cycles between US and UK electricity supplies and a recalcitrant Leonard Bernstein who insisted on occupying the hall for an orchestra rehearsal for most of the day; leaving the band and their support act: String Driven Thing; with barely any time to sound check before being ordered offstage by the band's roadie; Adrian. Nonetheless, despite the problems, which drove Mike Rutherford to throw his guitar to the floor in disgust at the end of the gig, the audience loved the show.

The New Year brought new challenges for the band. Now an established mainstream act in the UK, and with a loyal and growing fan base in parts of Europe, it was time to consolidate that success. The early part of the year was taken up with continued promotional duties for the Foxtrot album and fortunately, Charisma also had the wise idea to release a live album- at a budget price too: An idea, which the lads were initially against because they were still unhappy with their performances. However, the record company managed to secure the master tapes from two shows at Manchester and Leicester which had been recorded by a US radio company; the King Biscuit

Flower Hour. The resulting album; Genesis Live appeared in the summer of 1973 at a budget price, securing for it a decent position in the charts. Ironically enough, the album was later deleted briefly in the UK but soon reinstated in the Charisma catalogue when overpriced import copies started arriving.

The break that the release of that album gave the band proved to be a vital one with the new studio album proving to be something of a struggle all round. Perhaps the band was influenced by the growing domestic difficulties at home; 1973 and 1974 were to be years dominated by domestic political unrest, terrorist violence both in Northern Ireland and mainland UK, shortages, power cuts and the "Three Day Week" precipitated by an oil shortage. Into this environment, Genesis and Steve struggled to get to grips with an album that was to try and capitalise on the great success of its predecessor. Giving themselves almost three months to write, rehearse and record the album was surely enough time by anyone's standards. In fact, as several of the band themselves admit, they gave themselves almost too much time for the album. There was no shortage of ideas though; simply a matter of how to fit them all together into a successful whole, as Tony Banks remembers: "We had a few arguments about this at the time; actually because really there was too much material to go on the album. I wanted to kick off After The Ordeal, which I think is actually the worst song we have ever recorded.* I really didn't like that. I don't like the whole sort of pseudo classical thing. But Peter also said that he wanted to get rid of the instrumental bit at the end of Cinema Show and I said; 'We can't have that; it's great and it's got all the best bits!' So, we ended up with a compromise which was to keep the whole bloody lot on and as a result the album sides were far too long for vinyl".

By now, Steve was gaining in confidence both as a writer and as a player and his contributions to this album are among his most lasting from his time with the band. It is difficult to imagine this album now without Steve's soaring solo on Firth Of Fifth, and of course, his contribution to the band's first minor "hit" single: I Know What I Like. "It was Steve's riff that it was based on," recalls Banks. "We used to jam on it for hours and then I had the idea of playing it on the fuzz piano and organ at the same time. Because the piano was very out of tune with the organ; the whole thing had a nice quality about it. We knew we had written something that had single potential. It's unpretentious and quirky; I'm pretty pleased with that song."

*On his last acoustic tour; Steve dug out After The Ordeal, that particularly "contentious little number" as he wryly referred to it; dusted it off for the trio of Roger King on keyboards and John Hackett on flute to perform, and gave the fans yet another unexpected treat!

Brimming with ideas, the band were in a position to explore them and give a fuller creative rein to everyone which, from the finished result; certainly increased Steve's self-confidence and desire to push himself even further. "Having been involved with a bunch of guys who were a song writer's collective as they originally presented themselves; at that point I felt I hadn't really come up with any songs for the band. At that time I felt it was time to express myself spontaneously as a player. I felt it was never going to wash but I said; 'I've got a few bits that go like this (hums out tune to Dancing With The Moonlit Knight) or bits that could become solos and I said; 'What I am really all about is this, but I don't think you guys are really in this ball park, are you?' Phil said; 'Hold on, I think we've got something… and he did… I don't know exactly what he did but everybody was suddenly playing away."

Even the album's successor to Supper's Ready in the epic stakes; The Battle Of Epping Forest, a straggling tale of gangland violence taken from a newspaper article and yet another vehicle for Gabriel's growing cast of eccentric theatrical creations; was not without Steve's magical touch as Banks recalled: "The Battle Of Epping Forest was one of those songs that got way over embellished. It had a great backing track and a great lyric, but there was too much going on in between them. I recall Steve saying at the time that we should do it straight and that it didn't sound right any other way; and he was absolutely right. We should have kept it straight."

Already, Steve had begun to realise that the internal power structure within the band meant that he was going to have to struggle to get his ideas across. Genesis had begun with four song writers all determined to have their share of the musical cake and having stepped into Anthony Phillips' shoes he was faced with the remaining three writers' stony determination to leave things at the status quo ante stage. With that in mind, he opted to try a different tack for the new album: "I approached it from a player's point of view. I was not going to try and compete with the others in terms of songs… I didn't really try and write songs… I thought, 'I'll just give them riffs and that way they can reject them or incorporate them' and it seemed to pay off. I gave them a lot, not in terms of songs, but in terms of guitar riffs and I felt that was the best way to go. In those days the writing wasn't competitive, and that was very good because it meant that everyone was a composer and everyone was doing their own bit whether it was a bit of speeded up guitar in one corner or a little bit of oboe that Pete was doing or using it as a duck call or something (laughs). Which is where you get those lovely noises on Dancing With The Moonlit Knight where it all goes like a rather quiet lake. The bit that we used to call 'Disney', it wasn't wildlife (laughs) it was Pete who had removed the reed from the oboe. It was great because you got that feeling of experimentation... happy days".

With a hit single under their belts, the result of one of Mr Hackett's riffs, the subsequent album: Selling England By The Pound, saw Genesis consolidate their successes both at home and abroad. With three solid albums to draw from, the shows on this tour were masterpieces of presentation both musically and visually. Essentially, you could say that the 1973-74 tours in support of this album were a "Greatest Hits" package par-excellence, and nowhere was this more aptly demonstrated than on the band's tours in the USA, which Steve recalls very well: "I felt really at home in 1973-4 particularly when we were playing in America. I felt very much at home. I felt we were playing all the best numbers; we had three albums to draw from that I had been involved in. We had the best of Nursery Cryme; we had the best of Foxtrot; and we had the best of Selling England By The Pound. I felt that this was a mighty set that we were doing and I had belief over and above all the rest who felt that that album wasn't our greatest in terms of sound but it was a quantum leap in terms of sales."

The band even acquired the seal of approval from the aristocracy of English music when in an interview at the time of the album no less a person than John Lennon said that he was listening to Genesis! Praise indeed for the band. However, the USA was to prove a demanding taskmaster during this period. Having "conquered" New York the year before as they thought; the rest of America and Canada proved a much tougher nut to crack. The band undertook two extensive tours in the US between November and December 1973 and March through to the beginning of May 1974. Each tour had lengthy gaps in the schedule where it proved impossible to get gigs for a band carrying around as much gear and equipment as Genesis were by this time. After all; how many acts wanted a support act which could effectively outshine them and so, with the exception of a couple of shows opening for Lou Reed and Richie Havens, the band were headliners at all of their gigs which were not always well attended. UK Glam Rock which was the neat (but totally inaccurate) pigeonhole into which the band had been placed in the US was not a great success and it took a while for word to get round that Genesis was an entirely different proposition from that school. However, when the band did get an audience that were prepared to give them an unbiased listening; then the magic shone through and nowhere was this more apparent than at their Christmas shows at the Roxy Theatre in Hollywood in December 1973; shows which Steve still recalls vividly: "On the same tour where we were sometimes playing to packed houses and sometimes we couldn't get a gig anywhere. It was very much like an army and by the time we reached the Roxy we sat around there for a week or two not able to get a gig. Then we did those three nights at the Roxy; two shows a night and they were hanging from the rafters, they loved everything we did and they were to my mind some of the greatest gigs the band ever did because it was a small room. It was very powerful and I felt very much at home. I felt I knew what I was playing and I knew who I was... I was wearing a terrible jacket with strawberries all over it (laughs).

I was going through my phase of looking like the guy from Spinal Tap who had the moustache (laughs). There were things happening on stage; Pete and Phil were so loose and they would start going into comedy routines. At one point they would start doing this thing where I think Pete would start doing this impression of Alan Whicker* when Phil started doing the same thing and of course, the audience wouldn't know what was going on but the band were falling about; we were in tears of laughter. We did a Christmas show where in order to sound like Mickey Mouse; Peter took helium and he took too much and had hiccups for three days afterwards but for God's sake he went for it and he dressed up as Father Christmas and that was just great. Peter put in 1000% and really Pete was the reason I joined the band; it was he who replied to my advert and so for so many reasons I have affection for Peter over and above the ideas and the days when we sweated shoulder to shoulder. For me, I tend to come alive when I think of Selling England... I think I was able to infuse that album with the enthusiasm of a player and as an interpreter."

Fortunately for fans, there is a visual record of this period in the "Tony Stratton-Smith Presents Genesis In Concert" film, which until the advent of the recent 5.1 remastering project for the group's albums, was only available on bootleg copies. Looking at it now, you can see quite clearly the growing dichotomy between the rest of the rather anonymous players and the equally outrageous front man, who is just as anonymous in his own way, hiding behind various masks and other costumes as the surreal stories and characters that populated Genesis' canon of work were surreptitiously brought to life.

The fundamental problems of playing a live gig have remained fairly constant however, as Steve explains: "No matter what the size of audiences you are still coping with the same things every night. You are trying to deal with sound and the larger the place the worse the sound because you are trying to play and there is the sound of a 747 coming back at you (laughs) and

---

*English journalist and broadcaster, best known for his subtle brand of satire, and social commentary on his Seventies TV series Whicker's World.

it's roaring back at you. The idea is to try and get that 747 to play back in time at you. You ignore it and try to get through it. It is always a struggle playing live but it can be wonderful too".

It was on this album, that Steve came of age not only as a player but as an interpreter for the others too. His guitar solo on Firth Of Fifth, essentially a Tony Banks composition; is an established classic and amongst the greatest guitar solos ever written. I Know What I Like also demonstrated that he was capable of writing catchy music around which the rest of the band could create either long form epics or; shock horror: hit singles! Steve's versatility and dedication to his craft shines through the album at every level. Tony Banks' comments many years later about After The Ordeal seem particularly contradictory. He lists this track as the worst one Genesis ever recorded mainly because he did not like the "pseudo" classical style in which it was written. Steve's classical influences have always been part and parcel of his character and it was indeed strange to see Banks himself composing a "pseudo" classical suite many years later when he recorded the album Seven.

The tour promoting the album ended in the USA at the beginning of May 1974 and you would have thought that the band would have taken a well-deserved rest from activities but no such luck! By the middle of '74, the turmoil within the UK had taken a turn for the worse; Europe itself was wracked by unrest with student protests in France and Italy and the growing menace of IRA terrorism here at home. Not an atmosphere conducive to writing material based on mythology and pastoral Englishness. The pacifist ideas of the Sixties had finally died their inevitable painful death at the hands of the debacle of the Vietnam conflict and Watergate, and in the new era of realism that followed there was to be little room for the music that had been the norm in the years before.

Perhaps the band was already aware that the writing was on the wall for their particular brand of epic style productions. The brash new "music" of Punk that was to sweep like a tidal wave over the UK music scene a scant two years later, was already an enfant terrible just waiting for its opportunity. Pomp Rock had reached its creative apogee and its nadir with albums by Yes, ELP and Jethro Tull among others, that were the ultimate expressions of flash and pretension as much as musical content, and the public and the critics had already begun to overdose. Something had to change for Genesis too if they were not to suffer the same savage treatment that had been dealt out to others of their ilk.

Deciding to record away from the city, the band moved to Hedley Grange, former home of the "Great Beast" Aleister Crowley and previously frequented by the arch rock 'n' roll hedonists Led Zeppelin. Here in this rambling pile, the band began work on the album which was to divide not only the fans and critics but also their own members, and which has continued to do so ever since. Initial recordings done, the band then moved to a mobile studio in Glospant in Wales to refine the work and hone down the material into some kind of heterogeneous whole.

According to the band, the album was to be based around a concept; a brave step given the reaction to previous servings from this particularly maligned species of album in recent years! Two ideas were put into the pot for discussion; "The Little Prince" a children's story by Anton Saint Exupery; or Peter Gabriel's far earthier essay on the life of a Puerto Rican street kid called "Rael" in New York City. Eventually Peter won the day and started to write the "Story Of Rael" which was to become his own creative apogee (or nadir depending on how you view the resulting album) whilst the rest of the band threw themselves into the soundtrack to the story.

The resulting album: The Lamb Lies Down On Broadway was musically a million miles away from its predecessors. A work, which anticipated the harshness of Punk and yet remained firmly rooted in the progressive vein of storytelling and theatrical presentation. Even the album artwork and sleeve was geared towards that very idea although, to be honest; maybe it was also geared towards trying to actually give the listener at least a basic idea of what the album was actually about! Considering the realism of the story's setting; the story itself is incredibly dense and at times deliberately obscure. Musically however, it also brought out the best in the protagonists whose efforts bore fruit in many great collaborative pieces.

Steve recalls, "The bit on The Lamb… that we used to call Pharaohs, which became Fly On A Windshield; the bit that has no melody but is full of portent and has the idea of almost the Ben Hur rhythm; the guys in the galley (laughs) I thought…'Oh, that's good' and so the guitar became this sort of screaming voice over it."

Tony also looks back at that time: "It was a chance to do all sorts of improvisation. During the writing of this album we brought in all these little bits that we had. We set ourselves an idea and just improvised on it and some of them became more solid than others. There was The Waiting Room which was called Evil Jam and we just sat there and tried to frighten ourselves!"

In a recent interview, Steve shed some light on the difficulties that attended the writing and recording of such magnum opuses in the Seventies and how today's technology can be both a blessing and a curse when revisiting such projects: "In those days we were an active touring band and things were done very quickly by today's standards. So it all comes out in the wash. It wasn't Sergeant Pepper, six months in the making! We weren't able to do that and it took more like six weeks in the making that was just a fact of life. Albums took a month; they took six weeks; rarely did they take longer. The Lamb… took longer to write; that took about six months but we almost had it down to the point where we could guarantee that we would work six weeks; we could write and record an album in six weeks and then we were ready to go off on tour. Everyone has got the time now but obviously in the old days when you were in Island Studios; the clock was ticking and it was expensive and you are in a hurry; you have to get out. The difference is if you are a band that is working with orchestras that is going to take you longer. Larger arrangements and all this Genesis stuff was designed to be played live and I always had to think to myself; 'should I do an extra guitar overdub here? Because if I do, this means I really can't play this live'. So technology didn't facilitate that kind of thing then".

Peter Gabriel's decision to arrogate the writing of the story and the lyrics to himself was not perhaps the wisest decision. It certainly aggravated the situation that was already forming within the band with Gabriel's position being elevated to a position bordering on Godhood by many fans and some critics too, whilst the rest of the band had been relegated to being his "backing band". The position was not helped by his decision to copyright the story without reference to his band mates either! A situation which neither he, nor the band were really happy with. Peter became increasingly uncomfortable with the position he found himself in due to the adulation heaped on him by both the press and the fans and realised that in order to continue to have the same kind of control over his work that he had been allowed during the recording of The Lamb… he was going to have to leave because the rest of the band were quite rightly going to demand more space for their own contributions next time round. This was to be the same situation Steve was to find himself in a year or so later after the release of Voyage Of The Acolyte proved that he could function outside of the musical unit where his ideas were not necessarily getting the airing that he felt that they deserved, irrespective of whether they fitted the requirements of the band or not.

"Musically it wasn't fulfilling my needs or necessarily the needs of the others. Things started to become secondary to the story and there were bits of instrumental things that ended up being vocal things and so on," recalls Steve. "Maybe it was a bit crowded. Perhaps 'Crowded House' would have been a good title! (Laughs)."

Things were never quite as simple as fans and critics would have liked us to believe and the division of labour on this project was unusual to say the least as Steve explained in an interview at the time: "Peter took more of a back seat in the early stages and just let us get on with it. He was much more concerned with the lyrical side. We did half the music before we decided that Peter should write a story to go with it. We'd been working with the vague idea of The Lamb Lies Down On Broadway. That line seemed to stay with us. A great deal of music was written in the studio, which we'd never done before because time was running out on us. Previous to that late stage in the Lamb's development, much of the instrumentation was written in a house in the country and recorded with a mobile unit outside of a formal studio".

Tensions were running high in the band at this time. The uncertainty which Gabriel's departure and subsequent return to the band had generated during the previous few months, had not gone away. The lack of sympathy with which Gabriel perceived he had been treated during the trying times leading up to, and in the weeks after the birth of his first daughter; Anna had increased the tension. Steve's own problems were just as pressing; his first marriage had not worked out and the split had left him with an estranged wife, Hellen Busse, and a young son; Oliver. Steve recalls that his first marriage to Hellen was not a happy one: "We met in Germany, we were married for two years and we were plainly unsuited to each other. We were very young. This was very shortly after I joined Genesis. Also, I think, what you have to take on board are the pressures of a band that was constantly touring and it's a bit of a sailor's life - you are at sea most of the time! (Laughs) which is not necessarily conducive to domestic harmony".

The album took a while to complete, and indeed by the time the band eventually started their massive tour in Chicago in November 1974, it had still not been released in the USA. This was mainly due to Steve's hand injury, which took place at a post gig celebration he attended for the Sensational Alex Harvey Band.* The new album was backed by a completely new stage set up based around the story, which took rock 'n' roll to new heights of presentation... and pretension too! This was musical theatre at its most extravagant but launching it on an unsuspecting audience without warning them first did not always work. Neither did the gear on many occasions. "I loved the idea of playing it live and I wish it had worked better," recalls Banks. "The people that came to see us wanted to hear The Musical Box and

---

*Due to the stress Steve was under at this time (divorce) he felt that personal comments about Alex and the band reflected the situation with Peter and Genesis, resulting in crushing a wine glass into his hand. This led to the delay of the Lamb tour while the tendon in his thumb, which had been severed, was repaired and subjected to electro-therapy.

Supper's Ready - the things that they knew. When we started, we were playing in America to an audience that hadn't even heard it as the record wasn't even out at that stage. So, it was completely new music that they were hearing and it was difficult. We had so many special effects going which in the rehearsal room looked marvellous; but on stage they never all worked at the same time. We always had something going wrong. I hate it when something goes wrong on stage!"

Genesis' chief projectionist David Lawrence also remembers that on occasions, things went drastically wrong, none more so than on the first of the band's two nights at the Academy of Music in New York in December 1974. "This (the New York show) was going to be a good two nights; all the music press were there; and all the music people. Nothing could go wrong. In the past the New York shows had had lots of problems. The year before, someone had hi-jacked all of the guitars and held them for ransom; so we were more careful about this show than most. In the middle of the jam section (The Waiting Room) there is a long crescendo of sound getting louder and louder; the lights get brighter and brighter and then suddenly all the stage sound equipment went off; no keyboards; guitars; just Phil on drums. Backstage there is panic.

The band, all except Phil came offstage leaving him to do a quick solo. We were all running round backstage looking for the power supply board to see if a fuse or circuit breaker had blown. This took about two minutes as everything had been painted matt black; including the two big fuse boxes; which we could not find in the dark. When power came back and the band went back onstage to start playing again as if nothing had happened I think the audience thought it was part of the show and we got on with it. Unfortunately, the same thing happened at the same place during the next night but we were ready for it; this fuse blowing never happened again - ever! New York was fighting back!"

Steve appears happy in one of the rare bits of film from "The Lamb" tour, a televised segment from the band's gig at the Shrine Auditorium in Los Angeles in January 1975 that also shows him backstage at the gig.

"The Lamb" tour was certainly a defining moment in the band's life. A massive tour spanning the latter part of 1974 and through until the end of May 1975, the band brought their Lamb to markets throughout the USA, Canada and mainland Europe to mixed receptions. There are many stories associated with this tour, most of which must surely be apocryphal. But several are recalled in vivid detail by David Lawrence who remembers the band's initial show in Europe having to be rescued by fans who physically moved the stage gear from a broken down truck to the venue via their cars in the dead of night - people power in action!

The itinerary for this tour has always been confusing due to cancellations, re-scheduling and additions. An entire tour of Italy was cancelled because of the political situation in the country at that time. A similar situation took place in Portugal while the band was there. The dictator Salazar seized the country during the period when the band was playing two shows. Once again, Lawrence takes up the surreal story of what happened next: "The concert hall was a bit small, only seating around 2, 500 people and there was no power when we arrived. The dressing rooms were quite primitive and the feel of the hall was not good. After unloading the trucks and putting up the equipment; the local electrician, who could speak no English came in; and we couldn't speak Portuguese. He gave us three power cables and we needed five. A few minutes of head scratching told us that we only had half the power we needed and there was no earth. The electrician then took us outside to a pole in the street; he climbed it and clipped on our three cables to the top of the pole. Power was now on and live but we didn't want to touch it!

Using lots of gloves and towels to wrap around his hands, Peter managed to connect us to our power box without killing himself and we found an earth for the system via the trusty water pipe. Things were a bit basic in Portugal and we soon heard the sound of tanks outside the hall. It would seem that we had walked into a small revolution, which was about to start. Troops were walking around with guns in one hand and a can of beer in the other. A few shots were fired over people's heads and the place went mad. Head roadie Nick Blyth was running backstage telling everyone to arm themselves with anything heavy - the microphone stand now had more than one use! At one point half the crew were under the sound mixer with Craig (Schertz) shouting… 'Just like 'Nam!'*

Teargas was now being fired everywhere as fans were trying to get into the small hall. The army was trying to keep them out. The fans outside with no tickets were standing on top of tanks as they were driving around. It was all very nasty; the band went on and did the shows and during this time Craig had two guards at his side by the sound mixer. I had one by me, complete with automatic rifle and beer! This was not a good time to be in show business. When the show ended; all the army disappeared with the fans; leaving us to pack up and go.

*The Vietnam Conflict that despite a peace treaty signed by all parties in January 1973, continued until April 1975.

Around 2AM everything was in the trucks apart from our big mains cable, which was still connected to the outside power pole. The electrician had gone home and it needed someone to climb up the pole and disconnect the cable while it was live. Nobody was going to do this; so Peter picked up two pairs of working gloves and a hacksaw and shouted to me… 'You hold the cable; I'll cut it!' Peter cut through a 300 amp cable live and much sparking and we all ran to the bus. The drivers needed no directions on the way to go - out! A few hours after we had left Portugal; they closed the borders and had a small revolution; we were lucky to get out of that one".

The decision taken by Gabriel to leave at the end of the tour cast an obvious damper on the proceedings for all concerned, especially as it was not the first time he had departed the band to explore other avenues of expression; he had been tempted into film script work by William Friedkin in 1973 and had almost quit the band, much to Friedkin's horror that he promptly withdrew his offer to Gabriel when he realised that it could spell the end of the band. The doubts which that decision cast, had effectively driven a wedge between Gabriel and the rest of the band which no amount of diplomacy could hide and with his decision to leave now iron clad; the other members of the band began quietly to look at other avenues of work should the expected demise of the band take place once Gabriel's departure became public knowledge.

Another person who saw the band at this stage was Brian Gibbon who became Managing Director of Charisma Records. He recalls how he became involved with the band and also some of the difficulties balancing artistic requirements with commercial and financial realities…

"I was at Sony/CBS at the time and what actually happened was that I was head of the Buyers Department at CBS. Strat (Tony Stratton-Smith) came to us for a distribution deal and Maurice Oberstein who was the boss at the time asked me to look at it. He had already had a meeting with Tony and had shaken hands on it. Basically, I looked at it and had a meeting with Oberstein and said ' we can't do this. There is no way in the world we can structure a deal around this'. He said; 'well I have already shaken hands on it' and I said 'well you are going to have to go and tell Strat that we don't want to do it' and he said; 'why don't we want to do it?' and I said basically the company is in trouble and because I was Chief Financial Director and I wouldn't sign off on it. Anyway, what happened was that I went off to see Strat at the St Moritz in Wardour Street (laughs) and to tell him that we couldn't do the deal but he thought I had come to give it my blessing. I think he was very disappointed and at that time Oberstein had bought half a racehorse with Strat and he was none too pleased that it basically ended there. He wrote Maurice an extremely funny letter in which he said 'I'm glad I sold you the back end of the horse!' it was actually funnier than that but I can't remember the exact wording of it (laughs).

Then it transpired that about three months down the line Strat gave me a call and said; 'you were right' because I had told him in black and white and he asked me if I would consider joining the group which then consisted of B & C Records, Mooncrest and Charisma it was a loose group and I said "no". It just happened at that time that CBS always had an American boss and I didn't see that changing in any way even from the finance point of view my boss was based in Paris and then I had another in the States as well. I was the youngest Controller that Sony actually had and then Strat 'phoned me up again and said 'why don't we have lunch?' So I went in there as their Financial Controller and that is how it all started. I got to handle all the Genesis agreements, all the renewals and in fact I was the main contact for managers because they couldn't get hold of Strat, and Gail (Colson) was more involved with the marketing side. It was always difficult for independent labels with one or two big artists, it was completely synonymous with Chrysalis, Island and Charisma, and it was always difficult to have big artists and fund them and to do all the things that a major would do. We were always at that time looking to re-fund and get advances and distribution deals and that was the way it went.

Another thing that doesn't come out was in the early days we had to fund the tours; the bands themselves didn't fund the tours. The whole thing was funded by the record labels and that was quite an expensive thing to fund. It is all those aspects of promotion that people forget about. Bands like Lindisfarne, String Driven Thing and Genesis weren't doing enough gigs. They were doing gigs for about £50 a night but they needed funding in the interim to be able to perform and if they weren't performing… Genesis and Lindisfarne weren't performing, then we wouldn't have broken the records. They wouldn't have been in the same position as they were. They needed somebody to fund it to enable them to actually do it.

Those are the kind of things that people tend to forget about is that they were actually funded to go on the road, which to us was part of the promotion. There is no record company that doesn't want to have a hit (laughs) you know, if Steve had got in at a certain level with his first album then next time we would have wanted the next one to come in higher and it is completely naïve to think that any record label with any commercial sense would not want to do the best for their artists there was no luxury for us. We weren't an EMI! (Laughs) we wanted to break every single act we had on commercial terms."

Steve had already been compiling material of his own during the infrequent gaps in the band's recording/touring schedules and during 1973 and 1974 he had amassed a large body of material for which he was now unsure of finding a home for.

CHAPTER FOUR

The Acolyte Steps Out

The public announcement of Peter Gabriel's departure from Genesis was finally made via the music press in mid July 1975. Naturally, fans were shocked and upset. It even managed to take the band's long time chronicler and friend Armando Gallo by surprise. He had been led to believe earlier in the year that Phil Collins was deeply dissatisfied with the way things were going in the band and he had decided to leave so the final resolution took him completely by surprise: "I was leaving for California on a Monday and the week before maybe on the Wednesday or Thursday there was a presentation of gold discs for the Selling England By The Pound and they were finishing their tour for "The Lamb". Phil came up to me and said: 'You're leaving for Los Angeles and so I better tell you before somebody else does; I'm leaving the band' and I said; 'Really?' and he was getting this band together, which was Brand X. So I left for California and then in August and I find the news that Peter has left... what do you mean Peter has left the band? Phil was supposed to be leaving."

The uncertainty over the band's eventual future affected everyone and it was this uncertainty that eventually acted as a catalyst for Steve to bring himself to the realisation that the only outlet for his stockpile of material was to try to do it himself: "Casting my mind back, I think it was during 1974 that there was a slight lull after touring. In fact, that may have come as early as the end of 1973. Anyway, at one point I had the Mellotron at home in my bedroom and I seemed to spend hours doodling on it. One or two ideas got together because I was at the point where I was beginning to think to myself without the restriction of the band; 'I wonder what I can come up with?' I came up with one or two things that I was convinced that they were going to hate and that seemed to goad me even further into that direction and try things that I felt they would avoid."

Steve was also helped in one way by Gabriel's struggle to complete lyrics to deadlines, a position which was not helped by Peter's having to drive a five hour round trip to the hospital to see his critically ill baby daughter. This left Steve and the rest of the band with a lot of spare time on their hands as Steve recalls: "Some time back Peter was working hard on the vocals. A lot of the time my services weren't really called upon and I found I had a chunk of spare time. I started writing but not for any specific project; just a few melody lines and for some reason managed to assimilate quite a bit of material and very quickly had a lot more than I could use. Then I had six or seven months of solid touring and to keep myself sane in a very mechanical existence, I would write back at the hotel each night. That way I progressed and kept sane because in the early days I got very nervous on stage."

Following Gabriel's departure the mixed reaction to Steve's first solo success is something he recalls very well: "When Pete left nobody knew if the band's future was secure at all so arguably we had a no piece until we had all reconvened. Phil and Mike, luckily really brought that album alive. I didn't know how to write for bass and drums and it was great. But reaction to that album was mixed, of course. I had a hit with it, the album went silver and I was very proud and of course it was very positive for the band because people would think if Steve can have a hit on his own what can we do if we get together. It was great to be the captain of my own ship for the first time and it was very difficult to go back to being a member of the group again or even being a member of the crew again when you need the approval of the committee for everything.

So, there was a bit of jealousy there but it blew over very quickly. But having done I just felt what a delicious thing this is without needing the *approval* of everybody but having everybody's co-operation. I'm sure it's the same for anyone who has been in a band and you are no longer involved in angst-ridden rehearsals... From the very first night I knew it was going to be a goer".

While the rest of the band took their breaks; or in Phil's case immersed himself in the free -form Jazz of Brand X; Steve booked time in Kingsway Studios a dungeon like place, that was part of a Civil Aviation building, which sadly no longer exists. Even at this stage, he was still unsure if the disparate musical "bits" he had acquired would ever amount to anything other than a compilation of out-takes; he nevertheless proceeded to begin to explore those musical avenues which had been closed off to him for so long within the committee structure of Genesis. "The sessions were all evening sessions but I didn't seem to tire because of it. I made the album on an unhealthy diet of cigarettes and cups of soup from the dispensing machine! I was oblivious to everything around me while I was doing this thing. Of course I had the writing support of both my brother John and John Acock".*

Basing the album loosely around some of the stronger and more central figures of the Tarot might seem incredibly pretentious now but such a concept was not yet completely de-rigeur especially when it was handled correctly. "If you look at the titles on the album; they are all based on different pictures which the Tarot signifies. So I based a track like The Hermit on a particular card and it is very introspective. By looking at the cards and pulling out the strongest feelings, it mapped out a way of working. It was heavily symbolic although it was okay to be symbolic at that time. I think music then was at the point where there was very little in the way of cynicism. I think before it turned and people started not so much to review things as to assassinate them; you had a much broader canvas to draw from. I think you still had the idealism of the sixties plus the technology of the seventies which enabled you to do so much."

It must have been quite a culture shock for his band mates; Phil and Mike whose help he enlisted on the album, to be presented with substantially organised musical ideas instead of thrashing them out in the rehearsal room, which was the usual way that Genesis worked. "I remember starting the sessions with them and saying; 'I know we don't do it this way in the band but...' At that time we tended to work as a band in the rehearsal room and we got to hear everything that was going on".

In fact, Phil wryly remarked during the sessions, "Are you sure you wouldn't like to take four hours about it, like everybody else?"

Fans have often wondered why, given his decision to "go it alone" with Voyage... that Steve used two of the musicians from the very band whose clutches he was trying to escape from. The rationale behind that decision is not that difficult to appreciate as he explains, "I don't think I could have been able to talk to unfamiliar bass players and drummers and even to talk in a musical language which I had not discovered. I mean, for instance Genesis had its own terms for things. Like we didn't do things like shuffles and I shall enlighten anybody; Eric Clapton performing Hideaway; that's a shuffle. I didn't know that and Genesis used to call a shuffle a 'chugg', but imagine me saying to a drummer; 'can you do a chugg?' (laughs) They would say; 'Yer wot, mate? A chugg?!' (laughs). So I was terrified and tentatively I made enquiries and 'if I were to do some solo stuff, Phil, do you feel like playing on

---

*Sound engineer who worked with Steve on the production as well as playing mellotron, harmonium and piano.

it?' And he said, 'Yeah, sure'. He was playing on everyone's albums in those days anyway! And Mike was the same. thing; he said 'Yeah, sure'.

I had written one bass line, which was on the beginning of Ace Of Wands (hums the bass line). I didn't even know if it would work but he clocked it straight off. Not only that but doing variations and I think because they were very relaxed there was no pressure from the band on the uptake. They were just a killer rhythm section. They just brought that thing alive.

Having already worked out some of his musical ideas previously with his brother, whose input to this album was to be a vital component, Steve was able to have the confidence of bringing some fuller-formed ideas to the album without the usual round of haggling which attended any Genesis project. Even bringing a piece of music which he and Mike Rutherford had worked on several years earlier, and which had fallen victim to the "committee" stage of selection then in operation as Steve recalls: "There was one piece that Mike and I had written and we had rehearsed it around the time of Foxtrot. I was disappointed that we didn't use it then so I said to him; 'I really like that piece' and I had a long piece of music... 'Would you mind if we put that on the end?' He said; 'Fine'. He played on it and did a great version of it and I was very pleased with it at the time."

Steve was also able to finally find a home for some of the collaborative efforts between himself and his brother which had been around for quite some time too, as John Hackett recalls: "Steve was obviously writing melodies and we would try them out. Things like Hands Of The Priestess was written as a flute tune, as was The Hermit. There were guitar things because things like little harmony bits; descending passages and little bits that I had had and Steve would do something with it and put it together. We were messing around with tape recorders and I had a Tandberg; a stereo tape recorder and we were just playing backwards tapes and things like that and I was trying the flute backwards and that kind of thing on The Lovers and Steve has always loved classical music as well and because I was very much into classical flute by then; thence the classical influence on that album.."

The reaction to the album from both his band mates and Charisma records boss, Tony Stratton-Smith was very favourable too, explains Steve: "I went to Tony Smith* first of all, I think, and I said I would like to do a solo project; I've got it all worked out, how do you feel about it? He said "Yeah, sounds good, I'll have a word with Tony Stratton-Smith" so I had considerable support at the time, plus Phil and Mike who did an outstanding job in a

---

*Tony Smith is Genesis manager, and still handles the band's affairs to this present day. Not to be confused with Tony Stratton-Smith who was the managing director of Charisma Records and died in 1987.

fraction of the time it would have taken them to work on a Genesis album. They absorbed my ideas and immediately kicked in with great playing, I have to say. They made it sound like they had been playing those things all their life. That's always the mark of great players and intelligent musos."

Steve was fortunate in having a record company which was prepared to indulge him and he admits that the process was, to a certain extent, one of guess work and gut instinct: "The first track we did was 'Hands Of The Priestess' and I thought if we can first get one track down that sounds good then there is a chance we will come away with an album rather than a bunch of out-takes. So by the end of the first night we had recorded the twelve string, the flute part and the Mellotron and I thought it sounded so glorious from the word go.

The type of reverb that was used on the flute was a kind of reverb that I felt I hadn't really got on all of the Genesis albums. You know, the idea of music breathing. A type of reverb I heard on certain albums in the sixties. In those days we were using an Echo Plat,e which was something you had to physically move and recording at Aviation House, which had a nice sound. It also had a live echo chamber, which we used occasionally. I was thrilled at the way that track sounded and I fell in love with the process of music making without having to justify myself to a committee."

Steve told Melody Maker journalist Chris Welch at the time that he had wanted to work with his brother to use his capabilities on a full-scale project and this was the chance to do so: "My brother and I had always shared a great appreciation of music but we had never really worked together before. I had always wanted to because he is a really good player and even the stuff we did on this album doesn't show his capabilities. Technically he is a much better musician than I am."

Time strictures meant that Steve only had a limited amount of time to work on his project before reconvening with the remaining members of Genesis to explore the possibility of the band continuing. This had the desired effect of focussing Steve's mind sharply on the project and attending to it in ways which perhaps he would not have done, or needed to do, within the confines of Genesis. After all, this was his "baby" and he was ultimately responsible for its conception, delivery and subsequent nurture and as such he proved to be a loving parent. Certainly listened to now, one often wonders what might have happened if Steve had presented this material to the band instead of working it out for himself but such speculation really serves no useful purpose.

Voyage Of The Acolyte served notice that Steve was far more than the axe man in a rock band. He had been the bit player for Genesis for long enough and now he was finally master in his own house. The album is lyrically lush, musically adventurous and even the conceptual elements are drawn in such a fashion as to avoid the usual pitfalls and accusations of pretentiousness. Yes, it is a highly self-indulgent album. It had to be, there was room to be indulgent after sublimating his musical urges to the demands of Genesis, here was an opportunity which, at the time at least as far as Steve was concerned, might prove to be a once in a lifetime experience to delve a little deeper into his own musical psyche although even he admits that the entire project was a considerable gamble: "I wasn't sure when I started recording it if I would end up with an album or if I would have to abandon the project. I didn't know if I could steer it in anything like a cohesive direction. But after the first few sessions it seemed to go so well that I think I was pretty much in heaven as they say and it seemed to adapt a life of its own. I certainly wasn't afraid to be Gothic at that time; when it was considered gauche. So when I look back on the album I consider it to be a very 'seventies' sounding thing but even now, there are moments when I think; 'That was a good idea' in its more abbreviated moments, perhaps!" (Laughs)

For anyone listening to this album it is obvious Steve was more than prepared to let his imagination go, and wander in areas where previously he had feared to tread. He pays scant attention to musical conventions and it is obvious that if you don't know the musical "rules" you aren't aware that you are breaking them as he found out during the sessions: "I didn't realise that I had written something that was outside the range of the oboe; but Robin Miller our oboe player, was great and he was able to reach notes that regular oboe players couldn't play. No one told me that you couldn't do that! In a way less knowledge can be a very good thing. When Nigel Warren-Green who had been drafted in to orchestrate and score the orchestral parts of the album heard it he actually said; 'You must have a bloody good oboe player!' I think that too much training can leave you on a sticky wicket when it comes to writing things because your head can get filled up with so many rules and regulations about the things you can and cannot do. But it was done on an absolute high really; a drug free high (laughs). When it was finished I was absolutely amazed by it. I used to take tapes home and listen to them and I couldn't believe I had done it."

Fortunately, there were enough fans out there to embark on the musical adventure with Steve and the album achieved a healthy position in the UK charts, eventually gaining a silver disc. In fact, to paraphrase from the album's key track: The Hermit; the "mantle of attainment" no longer weighed heavily on Steve's shoulders; he had proven himself and waved his own magical "wand" and played an "ace". Even Barbara Charone, one of the writers for UK music paper; Sounds gave it the thumbs up: "Voyage Of The Acolyte confirms the talent Steve Hackett displays through his work with Genesis while promising good things for their next album".

The album was given its launch in London and the sleeve was later awarded "Album Of The Year" status. Steve's confidence was definitely on the up during this period, and he no longer felt uncertain about pushing himself and his material forward for consideration by the rest of the Genesis "committee" as he explained in an interview he gave to Barbara Charone at the time of the album's release: "I'm definitely more confident about submitting ideas to the band now. The album showed me that once I was happy with an idea there was really no reason why it shouldn't work. I wasn't particularly confident about my abilities as a writer and arranger before I did the album. In a band one relies heavily on the group for ideas. With us the strongest things are always group written, especially now. We want people to digest the album before we return to the road so that they will be aware that Peter is no longer with the band. If we went out as a four piece now and people hadn't already digested the situation they would find it difficult to accept. Its much easier for us to concentrate on the album now."

It was that next album and an uncertain one at that which Steve turned his attentions to next...

CHAPTER FIVE
Ripples Never Come Back

By the time Steve rejoined the rest of his band mates to work on the first Gabriel-less Genesis album, the obituaries for the band had already been written. No doubt, expectations of their demise had also been fuelled by the appearance of Voyage Of The Acolyte too but for Steve and the rest of the band no such thoughts had entered their heads. Yes, there was a gap to fill. Gabriel's presence was not something that could be taken lightly but neither was it of such sacrosanct importance to stifle the creative processes that the rest of the band was still more than capable of mustering.

In fact, it was precisely these creative instincts and urges, which had led to Steve, Phil and Mike becoming involved in projects outside of the rigid structure of the band. Phil had taken up residence with scratch band Zox And The Radar Boys for some impromptu sessions and low-key gigs out of which eventually emerged Jazz-fusion outfit Brand X. Mike had also finally found time to not only work with Steve on Voyage but also re-establish his connections with his friend and fellow Genesis co-founder; Anthony Phillips for some further writing and recording sessions for what would eventually emerge in 1977 as Phillips' first solo album: The Geese & The Ghost on which Steve's brother was also enlisted to play flute.

In fact, the variety of projects that the various incumbents were involved in led Tony Banks to remark, "Am I the only one writing material for this band?" He had ostensibly put his own solo album plans on hold, realising that the only hope that Genesis had of continuing as a going concern was to concentrate on the band. This was a view that was not necessarily shared by the rest of the band and with good reason. Fans and the music press are notoriously fickle at the best of times; and with the focal point of the band's success now out of the picture, how were they going to maintain the loyalty of the fans as well as keeping the press and record company on side? With the benefit of hindsight, the success of Voyage Of The Acolyte should have given the band a necessary boost. The album reached number 26 in the UK charts in September 1975 and it had featured three out of the remaining four members of the band after all!

The band had finally begun to emerge as individuals, none more than Steve and it was impossible to subvert those growing feelings of confidence and creativity as Steve himself remarked: "The difference was that everyone had become a slightly different person. I had had some solo success by then, in terms of being able to produce a whole album for myself. So, I was writing more material. I was actually quite bereft of ideas by the time we had started A Trick Of The Tail and I really had to think on my feet for that. Luckily by the time I had finished Voyage I only joined the band a day late so I was still able to contribute substantially to all the tracks on A Trick of The Tail…"

The band was every bit as inventive as they had ever been. However relations within the remaining members were a little strained at first. " I sensed that everyone was sensing each other out," recalls Steve. And we didn't have a singer; an appointed singer and so we were there to produce an album and find a singer to sing the songs we had written. It seemed much more shaky than history would ever believe."

The photos from the album sessions give an entirely different impression however, smiles are all round and the band look incredibly relaxed. " It is a very "up" album isn't it? Again I was essentially happy and that translates. We were rehearsing in the summer, I remember that during one of the first days of rehearsal, somebody who was running the place and it was in Acton; they had a lion cub who was literally playing on the floor like a kitten and I remember playing with this lion cub and stroking its head and it felt like horsehair and it licked me! The tongue was so rough and it was delightful (laughs). That was one of the most pleasant memories I have and if you see any photographs of that period, we are all laughing and you can see it becoming a happy band again…"

The band must have felt a certain degree of vindication with the success of the album and Steve recalls his feelings of the time: "Trick Of The Tail was marvellous because it was an album where Phil was singing for the first time and the band was being received by ever larger audiences. Although I loved Pete dearly and all his contributions it seemed as if there wasn't a blip, it was seamless the way we seemed to go from strength to strength. Having Bill Bruford in the band giving it the sanction of someone who had been in bands who were arguably bigger than us and suddenly he was joining us was great. And it feels to a certain extent the same now where I am touring with a band which has got well known individuals in it such as Rob Townsend and Nick Beggs."

Most recently, however, the band seems to have forgotten Steve's input from the very beginning of Trick... a situation he is at pains to clarify: "The funny thing is, I would quite like to put right something that I have noticed that the band are saying and they seem to have collective amnesia on (laughs). I was around for Dance On A Volcano from it's very inception. I remember us all going (hums the opening tune) because we all hit the accents together and I am credited on that track and the closing section is mine. It's true I wasn't around for maybe one day of rehearsal because I had to master my own album but I want it to be known that I was involved with that. We all became involved with other things that started as solo projects and Mike worked with Anthony Phillips on what became The Geese & The Ghost at the time and I suspect that Phil was doing Brand X and probably about twenty other projects too! (laughs) I think we all hoped that Pete would change his mind. He said he was going to tour the album and then leave at the end of it and we all hoped he was going to change his mind because we all loved him, let's face it."

The new album was everything that its predecessor was not. Whereas "The Lamb" had been raucous and on occasions, dissonant; A Trick of The Tail was lush, melodic and luxurious imbued with a sense of timelessness which was a welcome balm to the jaded senses. Tracks such as Ripples and Entangled merged and combined the talents of both Steve and Tony Banks in ways, which make it impossible to imagine them without either protagonist now. In fact, it is a credit to Steve's art of understatement; that a classic track such as Entangled, which many fans (myself included, I may add!) had thought to be primarily Tony's work; was in fact more to do with Steve: "I wrote the lyrics and the music for the verse. The chorus musically was Tony's and the outro was based on an arpeggiated figure that Mike came up with and on which Tony placed a choral effect."

Anyone who doubted that Genesis could rock was soon left in no doubt by the out and out rock that was Dance On A Volcano and Los Endos where the rhythm section of Rutherford and Collins blew everything away in their path and all of this from a band who at the time had still not found their new vocalist.

Cryptic advertisements referring to a "Genesis-style band seeking vocalist" were published in the music press both in the UK and elsewhere. Numerous singers sent in their audition tapes many of which were worthless. Tony's avowal in the music press that the band were not looking for a Gabriel sound-alike but a good performer who could handle being in the spotlight must have put some people off and by the time the album sessions were nearing completion, the band themselves must have been beginning to wonder if their search would ever bear any fruit. Collins had expressed no worries about this, even stating that if necessary the band would carry on as an instrumental act, surely something that was never really given any serious consideration by the rest of them. However, he had also expressed no desire to take the job on himself although others had viewed him as the obvious choice as Steve recalls: "Funnily enough, one of the first people to suggest that he should be the singer was Jon Anderson who came to Phil's wedding at the time. I said hi to Jon and we started very quickly talking about the band's future and I said I had just done a solo album on which Phil sang wonderfully. He said 'Why don't you get in extra instrumentalists and make the band stronger? Phil's got a nice voice you seem to be aware of that already.' I said, 'Really Jon? I don't think the band will wear that one really because they see him as the drummer'."

It took a rehearsal session with one of the handful of vocalists who made it past the initial tape audition stages for things to change Collins' mind on the prospect of becoming a singer. With the deadline for the completion of the album now looming; the band found themselves with an album of music and no vocals. Steve vividly recalls the day that changed Phil's mind: " Eventually we did take somebody into the studio to record and he sang a version of Squonk. He had considerable trouble with the melody lines because it was written by instrumentalists where the melody was up and down, weaving all over the place. Not an easy melody to sing and he found it very difficult to respond to it. Phil had deliberately stayed away on the day when we had the guy come in and we had been through a series of auditions by now. He was the best of the bunch but he had enormous problems with the melody. It was very uphill and he was sweating away trying to do it. The guy had a perfectly good voice but he just wasn't right for the part. So I remember Mike and Tony saying to Phil; 'what do you think, Phil?' and he said; 'I'll tell you what I think; I think it sounds fucking average; let me have a go!"

Collins duly had a "go" and before the band knew it; the album was finished and in the can, to everyone's surprise apart from Tony Stratton-Smith whose reaction on hearing the finished article with Phil's vocals was a masterpiece of understatement: "God, he sounds just like Pete. Sounds like you have found your vocalist, chaps!"

The band even managed to write more music than they could comfortably fit on the album, although this time there were no real arguments about leaving bits and pieces off. One track: It's Yourself, which appeared as the B side to the only single from the album was just such a track. "That was a song which we didn't think was up to scratch. We thought it was a bit Kensington Market which was one of the places that was the focus of the Hippy scene in the Sixties. Slightly ersatz and a bit like The Beatles on Social Security."

Part of the track was to emerge however, as the album's closing track; the rampaging Los Endos which also recapitulated ideas from several other tracks on the album almost into a musical C V of the album's finest moments.

The revisionists soon started re-evaluating the band and Gabriel's position in it from the initial standpoint of having him as the sole creator of the band's output to the total opposite. The bone of contention over song writing credits which had quietly festered for so long was effectively resolved on the new album by the crediting of individuals for their contribution to each track; a procedure which the band had considered on earlier albums, as Tony explained: "I'd said it before really as we had got slightly fed up because obviously in the very early days there was a tendency throughout the whole period with Peter to suggest that he was obviously the dominant writer and who tended to write most of the lyrics. You got this impression that he was doing all this while the rest of us were just sitting around watching him do his creative thing. Of course, Genesis were never like that... I just thought that people might have a better idea of where things actually came from".

Jon Anderson's comments about extra instrumentalists had some effect however. Tony had seen recent performances by Elton John's band which featured two drummers and he had remarked how stunning the performances had been. It was now obvious that another drummer would have to be enlisted to cover drumming duties while Phil was stage front wiggling his bum. There was no doubt in anyone's mind who was ideal for the job: Bill Bruford who had long been a hero of Phil's both in Yes and also in King Crimson. This almost didn't happen however, as Phil was afraid to ask Bill in case he said no and Bill was equally afraid of being turned down if he had asked to join - communication is a wonderful thing, isn't it folks?

"Bill came in and gave us all a big up," explained Banks. "When he arrived he was immediately cracking jokes and he dispelled any feelings of uncertainty and he jammed along with us ... he immediately put everyone at ease with his humour, which was great".

The subsequent tour for the new album began in late March 1976 in London Ontario and was a qualified success. Once again, the band played to their strengths with a set drawing on the finest moments from their previous efforts, which fitted seamlessly with the hefty dose of the new album material. Ironically, the first few gigs were played minus the epic Supper's Ready which Phil had expressed reservations about singing. Once in the set however, it soon became the jewel in an extremely glittering crown as Genesis confounded the critics who had now begun to spurn the very bands they had previously championed in favour of the brashness and dissonance of the then current flavour of the moment; Punk Rock.

The band's profile both at home was firmly on the ascendant although starting the tour in the US where Genesis was still a band which many people were unaware of was certainly a shrewd decision but also a potential gamble. The crowd reaction in the US was genuine and warm and to a greater extent, unburdened by the biased expectations, which crowds at home had for the band and their music. Commercially, A Trick Of The Tail easily outsold all of its predecessors establishing the band as one of the most popular UK acts of the time and proving to the fans and the critics that there was more to this band than a man masquerading as a gigantic sunflower!

The economic climate of the UK in the mid 1970's was firmly set against high earners and a band like Genesis that invested heavily in their stage presentations were, despite outward appearances, not exceedingly wealthy - in fact by the end of 1976 they were over £150,000 in debt! Having completed their tour, they took the purely financial step of recording the next album in Holland where their earnings would not be subject to the same crippling levels of taxation as were then current in the UK. Getting away from the UK and the distractions of the music scene was no bad thing and they were soon ensconced in Relight Studios in Hilvarenbeek, Holland.

Whilst working on this new album Steve finally came to the decision that was to shape his subsequent career. Genesis at this moment were very much on the up, and with one more push their futures would be secured and perhaps they could finally take their feet off the wearisome treadmill of album/tour/album that had been their lot since 1971. One thing more than any other had changed irretrievably, however. Steve's success as a solo artist had alerted him to the possibilities inherent within his own artistic character and it was increasingly difficult for him to subordinate himself to the band again. A Trick Of The Tail had not demanded this of him because he had pretty much exhausted the stock of ideas he had available to him for A Voyage Of The Acolyte; and by his own admission he had come to that album bringing little musical baggage with him to the table.

The new album was not the same. Steve now felt imbued with a fresh surge of creative ideas. Musically, the new album Wind & Wuthering harked back to Foxtrot, a deeply dramatic album and one, which Steve contributed to enormously. Eleventh Earl Of Mar, Unquiet Slumbers For The Sleepers and Blood On The Rooftops all bear his stamp. Tony Banks admits that Steve's contribution to the album was first rate: "There were things like Blood On The Rooftops which I didn't have a lot to do with in terms of writing but quite a lot to do with in terms of arranging. That was the first time that Steve's writing had really fitted into the band, and it was Phil's chorus with Steve's verse so it was the both of them and the two of them didn't tend to write so much for the band. That was really strong, that was a great track. Eleventh Earl Of Mar as well which quite a lot of the chorus parts was Steve's as well."

The sheer variety of musical ideas available was not just displayed across the album itself but even within songs, which was something that appealed especially to Steve. "One of the reasons we have so many different elements on one song, let alone on an album; is that if the listener doesn't respond to one thing; he probably will to something else. If you lose them at one point you will catch them somewhere else…"

However, once again the "committee" was weighted against Steve and it was the decision to include the lightweight Wot Gorilla over the fledgling version of Please Don't Touch that effectively forced his hand. "Please Don't Touch was something that Genesis rehearsed up originally and we didn't include it on the album because Phil could not get behind it. We did not develop it and I felt that it was a gem because the band didn't develop it. I felt; 'Hang on; here's one of my best ideas and we're not using it. Why are we including this one and not that one?' I became aware that the intensity of playing that was so important to me was not quite so high a priority for the others, as they were starting to relax a little bit more. I felt that I was coming up with far too many ideas for the band to fully exploit; explore is perhaps a better word and in order to develop I felt I had to work with some other people."

One musical idea, which Steve came up with, has been adored by fans ever since this album was released, and unusually for the band it was due to a technical problem in the studio. On the last day of recording the tape machine began to eat the tape rather than record it and this gave Steve the chance to try out another idea, which had been overlooked previously. "So Dave Hentschel, our engineer said; 'has anyone got any other ideas they want to try out?' And I had this idea of doing vocal loops. So the harmonies that you hear at the end of Afterglow are done with these vocal loops that were an idea of mine that wasn't a priority until we had the accident, because it meant that I could try the idea out. We had Phil sing on top of himself three times."

Steve's solo success may well have been the source of some rancour at the time. His desire to release further solo projects was viewed with a certain degree of suspicion as a potentially divisive threat to Genesis' audience at the time, especially with the re-emergence of Peter Gabriel as a solo artist that year. Ironic really, when it was Steve's first solo album that had effectively proven the loyalty of the Genesis fan base in the first place. "I was anxious to do a string of solo albums and this was something that worried both Tony and Mike. Phil wasn't in the least bit worried; he had been operating with Brand X for quite some time now but I think it was regarded as less of a threat because at least he wasn't pushing albums out under his own name but by this time everyone knew that Brand X was his band and he was going out and doing gigs with it so, perhaps if I had come up with another group title or something it would have been less of a hot potato but it did seem to create waves."

Wind & Wuthering is a much darker and dramatic album than its predecessor and a million miles from the then current heroes of the British musical critics and public. It is perhaps with a certain degree of irony that a song such as Eleventh Earl Of Mar ostensibly about a failed Jacobite rebellion could just as easily be a metaphor for the fickleness of the music press and music buying public who soon got bored of the so-called "New Wave" especially the lyric: "Bury your memories/Bury your friends/ Leave it alone for a year or two/Till the stories go hazy/And the legends come true/Then do it again/Some things never end." a brilliant observation of the cyclic nature of the music business perhaps?

Elsewhere too, Genesis proved that they had a fine eye for genuine pop songs. Your Own Special Way is a classic love song and anyone doubting the band's sense of humour should give the Tom & Jerry cartoon strip-styled All In A Mouse's Night a listen. In fact, once again the band suffered from an excess of good songs and the three that were left over; Pigeons, Match Of The Day and the superb social commentary on the injustices of the British legal system; Inside & Out should certainly have been included on the album.

Steve's commitment to Genesis' schedule ensured that his live swan song with the band was a memorable one. A massive world tour began with three nights at the recently refurbished Rainbow Theatre, a massive tour of the USA, and an enormously successful visit to South America. Genesis was one of the first European rock bands to play that continent.

Their success was finally confirmed by their triumphant return to London in late June 1977 for three sell-out shows at the massive Earls Court Arena, such was the demand to see the band at this time. Even though he was beginning to feel like a fish out of water within Genesis himself, Steve did manage to express his admiration for his fellow band mate and new boy, Chester Thompson who had been thrown in at the deep end on this tour. "I have become a fan of Chester's on this tour I hadn't heard much of him before we started playing together I had heard he had some involvement with Zappa's band and Weather Report which are pretty high credentials for any drummer. For a guy like that, working with us must seem like putting on another man's suit of clothes really; almost like an actor's role for him. Seeing if he can do it and he is really on another planet with us. He worked out great from the first day we started rehearsals he had already gone over a lot of our stuff in cassette form so he virtually knew it backwards when he started and that was great for us. All we were doing was drilling him on fine points really…

During interviews at this period, Steve managed to hide his feelings well, expressing the thought that there were still many areas of the US in particular that they had yet to visit and explore. Interestingly enough he also had the following to say when asked about the prospect of further solo outings by himself and the rest of the band during a telephone interview he did at the end of March 1977 at the end of the US tour: "I don't really know. I think we might sit down and discuss this but as far as I know no one was actually planning to do any but I think they are open to persuasion you know. It is not just me that needs the extra outlet…"

It is indeed a pity that perhaps that discussion never took place. Perhaps if everyone had relaxed their stiff upper lips a bit, the whole situation might have been resolved more amicably and a lot less painfully?

At the end of the tour, the band set to mixing down the masses of tapes they had from the previous two years' tours for a long overdue live album and it was during the mixing for that album; titled after Steve had departed, with a certain wry humour: Second's Out; that Steve finally announced that he had decided to quit the band for good. His reasons for so doing are as honest as his music and his own words on the subject should suffice for an answer: "I felt I had to work with some other people. I felt that I needed to paint pictures on my own. They had done great things but I felt to prove or to attempt that level of greatness for myself I had to do that outside the band. I was writing more and more but the band incorporated less and less. I had an abundance of ideas but it didn't affect the overall ratio of Hackett songs to; lets be honest, Tony Banks songs. Basically it was a two year decision, I didn't make it lightly and it didn't happen overnight."

John Hackett agrees with his brother's sentiments about leaving: "As I recall I was quite surprised when he left Genesis, but yeah… If you look back on it you could say I saw it coming. I remember he was a bit discontented. Well, we all whinge from time to time (laughs). As I understand it, it was because he wanted to do his solo stuff and there was a slight feeling from the others that perhaps that wasn't appropriate. Since then of course, they have all done their own things so what does it matter? He had such a strong creative talent and he wanted to take control of things himself and that is what he did and it has worked very well for him."

On the US promotional tour for Please Don't Touch, Steve commented: "After you've done one album yourself, an album which you're very pleased with and has sold well, you crave your own audience. There's no way that you are suddenly going to take a step back and accept a less responsible role. I've always wanted to work at my full potential. That's hard to do in a band when only a percentage is required."

It is interesting to hear the thoughts from the record company side of the coin however, as explained by Charisma's Managing Director; Brian Gibbon: "We always accepted Steve as having his own identity because we had done the first solo album with him and so there was no confusion in terms of his solo career. As there was no confusion with the things we did with Banksy and with Mike it was only that with Tony Smith, and I think this was a political thing; he wanted Phil to go to Virgin and I think that was more of a business thing. I never had any problems with any of the guys doing solo albums because they were almost doing it in downtime; they weren't on the road. I don't think anyone had a problem with him doing solo stuff; that wasn't a problem. They hadn't got around to it; he had because he wanted to work and do things. Phil had already started by that point with Brand X and that was his escape and I remember thinking 'Am I going to sell any of these? Probably not…' (Laughs) but yeah, we'll do it, we're his record label.

Steve appears to have had complete backing for his solo career from the record label Charisma, as Brian Gibbon recalls: "There was no doubt that we would put out Steve's stuff. We wanted to! And encouraged it. We didn't discourage any of them from the record company's point of view. We didn't grumble that we had a Brand X album or a Steve Hackett album because basically we needed to make releases every month and so that was never a problem".

He also has this to say regarding Steve's wish to have more writing credits, a frustration obviously felt by a musician who had shown just what he was capable of. Maybe being in a collective writing situation just wasn't going to work anymore. "The whole thing became a problem I think when Steve began to feel he wasn't getting a big enough share of the writing but I think the underlying thing is that he was perhaps asking for more than the boys were prepared to give at that stage, even though they did accept him as a full member of the band".

Steve may have felt, however misguidedly, that his solo work was not being given the same push as that of the band and/or Peter's solo ventures. Gibbon also goes on to air his views on the situation within the band regarding solo albums and how these were viewed. Remember that Peter Gabriel's option to divert his attention to the film script was rejected by the band, as total commitment at that time was required. Maybe a more mature group of individuals could see that solo work could be done whilst not taking away any momentum for the group. It is easy to view these things in hindsight but it does seem that solo options were not a hindrance to the artists and this wasn't the reason why Steve left. Gibbon continues… "There was this undercurrent that would push them to find another excuse but I don't ever believe they wanted Steve to leave - ever, and neither did Smithy. I tried to talk him out of it but it was a bit different to the Peter Gabriel scenario because Peter wanted to leave because they were going in different directions artistically. Steve wasn't going in a different direction; he just wanted to do what he wanted to do. They wouldn't have allowed him to make an album already unless… any of them could have made solo albums; it was written into their deals! Their deals said that they could make solo albums and that if they did, they had to offer them to us first. We had to have the option because Smithy might say 'I want a hundred grand for this' and I would say 'on your bike; if you can get a hundred grand for a Brand X album… great!' (laughs) but the solo albums were always written into an artist deal for two reasons. First; if the artist is worthy of a solo album, because some of them aren't; then we would like to have it and if he is not worthy then we don't want it. But the thing is that we would like to hear it and the third thing is it's a control because they usually have to ask our consent to do it. You don't want them to do a solo album too early in their career. So there are lots of controls in agreements like Greatest Hits and of course if they break up. Like it was in the case of Peter Gabriel leaving- it was like having a football team, like Ronaldo trying to go off and sign for Real Madrid (laughs). So it is a contractual control because you have given the group money for their albums not for the lead singer to be able to say 'cheerio' but that was an artistic thing".

Sadly, it appears that band politics did play their part in the lead up to Steve's decision to leave. The decision not to permit solo albums at this time, with the benefit of hindsight, may have been a wise one. Nonetheless, it was one which was bound to aggravate Steve given the fact that he had made the decision to record Voyage Of The Acolyte at a time when it appeared that Genesis may not have had a viable future, and when all of the other members (apart from Tony) had become involved with outside projects. By this time, however, opinions had become too deeply entrenched. Once Steve had made his mind up to leave, it was going to prove very difficult to persuade him otherwise. A situation, which has caused regrets all round since, as Brian Gibbon explains: "The Steve thing wasn't entirely an artistic thing, which was created by this situation, but then it led to other things. To an excuse to say you're not having that because they knew that would upset him and start him thinking if I haven't got a future here… It was nowhere similar to the Gabriel thing, that was a huge thing in terms of the band because he was the front man but that was to do with music; that was to do with wanting to try different things and the great thing was that another career was set up. Another big career was set up and we would have hoped that that would have happened to Steve as well. I don't know if Steve would ever acknowledge but he should never have left Genesis and he could have done both… which I told him! (laughs) Remember I am the record label; I wasn't managing him at that time and I asked him what was stopping him having a solo career and the answer was nothing, if you looked at it logically. It might have been a case of you can't do your tour if Genesis are doing a tour and so on but that is only logistics".

It is intriguing to think what might have happened had Phil Collins been at that particular meeting in time. Maybe the band's story might have taken an entirely different course. We shall never know. The split itself seemed to be amicable enough to the general public although Tony's ironic comments that once they knew he was leaving they mixed him out of the subsequent live album, certainly jarred a few nerves among the fan base. Indeed Steve's own comments in an American paper shortly after his departure outlining his reasons for leaving in perhaps a less diplomatic manner than might have been expected was to sour relations with the rest of the band for many years and divide the fan base even further. The balance of power, which had existed within the band throughout the period of Gabriel's tenure, had usually seen Tony in alliance with Mike, and Steve with Peter, with Phil usually watching from the sidelines.

Peter Gabriel's departure obviously weakened Steve's position and although he could convincingly argue the case that he was now a writer as well as a guitarist, he had produced a successful solo album when Genesis' future was in grave doubt, after all, but that cut no ice. Tony's gripe that he had effectively put his own solo album on hold for the band at this time really holds no water. Steve too, had scrapped much material to accommodate Genesis and he really felt that he could no longer tow this particular party line and make those kind of sacrifices which were obviously not being made by the others. If the material wasn't going to be used by Genesis, why should he waste it? Mixing down tracks, which he had heard hundreds of times for the live album; became a chore, which he could do without. The fact that apparently little effort was made by the remaining members to try and convince him to stay really says a lot about how much his contribution to Genesis had been undervalued by the band.

It must have seemed strange to be in a band having such success as Genesis were by 1977, yet knowing that you were about to walk away from it all. Steve recently gave the author his viewpoint on that decision and how it felt: "It felt great to be playing three nights at Earls Court and selling it out and me thinking; 'yeah, this band is up and flying, this has done everything in terms of the experiment' which Genesis always was for me. Genesis was never about making a fortune and having a glorious retirement; I still can't afford to retire even now - and I wouldn't want to! Good God, no. It did everything I wanted it to, and then it was time for a new model".

Hackett fans or "Hacketteers" as they have affectionately been labelled made no such mistake, and in many cases followed the exodus that had already attended the band when Gabriel had left and there is no doubt that the incarnation of the band which was left after Steve's departure had lost a certain charm and certainly a hefty slice of musical magic. Not that it stopped the band going on to even greater heights of success in the years which were to follow. And Steve remembers how impressed he was when he saw them after quitting: "When I saw Genesis at Hammersmith (1980) I was struck by what a great act they still were."

Upon its release on 2nd October 1977, Seconds Out reached the top ten in the UK album charts. As a resume of both Peter and Steve's time with the band it really is hard to beat and effectively drew a line under that period of Steve's musical development although it has to be said that the album as it stands does Steve little justice. It has become a standing joke among Hackett fans that Tony Banks' hand was on the faders during the mixing and Steve's contribution is buried in the mix. The fact that Steve himself was in many cases trying to make his guitar sound like a keyboard certainly doesn't help matters! Fortunately, there are several superb bootleg recordings from the 1976 and 1977 tours which serve as true testimony to his contribution to the band and it is to be hoped that the current excellent work of re-mastering the band's back catalogue of albums by long time producer; Nick Davis, might finally redress this perceived injustice. Whatever the realities of the situation, Steve considered that he had now graduated from musical university with honours and now the real musical world awaited him.

CHAPTER SIX

What A Carry On!

Without the safety net of Genesis to fall back on, Steve must have had thoughts of doubt about the wisdom of his decision to quit. If so, he certainly did not let the grass grow under his feet for long. The musical ideas which had occupied him for so long and which had remained without a proper home were soon to be given full treatment as he began to muster ideas and the troops for the album which he had passed over so much to make. Steve was at great pains to make his views on the reasons why he left Genesis and his rationale as a solo artist during several interviews he gave in the USA during the promotional outing for the new album. Sadly, not all of these interviews make for comfortable reading now, but they are interesting as a reflection of the state of Steve's mind at the time of the split and immediately afterwards: "It started taking shape in my mind a long, long time ago, certainly before I left the band, but the stuff on it is fairly current, stuff that I've written in the last year, although some of it dates back a lot further than that… not very much of it mind you! Some of it might well have been done by Genesis, had they shown more enthusiasm about some of the other things that I'd written."

Going solo was an uphill battle in so many ways. The critics and fans had been relatively kind to Steve's first effort while he was still in the bosom of the band, but now that he was out on his own, things were going to be radically different. That has to be said of his relationship with the record company too.

The problem was obviously an artistic one over details. Steve quite naturally wanted his work to be aired in the best possible light, however, artistic "temperament" and financial "realism" don't always mix although some viewpoints did not necessarily square with that of Charisma's Financial Director, Brian Gibbon: "It was open house and if you wanted to come in and see the press people or anything you didn't have to make an appointment. They normally did but if they were in Soho, they would pop in and see their record label and talk about whatever they wanted to talk about. It was a very hands on label so we were very sympathetic to the artistic side or whatever the artist wanted to talk about. So when it came to actually planning the actual promotions with them they were always involved with it.

When I managed to talk to Steve from the promotional side we would have everybody there as a team and I would invite any of the artists to come to the presentations I would make to the record labels so either they wanted to be there or they didn't. So when we had the likes of a Genesis playback, I would get the sales guys to come to the studio for the playback because that is so important a part of it and there aren't many labels that do that. All of the PolyGram boys used to love that and whatever the artist, they would be invited to the playback and the band would be there. They could talk to them and that was the way it was and that was the way we ran it".

Steve had already decided that the album was to be made in an environment where he was working with as wide a variety of artists as possible to bring his vision to life. Taking as broad a sweep of ideas as possible, his new album took in everything from heavy progressive rock to soul, ballads and typically English whimsy. Titled, Please Don't Touch the album showcased the diversity of ideas, which Steve had been brewing for some time. Typical of the adventurous nature of the material was the marvellously camp send-up of Agatha Christie's detective stories; Carry On Up The Vicarage, replete with sound effects and manic narration from Steve himself. He outlined his reasoning in an interview he gave for Good Times Magazine in April 1978: "A very large proportion of it had been written before I left Genesis. Because of the importance I placed on the material, I really wanted it to be recorded. With the band in the past, I found that certain things found favour and certain things didn't; the result being that I ended up scrapping a huge percentage of my material. Buy I felt that all of the songs on this album really deserved an airing. So, my impatience, combined with the desire to work with some other people, brought me to the necessary turning point."

Balanced against this was the marvellous balladry of Hoping Love Will Last, which was a song Steve had begun work on during his final period with Genesis but he had always envisaged it as being sung by a female singer: "I knew with a song like Hoping Love Will Last there was no way the band were in a position to do that. Obviously it was for a female singer and with all due respect to Phil, I couldn't imagine him singing that."

A chance encounter with Phil after the album was released, shows just how much opinions can change: "I remember bumping into Phil and Andi (Phil's first wife) in the King's Road and the two of them were saying how much they liked the album, especially the title track; and Phil said to me; 'It didn't sound like that when we rehearsed it' and Chester (Thompson) had done that and I felt that maybe if we had done it, then it would have come out great but Chester got a chance to shine on that. Originally I was questioning the part he had on that because it wasn't exactly the same pattern; it was a Weather Report pattern where the fast stuff was done on the hi-hat and he had two little things that sounded absolutely spot on and even now if I listen to that album I think, God it sounds like zombies trying to break out of the graveyard! (laughs). It's still a thrill for me because I tried very hard with that track".

Steve's choice of musicians and vocalists was inspired and in particular his choice of Randy Crawford for the vocal honours on "Hoping"... and Richie Havens on How Can I and Icarus Ascending took the album out of mainstream UK rock and gave it a flavour totally unexpected. Steve had inveigled Havens's support during an after-dinner discussion and the end results justified his confidence. He had already met Havens after the band's massively successful shows at Earls Court in June 1977 and Steve recalls the initial meeting that enlisted his help: "I wanted to meet him and I was wondering how to introduce myself when Dave LeBoult, his keyboard player wandered up and strangely enough started talking about Voyage Of The Acolyte, as he liked it. One thing led to another and I said I would like to meet Richie and Dave introduced me to him. He had just done a show and I am sure that he was shattered because he had put everything into it but he got up and shook my hand warmly for a long time. We got on well and I invited him to dinner a few days later. I thought that I would really like to work with him and the idea for a song started coming; even before he played the show I had heard him singing these lines in my head. I literally heard him singing the opening bars to Icarus Ascending. I didn't want to be pushy with him but at the end of the evening he said we should work together and I told him that I would love to do so."

Randy Crawford was a then unknown quantity in the UK and her vocal debut on Steve's album ensured her subsequent growing popularity here. Steve was looking for vocalists who could deliver his music in new and interesting ways and Randy certainly did that, " I met Randy in a nightclub and I can't remember the name of club but it was a club where I had originally gone to see Jaco Pastorius. I had gone along to see him because I loved the stuff he had done on Joni Mitchell's album. I was aware of what he had done with Weather Report. The opening act that night was Randy Crawford."

Randy was not well known here at the time, she had had no success here and very little success in the States. I saw her in this small club with a very small following who appreciated her every vocal pyrotechnic. It was similar to the Jazz audience vibe like when they do a solo manoeuvre with their instrument and there is a ripple of applause - all those things that are the stock in trade of the great Gospel/Jazz singers such as she is".

Nonetheless, the album had to contend with the savagery of New Wave, which by the autumn of 1978 was at its height. Strangely enough, the album did not receive any of the invective, which had been aimed at Genesis' last two albums. Indeed, both Steve and Peter's solo efforts were lauded as if these escapees from the excesses of Genesis were somehow above criticism. Perhaps it was the presence of a mainly American cast of musicians in the band that ensured that flak was minimal? Personally I have no doubts that it was the strength and variety of the material itself, which ensured its warm reception. There was no one thing that you could focus on to criticise, unless it be the very variety of ideas itself which was a point that Steve's then record company boss, Tony Stratton-Smith pointed out: "I think the punks would have been less able to assassinate this one than "Acolyte". I think there was a harder edge to it. There were areas where it was obviously more flowery. I wanted each track to be completely different to every other track so that there was really no central theme."

That is all too true, if you did not know who Steve Hackett was, there is nothing on this album which can really give you an indication at all of his former time with progressive giants Genesis. Not all of the critics were convinced, however, Steve Clarke of "Sounds" confirmed the above comments in his review: "It is both a measure of this record's random nature and its maker's lack of any strong musical personality that were it not for Steve Hackett's moniker being plastered all over it; it would be difficult to gauge exactly whose show Please Don't Touch is." So far so, good: Later in the same review however, he finally shows his true colours, "As a writer Hackett is no great shakes; he has ideas though usually he doesn't make the most of them. Often his melodies are annoyingly derivative."

Obviously Mr Clarke's sympathies lay elsewhere and the album's success in the charts must have been really galling for him! Musically, Steve stretched himself into areas which he had either never really touched before or into ones which he had wanted to explore but had been unable to whilst in the band. Even the album's title track a superb instrumental demanded more of the players than your average rock instrumental. "I still think that stands up as a piece of music that has still got teeth. When I did that I was a bit worried you know, the coming signs of madness; the Van Gogh swirls and so on, particularly the time signature sequence in it. When I heard it I realised that it was going to be very difficult to take because it was very extreme and it still is - its also difficult to play but it still works. It's not really Fusion either; its more of a Chinese Latin number really."

The album is chock full of weird and wonderful instrumentation including such archaic things as a psaltery, an ancient English stringed instrument. At the other end of the spectrum, however, Steve was not afraid to continue to embrace new technology including one of the first guitar synthesisers and computer technology abounded. As he stated in the album's sleeve notes, "And anything else I could lay my hands on at the time!" This was nowhere more in evidence than on Land Of A Thousand Autumns, where Steve fully embraced available studio technology in the shape of a computer called NECAM. "NECAM was the computer which we mixed the album on, although it wasn't all done by machines, but really what NECAM did was provide a kind of extra human memory, so it's a case of when you are in the studio you can mix on a computer or you can commit to tape and that has the advantage of being able to update it as you go along. For instance; if you want to bring up the vocals; you have got everything else dead right and you want to bring up the vocals; you can do that and you can adjust everything to the nth degree. Its just a wider degree of flexibility and I thought it would be rather nice because I had felt that the computer had contributed so much that we named a track after it."

Please Don't Touch certainly highlighted the sheer diversity of ideas and musicianship that were housed within him, although in all fairness, it is very difficult to imagine now, how this diversity could ever have sat comfortably within the confines of a band like Genesis! It always demonstrated that Steve was always prepared to work creatively with other musicians with the sole beneficiary being the resultant music as he explained at the time of the album's release, "Personally what I try to do now is - and what I tried to do on the solo album was - to make sure that everyone who worked on it was as happy with their performance as possible. If there was something wrong with it, I wanted to know why. And if they didn't like a song, I wouldn't ask them to do it. In fact, I had the reverse problem on Icarus Ascending, which Richie Havens sings on the album. Steve Walsh wanted to sing it and I had a problem because I had already given it to Richie. It's a pity, you know I would love to do two different versions and release them. But I had settled on certain people for certain songs and I think I made good choices. I worked very closely with all the people on it, and the problem if anything, is that because I worked for four months on the album, I need a breather from it now in order to be able to go back and enjoy it. Every time I hear it now I just think of all the sweat and the effort we put in to make it happen!"

The album was a struggle in many ways. Steve was still finding his feet both musically and in terms of production. The advice he was getting from the two different record companies (Charisma in the UK and Chrysalis in the USA) was often contradictory and led to some clashes. In the meantime, he continued to explore wider musical vistas: "That was a far more difficult album because by then I had left the band, and yes, I was nervous. I was doing far more than an album. Over the course of it I was forming a band. I didn't really have a game plan and really I wanted to do a number of pieces that I felt couldn't have been done within the auspices of the band. Having written a song for Randy Crawford and plainly that was always going to be a girl's song. I defy any man to sing a decent version of that! (laughs). It was an attempt like Jim Webb to bridge the generations in tracks like the romanticism of Hoping Love Will Last with the urgency of the title track where you have got a kind of fusion approach.

I think the choice of musicians had to do with the fact that my American record company at the time were showing a tremendous amount of enthusiasm whereas in England I think that I felt I was up against my own background and shadow boxing. It was made largely in L.A. but I didn't finish it there so half of it was done back home and I just ran out of time trying to do it there. I felt I had to come back to these shores to finish it off for all sorts of reasons. It's funny, it's an album that in part I am absolutely thrilled to have done and in another sense I felt that a lot of it is less than classic but what's classic is eternal about it. So I have mixed feelings about it as an album".

Obviously, with a band featuring as many famous names as this one did, touring with the recording musicians was not an option. Tour he must though, because Steve's fans were now keen to see their hero on a stage of his own. Steve had sworn that he would no longer be a touring artist and would content himself as a recording artist at the time of his departure from Genesis. Anyone who knows the man, however, will tell you that the equation "Hackett + Studio Album = Live Performance" is one which is as obvious as it is fundamental. Steve's brother, who has been a mainstay of most of Steve's subsequent touring bands summed him up nicely: "Steve is never happier than when he is onstage. I think he loves being onstage and he is his happiest when he is up there onstage playing his guitar. So, I think to just release studio albums for Steve would never be enough."

Even Steve himself admits that not touring for an album was something that was not really a sufficiently satisfying option. He needed the roar of the crowd as well as the barbs of the critics. "I realised several months afterwards, after swearing that I wouldn't tour I realised that I missed touring. The trouble is that if you are not touring an album all you have got is the critical response and the professional critics obviously the first time round will give you so much benefit of the doubt but the next time round it is much harder because the more you commit of yourself, the less new it is - the second production. It's that problem second album, isn't it?"

However, touring as a solo act wasn't necessarily that obvious to Steve and before he gave it any real thought it took someone else to point out that he could. "I was talking to someone at MAM (a promotions agency), Ian Wright who said; 'you know you can do some shows' and it hadn't dawned on me. I said; 'how am I going to do shows? I haven't got a band, I haven't got a line-up I had this guest and that guest...' and He said; 'well, you could put together a band' and the concept hadn't even dawned on me! (Laughs) I was trying to make albums that were hits, and that happens only to the very lucky few. Please Don't Touch had done substantially less well than the first album and I wondered why that was because I liked it just as much. People said; 'perhaps you need to promote it, perhaps you need to get out there and start doing it'.

So I started recruiting people and Nick Magnus was one of the first I saw. He was playing away in the living room of the house he shared with probably ninety seven other people (laughs) and I asked him; 'you can't do the sound of a church organ, can you?' thinking he'll never be able to do it with the two keyboards he's got, and he said; 'it just so happens I can because I have hooked up these oscillators...' In true boffin style he played something and it was just glorious and I thought; 'yeah, this guy is thinking along the right sort of lines...' And that was the keyboard sound you got to hear on Spectral Mornings".

Steve's fans are not only his most loyal supporters but also his harshest critics but at least they have paid for the privilege of speaking their criticism unlike the "professionals" such as Steve Clarke whose review was quoted earlier; who seldom buy the albums they review or pay for the tickets for the gigs they attend. Steve's first solo gig was at the Chateau Neuf on 4th October 1978 and which, surprisingly enough was not in France but in Oslo, Norway! His debut British gig was a few weeks later at the University Hall in Cardiff. The tour was a short one, consisting of about twenty dates in several European territories and also a handful of UK shows.

Going out on his own was every bit as nerve-wracking as his early days with Genesis: "I remember being incredibly nervous before the first gig in Oslo and that first gig went off so incredibly well. I thought if we can do this now then we can do it on other nights and that tour was great and we did wonderful business and audiences were fabulously supportive and it was wonderful".

Not everything on the tour was hi-tech and flashy and the Hackett entourage certainly didn't have the money for such things as Vari*lites*, something that Genesis started using in the early eighties.

The tour was a simple expedient of testing the waters to find out what the reception to the idea of Steve Hackett "solo artist" would be like. I am sure that Steve must have felt a certain amount of nervousness about those first gigs - he wasn't the only one! He didn't need to be nervous; the tour was a great success and fortunately did great business.

It was with a feeling of extreme trepidation that the author attended Steve's inaugural shows back in 1978. I had heard how important a part of Genesis he had been but now was my chance to witness that for myself. 1978 was a very important year for me musically. I finally got to see Steve's old stalwarts in Genesis for the first time at the massive Knebworth Park event which emphasised their now solid presence as rock superstars and a scant few months later I finally saw Steve and his new band in a much more intimate environment of Manchester's Apollo Theatre for an evening which was packed with magic, mystery and mayhem and that was just on stage! Anyone seeing Steve's first solo performances will tell you that they wove a magic which remained with you long after you had departed the car park and were home.

Once again, his mother remembers those early solo shows with fondness: "I remember the gig at Cardiff which was the first time I saw Steve and John on stage together there were lots of happy tears then. I had taken my mum and he played The Steppes for the first time and he said; 'I call this one Eric' (laughs) that was great."

Listen, if you can to any of the available bootlegs from that tour and you will soon realise what I mean. Despite the fact that the album had been recorded using a host of famous names and new and not so new technology, it is the sheer inventiveness of Steve's writing and his playing and the playing of his new band, which dominates the proceedings. The material from both his solo albums shines through a set which beggars' belief in terms of

*VARI*LITE is the brand name of one of the first automated variable-colour lighting systems, created by Showco a company from Texas, USA.

dynamics and driving enthusiasm. Magical soundscapes such as Land Of A Thousand Autumns and other worldly playing stood shoulder to shoulder with playful items such as Narnia and then to hear the sheer rock power of A Tower Struck Down amply demonstrated that Steve was more than capable of being the ring master in his own circus, surrounded by equally talented bandsmen determined to enjoy themselves.

He also continued the Genesis tradition of road testing as yet unrecorded material to gauge the opinion of his sternest critics: the fans, along with a playful nod at his previous band: I Know What I Like. The end result was a resounding success and one which certainly put Steve in a welcome position of knowing that not only could he pull off solo performances but that there was an audience more than willing to go along with him for the adventure.

The situation was not quite as easy for one of the members of that touring band, vocalist Peter Hicks, who was ensconced in a nine-to-five job at the time: "I was working in an office during the day and rushing up to London for rehearsals in the evening which became a nightmare scenario of sixteen to eighteen hour days. We were practising new songs; the songs I had learned from the albums and I had worked out the harmonies with Dik (Cadbury) and Steve."

This combination of long hours followed by the disorientation of travel made sure that Peter's opening night performance was one which he will never forget: "However, at the end of those gruelling days I was so confident and so familiar with Steve's intricate music that at the opening gig in Oslo I stumbled on stage and sang the first verse of Racing In A slightly out of tune and managed to get the verses of Narnia back to front." And Steve still let him have the job!

CHAPTER SEVEN

Towards The Spectral Morning

With his feet now firmly set upon the path towards a solo career, Steve continued to explore the new vistas that had opened up once the blinkers that had blinded him in Genesis had been removed. Always open to new ideas, one of the key people to assist his explorations over the next few years was keyboard player Nick Magnus whose previous bands had included a stint with The Enid. However he almost missed his chance to join as he recalls: "Steve saw my advert in Melody Maker and he 'phoned up. I thought it was somebody pulling my leg because Terry Pack from The Enid had a speciality of prank 'phone calls and he had done a couple of those on me. I thought this was another one. Eventually he managed to convince me that he was Steve Hackett and he said; 'I'll come down to your place and meet you and have a chat'. Even right up to the day when it happened I wasn't expecting it to. Of course it did and it was the whole shebang; there was Steve, and John came as well, so I had this nerve wracking and slightly undignified audition. They said; 'well, go on; play us something' and I just stumbled through a few things. Then Steve said 'Well, would you like to come up for a proper play around?' So, about two weeks later, his roadie; Ged Fitzpatrick came down in the van and picked all my stuff up and drove me up to London to the rehearsal room. It was just Steve and me in the rehearsal room and we ploughed our way through everything he could think of."

Of course, for any musician worth his salt; the ability to be paid for playing with the latest tools of the trade was also an added bonus, although not all of the new "kit" behaved exactly as it should, as Nick remembers only too well: "The Mellotron was a fantastic thing to play. I loved playing the Mellotron and when I discovered that part of the gig with Steve was having a Mellotron to play, I just couldn't believe my luck. They are only a pain on stage; they are always well behaved in the studio. Well; the one we had in the studio always behaved perfectly in the studio; it never put a foot wrong. The moment you took it on stage it sulked. The main problem was it didn't like extremes of temperature. It was basically; hot truck; cold gig; hot lights; cold bit in between sound check and gig and you would get condensation on the tapes. It would just dissolve the oxide off them and you would end up with brown glue on the tape head. So you would hold a chord down and then you would let go and you would hear a rustling sound of the thing rewinding and it hadn't rewound! (Laughs). So, we would end up with Ged (Fitzpatrick) sitting behind the thing with the back off just pulling the tapes down by hand as I was playing it. He did a fantastic job… he rarely missed a note! (Laughs)".

Nick had had no involvement with the recording of Please Don't Touch but he and the rest of Steve's new band were thrown in at the deep end with the short tour which opened Steve's solo live career in October 1978. The band had already started rehearsing for the follow-up to that album in September 1978 before the tour took place and several numbers from it were to be included in the set. Continuing to explore Steve found he had no shortage of ideas and the new album titled Spectral Mornings after the instrumental title track branched out into many differing areas. Everyday was Steve's first attempt to make an anti-drug song, very much a memory of the difficult times he had experienced with his first girlfriend and her addiction to "Cleopatra's Needle" and Steve was determined to exorcise the ghost of that particular relationship: "I had been involved with somebody who was a drug user in a very big way and it seemed that the more you put into that person; the less you got out. I was always trying to prop her up emotionally; always trying to get her to value herself and she was hell bent on a slow suicide, so I had seen what hard drugs could do to somebody."

In keeping with the rest of the album, Everyday was also devised very much as a live number. With the nucleus of a band now fully coalesced; it was important to maintain the live "vibe" of this and other tracks, which had been very much worked out in rehearsal room and concert stage. "It was a number which was born out of, to some extent, a song which I had written on a guitar but the actual arrangement as such was very much a rehearsal room number. The thing is that some of these things take more shape in the rehearsal room; some of them took more shape on the road. I mean; two tracks; Spectral Mornings, the title track and Clocks were included in the previous road show and I'd had the benefit of taking those numbers on the road and knowing just how ballsy they could be. So I wanted to ensure that the album had that kind of live feel. I didn't want people to say; 'Oh but you are so much better live'.

I wanted people to say; 'Yeah, really sounds like a live recording'."

The Red Flower Of Taichi Blooms Everywhere displayed his knowledge and appreciation of Chinese and Oriental music whilst The Virgin And The Gypsy was his very own homage to Dylan Thomas and D H Lawrence. "I hadn't read the book (The Virgin & The Gypsy) and funnily enough I didn't want to read the book. I sat down with some knowledge of the story and I had a Victorian book of flowers, so I thought I would try and string together a lyric using flower names. I was quite surprised and delighted to find when I read the book later; that he had included the word Marigold because it is both descriptive and a flower name."

Steve was never studiously inclined as he himself is the first to admit and yet; his leanings towards the classics of literature and music subconsciously informed his work even here, "Its funny I hardly ever read a thing while at school because they were always recommending us to read books and I always felt that these things were being forced on to us; shoved onto us and I never did. It wasn't until I left school that I found my own way into books. Some writers tend to write almost like musicians; certain writers have a rhythm to their writing,"

Fortunately, the school time experience eventually wore off and Steve's literary delvings have continued to influence his work, as has spiritualism, as he explains: "I was influenced by the Tarot when I did Voyage... and at that time I think I might have been more susceptible to the influence of gurus, and I use that term in its widest sense. Then by the time I came to Spectral Mornings where most of the lyrics were really based on the idea of spiritualism and the idea of survival. The title track Spectral Mornings itself was the idea of a spiritual release after all of this (corporeal existence). The flying feeling, the soaring, moments of that and it is still an interesting area and it does inform what I do but I think poetry more than anything else. I think while everyone else was trying to be 'Street Cred' around the time of Punk and there is still a hangover of that... nobody wants to be seen dead in poet's shoes and there's still a lot to reading Dylan Thomas".

Steve was never one to stand on ceremony and take himself too seriously, and Nick Magnus remembers his first rehearsal with Steve as an extremely pleasurable one: "The prospect was daunting but actually doing it was one of the most pleasurable days I can remember. Steve was so nice and it was at that point that I realised that other musicians; regardless of who they are; are human and nervous and make mistakes as well. And I thought; 'Oh God, Steve has played loads of bum notes!' So I didn't feel at all bad when I did too. I think that mutual realisation between the two of us made us feel very

Aged five - June 1955 *(Courtesy Mrs J Leaney)*

Aged six with John aged one - April 1956
(Courtesy Mrs J Leaney)

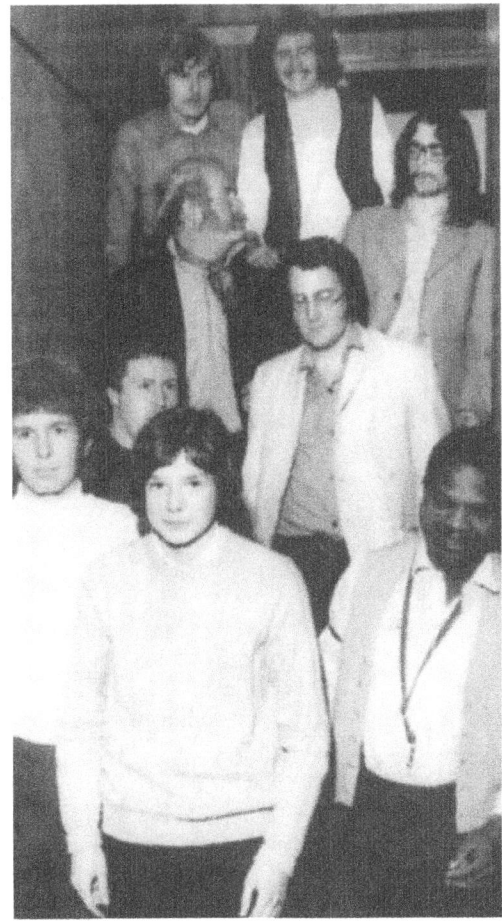

Quiet World 1969 - From top left; John Heather, Lea Heather, Sean O'Malley, Steve, Phil Henderson, Dick Driver, Neil Heather, John Hackett, Eddy Hines *(Courtesy Steve Hackett)*

Genesis - December 1972. From top left; Peter Gabriel, Steve, Phil Collins, Mike Rutherford, Tony Banks *(Courtesy Charisma Records)*

In Island Studios for the mixing sessions of 'The Lamb Lies Down On Broadway' - September 1974
(Robert Ellis/Repfoto)

"The Lamia". Genesis onstage at the Liverpool Empire Theatre during the
The Lamb Lies Down On Broadway' tour - April 1975 *(Robert Ellis/Repfoto)*

Performing with Genesis at the Palais De Sport in Paris - March 1975 *(Robert Ellis/Repfoto)*

"The Acolyte steps out" - 1975
(Courtesy Chrysalis Records)

1970's promotional shot
(Courtesy Charisma Records)

Happy days at the 'A Trick Of The Tail' sessions - 1975
(Courtesy Charisma Records)

"The windswept look is definitely in this year!" - 1976
(Courtesy Chrysalis Records)

Using the 'tapping' technique on the 'A Trick Of The Tail' Tour at the Hammersmith Odeon - June 1976
(Alan Perry)

Genesis on the 1977 'Wind And Wuthering' Tour. Left to right; Tony Banks, Chester Thompson, Mike Rutherford, Phil Collins and Steve *(Courtesy Atlantic Records)*

On stage in Liverpool during the 'Wind And Wuthering' Tour - January 1977 *(Alan Perry)*

"Landing lights in Liverpool". Genesis on the 'Wind And Wuthering' Tour - January 1977 *(Alan Perry)*

On the first solo outing. The 'Please Don't Touch' Tour - October 1978 *(Alan Perry)*

1980 promotional shot *(Courtesy Epic Records)*  Live in Boston - 1980 *(Roger Salem)*

Dik Cadbury
Boston - 1980
(Roger Salem)

John Shearer
Reading Festival - 1979
(Roger Salem)

John Hackett
Reading Festival - 1979
(Roger Salem)

Nick Magnus
New York - 1980
(Roger Salem)

Pete Hicks
Boston - 1980
(Roger Salem)

Performing at the Montreux Festival as part of the 'Defector' Tour - 1980 *(Roger Salem)*

comfortable and he was going through lots of ideas and saying; 'Can you do this?' and I would go; 'I think so' and by the end of the afternoon he was going; 'well, I can't think of anything else really; do you want the job?' I said 'yes' and that was basically it."

Dik Cadbury, another musician in Steve's first touring band also recalls his first encounters: "Having set the studio (Millstream) up I didn't think there was a full time role for me; I wasn't a sound engineer so I was looking for another post-Decameron gig and had just joined Pekoe Orange, a London/Kent based band playing original Dire Straits-ish songs. I loved the Little Feat vibe that they had and there was a serious push to get a deal. I think I played the last pub gig (The Pegasus in London) during the earliest rehearsal period with the new Hackett line-up. I had my shiny new bass cabs and amps I know that!

Then one day John Acock came into the studio and mentioned that he'd been asked by Steve if he could recommend any musicians for a band he was putting together and he had recommended me for the bass role. I got the call and got the job. At the audition we started with a blues jam and then Steve asked if there was anything I wanted to play? I had already wondered how the riff in A Tower Struck Down went, so Steve showed me and a couple of minutes later we were happily playing it together. He then revealed that the bass player on the session took an hour to learn the riff- I was in!"

In fact, although Steve had already written the basic ideas for the album; the recording process involved the rest of the band quite largely in the overall creative process as his brother remembers: "The thing is, as musicians it was a very exciting time because instead of having musicians coming in to do the project; it was a band and we used to rehearse together and then we would record the stuff and so I think it was a very exciting time for all of us, and certainly Steve was very up for the whole thing. There was something about... like getting it together in the country. But going somewhere overseas to do a project. There is a lot to be said for it. It was absolutely great. As far as the wildness goes; you know when you are recording there is an awful lot of hanging around that has to be done and when the Scotch is there, you need to get stuck into it!"

The intriguing thing about Steve's work methods to those who have seen him in action is that he always seems to have the ideas; fully formed in his head. He instinctively knows what a track should sound like but he has always been prepared to listen to the people around him in search of pinning down the performance that will define the initial idea that he has in his head.

He is not hidebound by musical rules and conventions and has always been prepared to take musical risks in pursuit of the bigger picture. It is a fascinating work method and one, which even leaves people who have known him for a long time, bemused, as his brother remarks: "It is an interesting thing about the writing, especially for that album because I had never really thought about it. I had always rather taken it for granted when we got together and did stuff that Steve would say; 'Well, I have got this... and I have got that' and we would put it together. Steve has never worked by sketching ideas out on a multi track as far as I know. He always had it in his head with the guitar; and he just had this aural vision. Steve seems to have this natural ability to imagine what he wants it to be like."

Nowhere was that ability to imagine what the end result should be like tested more fully than in the creation of the aural nightmare that became Clocks- The Angel Of Mons. "Clocks is quite a strange piece. It grew up in the rehearsal room and I spent two days trying to explain to everyone exactly what I was in about and it came at the end of a rehearsal period whereby at the end of it, you were totally washed out trying to explain this thing and remain articulate and feeling very, very tired at this point. And I said; 'Well, basically, it was written for a horror film score'. I was trying to retain that sort of suspense; almost to a time bomb feel and then it finally explodes."

Steve has always been prepared to give the musicians around him plenty of freedom to fulfil the creative process but always has his own mind set on what the final result should be, as Dik Cadbury recalls: "Steve came across as very reserved but clear in his mind about the direction he wanted the music to follow. On the whole Steve came in with his guitar sketch and a vocal melody where there were lyrics. In rehearsal he would usually start working with Nick (Magnus) to sort out the keyboard arrangements. The rest of us would quietly try things out or note things down so that by the time that he and Nick had sorted themselves out; we would have a pretty good idea of where we were going. With some songs Steve would have the bass parts in his head, which I would be shown, otherwise we just started running the number and fine-tuning it as we went.

Obviously we had the opportunity to pitch in ideas but mostly, if Steve said nothing then we assumed we were on the right track. I was given the role of vocal arranger. Steve was very keen to achieve the tight block harmonies of Crosby, Stills And Nash and Kansas and that's where my choral training and time with Decameron came in. With The Virgin & The Gypsy I confess I got carried away! Pete and Steve had their parts laid down and I got this vision in my head, probably inspired by 10cc's I'm Not In Love where one chord fades across another. I recorded the first harmony and then every time that

John (Acock) said; 'That's good, come and listen', I'd say; 'Just give me one more track' - I've got an idea'. They let me run with it and what came out has to be my best vocal performance."

Certainly, the end result was worth it and Spectral Mornings exploded into the UK charts giving Steve another chart success and the darker and more dramatic feel of the album was very much in keeping with the situation in England at the time. 1979 was another difficult year in the UK; the Labour Government of James Callaghan was in its death throes. The so-called "Social Contract" foisted on his Government by his allies; the Liberal Party was in ruins and the Trade Union movement was up in arms. Strikes, power cuts and pickets were the all too clear evidence that Britain was edging nearer to the "Anarchy In The UK" which the prophets of the Punk movement had been preaching a mere few months before.

Genesis had been forced to record out of the country due to crippling tax rates imposed on higher earners and Steve had been forced to follow suit. Spectral Mornings was recorded at the Hilversum Studios in Holland, which doubled as a radio station and headquarters for PolyGram, the distributors of Charisma's record product since 1974. Recording the album there might have been a relief from the social problems plaguing the UK at the time, but Steve remembers there being other problems to contend with: "Spectral Mornings was recorded at the beginning of 1979. It was very, very cold; sixteen degrees below zero and very little sleep! I used to come in at 3AM and the maids used to start making the rooms at 4AM! I swear they used to start at four! (Laughs).

"We recorded the album pretty much after we finished the 1978 tour," recalls Nick Magnus. "I think we started something like the second week in January 1979, we went over to Wisselloord in Holland and spent something like a month over there recording it and it was a wonderful, wonderful time. It was my first proper professional recording and the studio was great, it was a lovely studio and I think we were all sort of thrilled with the whole novelty of the situation and we had a cracking time. The food was wonderful- Indonesian food almost every day! The cleaners were absolutely lethal with their vacuum cleaners over there! If there was a vertical surface they could ram the vacuum cleaner against, preferably your door; they would do it! It was very cold; beautiful snowy weather at the time and the hotel that we were staying in had a gigantic lake outside at the rear, which must have had several feet of ice on it. You could not only see people skating on it but also people having car skidding contests on it!"

Life in the studio very soon took on a separate existence all of its own and soon developed a pace of its own. Late night table tennis and table football sessions with other bands inhabiting the same studio environment and a certain young flute player's incessant practising of Bach. Out of it all, certain moments stood out in Peter Hicks' memory: "The recording of the title track still remains one of the most moving experiences of my time with the band. There is something about that track that still makes me feel quite emotional. Then we had the lunacy of 'The Office Party' and of course, 'The Janitor' which you better ask Steve about!"

Bassist Dik Cadbury recalls a couple of the more surreal moments during the recording process: "I bumped into one of Holland's top session drummers; Louis Debij. He had recorded and toured with a Dutch band called Fungus in 1975 supporting Decameron (Dik's previous band) and had stayed with me during that period. John (Shearer) had just recorded the drum solo at the end of Clocks and I invited Louis to come and hear it. He asked John 'how many overdubs did you do?' John: 'none'. Louis: 'what are you - some kind of fucking octopus or something?'

Cadbury also recalls that the aforementioned track "The Janitor" wasn't without its moments either: "On The Office Party I remember really struggling with the bass pedal part. I was trying to replicate the steel drum in a calypso I'd heard on an album my parents had brought back from Trinidad (Carnival In Trinidad I think). After a while I gave up and said I would come back to it the next day. When the red light went on the next day it came to me straight away!"

Despite the carnival atmosphere of such tracks, there is a very wintry feel to the album; in many respects it is perhaps a hark back to the last album that Steve had recorded with Genesis: Wind & Wuthering, there are echoes of the same atmosphere and it was an interesting piece of Low Fi equipment that Steve had discovered during the recording sessions that brought a lighter hearted element to the album and the subsequent live show: "It was called The Optigon. I used to mess around with this thing. I found this machine, which was designed, for lounge use in Holland while we were at a place called Relight Studios where we had recorded Wind & Wuthering. It was an amazing machine; the height of kitsch in other words. On one side of the keyboard it would give you pre-recorded riffs with discs that you used to insert to achieve them. Again, it was supposed to be a moment of light relief."

The wartime experiences of Steve's own family also seem to have been brought to bear on the album. Steve's grandfather had served in the First World War and had been present at the Battle of Mons where the "Angel" had appeared. This incident was witnessed by over sixty thousand troops both allied and German, and depending on whose testimony you hear, the figure that was seen was either an angel or the Patron Saint of England: Saint George on a white horse, leading the British troops across No Man's Land on the first day of the battle, which was one of the bloodiest of that incredible conflict.

Although Steve would probably deny any innate knowledge of it; both Clocks: The Angel Of Mons and Spectral Mornings itself, are perhaps a requiem for the fallen in much the same way that Everyday was a tribute to modern life's own casualties? The noise and confusion of the battlefield are recalled with fervour in the frenetic former track whilst the latter brings to mind the quiet resolution of the morning after a battle and I can't help but be reminded of the closing sections of the marvellous film adaptation of Erich Maria Remarque's damning indictment of war: "All Quiet On The Western Front" with the ghosts of the slain marching into the distance accompanied by Steve's glorious soaring guitar solo.

Not all the album is of a serious cast however. The Ballad Of The Decomposing Man, which features the Optigon, brings a lighter moment to the proceedings. Mistaken for a protest about the chaos inflicted on the country by the conflict between the Trade Union Movement and the British Government, the song is in fact a parody of Music Hall star; George Formby! "It was really a straight George Formby parody. Probably a very bad impression of George Formby but nonetheless, it was meant to be humorous, I really wasn't thinking about any deeper meaning for the song. There come times when you do that but I don't want it all to be seen as serious as that... I think having a sense of humour is important."

That sense of humour was also demonstrated on a track called The Janitor, which was very much a throw away track and indeed it was thrown away until the initial release of Steve's albums on CD by Virgin Records in 1989 where it made an unexpected re-appearance. It had not been labelled on the master tapes at the time, and its re-appearance on the CD issue was as much a surprise to Steve as it was to the unsuspecting fans that eagerly bought the album! The track featured a spoken word run-out after the final track in which a disgruntled studio cleaner (AKA: Peter Hicks) fulminated about the mess that musicians made while working. Fortunately, this gem has since been restored to its rightful place as one of the bonus tracks on the new re-mastered edition: A delightfully light-hearted moment.

Steve threw himself into touring for this album with no less than two tours taking place during 1979. The first was an all UK affair but the second took in more dates in Europe and it was at one of them that one of the more surreal happenings that can occasionally take place when on the road, happened. Steve had a dedicated road crew, none more so than Gerard "Ged" Fitzpatrick; who was by all accounts quite a fiery individual and it was a local promoter at one of the German dates on the Autumn tour who incurred his wrath. As Steve's former manager; Billy Budis recalls, the guy was wandering round backstage checking that everything was okay but he had forgotten to wear his backstage pass. He was challenged by young Mr Fitzpatrick who obviously wanted to know who he was and what he was doing there: Due to language difficulties, and probably with much gesticulating, neither individual could make himself clear to the other and Ged resorted to talking with his fists and laid the poor guy out cold! No one ever forgot to wear their stage passes after that!

John Hackett remembers another amusing incident, which illustrated that life on the road, could have its funny side too, even if he didn't see it quite as amusing as the rest of the guys did: "I suppose compared to most rock bands we were actually pretty reserved and well behaved (and after travelling with them on several tours over the last few years the author can vouch for that!) I think I was probably much more uptight about things in those days in some ways and it was at the end of the tour and one of the roadies came on and thrust this custard pie in my face. It went all over my flute and I absolutely freaked out, you know; 'Look what you've done to my flute!' You have to laugh about it now."

By the time the second tour of the year was under way, Steve had already begun to form ideas for his next album, some of which was once again to be road-tested on the autumn tour. The guys, who had been enlisted a scant twelve months before merely to enable Steve to perform his existing music live, had evolved into a coherent and solidly creative working line-up. Revisiting an idea that was by now totally unfashionable; he launched a concept album upon an unsuspecting audience who had thought such things long dead and buried.

CHAPTER EIGHT

The Defector Speaks Out

As the Seventies gave way to the Eighties, the domestic troubles, which had plagued Britain, were replaced by a new era of international Cold War politics. At home, the British had elected their first woman premier; Margaret Thatcher and in the USA and Russia leaders; Reagan and Brezhnev were now in power, as determined to flex their muscles on the international stage as she was at home, as the Conservative Government set about bringing the Socialist North to heel in an exercise in political revenge that was to eventually leave the country bitterly divided.

Russian troops invaded Afghanistan and compounded the mistakes the British had made when they tried to rule that most ungovernable of countries. In the Middle East, the Shah was thrown into exile from Iran and American interests there were attacked and hostages taken. Against this background, Steve was to create one of his most challenging albums.

Challenging times were in store for all concerned. The late 1970's had not been kind to Charisma and had it not been for Genesis's runaway success with 1978's And Then There Were Three album which was the only UK album to achieve platinum status in 1978, the label's financial problems may have been considerably worse. In an interesting article in Music Week in September 1979, Charisma's founder; Tony Stratton- Smith had some very interesting and prophetic comments to make about Steve: "I feel that we have only seen half the potential of Steve Hackett and his last album (Spectral Mornings) was the first that had a 'band' feel. His next album in April will be very important to the company as it will be the first on the Charisma label in the States."

The new album: Defector, took as its basic premise the viewpoint of a refugee from the Soviet Bloc arriving in the West and his/her impressions of their new environment and memories of their old homeland. Of course, intriguingly enough, you could also stand this idea on its head and have the

"Defector" heading in the opposite direction and have it work just as well. As an idea it is certainly an intriguing one and with infinitely more merit than some of its predecessors in the field of supposed "concepts". At least, set in the context of its time and even subsequently it makes sense. What is fascinating to realise though is that at the time, Steve had no direct experience of the Communist East; he had never toured there or visited on holiday and yet here was an album that in its more successful moments; evoked a spirit and ethos totally in keeping with the subject.

The album's opening track The Steppes is a desolate windswept panorama augmented by the plaintive flute playing of Steve's brother. This is an album of light and shade, a creative process at which Steve is a master. The monochromatic Steppes are replaced by the garish vibrancy of Jacuzzi where the decadence of the West is given a jaunty flourish. An anguished plea for sanity is made in both Time To Get Out and The Show, which form a wonderfully contrasting set of bookends to the contrasting viewpoints of East and West. Nonconformity is urged in both tracks and the lyrics paint vivid pictures of both the mindless acceptance of dogmatic ideology that Communism espouses with the equally poisonous dogma of Capitalism.

The Show is also a brilliantly evocative examination of the demands that the rock 'n' roll lifestyle makes on its practitioners - a plea for sanity all round? Surprisingly enough for such a "political" album, Steve disavows that there is any deep political message in it: "I think that at the time there was a feeling that everything was going to explode. I know that I felt very depressed about the way the world was at the time. I suppose this was a much more cynical version. I just felt that everyone should just get the hell out of there. It wasn't a particularly political solution or anything. I think it was very apolitical; I hadn't formed any opinions I just felt that in the face of corruption a mass walk-out seemed the best way."

Once again, Steve had come to the table with his ideas well formed for the members of the band to work on and it is that freedom to be creative within the studio environment that Nick Magnus remembers: "Again, compositionally it was Steve's baby and obviously by then we'd had the benefit of a year together so people tended to input more into the process of actually recording and a lot of that was created in the studio. The spontaneity happened in the rehearsal room; that was when everybody pitched in and said; 'Why don't we try this? What would happen if we did that?' I don't think Steve would have been interested in people who just turned up and played solely what they were told…"

The band's creative involvement with the album grew to include co-composition credits shared with Pete Hicks on the anarchic Sentimental Institution and the cod heavy metal B Side; Hercules Unchained. Hammer In the Sand also finally took shape after nearly being abandoned, when Nick Magnus played it on the studio's Bosendorfer piano giving its final and unashamedly glorious romantic sound.

Not all the album was doom and gloom, however. Steve did manage to squeeze in another of his eccentric masterpieces in the shape of the aforementioned manic Sentimental Institution; a pastiche of ideas sending up the Big Band sound of the 1940's in a wonderfully camp outing down Insanity Lane which brought a lighter edge to the proceedings.

There is, of course, another school of thought that maintains that Defector of all of Steve's albums is a reflection on his departure from Genesis. Looked at from that perspective; Time To Get Out and Leaving are the tracks with the most obvious connotations in that department although Sentimental Institution too could be a wry look at the band in the guise of the "rich old lady" whose seductive powers Steve had finally eschewed; and both Jacuzzi and The Toast, the results of overindulgence in the hedonistic lifestyle which members of such well-known rock bands are "supposed" to take part in, perhaps?

Looked at in hindsight, even the promotional video for The Show, one of two tracks selected to be released as singles from the album, can be interpreted as either a dig at the faceless mandarins in charge of the Government or perhaps even the "suits" in charge of the record company. It featured two puppets dressed in pin stripe suits and bowler hats only to reveal Steve as the puppet master at the end! Wishful thinking? Or perhaps an indication of what was to come? An interesting alternative viewpoint from the norm and one, which has given some of Steve's fans pause for thought over the years.

For an album with such heavy weight ideas, the results were enormously encouraging. At his gig at the City Hall in Sheffield on 17th June, Steve was able to announce that the album had charted at number sixteen a hefty improvement on previous efforts., and it eventually achieved even better success, peaking at number nine, easily fulfilling Strat's confidence in Steve. In fact, 1980 was to be something of a high water mark for Charisma where, against the odds albums by Steve, Genesis and Peter Gabriel dominated the charts both in the UK and abroad. Once again, Steve was engaged in large scale touring for most of the summer and autumn including a slot at the prestigious Montreux Jazz Festival which was captured for posterity by the television cameras.

Touring also took Steve and the band to the USA for the first time, in the autumn, with an extensive string of shows which brought the Hackett brand of musical magic and mayhem to the other side of the Pond for the first time, promoting Defector as the first Charisma album to be released by the USA label; an exhausting schedule which was to have unforeseen repercussions in the near future. The touring schedule in the US was not helped by the fact that the record industry there organises promotion on a State by State basis which ended up being a nightmare for the band's tour manager Mick Angus, even indulging in some small deception due to American Trade Union rules which restricted who could work in their territories, which the band got round by having their sound and lighting engineer enter the US as "tourists"!

The touring life was not without its humorous moments though, as Dik Cadbury recalls: "Peter (Hicks) was notorious for his quick wit and especially in America where he was stopped by passers-by. Passing through the airport terminal in Buffalo and sounding a bit 'estuarine' (as he does), someone said to him:

Hey- you're English?
Pete: 'Yeah'.
Passer by: 'So how do you like fucking Buffalo?'
Pete: 'Never tried it'.

Passer by with a confused expression walks on by. Anyone with a fur coat would be asked; 'what's the bear wearing?'

He also had very irreverent titles for Steve's albums; The Voyage Of The Bakolite, Squeeze, Don't Crush; Spittoon Drownings; Defecator…."

What's that about having respect for your employer?

A potential "reunion" with Phil Collins almost took place at the Roxy Theatre in West Hollywood when Chester Thompson came backstage to inform Steve that Phil was in a bar next door and asked if Steve would care to join him. Sadly, Steve was occupied performing a show and asked if Phil would like to attend - sadly they never met!

The final gigs of the year in Italy also had unforeseen repercussions at the time which Peter Hicks remembers: "Sentimental Institution and It's Now Or Never were not received well in Italy; Sentimental Institution was an experiment and a lot of French and English audiences loved it but I'm not at all surprised It's Now Or Never was unpopular in Italy purely because of its musical origins - in the North it is considered to be a song from the South which even in a small country like England can sometimes cause a little friction. In the North of Italy they probably thought we were taking the piss."

Cadbury recalls the reaction to this particular ditty as being less than cordial too: "When touring in Italy Steve thought it would be a laugh to combine Elvis' It's Now Or Never with the Just One Cornetto jingle as an encore. O Sole Mio on which both of these are based is a Southern folk song and hated in the North and sacred in the South. So we finish the gig on the first night to rapturous applause, come back and do this number to be greeted with whistles and catcalls - the magic utterly destroyed! Our promoter takes Steve aside and strongly advises us not to repeat the exercise. Next night, Steve doesn't seem the harm and we go back, a little uncertainly in my case, and get the same reaction. Given my picture of Italy and the behaviour of dissatisfied audiences, I'm just waiting for the gunshot but we get away with it. This time the promoter backs Steve into a corner and makes it quite clear that we mustn't do it again (which fortunately we didn't). After that, a few gigs later our coach (yes, we were travelling by coach at that point) had all its windows smashed by dissident fans who couldn't get in for nothing and being a British coach we couldn't get replacement windows in Italy. So our poor driver had to cross the high mountain passes (in November) in a windowless coach, freezing his nuts off, to meet up with a colleague bringing a replacement bus from England to meet him in Lyon. We continued by Italian coach and travelled to France by train! You see, life on the road…"

CHAPTER NINE

Taking The Cure

By the end of 1980, Steve was able to take stock of his solo career to date. He had come so far from the artist prepared to colour in corners of other musician's musical artworks; to creating his own, fully formed masterpieces on a series of extremely broad and adventurous musical canvasses. The 1980's beckoned as a decade of further adventure and was certainly to prove to be one of the most challenging of Steve's career.

In 1980 Steve encountered the first signs of the differences in opinion with Charisma. He had realised that there was a demand for a live album from the last few years' successful tours. He would have been more than happy to release one, with numerous desk recordings from gigs at his disposal. Charisma appeared disinterested however, despite Steve's assertion that it was something that the fans wanted. Given the great success which had attended the Defector album and tour in terms of domestic and overseas sales; this was something of a mystifying decision by the record company. In fact, it was to be another ten years before he was able to release a live album but we shall come to that in good time. This did not stop him however, and he was soon at work on his new album.

From the perspective of the record company, a live album in much the same way as a "Greatest Hits" package is always viewed as something that can be used as a stop gap to keep an artists' profile high during a period of hiatus which was why Charisma were initially reluctant to the idea but not apathetic to it, as Brian Gibbon explains: "Charisma were not against the idea of Steve releasing a live album. The company were more interested in getting a new studio album. A live album was something that could easily be released at any point but at this time Steve was on a roll and Charisma were determined to keep that momentum going. Of course you always have your creative arguments with any artist and I can only tell you at the top level, life is full of politics and so I can't tell you what the promotion guy said or the marketing guys said or what the press guys said I can only tell you what Tony (Stratton-Smith) and I said. And that was that we would always try and be constructive and take on board comments and we could achieve it or that's not the right way.

I think that nobody wants to hear bad news but if you are an artist it is even worse or not even bad news but a difference of opinion. There was very little difference of opinion in terms of their musical input that was very important for us to let them get on and create their own music. It was always at the point of where we thought we were better because that was what we were employed for; we were a record label. We know how to plug; we know how to do the press and the promotion and I know how to work the sales guys. If you wanted to come to those meetings you were invited which is impossible to do now."

Meanwhile, just before Steve went on tour he found time to get married to Kim Poor at Chelsea Town Hall on 14th August. He had found the experience of extensive touring to be extremely wearying, especially after 1980's tour had seen him extend his touring itinerary to cover the USA for the first time: "It was the first time I had done an English tour, European tour and an American tour of two shows a night plus all the handshaking and a crash course in popularity - I found there wasn't much of me left."

The strain of the demands placed on him had even seen Steve spend time in hospital for treatment to stomach ulcers; a sure sign of stress so he ditched the elements of the rock lifestyle which were affecting his health; he gave up smoking and drinking and took up exercise - hardly the behaviour of a hedonistic rocker: "I had had some health problems during the period of Please Don't Touch where I actually ended up in hospital with ulcers. Around the time of Cured I thought; 'I really want to be healthy' When I was in Brazil; I was there for three months writing the album and I was doing a fantastic amount of exercise every day. I was really thrilled that when I got home I had managed to lose a tremendous amount of weight and I had become a runner again. So, I really wanted to clean up my act in a big way."

Steve played guitar to the track Voo do Coracao by Ritchie, an English artist resident in Brazil. The latter also incorporated a theme, which Steve was later to recycle as part of Jane Austen's door from the 1999 Darktown album. None of these tracks have been widely heard outside of their Brazilian marketplace although a recent unofficial compilation of "Hackett Rarities" has made them available to anyone keen enough to seek a copy out.

With live gigs becoming fewer in number at the time; it was not only Steve's waistline that was trimmed down. Upon the release of the new album: Cured, featuring a photograph of Steve wearing an enigmatic smile overlooking a sunlit Bermudan seashore; fans were shocked to see that the regular touring/recording band had been replaced by new musicians, and in one case by (shock, horror!) a drum machine! This was a purely economic reason rather than any personal conflicts with the musicians involved as Steve explains: "It was impossible to maintain weekly wages. I had a conversation with Bill Bruford funnily enough at the same time as I think I was about to disband. Anyway, he actually said; 'My band are driving me to the poorhouse' I think he had a band for about two years and had managed to keep it together. You see, the nice thing was that I was doing a fair amount of festivals and a fair amount of gigs at the time and regularly touring both in the States and here in Europe so it made sense to me that if someone said to me; 'Can you do a gig in Paris next week?' I would 'phone up the band and say; 'Right, chaps; we're off.' I was thinking along the lines of a much more traditional bandleader. In other words; it was like; 'Come on, boys; follow me we're off to conquer the Hun or the Frog!' (Laughs) That was great but it meant spending a lot of money and at the end of the day the gods of business had to be appeased; a shame really. The carpet was always pulled out from under one that way!"

Ironically, the above statement really reinforces what Brian Gibbon had already stated previously in particular with reference to Genesis in the early 70's. Artists seldom (if ever) had the individual wherewithal to maintain a band themselves without the support of the record company itself, a fact that is often overlooked by artists and fans alike.

Many speculated that there was some darker meaning behind the album's title, but nothing could have been further from the truth: "if you see the picture, its somebody sitting in the tropics and the idea came to me for the title because I thought who wouldn't be cured sitting in that situation? That photo was taken in Bermuda and it made me feel very well. I did a lot of touring and I did two shows every night and I lost a stone in weight and I became very, very tired from doing that kind of tour and so I took a break."

For fans still reeling from the shock of the abandonment of the services of Messrs Hicks, Cadbury and Shearer, an even greater shock was in store. Cured, featured a selection of much shorter one could almost say "poppier" songs all sung by Steve himself. This really should not have been such a surprise, Steve had always done backing vocals on his albums but he had finally moved centre stage in every way with this album. It took some while to get used to the idea of Steve becoming singer, I suppose it was a similar shock to that Genesis fans experienced when Phil Collins stepped up to the microphone. Familiarity had not necessarily bred contempt; but had certainly bred an atmosphere of complacency among Steve's fans - something that he was determined to avoid: "It was good, Nick used the drum machine and played keyboards and I played bass and guitar and sang and it still sounded like a band really. You wouldn't know it was just two people. I think from here on I do all the singing. With singing its like you can't get everyone to agree if someone has a good voice or not it's a very personal thing about singers and I enjoy singing enough to say I will do all the singing. Its far easier doing all my own singing than working with other singers really."

The decision not to continue with the now established touring and recording line-up took fans and members of that band by surprise as Dik Cadbury recalls: "I was very upset and very sad. I consider the time I spent with this band to be the highpoint of my musical career! There was a meeting during the last UK tour in 1980 where we aired our views on where we thought the band should be going, mainly from the point of view of the band members having creative input. I felt that certain members, given their head would strengthen the band and make it more a band and less a bunch of hired hands. Maybe that was unwelcome and to be fair to Steve, the band existed because he, as I see it, he left Genesis to be able to promote his compositions and talents. We should have known our place but I genuinely think we wanted to make things as good as they possibly could be, especially making the most of the astonishing talents of Nick's playing (already much in evidence but I felt not acknowledged enough) and Pete's lyric writing. I fear that encounter may have sealed our fate, although I believe Steve actually had a discussion with Bill Bruford about the cost of running a permanent band and possibly concluded that he couldn't afford us!"

Whatever the truth of the matter, the resulting album was a complete volt-face for Steve. The album has been labelled as "commercial" and yes, tracks such as Hope I Don't Wake and the upbeat Picture Postcard have all the trademarks of 1980's bubblegum Pop but even in these tracks there is an indefinable quality, which marks them out as a cut above the usual chart fodder. In fact, here was almost something synchronous about Steve's latest offering and that of his former band mates in Genesis. Both Cured and the latest Genesis album; Abacab stripped things back to the bare essentials to emerge leaner, and in Genesis' case, definitely meaner and it was intriguing to see the reaction to their respective new sounds. Genesis definitely got the worst of it; with fans at several European gigs booing the newer material!

Steve's fans were much more restrained in their reactions and the tour in support of Cured was received as appreciatively as usual.

Steve admitted in an interview he gave in Montreal the following year that part of his decision to change things so radically was down to lack of airplay and access to radio: "There is a change on the album. It is shorter songs; more simple; shorter songs a chance to sing myself It is a step in a more simple direction really; more mainstream if you like. The nice thing is, you see with the last album I couldn't get any radio play with the last album or the album before. Here in the States and Canada I had twenty or so radio stations playing those albums. Now I have over a hundred playing the album because there are songs so you see some of the reasoning behind it."

Unusually for a Hackett album, the main influence on Cured was definitely Steve's keyboard player; Nick Magnus with whom he shared compositional credits on several tracks - a first for a Hackett album. Nick's influence is central to the change in direction, which the album took as Nick, admits: "It was an experiment and I have to confess it was all my fault! (Laughs). It was just when the original Linn drum had come out because up until then the most sophisticated drum machine had been the TR808, and then the TR909 and apart from the 909 having sampled cymbals on it; drums still didn't sound anything like real drums and nothing did. So, when the Linn drum came out; I thought; 'I've just got to hear one of these'. I rushed over to Syco Systems who were the sole distributors the time and had a whizz through on one and immediately fell in techno lust with it. I had to get my hands on one and I thought I would never be able to afford one because they were £3-4000 when they came out and I thought… 'I know someone who can afford one…' (Laughs) So I rushed back and said to Steve; 'You have got to see this thing' and Steve was very keen too, so I dragged him over to Syco and gave him the full run down on it and he just fell in love with it too. I said; 'Do you think we might be able to use this instead of real drums on the next album?' And he was going; 'Oh, I don't know…' sharp intake of breath. So he bought one and we started recording with it."

Cured is a mixed bag of an album. You can hear Steve stretching out to embrace new technologies and ideas and deciding to take on the singing himself was certainly a brave step but much of the music is firmly rooted in the past. In fact, the album's closing track; Turn Back Time could almost be seen as wishful thinking! It is also ironic that despite embracing "New" technology, the presence of the drum machine is the one thing that makes the album sound incredibly dated when listened to now -something that Steve's music could seldom be accused of! The more traditional tracks such as

Overnight Sleeper and The Air Conditioned Nightmare; are exactly that and they stick out like the proverbial sore thumb. Hope I Don't Wake and Picture Postcard would have done quite well as singles but they lack that killer edge to divorce them from any association with Steve's past. Maybe this was down to a tacit admission on Steve's part of his own vocal limitations: "At the time I was learning to sing and trying to develop a vocal personality which at times ran contrary with my musical leanings. The point whereby some people were doing Jazz-Rock which I didn't feel particularly comfortable with. It wasn't a conscious decision to start writing commercial songs; I think one or two of them came out that way because of the use of the drum machine. The album had a more lightweight feel. In many ways it was more of a duet between Nick Magnus and myself. I was working with the limitations of my own voice rather than with people who had cast iron voices and so I think it was an album of finding my way."

For touring purposes, Steve eventually enlisted the assistance of two musicians whose credentials were already established in the music world. Chas Cronk, who was currently working as bassist in Rick Wakeman's band and who had previously played in The Strawbs, and Ian Mosley whose drumming had graced many a recording session and who was subsequently to become the backbone of progressive pockers; Marillion. Together with Nick Magnus and John Hackett this new look band took to the road in late August 1981 for another extensive European jaunt including the first gigs by any member of Genesis behind the Iron Curtain with two gigs in the then Yugoslav Republic in Ljubljana and Zagreb. A further appearance at that years' Reading Festival was broadcast by BBC Radio One's "Friday Rock Show" and subsequently widely bootlegged.

Steve even graced our TV screens here in the UK with a half hour live TV appearance filmed at the band's gig at Rock City in Nottingham for a brand new but ultimately short-lived TV series called "Video Sounds". It was also Steve's first commercial video release although not many copies surfaced. The live shows confirmed Steve's popularity both here and abroad and despite many fans' reservations about the somewhat lightweight nature of Cured as an album, there was no doubting the vibrancy of the material in the live context.

CHAPTER TEN

Taking The Long Way To The Camino Royale Via The Bay Of Kings

Anyone who had seen the events of 1981; a stripped back album of predominantly commercially-slanted songs featuring a drum machine might have been forgiven for thinking that there was nothing else Steve could do to take them by surprise. And they would have been completely wrong. The next eighteen months were to see some of the biggest changes in his career.

The following year began with high hopes for a new album but fan expectations were to be kept waiting. It was during this part of the 1980's that Charisma Records, a testament to the character and ingenuity of its founding father; Tony Stratton-Smith and to the eclectic mix of artists that formed its roster, came into conflict with the hard-headed business realities of the period. Success was increasingly dictated by how many chart singles your artists had and such qualities as "artistic integrity" became increasingly seen as filthy words. With their emphasis on album bands, and with a roster of extremely eclectic rather than mainstream artists; Charisma had pinned its contractual affiliations and its hopes to the shirt tails of its UK distributor; Virgin Records, itself another thriving example of small-time "Independent" success being assimilated by corporate necessity.

Steve once again pushed the idea of a live album their way but Charisma was determined to get another album out of him and with the emphasis becoming increasingly on sales figures; the idea of a hit single reared its head too. "I wasn't really aware of the situation with Charisma at that time. It became harder to work with them because they wanted to become more involved creatively with the product and the problems soon arose with a company that was in disarray itself. It can be very difficult if you are caught between departments. In other words A & R were starting to make comments and requests, which didn't fit the managing director's (Stratton-Smith's) idea. So it left me in the middle trying to steer a sensible course. As a result, Highly

Strung was a more difficult album. The circumstances around it were not as easy as I was defending my integrity if you like and that was why the album took eighteen months to take shape..."

In 1982 Steve's erstwhile band mate Peter Gabriel had allowed his altruism to get the better of him and his involvement with the good-intentioned World Of Music Arts And Dance (WOMAD) Festival in the summer of 1982 had become a financial nightmare. Genesis themselves were riding high on the success of the Abacab album and tour and were on tour in support of their new live album; Three Sides Live. Having heard of the problems which Peter was encountering, the band decided to help him out by organising the event which Genesis fans had dreamed of since 1975 - a reunion with Gabriel. Scheduled to take place at the end of their current UK tour, the gig was to be staged on Saturday 2nd October 1982 under the title: "Six Of The Best". For contractual reasons, they could not call it "Genesis"! The choice of venue and date were not particularly wise; Milton Keynes Concert Bowl is an okay venue for an outdoor gig in the summer but true to form, that old equation Genesis + open air made for an extremely wet day out for the sixty or so thousand fans who attended the event- I am still scraping the mud off after all these years myself!

Intriguingly enough, Anthony Phillips had been asked to take part in the gig, which was to be a fundraiser to help clear the outstanding debts of the WOMAD organisation. He had agreed to participate but was bizarrely subsequently advised by his then manager (Tony Smith) that it would not be a "good career move!"

Fortunately for all concerned; Steve was able to return to the UK in time from Brazil and his appearance on stage brought about the only complete reunion of the classic five man line up of Genesis if only for two songs: I Know What I Like and The Knife. As gigs go, it was a shambles; Gabriel forgot the words and looked at times to be extremely uncomfortable; but for anyone like myself who had never seen Steve or Peter on stage with Genesis; there was only one place to be that extremely wet Saturday evening!

During the lead up to the release of the new album, Steve was twice a guest on the music show Gas Tank on the newly established UK terrestrial TV station, Channel 4. Hosted by fellow Charisma artist; Rick Wakeman, it was during the second of these performances that fans got their first taste of the new album with a re-arranged (or should that be deranged?) instrumental version of Camino Royale. There was also an interesting conversation between the two musicians and a plug for an as yet unreleased collaborative album between these two musicians - obviously something that the A & R department at Charisma didn't approve of! Intriguingly enough, Charisma had recently refused to release Wakeman's Rock 'N' Roll Prophet album at this time, and he was to find himself surreptitiously dumped by the label shortly afterwards; which might make one wonder if perhaps Wakeman's comments during the Gas Tank interview with Steve were a little on the ironic side? It is also interesting that Wakeman then took the step that Steve was to take himself, several years later when he founded the short-lived Moon Records to release the album that Charisma had passed on. Both Rick and Steve are now the proud owners of their own recording facilities and labels but such things were really unheard of in the early 1980's.

Steve recalls the lack of direction that he was receiving at this time: "I think that the industry was seeking to re-invent itself and struggling to justify the old precepts by which things were fudged: The whole drive towards excellence. When you had a number of artists who were saying "you don't have to do that, you can do it on the cheap and it doesn't have to be good". Things were very image driven at that time. Basically it was brought home to me that what I thought was cutting edge; I was considered to be part of the Old Guard due to be swept away.

Whereas I felt in fact that what better badge of courage could there be than to say "I am an experimenter and I have said goodbye to success. I have walked away from a very successful band because I have belief in the power of musical ideas in themselves and I then went through a period of savaging in the press and basically if you weren't Punk then you were re-establishing yourself in the face of that and people were losing their jobs left, right and centre, including Chris Welch.
Strat wanted me to have a producer but the producers that were prepared to produce me, he didn't think were up to scratch! So, meanwhile I was losing time and I felt I needed an album each year; I was touring although I had abandoned the notion of having a regular band by then through the financial pressures of bankrolling a band from week to week but I did want to get back on the road in front of people.
And so, while all of that was going on I said; "well what do you think if I carry on recording because we are losing time here and don't you think it best to capitalise on the momentum?" So, I produced an album and a track that was a potential single. Unfortunately all of the mixes I had done of it were being rejected until I did a 12" extended version and that seemed to win the seal of approval. In other words, the thinking was within the industry that you could release the same piece of product twice; you could release a single version and an extended version and this may make things interesting."

Steve's new up front approach was all part of the fundamental rehabilitation of his own persona. For years, he had avoided confrontation. But now, as he was finally beginning to realise he had the confidence to tackle things head on as he had done by stripping things back to basics with his previous album; ditching the requirement to be a diplomat when it came to the feelings or opinions of musicians working with him in search of what he himself knew to be the right direction to pursue. At last he was not prepared to back down and the results were always going to challenge perceptions both Steve's own and those of his fans who had perhaps become a little too comfortable with what they thought their hero was all about.

Fans deprived of live sightings took comfort from his appearance at a special show at London's Venue Club on 13th December 1982 at which he showcased material from the as yet unreleased album before re-appearing to fans' delight on 29th January 1983 alongside his old band mates Peter Gabriel and Mike Rutherford for a special charitable show in aid of the Tadworth Children's Hospital appeal. This was not his first charitable effort; in November 1981 he had organised the "Poland Aid" concert aimed at providing medical aid for Poland after the imposition of martial law by the government of Marshall Jaruzelski.

The album, titled Highly Strung finally appeared in the shops on 23rd April 1983, preceded by the single Cell 151 on the 16th. The album's title ironically reflected the troubled background behind it and yet it is one of Steve's loosest sounding albums. Give It Away certainly sounds like a piece of advice from artist to record company executive... "When you lose your prized possession/Give it away. And perhaps also when looked at closely Steve had realised that it was time to move on himself, "When you lose your self-expression/It's just time to change direction/There's no need for more protection/Give it away." By this time, Steve was not prepared to subsume himself to the record company machinery; he had already acquitted himself as an artist and as such he was still trying to push himself further. The album also spawned a bona fide rarity; at least on this side of the Pond. Walking Through Walls, another intriguing album cut was given the full works on the US album with this extended version clocking in at almost two minutes longer than its UK counterpart.

Steve had always said that he needed time to "dream" his new projects into being, and he appeared to be taking this literally with some of the tracks from Highly Strung. "I've dreamed some marvellous melodies over the years - but they always used to go out of my mind by the time I woke up in the morning. One track; the third one; Always Somewhere Else I already had written but I wasn't going to use it until I dreamed I heard it playing on a car stereo and it sounded fantastic. But there are other things like Camino Royale which is an attempt to remember a tune I heard in a dream all about New Orleans; and Walking Through Walls which is based on a dream I had after reading a book by Carlos Castaneda. Both of those songs were conceived entirely out of a dream experience."

Certainly, the album took musical chances and Steve continued to work on his singing technique stretching himself beyond his usual range on tracks like Give It Away: Gradually breaking down his own limitations and developing a vocal style which he was comfortable with; which his fans grew used to as time progressed, and the initial shock of seeing him as singer as well as guitarist had begun to wear off.

Ironically, the album did spawn a hit single in the unlikely shape of Cell 151 which, if you are of a cynical cast of mind could also be seen as a reflection on Steve's relationship with Charisma. "It was ironic that it (Cell 151) was a success because it was a track that had been re-mixed eight times! (Laughs). It was always going backwards and forwards and I would be asking; 'Do you like this? Do you like that?' I constantly had the feeling that I was auditioning with the record company. It was an uncertain atmosphere and I wasn't sure of things. Even though I had success with that track, they decided that they weren't going to be involved with me anymore. Charisma wanted me to have a producer at the start and then they couldn't agree which producer it should be; so I said; ' well, do you mind if in the meantime, I just try and get on with it and start recording?'."

Charisma's problems left Steve with an album that he had every confidence in, one which he had invested a lot of himself in putting together as well; and with a hit single that, had Charisma had the financial clout, would have given them that much sought after chart success. Another track from the album really does show the fine line in humour that Steve displayed at a time when he must really have felt like screaming: India Rubber Man's ironic lyric... "The more I stretch the more you ask/Illusion has no end sums up the situation quite nicely. Weightless, meanwhile, based on Steve's experiences of hang gliding was just as much about facing up to your own fears and weaknesses which was something that Steve had finally begun to do for himself. The financial situation was not quite as black as it was painted however, as Brian Gibbon explains: "It wasn't that Charisma were in dire straits it was Strat getting fed up with the business and me wanting to get out as well. When you are at the sharp end of running something you get worn down. The objection to the live album was that I thought it was too early and

I thought he had more creative stuff to come out before a live album. To me it was as simple as that he had more creative work. We could always put out a live album because that's what you do. For me it is like putting out a Greatest Hits album too early like Wayne Rooney writing his book when he is only twelve years old (laughs). There is a flow with what a record company does; you put out full-price albums for as long as you can. If there is a huge gap and nothing is getting done or if Steve had said to me 'I'm not going to write anything for three years' then that's okay. We could put out a live album but there's got to be a reason for it or for a Greatest Hits and if you are still making albums, you know you can always bring out a live album if there is a gap in your recording. I don't think the fans were crying out for a live album as much as for a new Steve Hackett album. We might have had an argument about it but my argument would be why? Why aren't we bringing out a new Steve Hackett album? The live album we can bring out any time you like, and we can do anything you want with it".

Perhaps an example of artistic and commercial thinking not quite running in synch: Then there was also the decision to reject an all-acoustic project which Steve had begun considering back in 1980, "Firstly, so many fans were asking for a live album and I wanted to deliver one but Charisma were firmly against that. I felt it would have been the right move. The other was the idea of an all-acoustic album, which I had started doing in my own spare time with my own money as it were. I started recording that in 1980 but it wasn't released until 1983."

Once again, the situation was not quite as clear-cut as Brian Gibbon explains, "When I left Charisma, Steve approached me. I still had all the contacts with all the record labels there was a gap in terms of the management and he approached me because he was looking to renew the deal at that time. I managed Steve and I tried to get him a deal with the majors, mainly Chrysalis in the States but it was a difficult time for any artist to get a deal at that time. So the opportunity came about with Lamborghini who were an independent company with bucket loads of money. I thought this might be another little Charisma that might be right for Steve and we signed to them but they didn't fulfil any ambitions for themselves or for us really and so things ticked over for a while.

I suppose really they didn't have the wherewithal to promote it and I think that Lamborghini should have stuck with Pop and become like a RAK Records kind of thing. It was run by a chap called Mike Hurst who was with The Springfields so it was very much a poppy background. Basically it just didn't work out and I couldn't get it with any of the majors. The acoustic album was so far away from what they thought Steve Hackett should be that there was no vision there in terms of how to promote it. That album would have been fantastic on the old Charisma as a statement and I think it would have been accepted but trying to actually sell it to a new company who were thinking; 'this is an ex member of Genesis, we can only sell this as an ex member of Genesis but how can we sell an acoustic album?' With Charisma it might have been viewed as Steve's version of Brand X, it's not something he is going to do all the time but it's interesting, you know."

Steve soon found another record company with the right ethos towards his music. "Brian Gibbon approached me and he and I were involved for a while. Start was Brian's label. I continued to record but deals weren't always forthcoming however I did do something via Lamborghini Records which then went through Start and there is the chequered history of Bay Of Kings; an album I am still proud of that but which ended up going through a number of record companies before Camino eventually got hold of it."

Recording and releasing albums comprised entirely of acoustic music was something that was relatively unheard of in the early 1980's. The advent of "New Age" and MTV's "Unplugged" idea was still several years away and yet it worked. The album was a success in the classical charts and Steve even undertook a UK tour of smaller venues and university halls in support of the album with his brother John on flute. Not so much a trip down Memory Lane as a back to basics approach. "I started writing things that were as complex as my technique would allow but melodies were the things which seemed to be the most important. I viewed it as music without props and that pre-dates New Age and Unplugged so the derivations from the Classical and the Flamenco and folk and all these kind of areas are all there. I think it was a reaction against the dependency; the pyrotechnics of rock; the smoke and lasers and the dancing girls in the wings! (Laughs)".

The confusion that was primarily caused by bad advertising is reflected in the following extract from a review of Steve's performance at the Great Hall of Cardiff University, which was printed in the student magazine at the time...

"Concern over the competition with the bar meant that it was eventually closed during the performance. I think it would be fair to say that the Great Hall was not the best venue for this gig. I heard several comments afterwards, which ranged from 'boring...' to 'I could get into this...' so the new Hackett venture will lose him some support; but time will tell whether he gains acceptance with other audiences. The sight of the floor covered with seated bodies being somewhat out of place here. Anyhow, this piece of unashamed self-indulgence worked well if you were used to a 'Classical' style or were open to new ideas, but for those who were not, I assume the evening was a waste of time, well bad luck to them. The sound system left something to be desired but considering that Hackett was approaching the whole venture from a rock angle rather than a classical one it was inevitable; but the lighting, although sparse, was tasteful."

There were certainly no dancing girls at the shows but a lot of musical excellence, as Steve and John not only presented the new material but also a selection of wonderfully re-worked adaptations of existing classics from Steve's repertoire and the odd Genesis bit too. The album challenged the fans preconceptions of Steve as a musician yet again and it proved too much at one gig where the audience, who had been led to expect a full band show, were not best pleased by the acoustic setting they found themselves listening to. They gave the musicians such a hard time that the following night's gig was cancelled. The above review gives an idea of the mixed views which fans had over the new show but undoubtedly; bad or misleading advertising was the primary source of complaints rather than the actual content or performance of the shows themselves. Fortunately, the rest of the audiences were much more understanding and appreciative and the extensive tour for the album set the stage for future acoustic excursions which have become an increasingly common facet of Steve's music.

Steve could also take comfort from the fact that his gig at the prestigious Barbican Theatre in London in November 1983 was only the second sell-out gig of that year's season and the final seal of approval for his new approach came when no less an alumnus than Sir Yehudi Menuhin used a track from the album as part of the soundtrack to the documentary which was made about his music foundation: "From Kew To The Findhorn Foundation".

If Bay Of Kings could possibly lay claim to the title of the first "Unplugged" album, then his next effort was certainly one of the first albums under what is now the rather overused (and abused) "World Music" banner: Till We Have Faces, a title borrowed from a story by Steve's literary hero; C S Lewis whose work he had previously acknowledged on the track Narnia. The album is a ragbag of ideas. Many fans, myself included; were somewhat surprised, if not to say shocked by this album - I will be honest and say that on first hearing, I hated it! And to this day it remains my least favourite Hackett album.

Half the album was recorded in Brazil. Taking the basis of a Brazilian samba school of percussionists into the studio; this album is a drummer's wet dream. Every possible combination of rhythms is explored and stretched out in meandering paradiddles under which occasionally, you can hear a guitar. However, if you want an album that genuinely fits the definition of "Progressive" then this isn't your album. Each track features a different musical style from the basic Blues of Let Me Count The Ways, which was the first time that Steve had ventured out of the closet with his Blues vibratos. A Doll That's Made In Japan and What's My Name are the albums' sole concessions to what you would generally call "Rock" but at the same time have the influences of their respective countries; the koto features highly in the former, and the "Samba School" of Brazilian drummers is all over the latter; while Matilda Smith-Williams Home For The Aged, besides being the kind of title that you would have nightmares about during a game of Charades, is also a genuine hark-back to the anarchic humour that had been missing off Steve's most recent albums; especially the wonderful line: "And if you smuggle in another drop of gin/We'll take your hearing aid away".

Rob McIvor's review of the album in "Sounds" gave it a favourable and observant commentary: "It seems strange to think that this is Hackett's eighth solo outing yet he is still described as 'Ex-Genesis guitarist'. Over the seven years since he left he has produced some excellent music alongside the occasional real groaner. He's also taken to singing despite the fact that in all his years with Genesis he never once opened his mouth on record!
And it's in his singing that Hackett has made the most progress. On Till We Have Faces he handles a fair variety of styles, (whereas on previous albums he has tended to pitch all his songs around the same level) and comes up trumps every time. The opener, Duel brings in shades of Jim Morrison, Let Me Count The Ways follows a standard blues form, while the closing track, Taking The Easy Way Out finds our hero putting on his best romantic voice for a smoochy ending.

Hackett is also experimenting on the musical side. This album is far more percussive than anything that's gone before, using Brazilian drummers to generate excitement even when old Steve himself is at his most indulgent on the electric guitar.

Overall this is a difficult album to sum up. It certainly isn't commercial, yet it lacks any of the self-indulgence that has occasionally marred Hackett's previous work. It requires a lot of listening to, but I promise it's well worth it. My only gripe is that someone whose music is clearly rooted in the Eighties should use such an early Seventies style of illustration on the sleeve. It reeks of all the concept album/ surrealistic lyrics routine that Hackett has long since outgrown."

The percussive element was perhaps the most difficult part of the album for long standing fans to get to grips with. The simple fact was that this album did not "sound" like a Hackett album. Then again, what exactly is a Hackett album supposed to sound like? A question, which I am glad to say, has defied all logical answers since Steve's solo career began!

"The percussion was something else and in a way I thought of it as a learning experience; being involved with that amount of percussionists and rhythmic players. I would meet them and they would demonstrate their skills on the spot. In fact, recording in Brazil the restriction there was that I could only get access to a recording studio after midnight (laughs). Officially we were supposed to start at nine and these things always tended to conspire with circumstances and we would not get home until about eight in the morning!"

Sadly, Steve's intention to take the "Samba School" on tour with him did not materialise due to managerial problems at that time and the album remains one of the few for which Steve has never undertaken any live shows. He admits that taking such a group out on the road might have been a step too far for his audiences at home but also admits that had he had his way, "I think with hindsight, I would probably have gone even further with it and made it even more of a 'World Music' album, if that's the term, and abandoned all Western civilisation whatsoever. I still have performances of things that we recorded at the time."

Percussively driven as the album undoubtedly is, it has also fallen foul of the lazy approach of pigeonholing music merely for the sake of finding a peg on which to hang an individual project. Steve has always had far too much of an eclectic approach to his music as the albums released in the eighteen months between Highly Strung and Till We Have Faces, proved and that has often proven too much of a challenge for his critics and on occasions, it has to be admitted, his fans too!

"The banding of the album could have been a lot better. I often think that the way you arrange albums tends to colour people's view of them and therefore if you have something that is particularly rhythmic or ethnic at the beginning, people will say; 'Oh, its an ethnic album' or if you have something poppy they will say it's a pop album. I have usually found that the best thing to do is exactly what you wanted and then you have a good chance of pleasing the fans but at the same time you usually have a very good chance of upsetting the record company. It is very difficult to please both the business and the public and I think that over the years the business has become aware that there has been a distancing between their own tastes; imposing their own ideas instead of what fans actually want."

Till We Have Faces is an extreme album perhaps, but one which once again showed that Steve was prepared to take musical chances and run the risk of alienating some of his fans in the search for the direction that his "Muse" was taking him at the time. His next album was to take Steve back to ground he had already trodden many years before…

CHAPTER ELEVEN

Tuning The GTR

Faced with declining sales, minimal airplay; and little or no prospect of any live shows on the back of Till We Have Faces, Steve was faced with the dilemma of what to do next. By now, the marketplace for his particular brand of music was becoming increasingly narrow and every inch of it was hard fought for by the growing number of bands working under the deluded title of "New Prog".

It therefore came as quite a surprise to his fans, when rumours started to circulate in 1985 that he had joined forces with another axe man; Steve Howe to work on a group project. The idea of Steve in a group again after all his vicissitudes with Genesis took some believing. Steve Howe found himself in a similar position. Yes had effectively folded in 1981 and Asia had burned all too brightly and too briefly leaving him effectively in the same limbo that Hackett found himself in. Maybe fans would not have been so surprised by the new direction if they had understood Steve's frustration with the record industry at the time: "It evolved out of the frustration of doing albums which weren't getting a look in the American market place. I had done these things, which were a labour of love, but in America I got the usual response of; 'We'll take it if Phil Collins is on it'. I found that more and more people were interested in what I was doing only by association. I found the idea of doing GTR came out of the mutual frustration of two guitarists who felt the same way. So we decided to combine forces and put together a band which certainly had the potential for longevity, as opposed to doing the usual couple of acoustic guitars type project."

The opportunity for the two to work together had been presented to him during a chance meeting with Brian Lane who had managed Yes and Asia. Brian Gibbon recalls that Lane was interested in Steve as part of his plans for yet another super group; "Then we got to the situation whereby we started to talk to Brian Lane who I have known for ages and he is key at putting together super groups (laughs). He said; ' what is Steve doing?' I don't know if we had a party at Steve's house and Brian came along. He was managing somebody, probably Asia and he wanted to do something or Steve wanted to do something with the boys and that is really where GTR came from. To actually put these two guitarists together which was a fantastic idea and initially that worked. It worked well in the studio because there were the two principals; the two guitarists and they employed everybody else to be around them. I don't think Brian had much input there, he left the music very much to the artists so I don't think that in the studio there was a problem between the artists, so to speak it was again, when they got on the road".

"Then you get to the situation where you start doing things separately and you end up taking your own limo and stuff like that," continues Gibbon. "Steve Howe never had his missus on the road with him although they were the only two people that mattered anyway. So then you start to get this undercurrent, which I keep on, talking about again because initially it was very successful. It should have worked even though they are two very different people they could and indeed, should have seen that this could have been the goose that laid the golden egg and taken up from where Steve missed out big time with Genesis".

Whatever the truth in all this is, Lane had managed to steer the careers of many musicians and he had his sales pitch worked out. Currently managing the bandless Howe, he seized his opportunity over lunch one day with Steve Hacket. "Brian mentioned that Steve Howe was not doing much at that time; which paralleled my situation as I was between albums. He said that might be interesting, so I said I would meet Steve".

The meeting took place with the initial premise being that the two guitarists would work together on an album of material themselves but that quickly changed as they realised that to give the best chance of success to the project it would have to be toured. Lane's connections with Geffen Records ensured that there was initial interest from a major record label but they began to blow hot and cold and eventually Arista took the project on. Steve Howe recalls the unusual situation he found himself in after being basically unemployed for the first time, "Two months after Asia, the 'phone rang and it was my manager. He said what do you think about getting together with Steve Hackett and seeing what you might like to do. Both Steve and I are quite reserved in a way and we both approach the guitar from a writing point of view not so much from the long solo sort of perspective. It got more complicated when we had a band and in a way I think it was the band that made it more complicated than we had time to evaluate, because of having the other musicians pull and push. They had become, not arrogant but kind of confident, it created new imbalances in the whole thing because they felt that they had contributed to the whole success of the GTR thing but of course, Steve and I were the bosses; we were in charge. Well, that's how we started anyway".

In addition to the two Steves the rest of the band comprised a mixture of well known and lesser known people. Geoff Downes, another refugee from both Yes an Asia was in the producer's chair. Jonathan Mover an American session drummer who had previously worked albeit briefly with Marillion was enlisted, and bassist Phil Spalding was drafted in after working with the likes of Mike Oldfield, with Matt Clifford undertaking onstage keyboard duties. Vocalist Max Bacon had been plucked from relative obscurity after stints in two heavy rock outfits; Bronz and Nightwing, the latter of whom had actually covered Steve's track Cell 151 on their Night Of Mystery album a couple of years before.

The rest of the band did have a fair degree of input into the project as drummer Jonathan Mover recalls, "Actually Phil Spalding and I had quite a bit of input with regard to the writing but since we were the new guys along with Max Bacon we were told that we would receive writing and publishing credits on one song apiece. That song became the one I had most input into and that was Imagining but I also along with Phil had a lot to do with Here I Wait, Jekyll And Hyde; You Can Still Get Through and Reach Out (Never Say No).

The use of Geoff Downes was to prove beneficial in some ways to Steve because he introduced him to the budding area of midi technology and new guitar synths. Both musicians were keen to enlist his services as they recalled during a US radio interview to promote the tour:

(Howe) "It was nice to make contact with Geoff under different circumstances rather than keyboard and guitar in arm. This was great and I was really up for it when I heard about it because I knew that Geoff had a streak in him that wanted to do a little bit more in production and prove himself a little but there".

(Hackett) " Well, we wanted somebody who was a musician for a start, because we wanted certain areas of technology made available to us; this fretboard technology via midi to synthesisers and it was important to us that we had someone who was a bit of a boffin-type character'"

This assorted gathering found themselves ensconced in the Townhouse Studios in London for the recording of the album and also for a documentary video of the proceedings which was subsequently released by Arista in the USA only. The album sessions were protracted and by all accounts were not a tremendously enjoyable experience. The two protagonists were not natural bedfellows as Steve recalls "I found it difficult actually. I felt that somewhere down the line I got the feeling that he (Howe) was a spontaneous performer. I liked his work with Yes and I found that lots of the time in the rehearsal room we would have a great jam but by the time it found its way on to record some of its excitement was kind of ironed out of it."

That spontaneity however, did hit the mark on the album's single; When The Heart Rules The Mind, a massive hit on both sides of the Atlantic. "That was something that Steve and I wrote practically on the first day. He had the instrumental bit and I had the song; so we stuck the two together and I think it sounds very good. We had a very good mix of it which the record company rejected; they wanted another one."

Steve Howe was quick to point out that the original premise behind the project was to facilitate the two guitarists' exploration of the entire range of options available via their chosen instrument: "It was during the best phase of rehearsals, which happened early in the first three months of 1985. We used to send the guys out and the two of us would work out guitar parts. That was when we formulated the basic parts for what we did on the album. Though a lot of things changed in the studio, that was when we started getting the idea that we could work out and that the two guitars were complementary. I like working closely with one other person. That was the original flame. I suppose we were helping each other's song writing and by doing that we were able to feature each other's guitar playing. It was really a question of developing new sounds… it was an exchange of ideas and techniques."

During the course of the various interviews for the album, both musicians talked up the position of the new band with Steve Hackett referring to it as, "We hope this is going to turn into a long term thing. This is a debut album; it's a debut tour; it's a new concept of guitarists working together. It's a brave step for both of us." Sadly, many people still remembered the Yardbirds and other previous amalgams of talents that had promised much and had failed to deliver in the long term, and GTR was never accorded the wild reception in Britain and Europe that followed it in the USA.

The subsequent album, titled GTR became a massive hit in the USA where it was an AOR radio station favourite for most of 1986. Apart from the single and The Hunter, the rest of the album is a blatant attempt to fill the gaps left by Asia. Tracks such as You Can Still Get Through and Reach Out (Never Say No) are stadium fodder of the worst kind. It is amazing to think that the band featured two of the most inventive and revered guitar players in the world of rock and yet they were not allowed to produce the kind of material that would have been satisfying to them artistically. "There were various guitar parts that were left off the album. It was really the last time I worked under the corporate umbrella. Ever since then I have rued the idea of working with a mega company, who would want to stick their creative oar in at every stage. I think of it as a negotiation rather than as a record, very much in the way that modern successful Hollywood films are made."

The new look band undertook a massive tour of the USA and Canada throughout July and August 1986 before visiting the UK for a handful of shows and a meagre visit to Europe where they played to less than full houses. The show was the predictable mix of material from the GTR album preceded by solo acoustic sets by both guitarists effectively giving the audience "three bands in one" as Brian Lane was quick to point out.

Sandwiched in between the lumpen material from the GTR album were some genuine classics from Yes and Genesis which redeemed the show. The gig at the Wiltern Theatre Los Angeles on 19th July was even recorded by the King Biscuit Flower Hour radio show and subsequently released almost ten years later. The only European gig for which details have emerged was at the Alabamahalle in Munich on 22nd September 1986 and also partly filmed and broadcast on German TV. The footage reveals a band, which do not look at all comfortable despite all the media hype at the time. The irony of the success of the album was not lost on Steve: "It's funny that its probably one of the records that I found most difficult; yet it was one of the most successful things I'd ever done."

Even Steve Howe admits that the differences in their approach to recording were perhaps too diverse to successfully sit together within the same band: "We got on great during the writing period and then we asked for advice from our manager who wasn't perhaps the best person to bounce those kind of ideas off. But we also had our difficulties to the way we arranged things on tours; the way we all mucked around and I joined in on that and Steve perhaps felt that I shouldn't have done that and should have held myself aloof from all of that."

Reconvening shortly after the end of the GTR tour, work on the second album did not progress very far before the façade of unity crumbled, amidst increasing acrimony between the two main protagonists and legal proceedings which not only tied Steve up in litigation for a considerable period but also effectively hampered his next project. The fundamental difficulty appears to have been one of perception. Steve Howe had been used to a more democratic set up within Yes and Asia; where the members of the band were at least nominally equals all with a shared responsibility for the musical process and also a share of the potential profit or loss that accrued to any such venture resulting from their efforts. Steve Hackett on the other hand had effectively resigned from that committee structure when he had left Genesis and had the responsibility for organising his own projects ever since. "It all kind of spun round when we had problems that weren't really exactly about Steve and I," recalls Howe. "They were about the band and the organisation; the expenditure and all the problems that go with bands logically fell on Steve (Hackett's) and my shoulders but due to management we weren't able to sustain the concepts of the project which was pretty ludicrous. I guess in the end Steve and I felt that we were in almost different bands - we were in the same band but we felt differently about that band".

The problems associated with the album and subsequent tour are also recalled by Jonathan Mover, "Phil (Spalding) and I had finished our parts within a few days so I had a lot of time to kill while the others were taking care of the guitar and vocals. I decided to take a holiday in Europe with my girlfriend and when I got back I found that Geoff (Downes) had edited quite a bit of my drum parts and songs in order to make the record more 'accessible'. Meaning all the big drum fills and some odd time bits and pieces were nixed.

So, me and my big mouth told Geoff and Steve Howe to go and fuck themselves. I quit on the spot and walked out of Townhouse Studios. It was Steve Hackett who came out after me and persuaded me to stay and just go with it. His advice to me was to use GTR as a stepping-stone and use it as much as I could. I was pissed and hurt but I was lucky to have him looking out for me".

Despite the success of the album in the US, the prospect of a follow-up was not one, which Steve was particularly enamoured about. "I think it went wrong because of the people that got between the two Steves along with some greed and a lot of blame throwing," remembers Jonathan Mover. "You see Hackett with Genesis and Howe with Yes had two very different ways of doing things. Instead of coming together with the help of a manager and producer, they were driven apart. There was a lot of blame being thrown around for why GTR wasn't as big as Asia had been. So, instead of enjoying what we had done and where we could go with it; the wedge just separated them so much so that it became sad and un-enjoyable and a drag to be around, no matter how much I tried. When Hackett decided not to even show up in Devon for the writing/demo sessions for the next record, I knew my days were numbered. As much as I was angry with both of them for their silliness; my allegiance was with Hackett and I was not going to continue without him. I showed up in Devon with the others to start work on the next record and it's a real shame that it didn't happen because there were some great songs developing. But Steve never showed up and that really took its toll on me. He called me and told me he was done with GTR and would I still be interested in working with him on a solo project? I remember being crushed by it all and just decided to go home for the holidays and call it quits."

Steve Howe tried to carry the project forward after Hackett and Mover's departure under the title of "Steve Howe And Friends" initially with Phil Spalding and Max Bacon but that proved abortive. This was where the situation was to become horribly complex and it is over to Steve Howe to try and make sense of the resulting debacle: "The next phase was that Arista did approve a change of member in the band and Steve Hackett was replaced by Robert Berry. For a while this was a new venture. We weren't necessarily going to call it GTR because everybody understood that Steve and I had to both be in the band to call it GTR. So we invented this new band which got as far as doing backing tracks in the studio and then quite ridiculously allowed Robert Berry to leave and actually go and play with Keith Emerson and Carl Palmer in the group 3."

The contractual problems attendant on Arista's refusal to allow these recordings to be released because they consider them to be contractually theirs is compounded by the demands of the recording studio where they were made, also demanding that the recordings are theirs in lieu of unpaid studio fees. In short, it is a complete nightmare aided and abetted by an extremely dubious bootleg masquerading as a GTR demo recording of the second album which is actually nothing more than Robert Berry's songs augmented by a guitar mix of The Hunter which was not sanctioned by either protagonist! Confused? Good, because so am I!

Steve Hackett had also commenced work on a new solo album with a truly stellar cast; Chris Thompson; Bonnie Tyler and Brian May to name but three that were mentioned. The album; titled Feedback was sadly to remain in the cans for over ten years before the contractual problems attending its release and the final demise of GTR were worked out. "I think that Jeff Beck put it best when he said 'There's no way I am gonna stand on stage with another great guitar player'. David Palmer, who I have worked with put it quite succinctly… 'Is it a case of one guitarist too many?' I loved Steve Howe's work and still do. I suspect there is something about two guitarists working together that can cancel each other out. Yes liked to contest each other more while Genesis was perhaps more nurturing each other rather than sparring partners. I tend to work best when people love what I do and then I can be even better! I just want to get the best out of people. I don't respond to critics. Criticism at the song writing stage is fine. I didn't feel that the band was justifying its existence. It was losing money hand over fist and it was no longer enjoyable.

One of the Feedback songs we had recorded for the GTR album was Slot Machine which I continued with another guitarist of distinction; Brain May. That went the same way as Anthony and Mike's thing; we were going to do something together and it turned into my album,* but there were so many record company problems that I decided to go back to my roots with Momentum."

It was also highly embarrassing for the author to remember watching a broadcast of the UK "talent" show; "Search For A Star" a year or so after GTR had been launched and to see the band's vocalist; Max Bacon on the programme performing both The Hunter and When The Heart Rules The Mind and maintaining that the tracks were his own compositions - fortunately for all concerned he did not win the contest!

---

*This was the collaboration between Anthony Phillips and Mike Rutherford, which eventually emerged as Phillips' first solo album; The Geese & The Ghost in 1977 after Rutherford had to leave Phillips to it in order to concentrate more fully on the first post-Gabriel Genesis album, A Trick Of The Tail.

CHAPTER TWELVE

Gaining Momentum

With all the problems attendant on either the second GTR album or indeed a solo rock album, Steve opted for a second visit to the world of the "small orchestra" and prepared his second acoustic album. He had been writing acoustic material throughout the intervening period between Bay Of Kings and the beginning of 1988 as he remarked during an interview at the time of the Momentum tour: "Actually I was writing a rock album at the same time as this acoustic one and since the GTR thing I was working on a rock album with Brian May, Bonnie Tyler and Nick Magnus and the guys from my regular band. My brother John is on it; Ian Mosley is on one track and Chris Thompson does most of the vocals on it. Meanwhile, while that was being organised I did this acoustic album. In fact I had been writing acoustic stuff for three or four years since I had done Bay Of Kings. I decided to do this because it was something simple to record and simple to go on the road with and in a way; after the GTR thing, it's like saying I'm back doing what I think I do best."

Momentum, Steve's second acoustic album took the basic idea of its predecessor and moulded it into a much fuller formed and classically orientated album. Steve's technique had progressed enormously and he admitted that he had worked hard on the project: "They are harder to play this time; but they are... I tried to push my technique a lot more on this album. I wanted the pieces to be a bit more intricate. It's all nylon really; I have pared it down. There aren't any steel tracks on it but that is because I have got very dedicated to the nylon strung guitar. The nylon really is the real guitar for me, that's what it is. I think the nylon is timeless."

That was certainly the case with this album. Presenting tracks such as the percussive Cavalcanti and the wonderful tribute to his ex-boss Tony Stratton-Smith who had died of cancer the previous March, Concert For Munich. It had originally been intended as part of a soundtrack to a film about the "Busby Babes", the Manchester United football team who had lost their lives in a tragic air crash in 1958. Stratton-Smith's early career was as a sports journalist and he had been intending to travel on the same aircraft as the team but changed his plans. It was quite some time before he boarded an aeroplane again. Stratton-Smith through the auspices of Charisma's film subsidiary* was to make the film which sadly never materialised. The track was a suitably elegiac tribute to both him and the victims. Other tracks echo Steve's love of the Baroque period and especially his admiration for Bach and on the re-issued version of the CD some years later there was even a rendition of J S Bach's Bouree, previously made famous by Jethro Tull. The album was very much a reaction against the excesses of rock 'n' roll and once again showed that Steve was not prepared to be pigeonholed or forced into creating formula driven rock albums merely to satisfy the whims of record company executives. "I just wanted to get out and play to people without any fuss to show that I could do it without props; without the conglomerate and the big budget and so I started doing acoustic shows again. There were different pressures because what's delightfully simple on paper is frighteningly complex when you come to go out there and just play. There is in many ways much more pressure for the guy who is just sitting there on the stool, and the stage can become a very lonely place."

Certainly the show that Steve and his brother John, whom Steve charmingly referred to as "The Pharaoh of the flute; Prince of the pipes of Pan... King of the wind!" in his on stage introductions, performed a show, which charmed the audiences. Once again, Steve mixed performances from the new album and its predecessor with the occasional nod to his previous band mates, including both Horizons and the tribute to the concrete cows at Milton Keynes, and a certain reunion that had taken place there a few years previously in the humorously titled; Time Lapse At Milton Keynes. He also once again tried out unrecorded material including one piece with an absurd title: The Carrot That Killed My Sister! Occasional shouts from the audience for such unlikely Genesis tracks as Supper's Ready and The Knife, were given short shrift by Steve with a smile and the wry remark; "That was before the war!"

The tour was an extensive one taking in most of the UK and also with visits to mainland Europe in May and again in September 1988. Sadly the autumn tour of the US and Canada mentioned in the tour programme never

*Handmade Films, formed by former Beatle, George Harrison, and business partner Denis O'Brien in 1979 to finance the Monty Python film Life Of Brian and responsible for subsequent Monty Python films amongst others.

materialised. The entire project had been an artistically satisfying one but financially it had been the opposite. Poor advertising strategies had meant that the tour had failed to capitalise on Steve's presence.

This was very much a lost opportunity with fans attending not only from Estonia itself but other Baltic States, Russia and parts of Scandinavia where Steve's albums often had patchy, if any "legal" distribution at all!

There was even the bizarre threat of legal action by another artist to stop Steve's album being titled Momentum on the grounds that his band were called Momentum! Trying times abroad were compounded by the attitude of some of Steve's UK fans towards his latest performances as a letter received by his management from a disgruntled fan reveals…

Dear Steve

For many years now I have adored your music. I have all your albums and also all the Genesis albums and sincerely believe that their music lost something when you left them. But their loss was our gain because you produced your own superb sound and now my two children are in their teens and now appreciate the same 'real' music.

Thus when I heard you were on tour we decided that somehow we must attend your concerts. This was not easy because they live in Bedford, so I had to take my daughter to the Poole concert and I have two tickets for my son and I at Reading.

As far as we were concerned, the Poole concert was a great disappointment. Because of this I have cancelled my son's visit to Reading. We knew you wouldn't be in front of a great rock group but what happened to the Steve Hackett album sound? You hardly touched the electric guitar and instead indulged in a Spanish Classical guitar evening. I love the classical guitar but would expect to hear this at 'An Evening with John Williams'.

As dedicated fans of yours over many years we hoped we might hear the sound of Spectral Mornings but no such luck. During the preview of your tour on television there was no hint of what we might expect on stage. Please accept that three of your most enduring fans are not intending to buy your Momentum album".

Clearly there was no pleasing some people! Bizarre indeed because the press and television coverage for the album did indicate that it was an acoustic tour; the posters for the gigs featured Steve holding an acoustic guitar, rather than the usual rock star shot, and the fact that it was a tour in support of an acoustic album might have given the game away!

Steve's altruism reached its peak the following year when he, like so many other people heard of the intention of our government to forcibly repatriate the refugees from Vietnam who had fled by sea to Hong Kong, which was at that time still a British colony. Steve dedicated an incredible amount of time and effort into organising an all-star rendering of Rod Stewart's classic: Sailing: "1989 saw the beginning of our involvement in 'Rock Against Repatriation' for the Boat People. A lot of artists were involved in making yet another version of Sailing but in a way that wasn't really the point. We were looking for an emblem for the cause and the fact that they were boat people and that there was a song called 'Sailing' seemed perfect for it. A tremendous amount of people took part in the recording of that track. We also had an auction which became even more of a Who's Who of rock memorabilia."

Another example of his determination not to capitalise out of the plight of the people whose cause he was so willingly espousing, emerged when Start Records who still managed Steve announced that they planned to run a series of advertisements for their back catalogue of his albums on the back of the "Rock Against Repatriation" project. The advertisements were pulled when Steve's management objected.

Work on the abortive Feedback album had effectively been shelved by now as Steve opted, with the backing of a secure managerial team headed by his long time sound engineer; Billy Budis, who had already supervised the construction of the studio at Steve's home in 1989. This was the facility that enabled him to create many of his later albums. This facility eventually moved in 2000 to a new building, which Camino Records had acquired near to their offices and subsequently named MAP Studios.

With his contract with Start also at an end it was a long time before Steve was able to establish his own record label.* Meanwhile albums were licensed to other labels for distribution with Stephen Hackett Limited retaining the rights.

The vexed question of the long overdue transfer of Steve's early catalogue of solo albums to the now firmly established Compact Disc format was finally addressed by Virgin Records during 1989 with the albums from Voyage Of The Acolyte through to Highly Strung being transferred piecemeal. This was not without its attendant problems, however. The transferral was in some cases sloppily done and in one case, criminally done and all without Steve's knowledge to boot, as he recalled: "Virgin lost the original master of Voyage Of The Acolyte and so when the CD was done without my

---

*Camino Record finally came into its own as an established label in 1997.

knowledge, and without my co-operation; they used a production master that was, as far as we can find out; from Canada. In those days what you tended to do was use your master tape, which was first generation, then to the other territories, because you were dealing with vinyl, it was a copy so you got extra hiss. Obviously I have got a lot of pride in those early albums and I hate to see them going out slightly half-cocked."

Half-cocked is not the word most Hackett fans would use to describe the way in which Please Don't Touch was handled inserting a gap between Land Of A Thousand Autumns and the title track, which not only had not been present on the original album but which completely ruined the effect of the two tracks and had many fans returning their copies as faulty when it was first released! The situation was not much better with the remaining albums either and all of them suffered from poor production values.

The years of 1989-92 were tough ones as Steve recalls: "It was hard to find the deals but I realised I wasn't on my own. It was time for my own label, which has freed up a lot of artists. Occasionally we release things through other record companies such as A Midsummer Night's Dream album through EM because they may be able to give it a certain level of marketing budget that we can't give it ourselves. I realised it fairly early on with the advent of the Internet. I realised there had to be growth potential there because initially when people were selling via the Internet that was a fraction of what shop sales were doing and so it was still a time when people were testing the water and nobody knew if this private company idea was going to take off. We may have reduced record sales in shops now whether that is a good thing or not, I don't know."

All of this took a great deal of time and capital as Steve regrouped. A tantalising glimpse of his new sound was offered at a televised gig at the Central TV studios in Nottingham on 23rd September 1990, recorded as part of a new series of rock concert performances under the title "Bedrock". For this broadcast, Steve used a scratch band including Fudge Smith, the drummer from UK progsters; Pendragon, and Julian Colbeck who some fans may have seen the previous year with Anderson, Bruford; Wakeman and Howe. The performance was subsequently broadcast by the various UK independent TV networks but usually at some ungodly hour of the morning! The video was also later issued by Classic Rock Productions under the highly unoriginal title of "Horizons" and in greatly edited form. The show featured several brand new tracks, alongside classic slices of Hackett material, and certainly whet the whistles of fans eager for another slice of rock from the maestro.

The gloom was pierced briefly however, in 1991 with the long overdue release of a live album. Titled, Time Lapse there was a certain degree of irony displayed in the title. There was indeed a time lapse involved because the album featured two different gigs and two different band line-ups. The first half predominantly featured the music from the Nottingham TV show in 1990 with the rest being taken from a gig at the Savoy Theatre, New York back in 1981. It was almost impossible to see the join however and the album, initially released in Holland on the Dutch Crisis label became a popular item when it was subsequently re-issued by Camino Records.

Steve also encountered someone who was to play a larger part in his life during the last few years in the person of Joanna Lehmann who takes up the story of how they first met: "I was involved with a film production company and I had written a script which we were intending to turn into a feature film and there was a company called Zomba Music and Steve was on their books. They read the script and they decided that Steve would be a good person to approach because they thought he would like it and would like the idea of doing the music. So they arranged a meeting for a whole group of us and that's how we met. For the first eighteen or so months we worked together officially and after that we encouraged one another with what we were doing. If I was writing an article for a magazine or a book such as Our Dark Twin (Joanna's own book) it was Steve who encouraged me to write it in the first place. I had written all these ideas down and he said' This would make a book' and then with a lot of what Steve has been doing musically we have often talked about ideas together and what order to put something in on an album or individual tracks and ideas . So, essentially we have been creatively involved and I have always enormously admired Steve's innovation, strong sense of atmosphere and extraordinary talent as both composer and musician."

Contractual obligations with Steve's other record company; Virgin were finally laid to rest with the release in 1992 of The Unauthorised Biography, a compilation album with a difference. "Billy (Budis) and I sat down and we decided that we would include some tracks which hadn't received as much attention as some other tracks. So, instead of doing an album of stage favourites, we decided to include stuff like the Randy Crawford track; Hoping Love Will Last."

The album also featured two brand new tracks; Don't Fall Away From Me originally a bridging section to a song which he had been working on for the Feedback project with Brian May, and another delightful acoustic track: Prayers And Dreams which was intended as part of the putative soundtrack to Steve's first foray into the world of movies. Steve had written the screenplay to a life story of one of his musical heroes, Antonio Vivaldi. He had performed one of Vivaldi's guitar concertos together with an orchestra at the Royal Festival Hall in London several years earlier to great acclaim. The film; The Red Priest was based on the larger than life antics of one of the Baroque period's most famous talents. Steve explained in November 1991 in a feature for The Mail On Sunday's Roger Tavener, "Vivaldi was a 17th century hooligan with an incredible talent both for music and behaving extraordinarily badly". The film was to have been shot in London, Venice and Eastern Europe and was to star Andrew Strong (he of "The Commitments" fame) in the title role. As of yet, however, neither the soundtrack to this project or indeed the film itself has seen the light of day.

Another surprise appearance that emerged in 1992 was his collaboration with Austrian multi instrumentalist; Gandalf, a long-standing admirer who invited Steve to perform on the album Gallery Of Dreams. His contribution to the album can be heard on several tracks and Steve even performed at a gig by Gandalf at the Stadthalle in Vienna in the autumn of 1992* excerpts of which were included in the promotional video for the Face In The Mirror single from the album. Stepping out from the shadows that had long surounded his movements, it seemed that Steve was finally leaving the self-imposed darkness to re-emerge once again into the glare of the spotlight.

As we have seen, he had been far from idle and by the end of 1992 he was ready to take his fans on another musical adventure, one that was to colour his entire subsequent career.

---

* This recording has recently been released on CD and DVD under the title of "Gandalf & Friends".

CHAPTER THIRTEEN

There Are Many Sides To Steve Hackett

Despite the problems, which had attended one aspect of Steve's career or another over the preceding couple of years, he had not run short of ideas for projects. With plenty of material worked up, Steve opted to test drive some of it in front of audiences in the USA and Canada who had not had the pleasure of seeing him in concert for almost a decade: "I am routining new material in front of audiences to see what the reactions are like and also to shake those numbers up in front of a crowd and to get the input of the musicians I am working with."

Steve was obviously relishing his relatively newfound artistic freedom. With a secure management structure in place and proper outlets for his material, most of which was finally re-issued on CD in the States on the Caroline Records "Blue Plate" subsidiary, he gave the back catalogue as much of a push as he could. He undertook a proper US tour, trying out his new material and road testing the music and his new band in an environment, which he was evidently enjoying enormously: "Well, funnily enough the new stuff with the new band that I am touring with feels more like a band than either Genesis or GTR did. Its marvellous to work with a band again and it is something I have looked forward to for a long time. The material is mainly new material; I am testing new material in front of audiences before I record the majority of it. The studio stuff is mainly down in my own studio but the band does such fantastic versions of that stuff that I want to re-record it with this line up and we are very excited about it, the reaction so far has been very good. You can surprise people when you do it with musicians whom they might not have seen before. I think that when you come to work with people who are well known, their personalities are quite strong and people come to know what to expect; whereas I am always looking for the surprise element."

Normal service was certainly not long in coming and the fruits of Steve's labours emerged on 21st May 1993 with the release of Guitar Noir, his ninth solo studio album. Steve had moved centre stage in just about every aspect of his career and now he was to turn the spotlight in on himself with the most personal album he had released but the surprise element was still there. His own vocal range had improved although that may have been down to the fact that he was writing to his strengths now and having found his individual style he was prepared to make the most of it, as he explained at the time: "I continue to sing my own vocals and in fact I have changed the style of material to suit that I think. I have been taking a far more poetic approach to lyrics; I mean I write them down and see if they work on the printed page before I turn them into a song. I don't see the lyrics as an appendage to a song anymore. I am enjoying singing myself very much whether I sing flat all evening or I surprise myself and hit all the high notes; it doesn't actually matter to me in the same degree that it would say to a band that were concerned with creating say; 'radio friendly' material. I am not doing that; what I am doing is increasingly private. I write from the inside out much more now. I write about things that concern me."

This new turn was evident on tracks such as There Are Many Sides To The Night which examined the motivations for a prostitute's way of earning a living and the wry look at the obsession with commercialism in the USA; Little America are all written in a totally different fashion and cover subject matter which Steve would have steered well clear of on previous outings. There was even room for one of his more left-of-centre tracks; A Vampyre With A Healthy Appetite, ostensibly based around a newspaper report of the theft of several pints of blood from a New Orleans blood bank and delivered in a spoken word fashion using a megaphone. It became an unlikely hit in the new live set.

The rest of the band that Steve had enlisted for this project were all new faces to the fans although certainly in the case of Julian Colbeck, he had been on the music circuit for quite some time and had been a Charisma artist at roughly the same time as Steve and had appeared in the 1990 Nottingham TV broadcast. Drummer; Hugo Degenhardt had been selected from auditions: " I did the dreaded drum audition (laughs) one day we had several drummers in and I remember Hugo was the second guy and just as I turned around to make a cup of tea this guy just started on the drums and blew me away with the first thing he did on the kit, so I thought; 'that's him' and decided in the space of ten seconds. It was enough to convince me that Hugo was a must!"

The album was also more of a collaborative effort than any previous Hackett album. Not only did the band members make a more sizeable contribution to the proceedings but Steve also collaborated with Aron Friedman on the writing of several tracks. This was certainly indicative of a more relaxed approach as he admits: "There was much more collaboration going on. The guys were heavily involved on the creative side. Fifty percent in a way because fifty percent of the material was driven by acoustic guitar and on those ones I collaborated with Aron and there were a couple of tracks that I had done on my own and written and played everything but I also worked very closely with the technical team and that included Billy Budis. When Billy was critical as he often is; I listened to his criticism and tried not to take it personally."

The time spent getting organised with a new recording studio, record label and distribution deals, had also given Steve time to explore areas of music which he had always shied away from previously. It was not an easy period though, as he is at pains to point out: "You can never be 'new' in this business; you can be all sorts of things but you can't be new and there was a point where I was thinking; 'I wish I was new coming up with all of this stuff, and if I were twenty would that make a difference? If I were fifteen years younger would that make a difference? All the things that you don't really need but you think that people want and you think will make the difference. Then if you are lucky you arrive at the conclusion where you think; 'Oh sod it' and what I really need to do is be more myself and to self publish and the rest. Content, it has got to have content; a very uncool; very basic word isn't it; 'content'? Substance not just packaging."

His new stage show concentrated on the substance of the new album with practically every track featuring in the live set with the emphasis being firmly on the "new" although some old favourites were of course, included in the mix and a real surprise as Steve also opted to include another nod to his Genesis days with a stunning performance of In That Quiet Earth. Audiences in the US had also been given a sneak preview of his next project with the inclusion of the blues standard; The Stumble in their set. During the course of the rest of 1993, Steve made visits to the USA, Italy, South America and the UK in pursuit of bringing his work back to the fans who had been so loyal. It was almost as if a dam had been breached and the floodwaters were in full spate.

The show was not without its moments of unintended drama too. During a particularly fraught evening at the Swan in High Wycombe, Steve experienced the kind of technical difficulties, which he had not seen since his days in Genesis and to add insult to injury broke a guitar string during Spectral Mornings. His patience finally snapped when some wag from the crowd shouted out for "Supper's Ready" at which point Steve's response was uncharacteristically fiery but totally justified in the circumstances. (I wish I had a recording of that evening's gig!) Even the best of us have our breaking points and obviously on this particular evening, Steve had reached his, and his retort to requests for the likes of Supper's Ready from wags in the audience was understandable, if unprintable in a family publication such as this!

Concurrently with work on Guitar Noir, Steve had also indulged his passion for the blues with work on a collection of blues standards and new material written in that style which was to appear in early 1994 under the title Blues With A Feeling. Always a frustrated blues harp player; he finally managed to get his blues vibratos out of the closet where they had remained hidden for so long for an exercise that was more about enjoyment than it was about musical excellence: "I wanted to do an album where the solos are more important than the songs. Where blowing was more important than the songs and the reason that I was attracted to the blues a long time ago was that the playing; from the viewpoint of an aspiring guitarist, which I was in the Sixties; was where the innovations were happening in electric guitar playing and I always regard it with respect because there's nothing more exciting than hearing a really good blues solo... We are doing it for fun. It's a flexible line up and I don't know how many people will be in the finished project. I think of it as a band because its not a vehicle for songwriters; least of all me. It's more ... I'm quite happy to do covers of existing things. It's really an excuse for more aggressive playing really."

This album had been on the back burner for a very long time. As the source of Steve's musical inspirations, logic dictated that he should have recorded it long before. Logic and the record industry are seldom happy bedfellows though, "I had wanted to do something in a blues style as far back as the Sixties and really, at the end of the Sixties, beginning of the Seventies the blues boom that was died on everybody including me; and that kind of music was no longer finding an outlet. Meanwhile in my bedroom I would still be practising my blues vibratos and thinking; 'when can we use this?' So, I felt it was time to come out of the closet and say; 'Yes, you can do this stuff and you can be proud of it and you can really enjoy it'."

Certainly the mix of old and new blues was a healthy change from Steve's more usual offerings though not necessarily to everyone's taste. The important thing was not the style of music, which was being played. The key point that seemed to be lost on so many people at the time was that Steve finally had stepped out of his own shadow and had the confidence to record albums that satisfied him on every level. The emphasis with Blues With A Feeling was definitely on having fun, not something that fans had necessarily associated with him! The importance of the final move to the centre of the stage that Guitar Noir and Blues With A Feeling represent cannot be overstated. With these albums; Steve Hackett finally became the "whole" musician, which he had always aspired to be. Sadly, this new confidence did not extend quite as far as seeing Steve on stage with his blues harp giving us an evening of the blues but there were sound reasons for this, as he explained:

"Frankly I wasn't sure if the fans would appreciate and embrace it as much as I might. In a way it is like acting out of character. Another reason is that I didn't want to go out and disappoint fans by not playing anything for which I was known. I felt I would have been hamstrung between wanting to give an authentic blues show and not giving them anything more in relation to being accepted in the past. I didn't feel I had to deliver this live and I think it would be quite hard to do everything I did on the album live as well; play the guitar; harmonica and sing. The all singing-dancing-balancing act! (Laughs) It would be possible with a larger band obviously, with someone to take over the harmonica chores or guitar or strap a G clamp to my head and try to perform all three! (Laughs) I would probably need oxygen! (Laughs). That would be something, to do it properly, I would need a harmonica and would need to be somebody like John Mayall who used to have a harmonica strapped to him while he was playing organ. He was depending less on lead soloists and that was extraordinary in itself the way Mayall was. There was an element of self-sufficiency about it and I have never had the guts to do that (laughs). On that album I didn't let anyone else get a look in on the solos, you've got the harmonica player doing it and then the guitarist and the vocalist and they're all me! (Laughs)"

Steve's attitude towards his newfound freedom is tinged with a realisation of just how difficult he had made life for himself by refusing to compromise on his art: "I am working all the time and I think if it was up to me I would probably be releasing several albums a year and I would be touring more regularly but I think it is this thing of wanting to do things that are surprising. If I had settled for the easy comfortable ride and maybe stayed with Genesis one would have had the benefit of major investment; advertising; production and all of that but I think something is lost. I don't think I could have released an album like Guitar Noir on a major label and had them understand it. I don't feel that would have been possible. I wanted to make the best album ever."

Before the year was out, Steve had continued his touring schedule, taking in second tours of the USA and Italy and had toured again in Italy in 1994 with an acoustic duo with himself and Julian Colbeck. Fans had wondered why John Hackett had not been involved in this and Steve's other projects. Sadly, John had been involved in a car accident the year before which had left him severely incapacitated, and he was recuperating but not sufficiently able to participate at this time.

During 1994, Steve also took part in David Palmer's orchestral tour. Palmer, long time member of Jethro Tull and a classically trained musician and orchestrator had produced a series of orchestral adaptations of the music of Jethro Tull, Genesis; Pink Floyd and Queen which had been generally well received. Steve had actually played guitar on the Genesis album; We Know What We Like and he was invited to play on the tour which Palmer had organised to promote his latest offering in the series. Steve managed to fit in appearances at a couple of these shows before undertaking his acoustic tour of Italy with Julian and several festivals and even an appearance on the Golden Stag TV Festival in Brasov in Romania.

Once again, his decision to tour in an acoustic setting without a massive back line and laser show brought the music back to the people and the shows were very well received. Out of this tour, another original idea emerged. Steve had already pre-empted "Unplugged" and "World Music" with his Bay Of Kings and Till We Have Faces albums back in the 1980's. Now he would bring his audience one of the first (if not the first) acoustic live albums.

The album, There Are Many Sides To The Night proved to be enormously popular when it was released in 1995. Originally limited to a run of 1500 copies that soon had to be extended as demand for this item far outstripped supply. This recording was also to preclude a major development in Steve's output in the coming years.

With the release of the live acoustic album and no touring activity on the horizon in 1995, fans might have been forgiven for thinking that Steve was taking a well-deserved break from the treadmill. However, nothing was further from the truth and his next project was to set tongues wagging.

CHAPTER FOURTEEN

Revisiting The Past

Late August 1996 found the author ensconced in the managerial offices of Steve's record company having completed another informal chat with him about his career for The Waiting Room (the author's well-established Genesis magazine/web site). Steve had given me no indication about what was to happen next but when Billy Budis; his manager said; 'We have something we would like you to listen to' I was naturally intrigued. What I heard in the following hour or so left me completely gobsmacked! Many was the conversation I'd had with Genesis and Hackett fans over the years at gigs, or in the pub before or afterwards, chewing over the fat and speculating on the what ifs of Steve's potential career had he stayed with Genesis or if he had rejoined them. Over the years, he had been careful to distance himself from his previous affiliations with the band, sensibly steering clear of any accusations of trading off that association to enhance his current career.

So, why was I so astonished by what I heard on that August afternoon? Simply put, I had heard the results of Steve's decision to exorcise his past with Genesis once and for all. The recordings that had been played were to become the aptly titled Genesis Revisited album a few months later. The result was an astonishingly eclectic album, which I thought I knew. Instead of re-creating a faithful rendition of the tracks, which had been selected; each was looked at from new and fresh perspectives. A simple track such as For Absent Friends was given the Johan Strauss Waltz treatment and turned into a brand new delight. Your Own Special Way already a personal favourite, was souped up and given the soulful vocalisations of Paul Carrack and a brand new soaring guitar solo from Steve himself which took it to new heights. It was amazing that after all these years, not only had Steve dipped his toe into the heady waters of that period but he had also plunged headlong.

Nothing had been treated as sacrosanct; even tracks such as Firth Of Fifth, were given a complete overhaul. With the forces that were marshalled here for the purpose, including many people who had been associated with Genesis in the past in one form or another, augmented by the massive sounds of the Royal Philharmonic Orchestra; the end result defied description. There was even room for a genuine rarity with Steve's re-creation of a track which had been shelved at the time of the Selling England By The Pound sessions; Déjà Vu, which had been completed with Peter Gabriel's blessing. There were even several brand new (or not so new in the case of Riding The Colossus which had been written as far back as 1962 apparently) Hackett compositions, which fitted into the overall dramatic dynamic of the project. When Steve approached Gabriel for the go ahead to work on Déjà vu, he had his first inkling that Genesis themselves were about to revisit their own past with the first archive Box Set! Steve's reaction was suitably ironic:

"The two projects (Genesis Revisited and Genesis Archive) were actually completely independent of each other. I was already well into Genesis Revisited and I called up Peter and asked if he would mind if I used Déjà Vu. He said; 'Oh no, I don't know if you know that the band are doing a box set?' I said; 'Oh? What are they doing to my song, ma?' It was presented as a fait accompli and I offered therefore, to try and improve the more dreadful moments. I can tell you exactly what I fixed bits on; The Lamb Lies Down On Broadway, on Riding The Scree, and I believe Tony Banks fixed guitar bits on Hairless Heart. I re-did the solo on Firth Of Fifth because that didn't sound too good. You see the thing is that when we used to do live albums when I was a member of the band and I had quality control we only released the best of a year's worth of recordings. It just happened that this recording from the Rainbow… I felt it was very much scraping the bottom of the barrel so I didn't feel too good about things going out which were obvious mistakes."

There were numerous gasps of amazement and also disapproval from the purists when the album was initially released in Japan in December 1996 and the author's own thoughts on the project were mixed. Drastic re-workings of such revered tracks as I Know What I Like and The Waiting Room itself, humorously re-titled here as Waiting Room Only which were more effects ridden pastiches full of musical in-jokes did not always meet with approval but at least no one could say that they were boring!

So, after all those years of locking that part of his career so firmly in the "wardrobe" why had Steve suddenly decided to fling it open in such a dramatic and challenging fashion? The idea was so simple that it really beggars belief but it's over to Steve to explain the actual rationale behind this amazing project: "We were playing in Sicily and a fan turned up at the hotel and he had all the albums I had ever done. I signed them all and it took quite some time then he turned to his wife and pulled out another lot quite sheepishly and asked if I wouldn't mind signing these too; thinking that I wouldn't do it because they were all Genesis albums. I signed them all, thinking; 'why would anyone have the impression that I would be happy to sign my own albums and not Genesis ones'?"

That germ of an idea was to stay with Steve for the rest of the Italian tour and during the course of the plane journey home and a conversation with Julian Colbeck, who was Steve's keyboard player for this tour, the idea took firmer shape: "I said to him (Julian) 'You know I am always gonna be remembered for those Genesis albums above all no matter what I do'."

However, that basic idea was not sufficient for Steve. It would have been quite simple to re-record faithful replicas of those treasured songs but what would be the point of merely doing that? After all, the originals were still available so why re-paint the Mona Lisa? The idea of re-interpretation rather than re-creation was one, which appealed much more; after all hadn't he been the chief interpreter of the musical ideas of the others in the band rather than the initial driving force in the first place?

Even so, taking so many liberties with people's favourites could have had severe repercussions for our hero. Having already had the experience of working with an orchestra on adaptations of Genesis' music with David Palmer's effort a few years previously, Steve had already realised the potential that was there, which was still really under exploited and unexplored. Could it be harnessed to a fuller-scale project in which these songs were re-examined? "I often thought; 'I wonder what these numbers would sound like if they were re-recorded with the technology of now, putting my own studio to good use. There were always numbers that I had loved and adored and mainly I remembered those numbers often sounding wonderful live but feeling that the recorded versions of them were a bit disappointing. Things that were epically huge live, like Watcher Of The Skies on both the recorded versions; Foxtrot and Genesis Live; it didn't have the size and majesty I remembered playing it live to 20,000 people in the Palasport in Rome and having it fill that hall."

With that idea in mind, it then expanded to see if there might be interest between the other ex and present members for such an intriguing project. It was Julian Colbeck who suggested that it might be wise to contact the other incumbents for their views but soon the idea took on truly epic proportions as

Steve's original vision was expanded into an even larger soundscape: "We started kicking the ball around and he (Julian) said; 'maybe you should approach some of the other guys from the band and see what might come out of a quorum of guys from the band?' I thought; 'That's true' but more importantly for me; I felt that Genesis and the other progressive bands had all worked with each other in one combination or another; that maybe the public's perception of them was that they were one big band. That the similarities were more important than the differences?"

One thing was for sure, no one could say that Steve was anything other than either brave or insane to attempt such a project and certainly it was one that was going to require not only complete dedication but also a serious financial backer. Fortunately, they managed to secure the backing of Mercury Records in Japan who financed the recording under their Nippon Phonogram ambit. "It was a marvellous experience. It was very, very hard work and I thought if I am going to re-record these tracks, I want them to sound really good and I wanted the production to sound really good and I didn't want anyone to say; 'It would have been better to have had so-and-so play on it.' So, I really went to town on it and we used everything on it. We used Mellotrons; we used real orchestra. I realised that fans would still say that even though the originals were flawed in places; they still preferred it because it was the original people but then I took the attitude that there were certain tracks of Genesis that I considered to be classics; ones that I had taken part in. I felt that there are a tremendous amount of tribute bands around now, and I thought the time was nigh; if I was going to be remembered for this then I should now do the definitive Hackett version of these tracks."

Certainly the list of performers who appeared on the album in Japan and its subsequent issue in Europe and the USA, where it had its title changed to Watchers Of The Skies is a veritable "Who's Who" of rock; Tony Levin, Chester Thompson; Paul Carrack; John Wetton; Colin Blunstone; Pino Palladino; Uncle Tom Cobley and all really. Sadly, the collaboration between Steve and Tony Banks on a new version of Los Endos did not materialise and there were several other tracks that were attempted but eventually were shelved. Taking the natural criticisms of fans that would prefer the originals left un-tampered with into consideration; the resulting album explored and opened up this music to a completely fresh appraisal and if at the end of the day, you looked at the music in a slightly different way, then perhaps Steve has done his job.

Having speculated what it would be like if members of Genesis, King Crimson; Zappa and Weather Report would sound like together; not only did

Steve give us the answer with the Genesis Revisited album but also staged a handful of shows in Tokyo and Osaka in December 1996 from which a stunning live album: The Tokyo Tapes, emerged the following year, accompanied by the first video/DVD film from Steve since 1990's Central TV appearance. Done at the behest of the Japanese record company, this was Steve's first ever visit to Japan and one which he thoroughly enjoyed although it was quite demanding as his manager at the time wryly remarked, " We were there ten days but it felt longer! (Laughs) We hit the ground running; did all the tourist stuff; the rehearsals and did the shows and were back in time for Christmas"

Featuring Steve, John Wetton, Ian MacDonald; Julian Colbeck and Chester Thompson; this was truly an audio-visual feast for the eyes and ears as this ultimate supergroup romped through the highlights of their own back catalogues as well as that of Genesis itself. In many respects, the shows were like an old boys' reunion but one, which was enjoyable, all round as Steve remembers: "It was a very interesting line up; chock-full of pals. We had ten days' rehearsal, which was less than I would have liked. The Japanese were very attentive and it was great to work with the guys. I had worked with most of them before although I had never worked with Ian MacDonald. We had been friends ever since 1969 or 1970 even before I had joined Genesis, while I was in Quiet World and he was very encouraging to me. That was when he had just left King Crimson. He was around at one or two of the recording sessions and he was active in trying to find us management. The set we did included some of the things the other guys had been involved with; we did I Talk To The Wind; Battle Lines; Heat Of The Moment; In The Court Of The Crimson King; which were the songs that we had talked about…"

There was talk about a few other tracks being recorded for this project including a version of Los Endos that included Tony Banks, which didn't appear on either version of the album when it was finally released. The desire to "improve" on one's work is part of the intrinsic nature of any artist, and Steve has always been one for reinterpretation as he explains: "When you look back at any recorded work you think, I would do it slightly different now but the nice thing was that there were performances from musicians who weren't necessarily familiar with that material whereas fans of Genesis would probably know every note and it's cast in stone for them and that is understandable. But then when you are working with professionals who aren't in tribute bands and this is not to criticise those musicians who are, some of whom are fabulously good and play it better than we did at the time; you get a reinterpretation".

Another echo came back to revisit Steve at this time when the ghosts of GTR were resurrected by the release of the King Biscuit Flower Hour radio recording of the band's show from Los Angeles. An item of more curiosity value than any real lasting merit, it nonetheless, brought that particular facet of Steve's career under scrutiny again. One thing the album did succeed in doing really was to highlight the sheer banality of the band's own material when compared to the classic selections from the previous bands and solo material of the two principal protagonists.

The howls of protest that might have accompanied Steve's version of the Genesis classics were soon replaced by gasps of amazement when in June 1998 Virgin Records finally released the long overdue (it had first been mentioned to the author by Tony Banks in 1994) and much talked about first Genesis Archive set covering the period 1967-75 spanning the tenures of Anthony Phillips, Peter Gabriel, and of course, Steve Hackett. There was even a much-publicised "reunion" at Heathrow airport, which was a bizarre experience as Steve recalls: "It felt like being in the middle of a sandwich! (Laughs) Very strange get together for a reunion, which was as brief as a biscuit and every moment of which was filmed. What do you say to people who you haven't seen for twenty years?"

With that particular itch now well and truly scratched, Steve was now free to concentrate on consolidating their new record company, Camino Records and to work towards the final completion of the company's own fully working recording studio; MAP Studios. Distribution difficulties had hampered the availability of Steve's back catalogue of albums but with the proper machinery in place with the new record label, Steve was also able to re-issue several previously hard to obtain albums in re-mastered versions with many containing extra tracks as the flagship releases for the new label. Guitar Noir, Till we Have Faces, Bay Of Kings and Momentum were the prime beneficiaries of complete remastering and a surfeit of bonus track and demos including a couple of tantalising samples from the still unreleased Feedback project augmented the standard albums.

He was now committing himself fully to several projects, which had taken a long time to gestate even by his standards, as well as exorcising some of the more personal ghosts that had haunted him.

CHAPTER FIFTEEN
A Midsummer's Nightmare In Darktown

Steve had continued to write and record acoustic tracks in between his other more rock orientated projects with the intention that they would see the light of day at some stage, perhaps as part of another acoustic album. With so many irons in the fire; these tracks frequently got overlooked. He was quite surprised to find out that EMI Records had been keeping a weather eye on developments within his career and as they approached their hundredth anniversary as a record company it was decided that new material would be commissioned by their Classics Division as part of the celebrations. Steve's manager had felt that the acoustic/orchestral pieces might be right for EMI and made the deal for the album with them and both he and Steve subsequently developed the idea of consolidating them within the Midsummer Night's Dream concept.

"The A Midsummer Night's Dream thing came about as a result of a number of acoustic pieces which I had recorded and had on the back burner thinking this will probably go out on a small independent label probably at some point. There won't really be any interest from a major record company and I found that, on the contrary; EMI were very interested in my musical activities."

The project was not a simple re-telling of the Shakespearean play however, more a series of snapshots of some of the more important ideas and musical portraits of some of the principal characters from it: "I just thought it was such a lovely title and I never felt comfortable about calling one piece A Midsummer Night's Dream; I felt that was a disservice to Shakespeare, and people would have just said; 'Oh, you nicked that from Shakespeare' So, I thought, why not try and embrace it long form and try to write a suite of pieces or variations if you like; with repeated themes some of which I had begun to take as character portraits."

With EMI's backing, Steve was able to enlist the help of an orchestra once again as well as seeing the welcome return to active duties of his brother John who had finally managed a recovery from his injuries which at one point it had been thought would have curtailed his flute playing career entirely.* The album holds to the classical tenets of programme music. It is very much a modern day orchestral work but its roots are unashamedly based in the works of the classical "Romantics". Steve's love for the works of such composers as Rachmaninov and the manner in which they produced their music was an ethic, which he fully embraced in this project: "Involvement with this kind of project is where you realise that you are embracing very traditional kinds of material; you are plugging into an existing tradition and in order to embrace it fully you have to throw aside the idea of doing something 'new'. Really what you are doing is like looking at a statue; an existing edifice from a slightly different angle from the way that other people have looked at it in the past. I find that if there is a thread here it is in the idea of taking a mythological subject like we did with Genesis, explained with narrative and harking back to a tone poem".

That is indeed what the album is, a brilliantly evocative Tone Poem deliberately leaving its themes open to the interpretation of the listener. Some of the themes leave little to the listener's imagination but when the piece is based around an idea so wonderfully descriptive as Mountains Turned Into Clouds; In the Beached Margent Of The Sea and Starlight, there really is room for the listener to take their own flight of fancy and imbue the music with whatever slant they wish to put upon it.

Even though the album is classical in orientation, Steve was not worried about conforming to the strictures of the classical regime too much: "I told myself; 'Let's not worry if something sounds early Twentieth Century or late Nineteenth, or Elizabethan or whatever; let's not really worry about that but let each character develop'. For instance; Helena who for me represented unrequited love and I felt that it should basically be sad; but right at the end she is joined by the strings because her dreams do eventually come true. I took a very romantic approach to it."

The album was an enormous success, topping the classical charts and garnering widespread acclaim. I said in my review of the album at the time; that with it, Steve had come of age as a composer as well as a musician and time has not changed my opinion on that score. A Midsummer Night's Dream was, and is the work of a man driven by his art but confident enough

*He now plays a specially adapted flute with a curved section after the mouthpeice that enables the main body of the flute to come down vertically in front of the body.

of his own abilities to let the music flow in its own way without forcing it. That confidence was to continue to grow as Steve began to explore a sea change in his writing over the next few years.

With so many archival projects emerging from the vaults over the preceding couple of years, one would be forgiven for thinking that he had succumbed to an overdose of nostalgia but nothing could have been further from the truth. In between the visits to various parts of his past; Steve had continued working on new material in a variety of forms. His work ethos has always meant that projects come to ripen in the fullness of time but even so, his next rock album; his first since 1993' Guitar Noir had had an inordinate gestation period.

Darktown was to be a pivotal album in many ways. It was to be the first newly recorded album of his to be released by his Camino Records label; after having previous releases issued or licensed to various distributors.

By 1999 however, the Camino roster of artists contained several impressive names including Steve's former comrade in Genesis; Chester Thompson whose debut solo recording: A Joyful Noise had been re-issued by Camino, and the first solo album by former King Crimson member; Ian MacDonald on which Steve himself had also collaborated. The establishment of his own web site also ensured that he was ahead of the game in terms of being able to reach his target audience quickly and effectively and the creation of the Camino Records "web shop" made sure that fans searching for that elusive copy of one of Hackett's albums could now purchase it directly from the man himself.

Steve had already moved into areas that were a lot more personal on the Guitar Noir album and there were obviously a lot of things still preying on his mind, which gave the new album; Darktown a particularly dramatic cast. This is not an album for the faint hearted; far from it; "A nightmare themepark of an album from a man truly possessed" as the press release stated. It is a deeply personal and at times extremely angry examination of subjects, which Steve had avoided, in previous works. In fact, this album is an exorcism of thoughts, ideas and emotions; Steve's very own Primal Scream therapy if you like, which had obviously been locked up inside of his mind for years and which he felt impelled to release. The result is an album which it is difficult to imagine ever being released by a major label - if Steve felt that a major would not have understood Guitar Noir, then what their reaction to Darktown would have been is anyone's guess!

That is not to say that the album is without humour and the opening track;

Omega Metallicus is a guitar synth romp which paraphrases themes from a track from the as yet unreleased Feedback album but which had been included on the US version of the Guitar Noir album; Cassandra. Steve took great liberties with the credits for this one and it is very much tongue in cheek.

The humour is short-lived however; as the rest of the album deals with subjects as diverse as abuse in schools (Darktown); drug addiction and its consequences (Jane Austen's Door) and the manipulation of children by ideologues (The Golden Age Of Steam). Heady stuff and not the kind of material that makes for an album that is easy to listen to, but Steve has always been prepared to challenge not only his own preconceptions but those of his listeners, too and he certainly does that with this album. "There are some subjects which I have avoided in songs over the years because some of them were too painful to talk about but I got to the point where I felt ready to confront those demons in song."

Steve's own childhood experiences of school ground bullying and abuse not just by other children who can always be relied upon to be singularly cruel; but also by staff either through deliberate or unintended acts of abuse; are the subject matter of Darktown itself and this track bears close comparison to Pink Floyd's classic; Another Brick In The Wall (Pt2). It is every bit as dark; angst driven and emotional; a private nightmare made very public indeed: "The idea of in the last verse where I am talking about 'rabid animals' and I have spoken to people about this, and they have said that they get the feeling that once the parents disappeared at school; the teachers turned; they became something else; they became their true evil selves. I don't think I am paranoid, I have heard this from too many other people and I am assuming that other people have been through it.

Everyone is a victim to some extent at school and not just playground bullying but the incredible amount of power that is invested in masters and mistresses. You know, that feeling that as soon as the parents are gone, they start to change and their true aspect comes out. Whatever you are supposed to be taught or whatever it is you are supposed to learn isn't the point. There's another agenda and funnily enough there is a bit in Dennis Potter's The Singing Detective* where it's a school mistress who is absolutely relishing her power and I'm thinking; 'yes, I remember women looking like that, looking demonic. I've got you all now; I can do anything I want to you. You're never going to be good enough, you're going to be my victims for the next few years so screw the lot of you!' (In best Darktown voice) You know (laughs) 'I'm

---

*A critically acclaimed 1986 BBC television serial, and later adapted into a 2003 film featuring Robert Downey Jr. and Mel Gibson.

gonna give you nightmares!' That's the sub text, isn't it?"

The title track inspiration however, came from a poem by Steve's new partner; Joanna Lehmann as she recalls: "I wrote a poem and Steve liked it, so what was to become Darktown was inspired by it. The poem was called Underworld and the first part of the song is based on the poem. Sometimes it would be the two of us sitting down and talking about lyrics and other times we would be discussing a subject such as how we didn't like school so essentially we have always shared a lot of thoughts, feelings and ideas."

Nostalgia is a recurrent theme throughout the album; but not the romanticised ideal of remembering the past. Even a song such as The Golden Age Of Steam, ostensibly a memorial to its subject is much more involved that it appears on surface observation: "Well, you know the book; The Diary Of Anne Frank; her family's betrayal and discovery in a room in Amsterdam? Anyway, I had extracts of that read to me when I was at school and the book always haunted me: The idea of children making very effective spies in the Second World War. The idea came to me one night after I had been watching a programme about trains and the 'Golden Age' of travel. My mind did a sort of jump cut to what if the family had been shopped not by an adult but by a child? What if a child had been bribed by the Nazis? And the idea of the trains running on time oiling the machine; the machine of war."

Steve's reputation with attention to detail is legendary and he has been known to take hours over getting a single tone or chord sounding just the way he wants it. The shading in the corners which he was so dedicated to with Genesis is still something which he is concerned with even now that he is in charge of the entire canvas. On Darktown his attention to detail was augmented by the backroom boys with whom he had increasingly become involved. His former manager; Billy Budis has a long career as a sound man, indeed it was in that capacity that he first became involved with Steve more years ago than he cares to remember! Augmented by Ben Fenner and Roger King, whose own recording talents are not to be sneezed at either; this combination of talents gave Steve the ability to experiment more than ever before: "There were a tremendous amount of engineers involved and programmers; Roger King; Ben Fenner; there's Jerry Peal and Billy (Budis) engineered some tracks for me. What I tended to do is; I'll have an apparently finished track and then I will work on top of it."

Roger King had become an integral part of the Hackett set up in the studio by the time Darktown was released and the story of how he became part of the "Twickenham Mafia" was revealed in typically understated fashion by King during an interview on the 2005 tour: "I was sectioned! (Laughs) My own manager sent out a mass mail-out of CVs to management companies and record companies that she found in Music Weekly or whatever and found a management company about two minutes' walk from my front door and it happened to be Billy (Budis) and they needed an engineer/programmer. "

Roger was thrown in at the deep end with work on the Genesis Revisited project a "small scale project" as he so ironically refers to it; and has been there ever since as they say. His input both as a studio and concert musician has been first rate.

The end result is a highly polished and crafted album but one, which still has its soul and fire intact. Nowhere is that fire more evident than on Jane Austen's Door, an anguished examination of a relationship doomed by drug abuse. The demons of Steve's first relationship are dragged into the glare of the spotlight: "In her case she was going to do what she was going to do to herself anyway and there was an aspect of write-off about it. The person that I knew was no longer there in a sense, you know; the personality I knew had left and that is a sad indictment of drugs. It doesn't make sense to me that so many people were fucked up by LSD. And why my first girlfriend... I will always be asking 'why?' Why do people play Russian Roulette with their brains? Why the hell LSD? And if I could say to one kid out there; 'Don't put that fucking loaded gun to your head' you know: Don't do it!"

Having finally exorcised that particular ghost, it was nice to hear that the subject of the song had heard it as well: "I got to play it to her many years later, it was a song about her and she said it was like a ray of light getting through when you are in a dark cave. That's what she felt it was. She was speaking to me as an admittedly damaged person at that point".

Steve's work ethic had changed enormously too since his earlier efforts and indeed since his time in Genesis where the music was often served up in an almost pre-ordained fashion, Steve is much more prepared to work from the ground up these days: "I think Darktown had a lot of lyrical content which I wouldn't have been brave enough to include in previous years but I think that is something else that the music wants; for you to be brave as well and be prepared to possibly make a total idiot of yourself. In fact whenever I have sat in a studio about to work with people I have always been very unsure about the ideas I was about to present to them. Invariably those are the ones that end up being the strongest; the ones you are least sure about and that is really throwing yourself on the mercy of fate! I think that is because my previous experiences of working with a band and working as part of a collective was that you were expected to start off with something that was pretty substantial. I have since learned that it is not necessary to present a face that is fully made up; the less defined the idea; often the better because it allows other people to suggest things..."

Suggesting things was one thing, but as Steve was quick to point out; at the end of the day; the albums bore his name and he was ultimately responsible for whether they stood or fell by the demanding standards he set for himself: "I delegate a lot in my life in terms of business; but the music I will not delegate. I will not do that. I will not let someone play on it and see what it sounds like later. Sure, I will invite all their input; give people tremendous freedom on any project that I am working on but at the end of the day; I am the one who approves it and, I sound like a control freak I know, but it's the only way."

With the new millennium upon us and Steve in uncharacteristically fiery mode as the century turned, it was only the bravest of fans who would even begin to speculate where his muse would take him next...

CHAPTER SIXTEEN
Impressionistic Feedback

The advent of the new millennium was a period of reflection and looking forward for most people and Steve was no exception. The first year of the new century was to see Steve delving further into his past and at the same time expressing his thoughts for the future.

His first release of what was to prove a busy year was another surprise. Fans had become used to his excursions into the world of acoustic music but his collaborative album with his flautist brother; John now partially recovered from his injuries; was a real treat. Originally, Steve had been intending to record an album of all the acoustic pieces that he and John had performed during the various live shows over the years, but after John's accident, this idea fell by the way side and it was during discussions between the two of them that something completely different emerged: "John and I had talked about doing something for a long time. We hadn't worked together for a long time and frankly; I really missed it and we had talked about some possible flute and guitar combinations. We were originally thinking about an album that would have a mixture of things; a mixture of composers. I remember talking to Billy about one of John's suggestions, which was all the stuff that we played on tour over the years; the acoustic tours we had done; the adaptations of electric things basically written for flute but still close to both our hearts. John was very keen on recording that stuff and I think he still is in the long term but Billy said; 'Why don't you make it two separate projects? Why don't you do an album of Erik Satie stuff and do an album of the other stuff?'"

The decision to tackle the music of Satie might seem a strange one. Satie himself was one of the Impressionist school of musicians along with Debussy, Delius and many others. His work has a deeply individualised style, which separates him from so many of his peers, so in that respect the choice of Satie was a logical one. It was also another part of the rehabilitation of Steve's past. Satie had been an early influence on both Steve and John as the latter recalled: "It goes back along way I suppose really to when Steve and I were living at the flat back in the early days, even before he joined Genesis I think. We had an LP of Erik Satie and that was just when I had got into flute playing and there was some interesting flute playing on the album. I think I have always been attracted to his style of composing. I think that when Steve suggested doing the Satie thing, because they are originally piano pieces, I was wondering are these going to translate well on to the flute?"

The impressionistic and dreamlike qualities of many of the pieces eminently suited Steve's own style. Many of Steve's earlier compositions had an extremely impressionistic cast to them; he was always drawn to ideas rather than formulae and Satie's own somewhat unusual style appealed to both the brothers. The album was literally a work of translation with Steve having the most difficult job as he had to transcribe the original piano parts on to the guitar. Steve's grasp of the necessary technique is even more amazing when you realise that he has never had any formal training in this field, something which still surprises his classically trained brother: "Steve is an extraordinary musician. Not only does he have the rock background, which we all know, but he also has a tremendous understanding of classical music, which is amazing because he hasn't had the training. I am very much the trained musician and I don't mean that in any kind of superior way at all; I had to train; I found it very difficult and hard to understand. Steve was just a natural; he just picked up a guitar and whatever it was; working out chord sequences he has a fantastically good ear."

Certainly the resulting album is a charming work, which will surprise many with its familiarity. Satie's work may not be as well-known as that of Debussy, but it has been used in a surprisingly wide range of fields; film, television and advertising and many of the pieces which were selected for the "Hackett Treatment" will be instantly recognisable to most people. The Satie influence had been with Steve for a long time and in fact, the track Kim had been inspired by a Satie piece.

The album was put together in quite a short period of time but you would not know it from the quality of the music. It is an interpretation of the music rather than a slavish copy of the original although even John admits to a bit of unintended poetic licence on one of the recordings: "I realised that when I went back and listened to one of the pieces that I had left out one of the rests. I had read it wrongly and it is recorded now! (Laughs) Looking back on it now, I misread it but there's an element of poetic licence and we tried not to

Reading Festival - 1981 *(Alan Perry)*

"Highly Strung or nylon strung" Electric and acoustic tours - 1983 *(Mike Ainscoe)*

"Seven Of The Best!" Back with his old pals for one night only. 'Six Of The Best' reunion concert - 2nd October 1982
Left to right; Mike Rutherford, Phil Collins, Daryl Stuermer, Chester Thompson, Steve, Peter Gabriel and Tony Banks
(Alan Perry)

Performing live in Mansfield on the acoustic 'Bay Of Kings' Tour - November 1983 *(Andy Banks)*

Performing 'I Know What I Like' with Marillion at the Hammersmith Odeon - February 1986 *(Richard Nagy)*

Performing at the Manchester Apollo Theatre on the 'Highly Strung' Tour - April 1983 *(Mike Ainscoe)*

On the GTR Tour - 1986 *(Unknown)*

GTR at Manchester Apollo Theatre - September 1986 *(Richard Nagy)*

Performing in GTR with Steve Howe at Manchester Apollo Theatre - September 1986 *(Richard Nagy)*

"Big Hair, shiny suits and shoulder pads?" GTR in overblown mid-80's mode.
Left to right; Phil Spalding, Steve, Jonathan Mover, Steve Howe and Max Bacon *(Courtesy Arista Records)*

"Hackett & Hackett". Dueting with his brother John at Manchester Opera House on the 'Momentum' Tour - May 1988 *(Ted Sayers)*

Recording with Austrian musician Gandalf - 1991
(Author's collection)

Late 80's promotional shot
(Paul Cox/Caroline Records)

Richmond Hotel, London - Early 90's
(Author's collection)

Onstage with Gandalf - March 1992
(Courtesy Sony Records)

In the USA on the 'Tour Noir' - 1992 *(Bill Brink)*

Steve in 1992 *(Bill Brink)*

Steve and John during an interview for TWR at The Richmond Hotel, London February 2000 *(David Beaven)*

Live in Barcelona - November 1994 *(Carlos Noriega)*

"Konbanwa Tokyo" Steve with a few of his friends in Japan recording 'The Tokyo Tapes' - December 1996
Left to right; Chester Thompson, Julian Colbeck, Steve, John Wetton and Ian MacDonald *(Yuki Kuroyanagi)*

In Vivegano, Italy - July 2000
(Roger Salem)

Judging a knobbly-knees contest in Italy - 2000.
The contestants; (otherwise known as his touring band) Left to right; Ben Castle, Phil Mulford, Roger King, Gary O'Toole and Steve *(Helmut Janisch)*

The "Acoustic Trio" performing at the Auditorio San Domenico, Foligno in Italy - April 2002.
Left to right; John Hackett, Steve, Roger King *(Richard Nagy)*

Signing session at Borders bookstore, Fox Point, Wisconsin USA - August 2003 *(Kurt Lambert-Newgord)*

Performing for the 'Classic Rock Society' in Rotherham on the 'To Watch The Storms' Tour - October 2003 *(Richard Nagy)*

Onstage in Liverpool - October 2003. Left to right; Roger King, Steve, Gary O'Toole, Terry Gregory and Rob Townsend *(Richard Nagy)*

Steve's Mum - March 2009
(Roger Salem)

"Old boys' reunion" at the Shepherds Bush Empire - March 2004.
Left to right; Pete Hicks, Steve, Nick Magnus, John Hackett and Dik Cadbury
(Alan Hewitt)

Have sitar, will travel - at home 2009
(Alan Hewitt)

With son Oliver in Germany - June 2005
(Alan Hewitt)

Wedding day with Joanna
St Albans, 4th June 2010
(Alan Hewitt)

With Eleanor Rigby in Liverpool - 2010
(Alan Hewitt)

be too literal; we followed the notes but we wanted to make it a fresh approach."

Fans were delighted to see John back in action with his brother again and the album exudes a relaxed warmth which characterises their work. The selection of tracks also included some of Satie's more eclectic compositions and so as an introduction to his music not only do you get the glories of the Hackett brothers playing but also a healthy resume of the composer's musical works to boot.

As usual, Steve had been juggling several projects during the preceding year or so, including an album of "covers" with Jim Diamond who had featured so strongly on Days Of Long Ago on the Darktown album. They decided to wait for the right moment to release it. Fortunately, Steve had finally managed to complete his own studio and working on projects became slightly less pressured although one project that emerged out of this immensely creative period did put him under some pressure.

An American TV producer, Chris Ward had been inspired by a book; "Portrait Of A Young Forger" by a Polish Holocaust survivor; Marian Pretzel. He had survived the war by forging various documents for himself and fellow Jews. The book convinced Ward to make a documentary about the subject under the title "Outwitting Hitler" which was made and broadcast on the Showtime Channel in America although sadly it has not been given a broadcast slot outside of the U.S.

For this project, Steve used a selection of old and new music including a suite of pieces under the working titles; Janowska (the name of a concentration camp in Poland), Nightmare Years and Outwitting Hitler, which were to feature largely in a later work. Ward's initial insistence on using Steve came from him being a Genesis fan as he explained: "I am a big Genesis and Steve Hackett fan but the thought hadn't occurred to me until I was playing Steve's Walking Away From Rainbows and then later the Genesis track; Blood On the Rooftops. My instincts told me that Steve; who has that rare combination of talent and versatility; was the right choice for Outwitting Hitler. He was the only one I contacted about scoring the music - that's how sure I was about this. Let me add that at first, friends at Showtime felt otherwise. I had made the mistake of telling them that Steve had been the guitarist in Genesis. Of course, they came back saying that the driving sound of a rock band was totally wrong for a Holocaust documentary. Naturally, they ended up loving Steve's score."

Interestingly enough, the score not only featured the pieces mentioned earlier; but also extracts from Defector, and A Midsummer Night's Dream along with several other unrecorded pieces. Fortunately, Steve was used to working to deadlines and his score was completed in plenty of time. It always pays to have music "off the peg" so to speak!

2000 was an incredibly busy year; The Satie album was the first of a series of projects, which involved Steve. Another was his appearance on the first documentary about his old band mates in over ten years; "The Genesis Songbook" took an affectionate look at some of the band's better-known songs and Steve was duly interviewed for it. His time with Genesis was also brought into the spotlight again with the release of the second Genesis Archive set which covered the period from 1976 to 1992, effectively Steve's final years with the band and the era of Phil Collins. As if this wasn't enough Virgin also released Turn It On Again: The Hits, capitalising ostensibly on the success of the band's latter day "three man line up" material.

By this time, Genesis had gone through their final recording and performing incarnation with Ray Wilson fronting the short-lived Calling All Stations line-up. Steve had found himself out in the cold again when it came to consultations about the selection of material for the Archive project but it was a cynical marketing decision by Virgin which caused the most upset. At the time of the Genesis Revisited / Archive 1967-75 albums; Steve had been persuaded into taking part in the re-recording of a new version of Carpet Crawlers, ostensibly for inclusion as a finale to the first Box Set. Despite ill-informed reports in the music press at the time, no grand "reunion" of the musicians took place; everyone recorded their parts at their own studios and submitted them via other media, new technology sadly ensuring that there was no need for everyone to be present within the same studio and therefore no grand reunion, which everyone had imagined.

Steve also returned to live duties in the summer of 2000, with a short tour of Italy with a brand new band including Roger King, who has been a constant feature in Steve's recorded work since 1996's Genesis Revisited project. The band also incorporated Ben Castle; son of the legendary Roy Castle.* Reinvigorated by his recent work; Steve completely revamped the live set, dropping many on stage favourites in favour of material from his latest album; Darktown but also including a healthy selection of material from Genesis and even tracks from the Sketches Of Satie album.

Before the year was over, another archival project had finally been dragged kicking and screaming from the vaults. Steve had frequently made mention

*Roy Castle OBE 31 August 1932 - 2 September 1994 was an English dancer, singer, comedian, actor, television presenter and jazz trumpet player. He presented Record Breakers, a children's TV show for nearly 20 years. He recorded the theme song for the show himself and while presenting the show he broke several world records himself.

of the Feedback album which he had recorded back in 1987 with such alumni as Bonnie Tyler, Brian May and Chris Thompson. Bootleg copies of the album had surfaced but they were of an inferior stamp.

Eventually issued in September of 2000 under the title of Feedback 86, the album reflected a variety of facets of Steve's musical psyche. Tracks such as Cassandra and Slot Machine are out and out rock numbers and the latter's catchy hook should have ensured its success as a single had it been available. One track from the GTR period emerged in the shape of Prize Fighters, which had been performed as part of the GTR set in their tour: "Prizefighters was a track very much designed for GTR. Chris Thompson did a fantastic vocal on it. And Bonnie is a fabulous belter, she sings the first verse very gently and then she opens up and, bloody hell!"

The contrast between the male and the female vocals makes the song infinitely more successful than its solo voiced GTR version. Both Stadiums Of The Damned and The Gulf were topical songs both at the time of the album's inception and its actual release; the former outlining the obsessive and increasingly tribal behaviour of football hooligans (I won't call them "fans"); and The Gulf which explores the political situation in the Middle East which was soon to flare up again with the invasion of Kuwait. The "Gulf" in question could just as easily be the geographical one or the gulf between Christianity and Islam, either way an intriguing song.

One of the most surprising things about the album was the appearance on it of Queen maestro Brian May whom many would have seen as an unexpected cohort: "I met Brian in Brazil when Queen had just played the Rock In Rio Festival. Brian and I started talking and I said how much I liked his playing and he said; 'I remember you doing The Musical Box' and he said 'I liked the guitar playing on that'. I had no idea up to that point that he was aware of anything I had done and it was great to get that from one of my peers. So, that is how I got in touch with him and he and I had talked about doing something. I think perhaps we were talking about doing an album together and then his commitments didn't really coincide with mine at the time. I felt that I needed to get something finished and there were months between and so I said; 'Look, Brian I feel that I am going to need to play on with this…' He said; 'Well maybe it should be a guest appearance of me on something of yours' and we have stayed very much friends since."

Steve was also delighted to have the chance to work with Ian Mosley again on this album. After departing from Steve's band in 1983, he found himself working with Marillion whose star was firmly in the ascendant at that time: "Whenever Ian and I talk it is always an extension of our social life. I mean we immediately plug into that time when we were working together and doing two shows a night in America and flogging our guts out, you know? The nice thing about working with Ian is the sense of humour, which is paramount where that defuses many a difficult moment. It is always fun working with Ian, he makes it fun and it is important to me that people I work with; the people I have worked with the longest are the ones with the funniest sense of humour."

Steve's acoustic side was highlighted on this album by Notre Dame Des Fleurs, which had been a highlight of the 1988 Momentum tour. The piece owes its title to a book written by the French writer Jean Genet and his experiences in prison. Certainly this is an album that reflects the many sides of Steve Hackett and with such a marvellous cast of musicians it would surely have been a hit at the time but, better late than never, as they say!

Steve stepped up his touring schedule a notch in 2001 with another first for him; an extensive tour of South America after a handful of shows there back in 1993. This tour was not without its moments of drama. Apparently the local police force in one of the places where the band visited; held the band's gear to ransom before they were allowed to play, as Steve recalls: "The last gig we did in Rio was a bit hairy I seem to remember bits of equipment were turning up at the last minute... 'Yeah we'll have the lights here for the show in... five minutes' you know, and 'is that amp going to be alright?' You have to have confidence in the team that says 'It'll be alright' and you have to stay very calm. I know I got nervous before that Sao Paolo gig because the police had impounded the equipment basically to extract a bribe from us to enable the gig to happen. And the very last thing that went wrong before we were supposed to go on was that my guitar went stupid and suddenly I had to take the whole thing apart. The intro music was playing and already the crowd had been waiting three hours because of all the shenanigans with the police and I'm afraid for the second time on that tour I went... and I have just got to learn to control my temper. I think we had to pay $1000 just to get the equipment back."

The band (and their gear) survived the trauma and the tour was captured for posterity in the double CD, video and DVD release: Somewhere In South America. Once again Steve mixed the set up including a selection of as yet unrecorded material alongside a seamless mixture of classic solo Hackett tracks and some Genesis gems too.

As he had remarked earlier, there are usually bootlegs of gigs circulating soon after shows especially these days when recording technology has become so advanced and yet so accessible. Even so, it was a great surprise when later in the year, Camino Records issued what every Hackett fan had been dreaming of; a boxed set of archival recordings taken from various shows from the 1970's through to the 1990's. The initial success of the acoustic live album; There Are Many Sides To The Night back in 1995 had persuaded Steve and his record company that there was a market place for such releases. Housed in a nifty box and containing a detailed booklet; this set started a trend of recordings which has continued since. The set was also issued as two double CDs in Japan where a recording from Newcastle on the October 1979 tour replaced the Hammersmith recording from the boxed set which had been taken from the June 1979 shows. This release also included Feedback 86 as part of the package. The Newcastle disc was subsequently made available in the UK as a stand-alone "bonus" disc fitting nicely into the existing box!

Effectively giving the fans their own official bootlegs was something, which shrewdly deals with the bootleg problem and also brought money back to the rightful owners of the recordings whilst keeping the fans happy too. Steve must have taken some comfort that the idea was also emulated; albeit on a larger scale by his former band mate; Peter Gabriel who released virtually every show from his 2003 and 2004 tours as official "warts and all" bootlegs. Genesis themselves, as usual failed to grasp the nettle and despite talks about the release of a series of archival live recordings from the band's own collection of desk recordings; nothing has emerged to date and yet another golden opportunity appears to have passed them by. Selecting the material for this series was no easy task, however as he recalls: "It took place over a long time because we had the tapes and we transferred a lot of that stuff on to CD and DAT and just listening to them seemed to take forever.

So it seemed to happen in two halves. I was listening to so much of that stuff that it was driving me spare, frankly! Trying to access what was good and what wasn't. Let me try to be blunt... whenever I listen to a live thing; I want it to be perfect. I want every note to be great just like everyone else... You want all sorts of things to be wonderful and we were dealing with fixed mixes a lot of the time so there is only a limited amount of things you can do to fix things. Anyway we started off working on a bunch from each era and gradually by working on them thanks to the wonders of modern technology... working with Ben Fenner, I have to say he was central to this the fact that he has got multi band EQ and compression and so you can alter things. I prefer not to get in too close to it because essentially what you have got are very honest live recordings...."

However, the hassle did have its upside with Steve able to relive some happy memories with some of the gigs: "We listened to a lot of gigs from the

90's and it seemed like the Grand (Clapham Grand, London) was the most happening one. The Grand was a nice memory, there were a lot of people at that gig that I was glad were there. There were so many old friends at that gig that it would be virtually impossible to separate it from the idea that it was an event virtually in your own living room as it were; and wasn't it nice to get all those people together at that time? Like all home town gigs you get a little bit nervous that your grandmother is going to get in! (Laughs)."

Funnily enough, the author recalls Steve's grandmother was at that gig along with most of the rest of the Hackett clan and indeed, I remember that gig very well as the first time I ever had the pleasure of meeting Steve's mother and father.

2002 was taken up with an increasingly widespread series of peripatetic ventures which saw Steve performing a variety of different types of shows beginning with a series of acoustic trio shows in Japan, Hungary and Italy which saw the welcome reappearance of brother John on the concert stage. As if that were not enough; Steve also visited the USA and Canada and during the summer months for a short series of rock shows with his new look band. The long overdue return to the US was in no small part due to the establishment of a reliable record label to distribute the product in that particular territory. Steve was quite emphatic about the logistics of the touring situation in the USA during an interview he gave the day after his NEARfest performance in Trenton New Jersey: "It is not in terms of lack of support from the various territories; its just that you have to get that combination right of an agent putting you in the right sized places that you can actually fill and then hoping that you can make up the shortfall with merchandising and all that. It is the rock and roll equation which goes over and above music."

During both these tours, Steve continued to try out new material in both acoustic and electric settings. In the same interview, he gave the first indications of the direction his follow up to Darktown would take: "Some of it has got jazzy overtones; other things are more poppy maybe. Other things are more rocky; there are some comedic things. I try and make it a trip around the world every time I do an album. I try not to do albums, which are emotionally one-dimensional. The new album is less dark and more up than Darktown."

The results of these experiments were captured for posterity with a further series of live recordings including a first for Steve with the DVD/CD release of the complete acoustic show from the trio performance at the Petofi Csarnok in Budapest under the title Hungarian Horizons and a further release in what had by now been titled the "Live Archive" series taken from one of the US concert performances.

He also worked with classical percussionist Evelyn Glennie on a piece, which she had commissioned from Steve for performance by her highly acclaimed Rhythm Sticks Ensemble. Steve performed an improvised piece with Evelyn and the Rhythm Sticks Ensemble at the Bridgewater Hall in Manchester on 19th July 2002, a performance that was filmed for a national TV documentary about Glennie which has yet to be screened. Two days later the piece which he had written for her; The City In The Sea; was premiered at the Queen Elizabeth Hall in London. "She is a brilliant percussionist and drummer and she is also a fantastic marimba player," explained Steve at the time. "But she is from a classical background and the idea of us working together was her crossing over a little bit more into an area that isn't exactly rock but more of the avant garde as it were; but it is with her with her tongue firmly in her cheek, you know and there is a lot of humour in her stuff. I am joining her in Manchester to do something, which is entirely improvised, and then there is something, which I have written for her, which we are doing at the Queen Elizabeth Hall in London. I am trying to talk her into doing an album together because that might be very interesting and it will be very different to anything I have done before".

It still remains to be seen if this intriguing pairing will work on a fuller-length project in the future, with both artists' schedules remaining incredibly busy, finding time to organise such a project would be the main stumbling block to any such activity but once again, Steve has continued to push the musical envelope and work in different and stimulating environments.

All of this was grist to the mill as he also continued to work on his next album which was to be his first brand new rock album since 1999's Darktown.

CHAPTER SEVENTEEN

Sunshine After The Rain

Another extremely busy year for Steve arrived in 2003. First to appear was his contribution to the latest album by Gordian Knot; "Emergent" which featured Steve alongside Bill Bruford for the first time since the Genesis Revisited album. This was to be a taster for the long awaited new album.

May 2003 saw the release of To Watch The Storms, Steve's fourteenth studio album and one whose title is completely misleading. If Darktown was Steve's effective anger management album; then To Watch The Storms found our hero in a much happier frame of mind. Continuing the personal approach to his work, which had begun, on Guitar Noir, this album was every bit as intense as its predecessor but instead of examining the things that made him angry or sad, here we have a look at more of the things that make Steve smile. The album contrasted completely with its predecessor which was also part of Steve's rationale both for his studio work and his live shows: "What I find is that contrast between different musical styles is what really works for me. If it was jazz all night that would be very boring I think; if it was all sweetness and gentle ballads all night that would also be very boring for me. I think a live show covers a tremendous amount of bases."

This is another nostalgic album as Steve effectively gives us a series of looks into his own photo album of memories from another of his "list songs" in the shape of Strutton Ground which plays on the names of places in much the same way that The Virgin & The Gypsy had done with flowers all those years previously alongside some personal reminiscences: "A Friend said; 'It's one of your list songs again, isn't it?' I did the same thing with The Virgin & The Gypsy. This time it was places and yes, some of them are personal references; Jobson's Cove is this place in Bermuda. The Butterfly House is near here in Syon Park and I always remember the first time I went in there and all these butterflies settled on me and I felt like a giant surrounded by fairies."

The Devil Is An Englishman is the first cover version to appear on a Hackett album and a gloriously over the top performance it is too. Originally recorded by Thomas Dolby for the Ken Russell film Gothic, a biography of the poet Byron, but never used in the actual soundtrack. Steve's vocalisations are as manic as Lawrence Olivier on an LSD trip! It was obvious that he had a great deal of fun with this one and it would have made a great video too, as he remarked at the time: "It's a kind of spoof, psycho-disco number. It's basically a comedy number. It would make a very good video I feel, but you know making films is a vastly more expensive business than making albums. I always figure that by the end of the day, by the time you have made a slightly dodgy video you might have been able to go out and hire a really magnificent orchestra so I tend to invest in the musical side, at the expense of the visual side. I don't think I am a particularly visual act". A strangely contradictory comment from someone whose music has such a visual slant to it!

Frozen Statues and Mechanical Bride take on more serious ideas with the former being inspired by Leonard Sachs's books on a medical condition, which effectively renders the sufferer immobile. Mechanical Bride takes a wry view of man's inhumanity to man and his fellow creatures: "I remember being at a charity dinner party and listening to these two people discussing how many grouse or whatever they had bagged and I said to them; 'Wouldn't it be fun if the animals could fire back?' and they looked at me as if I had gone crazy and walked away. Yes, it is a protest song… at the end of the day it was all about innocent men dying in the electric chair and being tortured to death; state sanctioned torture and the idea that any civilised nation could do things like that rests very uneasily with me."

Wind, Sand And Stars was inspired by the work of Anton Saint Exupery whose work; The Little Prince had been in the frame for Genesis at the time of "The Lamb". The title is from his work about his time as a flying postman in the Spanish Sahara in the 1930's and evokes all the sense of desolation of that region and also incorporates some of the rhythmic ideas that Steve gained from his work with renowned orchestral percussionist Evelyn Glennie.

Brand New is perhaps the closest to a straight love song that you could expect from Steve but it is counterbalanced by his rendering of the haunting Daphne Du Maurier tale; Rebecca and love lost in This World. The Silk Road takes us down the path of "World Music" which Peter Gabriel has worked so much to promote. Steve however, had very much precluded the use of "ethnic" sounds, instruments and musicians with his 1984 album Till We Have Faces, and this track was inspired by oriental lyric poetry such as the Japanese "Haiku" verses which are usually very short. " It is named after a specific trade route and the journey is everything. Lyrically it borrows from oriental poetry where you get two line stanzas that accompany calligraphy that accompanies oriental stuff… It wasn't just indigenous music sold to you as world music because really what you are getting is folk music of a particular region… and the imagination runs riot on the whole thing; the idea of having a rhythm that's common to Brazil and Africa twinned with a Cantonese koto. I wanted people to think 'Oh, I wonder where in the world this comes from'?"

Once again, this particular track showed just how open Steve is to the suggestions of the people around him and on this particular occasion, it was to be his engineer/keyboard player Roger King who made a substantial contribution to the end result. "I love working with other people when they will come up with an aspect of the arrangement that is absolutely crucial and it might be something they have picked up on in the lyric; or something harmonically. Roger put that one together. We had worked on it and he constructed it rhythmically from my basic parts."

We have the drunken Polka band taking the stage in Come Away where Eastern European mazurka music meets the heady world of western rock 'n' roll; a generic pub chain name was utilised in the title of The Moon Under Water, another one of Steve's acoustic numbers inspired from this very unlikely setting: "It is a local pub name actually, which I thought was wonderful. I had never heard of it before someone mentioned it on the train as I was going home from a jazz gig. I thought it was a wonderful idea… this bunch of drunken guys were talking about The Moon Under Water and I thought it was a great title. It was an acoustic piece and a fairly festive one. My acoustic stuff in general tended to be slow and peaceful. This one keeps motoring."

Perhaps the most personal track on the entire album is Steve's wonderful tribute to his artist father: Serpentine Song. One of the most beautifully observed portraits that Steve has ever committed to record and one which rounds off the album in fine style. An unabashedly rose-tinted closer and one of his favourites: "Well, it's a stroll through Hyde Park through the seasons, because it refers to rain; sunshine; snow; autumn; so in a way it refers to all the seasons. It's all those strolls I have taken round the lake put into one. Its also dedicated to my dad who sells paintings alongside the railings of Hyde Park on the Bayswater Road side and he still does that every Sunday."

To Watch The Storms is Steve's most diverse album with a virtual showcase for every style he has explored during his career appearing throughout its thirteen tracks; and in fact it was referred to as "a street with thirteen bungalows on it; each with a different frontage" by one percipient observer! Also if you were lucky enough to get hold of the special edition of the album or the Japanese edition; you were treated to additional material not available on the standard version including such gems as the tribute to the halcyon days of the blues scene and Paul Butterfield; Fire Island; and the manically humorous Marijuana Assassin Of Youth. The album is very much the world in miniature, which is precisely what Steve intended it to be: "I allowed myself to get lost in the world of sound and lyrics and the attempt to paint atmospheres with music. If you think it's almost like a film for the ears rather than the eyes. I was trying to take people off on a journey to many different places and times."

To Watch The Storms was also to be the album that finally brought Steve home to the UK concert stage for the first time in ten years! An unlikely series of acoustic shows took place before this, however, as he returned to the States for a series of impromptu solo acoustic gigs in the setting of several stores in the Borders bookstore chain during August; shows at which he continued to perform music which he was working on but which had not yet reached a status of "finished".

As if by contrast to that; he was also invited to take part in the twentieth anniversary celebrations of the Hard Rock Café in Japan. Here he performed in the company of such heavy rock alumni as Nuno Bettencourt; Paul Gilbert and Led Zeppelin's John Paul Jones, (the latter of whom was to be Steve's special guest at his show at the Shepherd's Bush Empire Theatre during Steve's subsequent UK tour) in a series of gigs under the title: "Guitar Wars". These shows were recorded and subsequently issued in Japan as a CD and DVD under that title but this release has not been given a distribution elsewhere yet although to be honest Steve's performance was not his greatest!

Steve rates his new band in the same league as the band that created the awesome live trilogy of tours for Please Don't Touch, Spectral Mornings and Defector and it was difficult to disagree with his assessment of the new players: "There's been perhaps one other rock album I have done that's like this and that was Spectral Mornings - an album that was made with a really fine band. It's the same thing on To Watch The Storms; a really great band put this album together; so quite apart from what anyone thinks of my playing; I can stand back and be a fan of everyone else's playing. Gary's drums which are second to none on it. Rob's extraordinary woodwind work and brass work and Roger's extraordinary... well, basically co-production with me, and computer work, as well as his own literal playing. His stamp is all over it. Not to mention John's fabulous flute."

The new musicians were drawn together by the usual mix of auditions and in the case of Gary O'Toole, he was spotted by Steve's manager who took Steve to see him playing with Manuka who were Aron* and Jeanne Friedman's band.

A comprehensive UK tour was organised for October including a first time visit to both Dublin and Belfast for Steve as a solo artist, and all too rare visits to Scotland and Wales to boot. The show which was presented here was, in most respects, the same as that which had been performed over the preceding couple of years in Italy and South America but with such a lengthy gap between this and his last UK tour, the fans were eager to hear their hero again and the gigs were very well attended, many being complete sell-outs.

With such a varied catalogue of albums to draw from, he was not short of material to perform but once again the emphasis being on the newer albums. However, fans were not deprived of their share of classic cuts from Steve's back catalogue and once again several nods to his time in Genesis including a truly awesome rendition of Hairless Heart. In fact, tongues were soon set wagging with reports that Tony Banks had been seen in the audience and deep in conversation with Steve backstage at the gig at the Shepherds Bush Empire Theatre, where there was also a reunion of sorts backstage with Nick Magnus, Peter Hicks and Dik Cadbury from Steve's first touring band along with his brother, parents and many other friends and relations. Fans were soon treated to another live recording from this series of gigs when yet another volume in the "Live Archive" series of official bootlegs was subsequently released, compiled from several shows in the UK and in Europe.

*Aron Friedman had collaborated on the Guitar Noir album and just like the rest of the guys, he proved to be an inspired choice!

CHAPTER EIGHTEEN

This Vast Life

Barely a scant few months after the end of the To Watch The Storms tour had ended, Steve was back on the road both in the UK and in Europe with what ostensibly was viewed by many as simply an extension of that tour. Those who opted not to go and see the 2004 shows soon regretted their decision however. Steve had taken on board the suggestions of his fan base through the Internet and had drawn up an entirely different set. There were gasps when he opened the show with Valley Of The Kings from the Genesis Revisited album but they were as nothing compared to the surprise when he made his introductions to an unexpected Genesis classic: "This is a song that was intended for a drummer to sing and tonight we have Mr Gary O'Toole to sing it for us. This is Blood On The Rooftops"

Steve had always included references to this track in his acoustic medleys but here it was in its entirety for the first time ever and I am not ashamed to admit that on the opening night of the tour in Dartford, yours truly was in tears by the end of it! Without doubt, the 2004 set list was the most representative that Steve had ever played. He drew upon virtually every album from his own catalogue including the extremely belated debut of Hammer In the Sand in the live set a mere twenty five years after it had first been written! He installed several Genesis classics in between them for good measure. If there were any quibbles over not playing one track; they were more than compensated for by his selection of others to give as broad a picture of his career as it was humanly possible to cram into a scan two hour show, which whizzed by so quickly it felt like minutes. Once again, there was even space for a brand new track; a supercharged rocker titled during the tour; A Dark Night In Toytown but subsequently re-titled on the next "Live Archive" release as If You Can't Find Heaven; one of any number of tracks which Steve continued to hone into shape for future use. The tour was also captured for posterity by the DVD release: "Once Above A Time" which was filmed at the final gig of the tour in Budapest.

The live recording was also accompanied by Steve's first rock DVD since 2001's Somewhere In South America and once again, it captured the essential spark of his concert performance perfectly. The no frills approach to these releases ensured that they reached their target audience at a very reasonable price.

Steve also found time during the course of that year to be reunited with his old keyboard chum, Nick Magnus to work on his own project: Hexameron. This was an album that was to feature an almost complete reunion of the original Hackett touring band with appearances by Peter Hicks, as well as John Hackett, with a day in the studio that Steve enjoyed immensely: "My involvement with Nick, we did a very long day. We had intended to get everything done by six o'clock and I said; 'Have you got any others?' He said; 'It would be great if you could do this.' I think I staggered out at midnight! (Laughs). We really had given it a good go. Lovely to work with him again".

Steve had also contributed to the album by his former drummer Ian Mosley, a collaborative effort with Ben Castle under the title of "Postmankind" which had been issued on Marillion's very own Racket Records imprint. Nick's album was one of the best releases of the year and it spoke volumes for the friendships that still existed between the various incumbents that they were still glad to help each other out.

In and around this flurry of activity, Steve also managed to dedicate some time to help his brother make the bold decision to emerge from the shadows and complete work on his own debut rock album. John had already produced a well-received flute/piano album titled Velvet Afternoon in 2004 and as the year progressed he found time to complete his first foray into the world of rock with Checking Out Of London, released at the beginning of 2005. Once again, the album featured Nick Magnus, alongside John and Steve with lyrics written by John's long time friend Nick Clabburn. Steve was extremely supportive of the effort John had made on this his first rock outing. In some respects it took Steve back to his own beginnings:

"Because it was John's first rock album under his own name; my feeling was that I hope John would get to the point where he was very happy with it and in love with it. I was always trying to steer him back to himself. It doesn't matter what I think; it's what you think; it's your album. It is lovely to see him flower like this. It gives me great pleasure and I am pleased to see him happy with it. Two magazines have already chosen it as their album of the month so it can't be a fluke. I know this feeling when you first do a solo thing and you are wondering if you are going to sell two copies or not. It is ironic that we both finished our albums on the same day. We had worked on each other's albums and that was a lovely synchronous thing. So, in a way the projects are twinned in more ways than one."

Steve had already stepped centre stage and so it was great to see him rendering such sterling assistance to his brother's first attempts in this notoriously difficult field. John's efforts were rewarded by glowing reviews including "album of the month" in Record Collector's round up of releases. Steve was also far more complimentary about the latest re-working of some of his Genesis past in the shape of the Platinum Collection, yet another marketing device from EMI but this time one which served as a very useful showcase for the work which the band's producer Nick Davis had been doing on the long overdue re-mastering, as well as being a useful introduction to the floating voters still unwilling to investigate the band's back catalogue: "Nick is in the driving seat with this and he did such a good job to be honest with the live version of "The Lamb"... It was never designed as an album in the first place and he did such a good job with that. Nick is a very hands on guy. On the Platinum Collection there is a particularly nice version of Afterglow. If these are restorations he has broadened the picture. He has been very thorough and he does listen to everything in the sound field. I don't know how he does it. Maybe he does it a couple of bars at a time because that stuff is replete with detail and it is easy to miss something."

2004 saw Steve's latest album book-ended by several more archival projects. There has always been considerable interest among Hackett fans for the release of the handful of TV appearances from the late 1970's onwards which they are aware of. Many of these items have appeared on bootleg video or DVD copies and it was refreshing to see that the TV company responsible for the earliest visual document of Steve's solo career was issuing it on a DVD. Taken from a TV studio performance from his first tour in 1978 titled "Spectral Mornings". This release captured the essence and magic of those early performances and was welcomed by the fans. There are several other similar tantalising items in the vaults, which may make for a similar release at some point.

Steve's own album reinforced his status as one of the country's most innovative and creative composers of orchestral music. Metamorpheus is a large-scale orchestral examination of the Greek myths of Orpheus and Eurydice - a mythology that examines the fundamental questions of life and death. Once again, this album had evolved over a lengthy period. Many of

Steve's albums can certainly be likened to a fine wine that is left to rest upon the lees until its full vintage and flavour can be released and Metamorpheus fits snugly into that category. Metamorpheus as an idea, had been with Steve almost as long as the A Midsummer Night's Dream album, and similarly to that project; the diversions of Steve's efforts to other projects which were perhaps easier to accommodate, resulted in a lengthier gestation period which gave the finished result a much fuller form: "I recorded most of the guitar work back then in 1997. I think it must have been hard on the heels of A Midsummer Night's Dream and then I had to leave it for a number of years whilst a number of other projects took precedence because they were easier to deliver."

The project also saw Steve reunited with one of his former colleagues from Quiet World; Dick Driver, who in the intervening years had become a well-known bass player and through his work with several orchestras, he was able to assemble the core ensemble that became the "Underground Orchestra" for the album. Once again, Roger King and Ben Fenner ably assisted Steve in the studio. In fact, some of the inspiration for the album was derived from that meeting with Steve's childhood friend Trevor who had suffered from polio and who had opened Steve's eyes and ears to the world of orchestral music. The experience of hearing this music for the first time had stuck with Steve as he recalled how the dramatic closing moments of Metamorpheus, all full of portent and drama were born: "First of all, as a child I felt so uplifted by that piece (Tchaikovsky's Piano Concerto in B flat Minor) of music. It was instant, and there was this thing we all flew with the angels, there were no cripples; and that melody flew so high. It was so touching and so wonderful and it touched me with sunshine. I imagine what it must have done for Trevor. It must have given him wings and that little old piece of music has got its influence in the very last piece; Lyra on the new album because you have the same four notes, and I have the same melody which goes on and on except that I don't develop it thematically. I just develop it chordally and that's the nod to Tchaikovsky. It is my own way of making that fly because I find that is this album probably at its most emotional. It is at its most sad and yet it's most triumphant at the same time. I deliberately wanted at the beginning… there is this sound of timpani; a piano; a bell and a gong all being struck at the same time to give it a huge bell sound. It's both a wake up call and a death knell and everything; life and death all in one."

The album draws together many fundamental ideas; the idea of music as a healer; sorrow, redemption; tribulation. Not necessarily ideas that lend themselves easily to the listener but when has Steve ever made things easy for himself or his listeners? Austere in style; this is music that demands that the listener pay close attention to it and then to firmly draw their own conclusions from the hearing. There are echoes of previous works throughout; reinvented and rejuvenated in fact, it is as though listening to parts of the album are like looking backwards on time through a frosted window seeing echoes of things that have not yet come to pass, if that makes any sense? If any one album can be said to represent the sum of all the parts that constitute Steve Hackett; then Metamorpheus is it.

"I suspect that the Orpheus myth provides the sub-text to every musician's life. The myth claims to do all sorts of things; it is claimed that Orpheus is a healer; and he tries to save life with his music. It brings in ideas of rebirth; many things. As a religion, Orpheus was as important to the ancients as Christ is to people today and so I am going back to an older; some would regard it as a pagan religion or philosophy in order to set this music in a context."

It was also fortunate that Steve had the assistance of his new partner; Joanna Lehmann, and her knowledge of Classical Greek Mythology proved very useful as he was working on this project, as she recalls: "Metamorpheus was something else I was involved with. Obviously Steve was doing all the music so it would be a case of suggesting in places what energy might reflect what was going on in the story and what the undertones were and how that would affect the music. That was something we would discuss a lot. Sometimes we would be together while Steve was composing bits and pieces. I can remember specifically when the bit where Eurydice is trying to escape and she dies, and Steve actually composing it as we were talking about what was happening and how you create a dramatic effect to a story in music when you are not actually using words, The atmosphere of that message is so powerful and it means so much."

Steve was wearing his musical influences very much on his sleeve with this project but that is part and parcel of the fascination with his music; actually finding out what inspires him to create the music, which in turn inspires his fans: "Sometimes I am quite happy for it to be uncovered and say yes; that's what that is and that's a variation on a theme and a lot of classical music works in that way as do other forms. That's part of what it is all about as long as you feel it, I figure it is all right. I think I may have upset Tchaikovsky or Borodin or Bach or any number of people who may have had an influence on this and I think Rachmaninov put it very well when he said; 'I am not seeking to be original, I am just trying to get down the music that I hear in my head'. Then there is the traditional stuff such as I Know Where I Am Going, which I have not credited because it is a traditional theme. I think most people know it and it will be spotted as a variation on a traditional theme but I wanted to give it one overall title; the piece that is eighteen minutes long: That Vast Life. That really is the love theme and beyond really."

If you like, Metamorpheus is a encapsulation of all the essences that make up the fundamental facets of Steve's character; romanticism, spirituality; understated humour; determination; stoicism; all of which make the musician whose story has been told all too briefly in these pages. It also saw the recycling of those elements which had first seen the light of day as parts of the "Outwitting Hitler" TV project a few years previously with those themes re-worked as parts of the new album.

Unusually the emphasis of the 2005 series of tours, which took in another extensive trip around the UK, visits to Germany, Spain and Italy, and also his first extensive trip to the USA and Canada since the GTR tour back in 1986, was firmly on the acoustic side of his music. Metamorpheus being predominantly an orchestral album was almost impossible to tour without those resources and so, in an almost deliberately perverse act; Steve opted for an acoustic trio performance featuring himself, Roger King and his brother who had now managed some recovery from his injuries. For fans wondering why Steve was not taking to the highways and byways of England with an orchestra his answer was quite simple: "Obviously with the size of production that Metamorpheus has, much as it would be nice to take a hundred people or whatever on the road, that would be tricky. The fact was that we were talking about doing some acoustic shows and the album was nearing completion when the possibility of some trio shows came up. So in a sense it is a tour to support that. It is really an excuse for a family outing (laughs)"

Even Roger agreed with Steve's reference to these shows as music without "props" although of course he did so in his own inimitable fashion: "It is harder; the mistakes are louder! (Laughs). It is the stuff that makes the grade as a cut down arrangement really. That's why we aren't doing anything major with Metamorpheus; a large-scale orchestral work simply doesn't work with three people unless one of them has twelve hands and is an immensely capable keyboard player! (Laughs)."

Once again, the live show derived much of its impetus from the existing acoustic music in Steve's repertoire but, as if to keep us all on our toes, there were a few surprises not least the wonderful trio version of After The Ordeal; that "contentious little number" as he referred to it onstage. Adapting some of the standard rock instrumentals for the trio gave many of them a new lease of life especially the re-working of Hands Of The Priestess coupled with The Red Flower Of Taichi Blooms Everywhere. The show also introduced us to solo performances by John and Roger of their own compositions giving a broader flavour to the proceedings and indeed, he continued the process of trying out material which may or may not surface on one of his numerous ongoing musical projects. This is all part and parcel of the fundamentally organic approach, which Steve has to his live shows:

"The set has always been an updateable set rather than the idea of 'we will now go out and play you the new album'. The same holds true with rock shows, I tend to add and subtract rather than force the entire new work down your throat whatever it happens to be. There comes a moment in the rehearsal room when you say; 'This is possible' and despite the fact that technology has moved on, to the fact that it is possible to play virtually anything, we do like to keep it as live as possible. It is nice that we can deliver what we do without being sequenced... mimed! (Laughs),"

This was the first time that his brother had accompanied Steve since 2002's shows in Tokyo and Budapest and it was obvious that John was relishing the prospect of playing with his big brother again: "It's terrific. I am enjoying it very much. I am a little bit heavier than I was twenty odd years ago though! (Laughs). It has been great to be on stage again with Steve and even with Roger!"

They say that the sign of a band that is relaxed and enjoying itself is the banter that flows between the members, if so then this was an exceedingly happy ship all round. Roger King had already become an integral part of Steve's studio set up and his acerbic wit was on ready display during the tour and during interviews, especially on the vexed question of what it was really like to work with Steve. "Utter misery! (Laughs)." John was quick to point out that the trio was an extremely happy one, too: "I must say from my point of view with these two guys on stage the humour on stage helps me play better because it really relaxes me."

Even the selection of venues on the tour was eclectic to say the least. Normal venues were on the itinerary but I have to say that I haven't often seen a gig such as this in a church but several were visited on the tour both in the UK and in Germany. Perhaps the vote for most unusual venue of the tour goes to the Carnglaze Caverns in Liskeard, Cornwall that was a slate quarry - complete with resident bats! An appropriate gig for a "rock" show you might think, and yes; all the clichés were duly trotted out at this one! My vote for best comment however goes to the manager of the venue who offered free beer to anyone who could get a signal on their mobile 'phone! The venues were usually intimate and ideal settings for the kind of music that the trio were performing. That isn't to say that larger halls didn't figure in the itinerary too. Steve managed to sell-out the prestigious Queen Elizabeth Hall in London from which another live recording was made and released to the expectant fans within a scant month of the gig taking place!

Nostalgia even featured in at least one of the German gigs. The last show of Steve's trip to Germany was at the annual Loreley Festival in St Goarshausen on the picturesque banks of the river Rhine. Steve has very fond memories of the first time he played this particular festival back in 1976 with his old band of reprobates in Genesis. Amazingly enough that was the very first Loreley Festival and here he was back again twenty nine years later although this time with no repetition of the incidents which had made that first performance so memorable - apparently according to Steve; there was a drugs den set up next to the stage which was raided by the police and subsequently set on fire by the disgruntled drug dealers; leading to the precipitate removal of the band from the stage for their own safety!

No such behaviour was in evidence this time, but a scorching hot day for a gig. Over the last few years, Steve has become much more relaxed in his playing; the intensity of ideas is still there in the music but the man himself has loosened up considerably and it was marvellous for the author to see a completely relaxed Steve, grinning from ear to ear as he was invited to "jam" on stage with Mother's Finest during their performance at that same Loreley Festival - probably the closest I will ever get to one of those impromptu jamming sessions that he used to take part in! Not only that but it was also a delight for the author to have the opportunity of meeting Steve's son Oliver and his girlfriend Dagmar at a couple of these gigs. It really was wonderful to be privileged to watch the "reunion" between Steve and his son during these gigs and it was obvious that Steve is very proud of his son; and he of his father too! And it is to be hoped that they will continue their obvious rehabilitation in the coming years!

His past has been well and truly revisited and revamped especially with the superb work done by himself and Ben Fenner on the re-issued Voyage Of The Acolyte, Please Don't Touch; Spectral Mornings and Defector albums which finally addressed the many complaints about the original CD versions. The new versions of these classic albums were finally issued to an expectant fan base on 19th September 2005. Unlike the previous versions, these had been organised with Steve's full and active participation in the re-mastering. Finally using the original UK master tape versions of each album, it was possible at last to sonically bring these albums to the same standard that had been intended when they were recorded. Replete with extra tracks including several that had been rescued from unorthodox places (the tape of one track had apparently been found in Steve's father's garden shed!).

Ironically enough, Steve has recently unearthed still more tapes from the mid 70s whilst helping his dad move home. So there is still more treasure to be heard at some point although as yet Steve has not had time to listen to the material as he explains: "Funnily enough, once again in moving dad to this area, some old tapes have come to light. Now I haven't had time to go through these yet because we have still been going through things that are his. I think there may be one or two things that have a future from that time. I don't know, much the same as the long version of Shadow Of The Hierophant and I was very pleased that that one came to light after thirty years!"

The remaining albums; Cured and Highly Strung were finally given the 'Ben Fenner' treatment and issued to an eager public on 30th May 2007, completing the series. The albums were amazingly transferred during a short break between the British and European legs of the 2005 tour! It was interesting to hear some of the alternative versions of some of our favourite Hackett tracks as well as finally finding a well-deserved resting place for a few B-sides too.

Another surprising re-issue had also appeared shortly before the start of the UK tour. Camino, in association with Gramy Records in Hungary; a label specialising in limited edition vinyl issues; decided to release the Sketches Of Satie album in this format for collectors. Made from virgin 180-gram vinyl the album was issued as a strictly limited edition of a mere 500 copies, which are now highly sought after by collectors.

As Steve remarked to me during the 2005 German tour; "Perhaps I need some time to dream some more". His brother jokingly replied when asked by a fan on that same tour, what Steve's next musical project might be, that it might be a skiffle album. Who knows? Even Steve himself isn't sure but he did give some inkling about the possible shape of the next project during an interview given to the author during the UK tour: "It has been a busy time finishing Metamorpheus and going on tour with this. I can't be in two places at once and so I am saying to people it will be done when it's done; the next rock thing, for lack of a better word. I hope there will be some orchestral moments on it since we have discovered the new augmented team. "

Steve's dreams have certainly taken him to some very bizarre places, which is of course, a major part of the fascination his work holds for his fans, but maybe people should take courage from his own work ethic: "In some ways I try not to come up with things consciously. I wait for them to nudge me; and then if they have bubbled up from my own dark recesses, that's fine. If it is something that I have unconsciously misappropriated from somewhere else, then that's unfortunately the name of the game. You would think that all the juxtapositions of all the styles have already been done and I might think 'I haven't heard anything new for two years'. Then suddenly I will hear something from somewhere and; 'Ah, that's interesting… maybe I can take that idea further. Often unlikely constructions usually start with some kind of accident. It can happen in the studio; if something is switched on which shouldn't be or there will be some noise from outside, which sparks something else off. "

Never one to rest on his laurels, the indefatigable Hackett continued to unpeel the layers of what can only be only described of his very own "musical onion" with work on yet another rock album. Taking its cue from many of Steve's previous outings, this new (and at the time, untitled) opus grew out of many different areas and influences. Some have taken longer to come to fruition than others. For example, Steve's love of Bach has long been known but it is only recently that he has begun to seriously contemplate an attempt to visit some of that master's music himself. As usual, Steve has not taken the easy path even there. One piece that was being considered for a possible "Bachian" tribute is the Chaconne, a twelve-minute masterpiece that demands the highest standards of excellence from anyone playing it. Steve's current version utilises the recording techniques that were prevalent when that earlier interpreter of Bach, Andres Segovia was alive. The resultant version is astonishing in both its warmth and musical accuracy. He continued to record several Bach pieces as well as other acoustic pieces which would eventually form the basis of a tribute project, including a studio recording of his marvellous tribute to Andres Segovia, which formed such an integral part of his 2005 acoustic tour setlist.

Hackett has never been one to give himself or his fans the easy option and this latest rock album demands a great deal from the listener on so many levels. Even with songs such as the cover version of Bob Dylan's Man In The Long Black Coat, there is much more going on than meets the eye: "I loved the lyric; 'the old dance hall on the outskirts of town' now that to me…. my own version of that was Eel Pie Island and that is exactly what that place was. That was a place I escaped to at the time when it was illicit for me; I was an under age drinker in a place where I am hearing wonderful music."

He has always been fascinated by the romance of places as much as of relationships and once again; his love affair with his own hometown of London comes to the fore in the effects-driven Down Street, which apparently was the Tube Station by which Churchill and the Wartime Cabinet would have escaped if the need had arisen. Owing as much to the London of Dickens and Fagin, as to the multicultural city of today; this is an extravagant visit to Steve's very own Twilight Zone, replete with a cast of characters from the works of such masters as Dickens and Stephen King, all led by the re-appearance of the psychotic Lawrence Olivier-type character who first appeared on The Devil Is An Englishman.

The same can be said of both On The Transylvanian Express and its vocal counterpart; A Dark Night In Toytown both of which are further nightmare rides in the monstrous theme park of the possessed which Steve peoples so many of his albums with. In fact, many of the tracks on this and the albums immediately preceding it can be fairly said to be reflecting the child in him, who never grew up; always with a slightly macabre and essentially English twist to the characters though. Very much the "grim" in Grimm's fairytales in fact as Steve points out, even here there is an element of sly humour: "All of my spooks are not supposed to be taken seriously. They are more haunted house than real. Yes, it's Pinocchio meets The Wizard Of Oz."

Or perhaps the typically English horror of the Hammer House Of Horrors film productions, the track is certainly redolent of the classic coach chases from several of those films as the demonic Count Dracula flees from the doggedly determined Dr Van Helsing - wonderful stuff and not at all to be taken seriously! Hide behind the sofa when you are listening to them if you will, though!

In between the drama or perhaps, the melodrama, there are candyfloss moments too such as the wonderful Forties' pastiche Why which evokes the spirit of that Sentimental Institution we all know so well: "It was my chance to use the Optigon again. I kept it very short. Originally it was that length then I wrote some extra verses, recorded them and tried to sing them in the kitchen laughing my head off. There is aversion of that where I can't control myself and I can't stop laughing so much. I was going to tack them on but I thought there might be the odd thing that might be offensive to some people. So I think the only time I have been potentially offensive to people is 'cremation won't be long' (quiet chuckles) I could go on about it endlessly (laughs) but it is a very short song for obvious reasons. It is 'End Of The Pier' stuff which is why right at the end of it you have the wind blowing as if you were on the seafront or the pier."

Although it may not always be evident straight away, Steve's love of humour is always there, informing his work as he explains, "I do love silly humour, old Victorian style humour; belly laughs; slapstick. I'm not very sophisticated but I do like Monty Python of course. Everybody did; we all still do. Who else? Derek & Clive, still raises a laugh, God bless 'em, they're dead now aren't they, Peter Cook and Dudley Moore. I remember a Melody Maker awards around 1977 where they were giving out the prizes and I was receiving one for Genesis being top live act along with Bill Bruford, and they were doing it in character as Derek & Clive and swearing at everyone they were giving an award to (laughs). I remember Rick Wakeman giving them a plastic lobster - but you have to know the album of course! (Laughs)." Indeed, that very album was regular listening on the tour bus during Steve's 2005 German tour.

Steve summed up best the way in which he views his own work these days in another recent interview: "I think that what we do here is make test tube babies basically. We mix this tremendous amount of real and sample. Basically we have conversations and then we try to put into effect. It is the two of us (Steve and Roger King) sitting down and taking our time over what happens next. It is a very unhurried pace. We do whatever it takes to get the sound; if it is the performance, whether its man, woman or …it if it moves, we track it!"

Steve has always maintained that he is no longer a team player but this does not seem to be the case where his working relationship with his long-time colleague Roger King is concerned, if the comments by the pair of them in a recent interview are to be believed. "It's about half way between there, Steve writes the song and my job is as a programmer and keyboard player and, I guess recording engineer too. They are all Steve's songs but I am sure he won't mind me saying so; he isn't terribly technically literate; certainly not as a computer operator!"

"I'm a humble guitarist and I like to have conversations about what happens next. I think the danger is that, in the last… how many years would it be? Twenty-five years or more? Thirty years perhaps? Guys can make albums on their own but it is nice to sit down with a mate and say; 'what do you think? I'm not sure about that… maybe we could try such and such?' Which is a million miles away from the idea of the composer sitting down at one time with the score sheet and it was set in stone. This is a very flexible way of working and I think it is wonderful. I do get frustrated that I can't have a fader and just turn something up but that has to be agreed in increments and sometimes the simplest things that were done in the old fashioned way of working seem to be much more difficult to do now but the amount of choices you have now currently is fantastic. Just to be able to produce work that is both in time and tune".

The new systems of working that are in place now, have freed up Steve and indeed the rest of the people with whom he works, to be able to explore much more fully the diversity of sounds that they are seeking for each track as Roger King explains: "That's the point I think about building the mix from the very first note you play and then if there is a query about whether a certain sound fits, or a search is on for a sound to do a certain job. There is no longer a question mark about whether it will work eventually when you have got the mix up; because you have already got the mix up. If it fits, then it fits; if it doesn't then it is never going to fit which is the big advantage of building the mix from the first beat...."

Even unlikely sounds can come in useful and even an artiste's illnesses have their uses: "One day a few years ago I had a horrendous cough and I thought; 'let's not let this go to waste' and so I sampled it, and that appears at the beginning of one of the new tracks on the album. I am quite pleased about that, that it was my own cough and I didn't have to use somebody else's. It is a much more virtuoso cough than the tiny cough that appeared on A Tower Struck Down... I was at RADA for months! (Laughs)"* I suppose it gives an entire new meaning to the phrase "suffering for one's art"!

For an individual as introverted as Steve undoubtedly is; his work over the last few years has seen a growing willingness to examine subjects of a much more personal nature than would be expected. His latest work continues that thread; dealing with an ever wider range of subjects including another thought provoking protest song in similar vein to Mechanical Bride on his previous outing: "The Fundamentals Of Brainwashing is the idea of not being hoodwinked by 'experts'. Have some kind of political opinion even if you can't take in all the detail. In a way it sort of clamours for peace. It is a protest song. It's that I think too many horrors have been perpetrated in the name of patriotism and religion and so that's it".

With the album in the cans and negotiations under way for its release in the various territories, Steve has continued his work on many of the numerous projects which tend to overlap one another and Steve continues to explore other areas of endeavour, some of which have been mentioned above.

Wild Orchids, his most recent rock album, was eventually released by Camino on 9th September 2006. Another roller coaster of an album, there is

---

*The Royal Academy of Dramatic Art in Bloomsbury, London, generally regarded as one of the most renowned drama schools in the world, and one of the oldest drama schools in Britain.

something for every shade of Hacketteer on it. The mania of Down Street, the acoustic glory of Set Your Compass and some hard rockin' too in the shape of On The Transylvanian Express. His wry observations on the situation in the Middle East are expounded on Cedars Of Lebanon. Another album that proves that Steve Hackett refuses to be pigeonholed. Originally, this track had been slated for Richie Havens to perform on but sadly that was not to be but Steve's own version is just as emotive and powerful.

Flying in the face of convention, his newest project is an album dedicated to the music of such craftsmen as JS Bach. Not an album intended for the charts certainly but one that posed its own challenges as he explains: "The new album is an acoustic one that concentrates on classical music this time; six pieces of Bach one of… various composers. I am very proud of it too. As ever there are still a few things that need to be negotiated. This is different, this is like joining the ranks of all those who have played Hamlet, it is the equivalent of climbing Everest for any musician. At the very least it is technically demanding but beyond that there is the simplicity of it and Bach is the most fluent of chord smiths!"

On the vexed subject of a reunion with his old bandmates in Genesis, I will give Steve the final word: "I couldn't possibly comment at this stage. It all depends. Live work and all that and reunions and all that stuff. I can't deliver anything there. I can't reunite everybody; all I can do is turn up at the meetings and say; 'Yeah that's it; that will be great and if you are up for it; then I am up for it' and if it doesn't happen it won't be my fault."

Events took a surprising turn with the announcement in November 2006 of the reformation of the Banks / Collins / Rutherford line up of Genesis for a series of shows throughout Europe and North America, although what eventually took place as the Turn It On Again Tour was not what had originally been envisaged, as Steve explains: "As you know, I was approached, along with Pete and the plan was to do The Lamb Lies Down On Broadway. I said 'yes', Pete said 'no' after we had all met up. Of course with an album like that it would be important to do it with the original team. An idea that seemed like a goer has been put on hold, if not completely dismissed. I don't know why Pete didn't want to do that. Perhaps there are pressures that he feels which we don't. I always thought that if you took a more broad view of the band's history it would be easier to take things from different periods even if one concentrated on the so-called 'classic' seventies period. I think that would have been easier for Pete but I am only guessing. I don't know, apart from being positive about a potential reunion and I have given it my blessing and if Pete needs me, I'll be there."

Steve is also very happy with the new Genesis remasters too. The 5.1 albums that are currently available certainly give every musician his chance to shine and he is particularly pleased with how his guitar contributions have sonically improved in the remixes of those early albums, especially on Wind & Wuthering. Steve also gives some very honest and affectionate recollections of his time in the band in the additional DVD interview footage that accompanies the releases.

It is difficult to credit that in the last twelve years, Steve has probably released more studio and live projects than at any other time in his career. The new studio album was his ninth in that period, an astonishing work rate by anybody's standards!

CHAPTER NINETEEN

Paying Tribute

Wild Orchids was no sooner in the cans and on the shelves, than Steve was hard at work on several other projects. As he has said on many times, his work sometimes overlaps and projects are sometimes put at one side while the muse is beckoning in another direction. However, the last two years have also seen their share of stressful personal issues as well as musical explorations. The health of Steve's father; Peter who has been suffering from Parkinson's Disease for some time has been of some concern to the family and it was only recently that Steve and his brother managed to find accommodation which was suitable for such an independent-minded man to continue living an independent life albeit under the close and watchful eyes of a very supportive family unit. In fact, more recently still, his father has moved to Sheffield to be nearer to Steve's brother John and their family.

Sadly, his marital relationship saw Steve and his wife leading even more independent existences and they divorced in June 2007. Steve was fortunate to have already met Joanna Lehmann who is now his partner: "Fortunately I met Jo, who has been a wonderful support for my family and me".

The fact that Steve has continued to explore the musical avenues dictated to him by his muse has resulted in even more unexpected twists and turns to his offerings. He may not have had too much time left over for dreaming with so much turmoil in his recent personal life but the musical results have been astonishing. Having already secured his reputation as one of England's finest composers for the acoustic guitar with his previous albums Bay Of Kings and Momentum, along with a well-deserved reputation for musical excellence and a keen ear for a fine melody within the orchestral format with A Midsummer Night's Dream and Metamorpheus; Steve's abilities in both fields are well established and well respected by both fans and critics alike - A Midsummer Night's Dream and Metamorpheus in particular have garnered some of the best reviews of a Steve Hackett album seen in many a year!

His latest acoustic album; Tribute expands the envelope even further with a work which embraces the romance and warmth of Baroque and later masters' work with some of his own compositions written in the same style and imbued with the same spirit. Another work which harks back to Steve's earliest influences it is perhaps best explained in his own words: "For years now I had thought that I must have a go at some of the material that is the most beautiful and most difficult that I have heard played. Most of this music was written without regard to the limitations of the guitar; pieces that were written for solo lute or violin and which translate very well because you are often moving from four to six strings. Originally I was going to make it a tribute to Segovia and then I realised that there were other pieces I hadn't heard him play but which were just as good. So I thought it might be better if I did a tribute to various people.

Playing the pieces that had haunted me for years and years, pieces that just wouldn't go away! So it was an exorcism but a nice one; laying old friends and ghosts to rest. I just felt that the quality of the music was so great that even if I did a half way decent job that would still come through and because I am not trained, what I have brought to it is my feeling and my love for it. I haven't had to beat myself over the head to do it and I haven't had any raps over the knuckles. I haven't had to learn this stuff and because I have gone my own sweet way I can tear up the rule book."

Tearing up the rule book is certainly something which Steve has done with astonishing regularity throughout his career but even so, by breaking the rules this time; he has managed to come up with a work of beauty which pays a great tribute to the masters who were among his earliest influences. Getting to the stage where he could fully explore this music was a long-term project though, as he readily admits: "The Gavottes were my first introduction to classical music and when I first heard them I went 'Oh, wow!' Those early recordings made me think and wonder one day will I able to write music like that. In the back of my mind there was the thought that one day there will be a band that takes a blues influence and a rock influence and combines the two. It didn't exist at the time but in my dreams. Then bands did appear that were like-minded in their influences and of course, to some extent, Genesis facilitated that."

Many fans, the author included, have wondered why, given his passion for orchestral music, why Steve has never really given time to performances with an orchestra. I put this question to him recently, and here is what he had to say on the subject: " I played at the Barbican with the London Chamber Orchestra (1983) doing excerpts from a Vivaldi guitar concerto and I found it thrilling but at the same time I thought that... these guys are all reading and if I mess up on the repeats (laughs). It's an extraordinary thing, you can't look at each other like you can in a band and go 'ah, someone's missed his cue' and we can change it all. You can't do that with an orchestra, it's got to be right. So I have done a tiny bit of that and maybe we would do something in the future. I say 'we' because it would have to be me and someone I am very familiar with who might be conducting it from the keyboard or the violin, it would have to be something..."

CHAPTER TWENTY
Out Of The Tunnel's Mouth

The last couple of years have been fraught with difficulties for Steve with his divorce and legal situation affecting his back catalogue and commercial concerns. It is against this background that he has continued to try to work. One unfinished album has effectively been put in limbo by these wrangles and will probably become a latter day "Feedback 86". Steve himself explains a little about the current situation: "It has slowed down the writing and recording of this album but nonetheless, I think that it colours it in a way because when you have to fight harder for it, it is more personal and I will use an American word; meaningful. It has been about eight months in the making. It was my third attempt at finishing an album due to various reasons, which I can't go into. Basically I realised I had a short window of opportunity to write and record very much on the run. This album probably has more electric guitar work on it than any other album I've done. Since I did Tribute, which was an album that featured at least six pieces of Bach, that scratched that particular itch, I thought it was time to be that hooligan again. (Laughs)

The thing about the electric guitar, I started buying electric guitar tracks when I was... let's just say it was fifty years ago when I started and I used to buy electric guitar records usually with the thought 'I'm buying this because it's the most exciting sound around'. The sound still isn't right and in a way I am still looking for something more exciting than The Shadows but it wasn't really until The Stones did I Wanna Be Your Man that an electric guitar solo blazed. Brian Jones' bottleneck solo on that just blazed for me and it was like seeing and riding a Harley Davidson for the first time, the thrill was just monumental."

The Genesis connection has continued too, with the impending re-issue of the remastered live albums, which have once again benefited from the work of Nick Davis as Steve comments: "I have been so bloody busy lately I haven't had a chance to contact Nick and say what a fine job he did on them. Once again they will be released at the same time as my album, same sort of time frame. I don't think I have ever released an album that hasn't clashed with something from Genesis! (laughs) I love that stuff, it is a glorious retrospective, whereas people have been talking to me recently about reformations and I have had to say I am too busy with my own stuff to think about that".

As a result of these problems, Steve started work on a new project from scratch in early 2008 whilst continuing to work with a variety of other musicians on several projects, including the recent acoustic album Prelude To Summer by his brother, John. He has also found time to work on Simon Collins' new album; U-Catastrophe, (he appears on the track Fast Forward To The Future). It is this freedom to experiment that Steve enjoys, "People like Gary Husband for instance, who I have worked with recently, and who gets to play drums with Level 42, and keyboards with John Mclaughlin: I mean, how clever is that? I have really enjoyed working with all the guys in the band. I enjoyed working with the Genesis guys; that was great to be part of but then it was equally inspiring to work with Richie Havens who hadn't really heard the two songs he sang on Please Don't Touch but was able to make them sound like he had been singing them his whole life. I loved working with my first band. I loved working with all the bands. It would be unfair to single people out, really".

Steve's collaborations have not always been those his fans would necessarily expect though. From the unlikely collaboration on the David Palmer (ex Jethro Tull) series of rock orchestrations, to more recent ones with Gandalf and more recently still, Hungarian Jazz artist, Djabe. Steve explains how some of these unlikely pairings came about: "I recorded stuff for David Palmer and I can't remember if he put the orchestra on before or afterwards so the orchestra and I were not working side by side. Similarly for the live shows I did. Although I was on the bill I was doing a separate set so I wasn't playing those numbers live because he was doing a show that comprised numbers from Pink Floyd to Led Zeppelin, so once again I got to do my bit separately.

Gandalf got in touch with me. I didn't know his stuff at that point. And I went to Austria and I had never been there before or done any gigs there, and I am about to go there again soon with Djabe, funnily enough, and I spent time with his family, recording in the house. It was all very relaxed and I have done live shows with him coming on as a special guest.

With Djabe I get up and jam with them. Sometimes we do a twelve bar, sometimes we do Firth Of Fifth - it's that informal, and the last time I played with him, which was in Sarajevo, which was a trip in itself (laughs), they had rehearsed up a version of The Steppes. Everything was going wrong before the show, a keyboard hadn't arrived and I couldn't even plug in and get a unit working and the amp was all wrong. I had a bit of a tantrum and suddenly things magically started appearing and luckily we were able to rehearse up that number and a couple of others; we did, In That Quiet Earth as well, so we did three things that were well known from my history and other things that were way off the map but it is a lively improvised show."

Over the last couple of years Steve has kept his hand in with gigs in a far-flung variety of territories including a show at the prestigious Penang Island Jazz Festival in Malaysia. This year, 2009, he has returned to the world of the rock show proper with a series of shows in Italy which, showcased not only some new and as yet unreleased material, but also a new band line up, where alongside regular stalwarts such as Roger King, Gary O'Toole and Rob Townsend, was the phenomenal bass playing of Nick Beggs. The shows drew on a mix of old and new material although for fans who were expecting Steve to perform material from his most recent rock album; Wild Orchids, this was not an omission on Steve's part. As he pointed out, when I asked him why there was no material from that album in the live set, he explains: "Songs that grow up in the computer are harder to perform than songs that grew up in the rehearsal room. So a song like Down Street, for instance, we were up to about two hundred and twelve tracks on that! Then you have got all the multi-layered vocals that are on Set Your Compass, where there's ninety zillion of me! That's me and Gary O'Toole tracked up on that one. So, that would be hard to do. I could stand there and mime to it but would everyone mind if I did that? (Laughs) And there are songs like The Golden Age Of Steam from Darktown which is samples doing an impression of the Royal Philharmonic and again, I would be happy to stand there and mime as I know some have!"

Many fans were surprised by the presence in Steve's latest touring band of Nick Beggs whom many of us remember from eighties band Kajagoogoo.* Begg's pedigree and love of music are evident to anyone who sees him play and he recently explained how he became involved with Steve: "I was a fan of his solo work from the get go. We met at an EMI conference back in 1998 when I was playing for Belinda Carlisle. He was presenting his new remastered back catalogue and we spoke about my sound, which he really

---

*Kajagoogoo's original line-up reunited in 2009 to tour the UK for the first time in 25 years.

liked. We hooked up for tea and said that we should work together at some point. Eleven years later, here we are".

There are plenty of other "new faces" on this project too including one surprise for Genesis fans. "There's Chris Squire, for instance, he is on a couple of tracks on bass, the first track Fire On The Moon. Nick Beggs shares bass chores with Chris on one of the tracks called Nomads. Obviously Roger (King) is all over it as he has recorded, engineered mixed and played on it, and often he made the tea although his tea making isn't as good as mine! (Laughs)

We've got my brother John on it on Last Train To Istanbul and Rob (Townsend) on it, and Ferenc Kovacs (from Djabe) on it on violin. We have got Christine Townsend on violin and viola; Dick Driver on double bass, both of whom were part of the Underworld Orchestra for the Metamorpheus album. We have got some girl singers on it; we have got Amanda and Joanna Lehmann; we've got Lauren King (Roger's daughter) and Anthony Phillips on twelve string".

Steve also explains how he managed to get such august personages to play on the new record: "I had to sleep with them all, of course for several nights and I'm so sore but it was worth it! (laughs) It's been a hard life, which is why I have had to pour cold water on it for so many years! (laughs). The amazing thing about Nick (Beggs) is that people think of him as a reformed pop star but he has worked with so many people who have operated in so many different areas in music from John Paul Jones to… so that tells you he is a bass player's bass player and also a great Stick player. He is very clever and the lovely thing was, he was sending me stuff to listen to on the Internet and to play back on computer. It was a bit like in each case he had found the bass sounds that everyone had used on the original; the same sound with the same mixes but with the bass much louder and he had been absolutely bang on. It was marvellous I think he wrote all the parts out, learned them all and he was spot on".

Having been fortunate enough to take in some of Begg's first gigs with Steve, the author can confirm that he is without doubt one of the finest purveyors of both bass and Chapman "Stick" that I have ever seen. But his work ethic extends beyond that as he explained how he went about learning the parts for these shows: "It was my intention to know everything I needed to know before I set foot in the rehearsal room. So, I worked on it all over two months prior to that. I wanted to hit the ground running and not hold up proceedings, so I wrote out every tune and then consigned them to memory".

This is quite true, while out on the road with Steve in Italy in March 2009, Beggs was duly transcribing bass parts during his spare time before the gigs for another band he was due to be performing with later in the year.

The new album; Out Of The Tunnel's Mouth continues the trend of the last few Hackett projects. There is homage to the blues: (Still Waters), a wonderful marriage between Flamenco and electric guitar (Nomads). The emphasis this time is most definitely on the electric guitar and there is more of Hackett the axe man on this album than any other since 1999's Darktown. The theme of travel continues not only in the album's title and cover, which shows Steve carrying a guitar case emerging from a cloud of steam from a steam engine (called The Dragonslayer for those of you who want to know such details) to the album's closing cut; Last Train To Istanbul, which once again merges the musical influences and heritages of both East and West. Fans wondering if many tracks from the album would feature in the new live show soon had their answer; Fire On The Moon was road-tested in front of audiences in the early part of 2009 along with Storm Chaser, a track from the collaborative "Squackett" project with Chris Squire. By the time the album was ready for release, several of the tracks had become stage favourites. In fact the album was better represented live than several of its predecessors. Steve explains the rationale behind this: "It is a very interactive world these days, and I realise that I have to try and keep people happy... what kind of music would you like to hear as an audience? Largely what I do is a response to that. I don't want to go out disappointing people. I am not a firm believer in going out and playing the latest album and playing it all perfectly perhaps, and then people afterwards saying; 'yeah, I really wish you'd done the old stuff!' (Laughs).

Chris got in touch because he wanted to do a Christmas album (Chris Squire's Swiss Choir) and he wanted someone to play guitar on it. I said' 'yeah, sure' I'd love to work with Chris Squire on anything. Chris Squire is part of my record collection! (Laughs). Simon Phillips, I very nearly formed a band with Simon Phillips, Keith Emerson and Jack Bruce... name drop, name drop! (Laughs) We did all rehearse together in the early Eighties and it looked like it was going to be a four piece comprising the four of us. Then everyone suddenly went off and did something else so I always remembered Simon from that. Then he did something else I had been involved with; Rock Against Repatriation, he was drumming on that. Then he came to a show I did in California some time back in the nineties. He said; 'I've just been through a divorce' and I'm recovering from that now, and I'm working and I felt it would be lovely to work with him again. Now I know what he was talking about when he said 'recovery' because it is an important part of what I am going through, setting things straight after that. Once again it was wonderful even though we worked at a distance where stuff was sent to him and came back perfectly in time (laughs) as it does when you are working with someone who is such a consummate professional. He was excited about the idea of working with myself and Chris".

The real surprise for Genesis fans though is the presence of Anthony Phillips on the album. Fans have speculated for years what it might be like if these two marvellous instrumentalists had the chance to work together. Now we know. Phillips appears on two tracks. Steve explains how this magical pairing came about...

"I was trying to get Ant to play on a track I had done for the unreleased album I have at the moment. The one that's in litigious difficulties shall we say. At the time he didn't quite do that but over the course of a couple of years or so he and I would get together for the odd soiree and I think on the day that he came in and recorded he said; 'oh I thought we were just going to rehearse this?' I said; 'well I've got someone here if you want to put something down'. I said; 'look, perhaps it's best if I go out of the room because the last thing you want is another guitarist breathing down your neck while you are doing this'. He said; 'that's a good idea' and he recorded this chorus on Emeralds And Ash. I said; 'look, this one's not in a guitar friendly key; the chorus is in B flat' and he immediately said; 'well I'll tune down a tone so when I am playing C it will be in B flat'. Anyway, whatever it was, he tuned down so for B flat he was playing C and I said; 'that sounds good'.

The lovely thing is, the twelve string sounds great when someone else is playing it and when I am playing it, it's such hard work. (laughs) Although I love it I can't be objective and I said; 'that sounds great' and he said; 'that's because it is open strings' and the resonance of it was lovely. He went and did that track and then he said; 'come and have a listen!' So I came down from upstairs and I said; 'That sounds great; it sounds lovely'. He had recorded two tracks of twelve string and I already had two tracks of electric guitar which were arpeggiated. For the trainspotters among you they were put through a rotary effect in simulation of a Lesley cabinet and I had done my part in octaves. So, what sounds like one glorious guitar is actually about four and it sounded so nice on that chorus. I said to Roger (King) 'why don't we create some extra bars of that so that we have that guitar feature happening on its own?'

It really did have that early Genesis sound and Roger also put an organ sound with the repeat of the same pattern and it really had... It's funny I have often felt threatened when people have said 'Oh, that sounds like Genesis'. I have been trying so hard to do something different but when it's twelve strings of course it's going to sound like Genesis! Because multi-layered twelve strings *is* early Genesis! It wasn't as if I was trying for an early Genesis feel, it just happened naturally. I just wanted to get the two of us working on something and see whether it could happen.

I remember bumping into Ant years ago on a bridge over the Thames, and I was on my way to see something at the Hungarian Cultural Centre. I saw Ant and he said 'hello' and I said to him; ' You know Ant; I think if we'd been in the band together at the same time there would have been no problems' and he laughed at that and years later here we are doing something whereby I gave him the space to do what he thought was right for this thing. This was like the way it was with Genesis when Pete didn't want anyone there when he was doing vocals and I understand that totally. Really, you don't need an audience; you are connecting with the music. It was beautiful and I am not just saying that because it is politically expedient for me to do so because he happens to be on the album. He played and it was gorgeous and it is my favourite moment on the whole album".

A fascinating thought - Steve and Ant together in Genesis! At least we finally have an idea of what these two exponents of their craft sound like together and fans will be delighted with the finished result. Anthony Phillips certainly was as he explained to the author recently...

"I remember at one point the entreaty was something along the lines of 'I don't mind what you play just come along and play Serbian toe flute.' And I remember thinking... 'Okay it's pretty relaxed if I can come along with the old Serbian toe flute'. So, I didn't come along with a Serbian toe flute, I came along with a twelve-string that was played very little over the summer, because I was involved with all this building work and stuff, and the studio was mothballed. It was one of the most pleasant and easy sessions of my life and I know it sounds like a cliché and to turn up with a twelve string but I thought I was turning up just to listen to a couple of things and then think 'shit! I haven't got any ideas' and go away and say 'sorry mate, I can't add anything' and I am not being falsely modest, I really did think that. I was definitely not going along in my mind to add stuff on the spot but he played me this song, which was in B flat. Because my twelve-string was tuned down a tone and was in C and therefore had a lot of open strings, is much easier to play.

So it was real serendipity working overtime and the chords were reasonably simple and that sounds incredibly denigrating but what I mean was that it wasn't incredibly difficult to learn and it was very nice as well. So it was easier to just kind of duck into and interweave and do a little bit of mucking about without going too far off. It was just one of those odd things where you start playing and you know… because often when you start playing, people go off in huddles and go 'hmm, maybe' and then you keep trying things and the more things you try the further away you go. This was the reverse, really. Everything I tried they seemed to like and so I found myself recording the choruses of that song.

Steve went out of the room, which is the normal thing he does and I found myself recording with Roger (King) who is delightful. Not a pushover, I know my timing always seems to speed up a bit like the old Mike Giles story of going home and practising with a metronome. I did tend to speed up a bit and they might have done a bit of moving afterwards but it wasn't like just one take and then 'Oh, can you repair that, Roger?' I did retake slightly but it was good fun and they double tracked it with a higher inversion and it was fine. Everyone seemed so happy and it had taken so little time.

The first one I did was the almost Country type (Emerald And Ash) and the other one was Sleepers. That one he said was just a complete long shot and he said; 'Can you add anything to this?' And I listened to it and thought 'no' (laughs) but then it didn't seem to be right for twelve-string and I just started mucking about again. It was in… anyway, I was in B minor which seemed to work. I don't know but Roger was saying 'well, actually that really does work, why don't you just try and develop that?' Then they started stripping down the track and they said; 'Maybe we will just use a section where we just use all the guitars…' and it seemed to work nicely. That was a lot looser, I was just vamping around on that one and the track sounded great. So that was it really. An hour and then out to supper! (laughs) And I didn't have to come back! (laughs) That was great fun and very enjoyable indeed. Roger just couldn't have been any more delightful. Steve was very easy and it was just perfect really - even the neighbours enjoyed it! (laughs)"

That is typical of Steve all over though, always determined to get the best out of the people he is working with, whoever they may be. One thing that Steve admits to is that these days he is much more pre-occupied with writing than practising: "The weird thing is that I prefer trying to write than practice. I always think that time spent practising should be time spent writing. Maybe little twiddles become tunes. I like to push myself, I always have done, and maybe something that I couldn't play today will become something tomorrow because it was too bloody difficult! (laughs). I don't try to do things that are difficult just for the sake of it but you hear certain people do certain things and you think, 'well, that's possible, isn't it? Why can't I do that?' I have always had the feeling that I am filling in for someone who is much better than me, you know, this guy's going to show up tomorrow or the next day! (Laughs) I always want to be better than I am".

Some of the legal problems mentioned previously, were finally resolved when the disputes were brought to a close in court in November 2010. Steve does not have any involvement with Camino Records now and the previous website stevehackett.com no longer exists. He enjoys his involvement with his website www.hackettsongs.com and he continues to move forwards jointly managing his career with the team he has been working with since autumn 2008.

CHAPTER TWENTY ONE
Squackett & Other Tales Of Mythology

Steve's touring schedule has continued throughout 2010 with the second leg of the appropriately titled "Around The World In Eighty Trains" tour, which took Steve to many far-flung places, as well as another extensive tour of the UK and Europe.

In between bouts of touring he has continued to work on several projects the most intriguing of which as far as the fans are concerned is the Squackett album, which he has worked on with Yes bass man, Chris Squire. Many fans (myself included) were very surprised to hear that Steve was working with another member of Yes after the GTR debacle but Steve explained how it came about in a recent interview with the author…

"I think Chris wants it to be a hit. Personally I am always pleased with a release. I get the feeling it will find its feet and it will find its place. It has elements of progressive rock and classic rock and almost smooth easy listening. It bridges the gap over all those things in a way that some of the work of Tears For Fears did. It has been self-funded, there is no Executive Department that has to be accounted to for how long we spent in the studio. So it has got this rootsy thing about it and I think that there was a natural harmony between Chris and myself. Sometimes we wrote things separately and then brought them together. Other times we sat opposite each other and the song writing process flowed very easily. It seemed that we were instantly able to come up with ideas together as if we had been writing together all our lives. There didn't seem to be any competitive element.

Chris has unique ideas about where sections ought to go in the music and he would say 'why don't we use this bit here and that bit there' and I tried to be as flexible as possible because I have often likened the song writing process to kicking around a football; one person kicks it, another kicks it back, we dribble around a bit and then eventually score a goal, hopefully. There is another side to this though when you stop kicking the poor little creature and act as the glue and figure that you have just got to stick to this ball in some way and that is the aspect of team playing that hasn't always come naturally to me because I always cared so much about every note.

I worked on Chris' Christmas album (Chris Squire's Swiss Choir) he then worked on a solo effort of mine, which hopefully will be released soon. Some of the tracks were initiated by each of us, but along with Roger King we developed them all together."

Indeed, as has long been the habit with Steve, new material was road-tested during the 2010 shows with one work in progress being given an airing to gauge audience reaction. Steve explained the origins of the new track; Prairie Angel to the author…

"Whether or not Prairie Angel remains a title, it's a working title. I do like what we did with it but at the moment it is just a short section of something; the kernel of an idea of something that is yet to be. The title I got from Jack Kerouac and it was the description of a young girl that he and a pal had seen on their travels and they both thought she was beautiful and she was described as a 'angel of the prairie' and you get the feeling of the remoteness of the landscape dotted around with a few figures; the wide open expanse of the prairie that I saw on my travels as a child in the 1950's this idea of dry brush with nothing around struck me…."

Fans who attended the shows were not only treated to the new material but those who were at the London gig also had the added treat of watching Steve perform with long time friend John Wetton and also with Steven Wilson during the gig. Fortunately for those not at this show, it was filmed for the Fire & Ice DVD release; something else for Hackett fans to revel in!

For one who has previously declared himself averse to being part of a team, recently Steve has lent himself to an increasing number of collaborative projects. His work with Chris Squire has been the most discussed but far from the only one as he himself describes…

"I worked with two very interesting people back to back one day after the other. I worked with Steven Wilson (Porcupine Tree) one day and Gary Husband (John McLaughlin/Level 42) and the interesting thing was that each one was in a very different style. Steve wanted me to play very spontaneous stuff, which was treated as data. I did lots of different solos, lots of different styles and he wanted something that was uncharacteristic and finally we hit on some really wild sounds for it.

Then on a subsequent day I did some nylon for it but that was done at home. Then the following day I worked with Gary Husband and that was completely different. That was very much a performance with him sitting through it and saying 'I like that' or 'I'm not so keen on that' and 'I think we can improve on that' so we were refining it on the spot but they were two completely different ways of working but both produced fantastic results... I did something recently with Rob Reed of Magenta. That came out beautifully as well. It's almost like being the proud father of triplets really..."

Steve's collaboration with Gary can be heard on the latter's Dirty & Beautiful album released last year; the collaboration with Steven Wilson on his Grace For Drowning album, while the work with Rob Reed remains as yet unreleased. There is also talk of Steven Wilson taking parts of Steve's back catalogue in hand to produce 5.1 remasters. His work on the recent King Crimson re-issues has gained critical and public acclaim but there are still problems surrounding this material as Steve explains...

"There is every chance of it (the 5.1 remastering) providing that the source material exists. It is difficult to say but I hope that the original masters will show up in their (EMI's) vaults. If they don't it will just be another Egyptian tomb pillaged by heathens!"

With most of the legal problems also resolved it means that Steve might not have to make another album in the living room. That said, if the results are as good as the last album; then maybe that is precisely where he should continue recording! The days of record company interference are long gone and artists can continue their own careers with a degree of freedom, which was unheard of when Steve commenced his career, as he comments...

"I suspect that along with a lot of other people, it felt that the music business was in the doldrums for so long and people have finally got rid of the shackles, and that period of the 1980's where you had the sense of music in chains with executives calling the shots. That era is past..."

More recently still, Steve announced his engagement to new partner; Joanna Lehmann on 14th February 2011. Her encouragement and practical assistance over recent years cannot be understated and it is to be hoped that the couple have a long and fruitful artistic life together. As Steve stated in the announcement, Joanna's presence has certainly put fans at ease and her cheerful and practical manner have certainly been of great assistance to the author. The couple were wed at St Albans Register Office on 4th June 2011 and hopefully a bright future awaits the happy couple.

CHAPTER TWENTY TWO

Exploring The Shrouded Horizon

Barely had the dust settled on Out Of The Tunnel's Mouth than Steve was immersed in work on several other projects. His constant touring during the previous couple of years had been born out of necessity to a certain extent, but had nevertheless served to expand his fan base and bring his music to audiences in places, which seldom get to see a musician of his calibre. His follow up to it however, as usual with Steve's work, had a more convoluted history than you might expect as he explained in a recent interview with the author…

"Oh God, I started it much earlier. Work normally starts on an album about a year before its release but this one started much earlier because of several other projects that followed it and I was in the time of troubles (laughs) and I recorded this stuff then put it to one side. There was a whole album and then I started plundering bits of it for this project I was working on with Chris Squire and so it has been backwards and forwards. Now Out Of The Tunnel's Mouth was my third attempt at doing an album. After that I started to work on more material, which I was able to put together with the earlier recordings once the legal problems were over…"

With so much material ostensibly to choose from, including material, which the author heard back in 2008, there was to be no shortage of tracks to choose from on this one and Steve even expressed the opinion that this album might be his very own version of a certain contentious album from his days in Genesis…

When details were eventually announced about the new album, fans were taken by surprise by the decision to release a two disc special edition. Certainly there is a lot of music here to digest and as usual, Steve has taken his own slant on where the musical journey will take us, the listeners. One thing he was at pains to avoid though was the accusation of using "filler" tracks to pad things out...

"Funnily enough, many of the tracks that were on Japanese editions came up for use. I used quite a lot of things that had been available on Japanese editions on the special edition. These things weren't available in the rest of the world, so I have tried to make this extra CD not just any old tat but stuff that I like. You have heard the term 'bonus' tracks or the term 'bogus' tracks (laughs) you know the one where you have a bit of hi hat going or 'alternative' mix where you go, 'one, two three, four' (in best Spike Milligan voice) so we haven't done that..."

The resulting album, Beyond The Shrouded Horizon was released on 26th September 2011. Even its title, as evocative of its predecessor, Spectral Mornings, came from a quite unexpected source, as Steve reveals...

"The language of the sea and the call of the unknown adventure was the original inspiration. The idea was then developed further, but it wasn't a direct lift and it has been kicked around a lot, backwards and forwards..."

Even on a standard (if one can use that word to describe work by Steve), album there is always a variety of different styles and playing to absorb but here even the kitchen sink has been thrown into the mix. You are taken on another travelogue or, perhaps to use a less well-worn phrase, this album is Steve's audio diary of places and people. The journey isn't your usual one though. One moment we are on the shores of Loch Lomond, the next you are staring at the Two Faces Of Cairo before being dragged kicking and screaming into Steve's very own spaceship for a voyage round the universe for Turn This Island Earth. Not your usual fare by any means!

How did he do it? Well, some of the tracks had a more easy gestation than others and others a lengthier one as Steve explains in the case of Prairie Angel/A Place Called Freedom...

"Prairie Angel became a song that continued some of the same themes but I felt that some people might be more interested in the song and others might be more interested in the instrumental aspect, so I banded them as two separate things so it became Prairie Angel and A Place Called Freedom so there are themes that go throughout the album. There was one theme that was a riff that we had around the time of GTR with Steve Howe and Jonathon Mover, and I have credited them on it. It was something that I liked in GTR but we didn't develop it. I have certainly developed it on this album- not just as a rock thing which is how it started, but also it becomes an orchestral exercise and starts using whole tones with the orchestra doing all sorts of weird and wonderful things…"

Two Faces Of Cairo had its origins in a trip that Steve and Jo took to the land of the Pharaohs, but one with unexpected results…

"Jo and I visited Egypt and I was so excited about the remote possibility of seeing the sights because we were only there for a day believe it or not, and we were dashing around like crazy. In that one-day we saw the Pyramids, the Sphinx and we had a trip down the Nile. So while I was there I was scribbling away furiously in a notebook because I was getting so many phrases. I was standing next to the Sphinx on a sunny day just like it is supposed to be on the postcards and you've got no sun hat! (laughs). A little later in the day after we had been wined and dined and feted, we were driving past this area where the tour guide was saying, 'Oh these are the people that live in the tombs. The authorities have tried moving them, but they like living there'. And what you could see was twilight and unlike any other street where you would see a lot of people, there were no street lights so all you saw was shadowy forms. I only got a glimpse of this but the image was so strong and I thought, 'yeah, Cairo really has got two faces'…."

As usual, Steve has continued to work with a wide variety of musicians to help bring his musical dreams to life. Apart from the now established band of musicians whom Steve performs with on stage (and in the studio), he has been able to call on help from some other stellar talents this time round including both Chris Squire and Simon Phillips, and that power trio gets its moment to shine on the album's blues track; Catwalk as Steve explains…

"That's a blues trio with myself, Chris and Simon so you can imagine how that sounds. Scary, yeah. It's quite brutal in a basic bluesy way but I am proud of it because I had been nudging at the blues stuff for a long time and I had never managed to get it quite that brutal! (laughs). It's quite a thrash…"

Once again, the input of Roger King not only in terms of his keyboard playing but also the production values which marks the album out as a cut above the rest, has been invaluable and has drawn comparisons with the great Sir George Martin from several fans. His input is gratefully acknowledged by Steve…

"Roger will always bring something to it that I hadn't thought of. Sometimes he will fight me on issues but I like to think that we take on each other's point of view and I think that is necessary."

There are echoes of previous work throughout as well, which inform but never overwhelm the finished product. Steve's wife Jo, has had a notable hand in the lyrical content of the album and it has to be said, that lyrically this is probably Steve's most impressive effort to date with some startling images throughout although the one which has probably got the fans scratching their heads more than any other is Looking For Fantasy, a delightful composite picture as Steve explains…

"It really is a composite of a lot of girls and women who are part flower child. It gives a sense of lost innocence and reflection on a gentler world. It's about so many people and what they believed and what they followed and whatever they later became…"

I think that memories of Steve's mother and his first girlfriend, Barbara, are evident in this song and nostalgia has always informed Steve's work but never has it descended into sentimentality. Characters are always drawn in vivid detail, fresh and startlingly alive.

From the glories of sixties London to a trip around the universe, the standard version of the album closes with Turn This Island Earth, a definite homage to the 1950's classic Sci-Fi film This Island Earth, and without doubt a nod in the direction of Lost In Space too. A track already of epic proportions when I first heard it back in 2008, the end result, although slightly shorter has lost none of its majesty although some might be surprised by Steve's comments on it…

"The song doesn't follow the storyline of This Island Earth. Completely escapist, it is pure fantasy but it addresses some of those same issues that I suspect we did on Watcher Of The Skies. We have got the space theme; it's of Earth but… we keep on switching from a view of Earth to one of Earth from somewhere else and there is dream imagery associated with that… That was originally going to be the first track, because it is very long, it is opus length. And the odd comment started coming in 'Oh God, people are going to have to wade through that before you get to the rest of it! (laughs) Can't we have a few hors d'oeuvres before the main course?' "

Well if I may continue the gastronomic analogy for a moment, the canapés are served up on the special edition including the Four Winds Suite, which as I suspected also owes something to Steve's old band mates…

"Yes, I was working on the idea of four winds then (back in 1977) and it ended ups as Wind & Wuthering so in a way it was that. There was no song called Four Winds and on this album they are all separate instrumental pieces, all very different in nature…"

Even the tracks which have appeared elsewhere before do not appear to be out of place and one, Enter The Night which has been around under a plethora of titles before (Depth Charge, Riding The Colossus) has been dusted down and finally given the lyrics which, I for one always felt that it deserved.

For a man who has eschewed working as part of a team, Steve 's recent series of collaborations may take some by surprise. His work with Rob Reed of Magenta has yet to see the light of day but his recent collaboration with the enfant terrible of Neo Prog, Steven Wilson has recently appeared on Wilson's Grace For Drowning album, another thought provoking effort which fans of both musicians will appreciate. Other collaborations are still merely the subject of speculation at the moment including the truly frightening prospect of working with modern guitar hero Joe Bonamassa and Jason Bonham among others.

The Squackett project is now the subject of record company discussion and should see the light of day soon, and with it the tantalising prospect of seeing Messrs Hackett and Squire on a concert stage together at some point. Speaking of concert stages, Steve was back on the road in November 2011 to promote the new album on his Breaking Waves Tour bringing his own brand of music to a venue near you.

The live DVD Fire & Ice recorded at the Shepherd's Bush Empire in 2010 gig is the latest release and a documentary about Steve's career is also in production and should be available some time in the not too distant future. So as stated in the close to the previous edition of this book, there are still many more musical voyages for us with this particular acolyte!

APPENDIX 1

Encounters With Hackett

I thought it might prove a useful insight to dedicate this part of the book to the memories of a few fans with their very own "Encounters with Hackett" section, so over to you, guys...

Back around the time period of To Watch The Storms I recall driving home after a bad day at work on a hot summer's day. I was trying to drown out the frustrations of the day with some blaringly loud classic rock from a local Philadelphia radio station - which frankly was not working!

Whilst driving the radio DJ announced that Steve Hackett would be playing Borders Bookstores for a limited US promotional tour. I was in total disbelief having seen him the summer before at the Theatre Of Living Arts on South Street in Philadelphia to a sell-out crowd. I was thrilled and suddenly the stress of the day vanished as I feverishly scribbled down the information verbatim from the lips of the DJ onto a small scrap of coffee stained paper in my glove compartment while dodging oncoming traffic.

When I got home, I was still in disbelief and so I called the bookstore to confirm his appearance. There were in fact, two performances in Philadelphia; one in the city centre and one in a suburb called Bryn Mawr. I was unable to make the Philly show due to it being a mid day performance during the week but the Bryn Mawr show was on a weekend and so I carefully made my travel plans.

Not knowing what to expect I showed up four hours early. I was astonished to see that I was the only Hackett fan there. Initially I feared that I had got the date wrong, but those fears soon subsided. I walked around the store until I saw a clerk setting up what appeared to be a mock stage (basically a chair and a stand) and a few rows of benches. I took my place prominently at the front beside what appeared to be Steve's seat - a mere four or five feet away! Sure enough, as it got closer to show time, people started to pile in. By the time the show was set to start the place was overflowing with Hackett fans filling not only the seats but the upper levels of the bookstore overlooking the performance area, the stairwell (which had a decent view overlooking the stage - although probably a major fire hazard!) and everywhere in between.

Steve appeared out of a side "Employees Only" door to thunderous applause. After a short tune up, he jumped right into his set list. The intimate setting was incredible not just because it was a small stage or because it was just an acoustic guitar, but also because he played right in front of me! I sat there listening to the music while studying the fiery fretboard tremble under Steve's able fingers. Incredible! There was no back up band, no lighting beyond the pale incandescent lighting from the store ceiling above, and no smog machines… just Steve - and his showmanship prowess on the guitar, and mastery of the crowd shone through! Without doubt it is one of the most incredible concert experiences I have ever had! If not the most incredible concert experience I have ever had.

After playing a decent (and long) set of tunes, Steve fielded questions from the audience and actually stayed to sign autographs and take pictures with everyone in attendance who wanted one. Being at the front I was one of the first to shake his hand and thank him for the day. He graciously smiled back and signed a few items while posing for a picture. Hackett was a real class act. He was extremely appreciative and humble and just a pleasure to listen to and talk with. As someone who interviews musicians and bands as a freelance writer from time to time, one of the greatest concerns I have is meeting someone whose music you really love only to find out that they are a total jerk…then the music is ruined forever. Meeting Steve and experience his music this was nothing short of wonderful. I left that show a bigger Hackett fan than I had ever been before.

David Negrin
(David also runs the excellent World Of Genesis website)

* * * * * * * * *

I used to make a point of meeting Steve after every gig - beyond the obvious reason of being a huge fan but because of the trouble he took to meet everyone who took the trouble to meet him and the following episode epitomises this best…

I stood at the back of a long queue of fans who were waiting to meet Steve at an end of tour show at Hammersmith Odeon in 1980 I was about to turn 16 I think. Anyway, when it was finally my turn you could tell he was tired, but being the last person in line it was obvious he intended staying the course.

But I had an unusual request... I told Mr Hackett that I had been busy learning a number of his acoustic pieces but was stuck on a section in Racing In A and asked if he could explain to me how that part went. Steve began to play air guitar to explain it but then decided it would be easier if he could show me on a real guitar. Imagine that! Steve going to get his guitar to show me how to play a section - and at the end of a long tour, a long show and a long line of fans he had just met! Alas, the crew had packed the guitars away and so the opportunity was lost but the memory lives on - Steve Hackett is one classy guy!

Peter Matuchniak

* * * * * * * * * *

I first met Steve on the To Watch The Storms tour in October 2003, which was the first time I had seen him since 1980. I had sort of lost touch since then but had rediscovered him with the release of Darktown. To Watch The Storms was such a great album that I was really looking forward to seeing him again. I was also looking forward to revisiting the Newcastle Tyne Theatre, which is a fantastic intimate venue a bit like a faded Opera House where I had seen a storming set by Keith Emerson and The Nice the previous year.

Steve's set exceeded my high expectations although you probably know how good he and his band are live. I hung around in the bar after the show with a group of fans who indicated that he might appear for a meet and greet. Sure enough, after about thirty minutes he and the band did just that and took time to speak to all of us in turn. When it was my turn I asked him about the unusual guitar he was using (Like a Les Paul with a whammy bar). I was interested to know about this because I play a bit of guitar myself. What surprised me was the considerable amount of time and detail he spent answering my question together with other details of his guitar rig despite having probably been asked the same question many times before.

He also asked for details of who I was and I said I remembered two particularly triumphant Genesis concerts, which I had attended at the Glasgow Apollo in 1976 promoting A Trick Of The Tail. I also wanted to let the rest of his band know how great they were. I was so pleased with how well the evening had gone that on my return I arranged to see him again at the Fairfield Hall in Croydon two weeks later. I have met him a few times since after his concerts (I hate the term "gig" his concerts are too special for that). He always strikes me as a really genuine, sincere and friendly guy and it is great that he takes time out to meet his fans.

John Coulson

* * * * * * * * *

It all happened because of the Official Genesis Forum, which I joined in 2004. Through that forum I met Tomi who was a Genesis fan who lived in Greater Vancouver BC as do I. At some point in 2005 I read that Steve would be touring with the acoustic trio and the closest to us they'd be playing would be Seattle. I told Tomi about this and he was interested in going, so I reserved two tickets.

On the day of the gig (10th October 2005) Tomi had been in pain all day and it had taken us several hours to drive to Seattle but that all seemed to disappear when it was his turn to speak to Steve at the meet and greet after the show. Tomi asked him when he was going to play Vancouver (during the show Steve had told a story about how his family had spent a short time living in Vancouver and Steve had asked if there was anyone in the audience from Vancouver and apparently there were quite a few of us). In response to Tomi's question, Steve said he would love to play Vancouver again. I think we also told Steve that Tomi and I had met through the Genesis Forum and that we were good friends... the rest of that conversation is a bit of a blur.

Then it came to my turn to speak to Steve. I had also brought along my copy of Armando Gallo's I Know What I Like book in the hope that both Steve and John would sign page 147 where there is a photo of the two of them as little boys in short pants, plus there's a photo of them a number of years later with their parents. He turned to whoever was on his right and said; 'isn't that a nice picture of mum?'

Both Tomi and I had forgotten to bring a camera and so I shall be forever grateful to Ian, another Canadian from the Vancouver area. He had a digital camera and took a photo of Tomi, Steve and I and then e-mailed it to me the following day. Perhaps I can again thank Steve for taking the time to do that at the end of a long meet and greet session. I will never forget how great that moment felt. Long before we had met, Tomi and I had both seen Steve's electric band in Vancouver but I didn't know that Steve met his fans until I read about it on the Genesis Forum. That night in Seattle we did not know that the pain Tomi was experiencing was caused by the cancer that would take him from us a year later.

Laurel Axam/Tomi Inkinen R.I.P.

I've had the pleasure of meeting Steve on numerous occasions. Most of these have been at gigs, Steve's natural habitat! The first time was at the De Montfort Hall Leicester back in 2003. I hung around the venue foyer in the hopes that I might catch a glimpse of the man himself. A few dozen fans had the same idea as well. After the gig, he signed autographs and posed for photos with people. When it came to my turn, I was so tongue-tied at meeting him that I could hardly speak. I pushed a few Genesis CD covers at him, he signed them and then he stood with me for some photos before retiring to his dressing room. I drove home to London with a big smile on my face. I had met one of the former players of my favourite band; the man who had written and played on some of my favourite songs. My only disappointment was that the photos taken of me with Steve didn't turn out. That'll teach me to get a cheap camera! Still, I had the memory of meeting the man, and if nothing else I could live with that.

The next time I met Steve was a year later on his acoustic trio tour. I managed to end up being invited backstage at the Queen Elizabeth Hall. One of the tour crew (that dodgy bloke on the merchandise desk) asked me for a hand with a few things and in return asked me if I wanted a drink backstage. How could I refuse? After making our way through the maze that is the backstage area of the hall, we entered the green room, where a small party was going on. This was a highly private occasion with what looked like family and friends only; I felt like I was gate crashing. Alan Hewitt handed me a glass of champagne and told me to go and mingle while he went and spoke to a few people. Me, mingle at a backstage party with Steve Hackett? How on earth did I end up here? Alan rescued me from the corner I ended up hiding in, and introduced me to Steve. After a very brief "hello", Steve was collared by someone else. Shortly after that, I left in order to get the last train home, but not before bumping into Nick Magnus on the way out!

My next meeting with Steve was to do an interview for The Waiting Room in 2006. Alan felt that I was now ready and trusted enough to 'go solo' and do an interview without him having to be there. That and the fact that he lived in Liverpool and I lived just a couple of miles away from Steve's studio…

After finding the right door, I knocked and waited. I don't know why, but it took me by surprise when Steve opened it. I wasn't expecting him to be the one to open the door. I know that's silly, as who else would be there to do it? Steve invited me in and made me a coffee (even apologising for the lack of milk) before inviting me upstairs to the control room while we waited for Roger King to arrive (he was to help out by answering some of the more technical questions I was there to ask). It's the most bizarre thing to be alone with someone you admire and be chatting idly to them. As soon as Roger arrived, I switched on my pocket recorder and we did the interview. Throughout the interview, Steve would always pause before answering in order to consider his answer. What this did was allow him to provide carefully measured answers, especially when the subject of Genesis was broached. I wasn't there for any gossip or dirt, so there was no reason to expect any. Steve was clearly used to being interviewed, as when he answered a question it would be a lot more than a simple 'yes' or 'no'. Once the interview was over, I had Steve and Roger sign a few things for me (why not? This was as good an opportunity as any other!) and they even posed for some pictures. I was cheeky enough to ask Steve to take a photo of Roger and I standing at the mixing desk.

I can't think of very many other musicians who will make the time after playing a gig, to come out front and make themselves available to fans. Okay, so it's not guaranteed that he'll do it at every gig, bit for those gigs he does, it gives those fans who are willing to wait, something special to go home with. Whilst waiting in line for autographs, I have been able to hear him chatting to fans. He must get asked the same dozen or so questions at every gig, however each time I've heard him answer, it's sounded like the first time he's been asked it. Not once have I heard him say 'oh not that one again' when asked about getting back with Genesis or if he and Tony Banks still talk. Other rock/pop stars take note: this is how it should be done...

Stuart Barnes
(web master TWR online web site)

APPENDIX 2
Album By Album

Canterbury Glass - Sacred Scenes And Characters
ORK Records ORK005, 1968/2007

Kyrie / Nunc Dimittis / Gloria / Prologue / We're Going To Beat It (Battle Hymn) (Demo)

Neither this album, nor the next one are Steve Hackett albums but without either of them Steve may never have got off the ground and so it is only fair to acknowledge them here. This album has had an extremely long gestation period, being written and recorded in 1968 and only finally gaining a release in 2007. The album is certainly in no way a representation of Steve's music and in fact, Steve's contribution is limited to one track: Prologue. It is a wildly psychedelic romp in which he can be heard riffing away in the typically over the top style of the time - it was the Sixties after all, folks! One for serious collectors only, really.

Quiet World - The Road
Dawn Records ESMCD 776, 1970/1999

The Great Birth-Theme / First Light / Theme / Star / Theme / Loneliness And Grief / Theme-Change Of Age / Christ One / Hang On / Christ Continued / Body To The Mind / Traveller / Let Everybody Sing / Theme / Children of The World / Change Of Age / Love Is Walking

Two years on, and this album represents Steve's first serious efforts in a recording environment. Another product of its time, it does have some interesting moments and some very good playing if you can get past the incredibly naïve evangelical message that forms the backbone to the album itself. This is a sugar-sweet confection of ideas many of which really are hangovers from the "Hippy" ideal, which by 1970 had died an extremely painful death. Even as a product of its time, I would have to say that it was several years too late to really stand any chance of gaining an audience. Steve's contribution is much more noticeable here although once again, it is very much subordinate to the other players. If you are a fan of English psychedelic, then this is definitely an album that you will enjoy otherwise… enough said!

Voyage Of The Acolyte
Charisma Records CAS111, 1975

Ace Of Wands / Hands Of The Priestess (Part 1) / A Tower Struck Down / Hands Of The Priestess (Part 2) / The Hermit / Star Of Sirius / The Lovers / Shadow Of The Hierophant / Ace Of Wands (live at the Theatre Royal Drury Lane)* / Shadow Of The Hierophant (Extended playout version)*

* Bonus tracks on the 2005 Virgin Remastered edition.

Steve's first proper foray into the world of the solo musician and a brave step to base an album around a concept as unusual as the Tarot cards, especially in 1975 with the New Wave about to break upon the shores of the UK. Opening the album with the by turns manic and luxurious Ace Of Wands, this track conjures up the image of a somewhat demented magician experimenting in his laboratory with an experiment which he seems unable to master. The use of well placed sound effects; bangs, whistles etc adds greatly to this impression and the vibrancy of this track made it an instant stage favourite.

Hands Of The Priestess Pt1 by contrast, is a much more sedate and luxurious composition combining the marvellous sounds of twelve string guitar, Mellotron and flute to create a delightful soundscape which in turn leads into the aural nightmare that is A Tower Struck Down in which everything including the kitchen sink, I suspect; is thrown into the attack; this is an unabashed assault upon the senses only resolved by the apparent destruction of the tower; and the ensuing calm and tolling of bells which leads once again to the calm of Hands Of The Priestess Pt2 which restores some sense of normality to the proceedings.

The Hermit is another wonderfully described aural picture delightfully painted by the combined musical and vocal talents of the musicians involved to evoke the deep sense of mystery and sedate power which this card represents.

Star Of Sirius, is not an evocation of the Tarot but instead something even older perhaps? I don't know if Steve had read Homer (the Greek one not Mr Simpson) before he had worked on this project but the reference to "amber stained evening" to me echoes the words of Homer and the "Wine dark sea" of The Iliad. Stately, restrained and magical this track brings an earlier age to vibrant life.

The Lovers is a delightful but all too brief description of love's young dream as it flourishes and fades into the doom-laden Shadow Of The Hierophant, a mythical creature whose shadow forecast doom. Steve's own thoughts on his career position may (if you wish) be read into this track. Is he the person who is… "lost in thought in search of vision" ? That musical vision has continued to grow ever since this album was released. A strong debut album and one which succeeds in describing the elements and characters of some of the essential cards in the Tarot pack along with other essential ideas that were to mark Steve's individuality as a musician and composer over the coming years.

Please Don't Touch
Charisma Records CDS 4012, 1978

Narnia / Carry On Up The Vicarage / Racing In A / Kim / How Can I? / Hoping Love Will Last / Land Of A Thousand Autumns / Please Don't Touch / The Voice Of Necam / Icarus Ascending / Narnia (John Perry Vocal Version)* / Land Of A Thousand Autumns - Please Don't Touch (Live)* / Narnia (Alternate Version)*

* Bonus tracks on 2005 Virgin remastered edition.

Steve's first proper "Solo" album appeared in 1978 and confirmed that the success of its predecessor had not been due to the Genesis associations attached to it. This is an extremely adventurous album right from the outset of the album with Steve's wonderful homage to the Narnia Chronicles of CS Lewis and the delightfully camp send up of the murder mysteries of Agatha Christie in Carry on Up The Vicarage; if nothing else these two tracks certainly demonstrated that Steve's sense of humour was gloriously alive.

Choosing to dissociate himself from the Genesis tag and instead immersing himself in the sounds of the US rock and Soul scene, his choice of musicians and singers on this project was nothing short of inspired. Hoping Love Will Last brought the dulcet tones of Randy Crawford to the attention of listeners in the UK for the first time whilst Woodstock veteran Richie Havens brought his glorious smokey vocals to both How Can I and Icarus Ascending. Instrumentally too, this album brought a wider range of colours to Steve's palette including the use of early synthesiser technology to augment Steve's uniquely quirky playing - who else in rock would use the medieval Psaltery on an album but here it is! Certainly another album which marked Steve out as being a cut above the rest!

Spectral Mornings
Charisma Records CDS 4017, 1979

Every Day / The Virgin And The Gypsy / The Red Flower Of Taichi Blooms Everywhere / Clocks - The Angel Of Mons / The Ballad Of The Decomposing Man / Lost Time In Cordoba / Tigermoth / Spectral Mornings / Every Day (Alternate Mix)* / The Virgin And The Gypsy (Alternate Mix)* / Tigermoth (Alternate Mix)* / The Ballad Of The Decomposing Man (Alternate Mix)* / Clocks - The Angel Of Mons (Single Version)* / Live Acoustic Set : Etude In A Minor - Blood On The Rooftops - Horizons - Kim / Tigermoth (Live)*

* Bonus tracks on the Virgin 2005 remastered edition.

Written in the depths of winter and on very little sleep apparently, there is nothing of that to show on this, Steve's acknowledged masterpiece. Justly famed for the title track which still rates as one of the finest guitar instrumentals ever written; the rest of the album isn't far behind either. Steve's willingness to experiment with the sound of both music and vocals is plain to see on this album. The delightful word-play that is used on The Virgin & The Gypsy based round the various wild flowers of the English woodlands and meadows is coupled with an earthy acoustic guitar playing totally in harmony with its subject.

The Red Flower Of Taichi Blooms Everywhere brings a touch of the Orient into the album in a delightfully enigmatic and evocative track. War time subjects are also dealt with in dramatic form with the tale of a ghost pilot; Lost Time In Cordoba and the aural assault on the ears that is Clocks - The Angel Of Mons. Everyday deals with drug addiction in a realistic and dramatic fashion; and despite Steve's own insistence that The Ballad Of The Decomposing Man is a parody of George Formby; many people have seen it as an extended metaphor for the state of industrial relations within the UK at the time. A marvellous mix of reality and fantasy makes this album one of the finest that Steve has ever committed to record.

Defector
Charisma Records CDS 4018, 1980

The Steppes / Time To Get Out / Slogans / Leaving / Two Vamps As Guests / Jacuzzi / Hammer In The Sand / The Toast / The Show / Sentimental Institution / Hercules Unchained* / Sentimental Institutuion (Live at the Theatre Royal Drury Lane)* / The Steppes (Live At the Reading Festival)* / Clocks - The Angel Of Mons (Live at the Reading Festival)*

* Bonus tracks on the 2005 Virgin remastered edition.

A scant few months separate Spectral Mornings from Defector and Steve's writing had come on leaps and bounds and he was now ready to tackle (shock, horror) a CONCEPT album! Defector the wonderfully imaginative story of the aural and visual impressions of a defector from the Eastern Bloc on his arrival in the West. As usual though, Steve uses the mixture of music and lyrics to convey the story in a witty and observant fashion from the windswept homeland of The Steppes and the realisation that it is Time To Get Out and the deeply poignant Leaving and Hammer In The Sand both of which evoke all the sadness of departure from all you have ever known as home in pursuit of a "better" life. Jacuzzi and The Toast evoke the decadence of Western society and The Show is a brilliantly stated plea for toleration through music. Steve's wonderfully understated and immensely playful sense of humour is also given full rein on the delightfully tongue-in-cheek Sentimental Institution, which is also another wonderful reference to some of Steve's earliest influences where some of the great band leaders of the 1940's ; Artie Shaw; Benny Goodman are name checked here.

Cured
Charisma Records CDS 4021, 1981

Hope I Don't Wake / Picture Postcard / Can't Let Go / The Air-Conditioned Nightmare / Funny Feeling / A Cradle Of Swans / Overnight Sleeper / Turn Back Time / Tales Of The Riverbank* / Second Chance* / The Air-Conditioned Nightmare (Live at the Reading Festival)*

* Bonus tracks on the 2006 Virgin remastered edition.

Always one for taking musical adventures and risks; Steve took the biggest gamble of his career since leaving Genesis with this album. Investing heavily in the new upcoming technologies including the first drum machines; Steve ditched the comfort of existing formulae and stripped things back to basics. Finally taking centre stage as the singer of his own material; Steve's first steps in this direction were not immediately well received by his fans and this is an album that still divides them to this day. Looked at with the benefits of hindsight, however; Cured is an extremely important album for Steve. His rock sensibilities are still here on such live favourites as The Air Conditioned Nightmare and Overnight Sleeper, but sandwiched between them are tracks which should have seen Steve's emergence as a writer of crafted "Pop" songs too. Hope I Don't Wake and Funny Feeling in particular have all the essential trademarks for any prospective chart single and yet still carry Hackett's distinctive stamp. Cured is a difficult album because it is a transitional one and the transition which it heralded is still being felt in Steve's music some thirty odd years later.

Highly Strung
Charisma Records HACK1, 1983

Camino Royale / Cell 151 / Always Somewhere Else / Walking Through Walls / Hive It Away / Weightless / Group Therapy / India Rubber Man / Hackett To Pieces / Guitar Boogie* / Walking Through Walls (12" Version)* / Time Lapse At Milton Keynes*

* Bonus tracks on the 2006 Virgin remastered edition.

Steve's next album gave him the one thing, which had so far eluded him: a hit single. Cell 151 grazed the UK charts on its release and at the same time reassured his fans that their hero was still capable of writing great rock tunes. Of course, they were rock tunes with a difference; Weightless (relating Steve's first experience of hang gliding) for instance was not your usual rock formula, nor in fact, was it any such navel-gazing but more a wry piss-take on the pretensions of rock stars. Nor indeed was the witty send up of James Bond films in Camino Royale. With his tongue firmly in his cheek, Steve also allowed his new band some "Group Therapy" with the instrumental track of the same name. Once again, he had proven that unusual subjects were to be an increasing part of his stock in trade but the music remained as fresh and vibrant as ever.

Bay Of Kings
Start Records SLP10, 1983

Bay Of Kings / The Journey / Kim / Marigold / St Elmo's Fire/Petropolis / Second Chance / Cast Adrift / Horizons / Black Light / The Barren Land / Calmaria / Time Lapse At Milton Keynes* / Tales Of The Riverbank* / The Skye Boat Song*

*Bonus tracks on 1994 CD re-issue.

If fans had just about got used to the shock of Steve singing and using new technology; another surprise was in store later in 1983 when he unleashed his first salvo from the "small orchestra" in the form of a totally acoustic album. Bay Of Kings had its conception at the beginning of the 1980's but record company intransigence meant that the album was shelved until Steve was able to release it via a more sympathetic outlet. There had always been acoustic material on his albums before but here at last was a showcase for the other Steve Hackett. Serene and beautiful and conforming to the tenets of classical melody; Bay Of Kings won Steve many new fans; not least Yehudi Menuhin who used a track from it in a documentary later that year - praise indeed!

Till We Have Faces
Lamborghini Records LMGLP11, 1984

Duel / Matilda Smith-Williams Home For The Aged / Let Me Count The Ways / A Doll That's Made In Japan / Myopia / What's My Name / The Rio Connection/ Taking The Easy Way Out / When You Wish Upon A Star / The Gulf* / Stadiums Of The Damned*

*Bonus tracks on 1994 re-issue.

Just when Steve's fans thought that he could not possibly surprise them any more; he did exactly that with this, his next album. Without doubt this is the album, which divides Hackett fans more than any other. Recorded mainly in Brazil and utilising their percussive music style this album can perhaps be viewed as one of the first examples of "World Music" that had then been released. We take that for granted now but back in 1984 this was a hard musical pill to swallow especially for fans that had had to cope with so many other changes of late. The album suffers from a paucity of material with only the single: A Doll That's Made In Japan and the riddle-like What's my Name? rising above the mediocrity of the rest of the material although the wonderfully acerbic Matilda Smith-Williams Home For The Aged did prove that Steve's sense of observation and humour were just as vital as always. The album was re-issued in the mid 1990's by Camino, and with the benefit of remastering and a re-ordering of the tracks, is now a slightly more acceptable proposition although not one which will ever be in my top five Hackett albums, I'm afraid.

GTR
Arista Records ARC 8400, 1986

When The Heart Rules The Mind / The Hunter / Here I Wait / Sketches Of The Sun / Jekyll And Hyde / You Can Still Get Through / Reach Out (Never Say No) / Toe The Line / Hackett To Bits/Imagining

Steve had always steered clear of re-joining any form of "Super Group" after his departure from Genesis and so many fans were wondering what was going on when this album, co-written with Yes alumnus Steve Howe appeared. This is an A & R man's wet dream of an album and it certainly took the US market by storm. An album that saw Steve bite the commercial bullet very much in order to replenish the coffers rather than satisfy any real artistic urge. Certainly there is no doubting the initial quality of tracks such as When The Heart Rules The Mind and The Hunter but the bulk of the album fails to rise above predictable mediocrity and fortunately Steve was not to remain hitched to this particular wagon for very long!

Momentum
Start Records SLP15, 1988

Cavalcanti / The Sleeping Sea / Portrait Of A Brazilian Lady / When the Bell Breaks / A Bed A Chair And A Guitar / Concert For Munich / Last Rites Of Innocence / Troubled Spirit / Variation On A Theme By Chopin / Pierrot / Momentum / Bouree* / An Open Window / The Vigil

* *Bonus tracks on the 1994 re-issue.*

A welcome return to the acoustic field saw Steve refine and hone the music that inspired him so much. Without doubt, this album has its roots firmly set in the Baroque period. It is a wonderfully polished work with several tracks eminently suitable for performance in the concert halls and opera houses of the UK and elsewhere. It marked Steve's coming of age as a composer of music of merit outside of the world of rock 'n' roll. The performance level on this album is far in excess of its predecessor and the result is an album that conforms more directly to the precepts of classical music. Austere in places but always tinged with that inherent sense of warmth that colours most of Steve's work.

Time Lapse: Steve Hackett Live
Crisis Records 500 001-2, 1991

Camino Royale / Please Don't Touch / Every Day / In That Quiet Earth / Depth Charge / Jacuzzi/ The Steppes / Ace Of Wands / Hope I Don't Wake / The Red Flower Of Taichi Blooms Everywhere / Tigermoth / A Tower Struck Down / Spectral Mornings / Clocks - The Angel Of Mons

At last! After years of requests from the fans, here is the live album that they had wanted. Steve had wanted to issue a live recording in the 1980's but met with resistance from his old record company. Fortunately, in this instance the wait was worth it. Combining two performances from two bands with almost a decade separating them this album married the excitement of the classic Hackett live tracks such as Please Don't Touch and Spectral Mornings alongside brand new material such as Depth Charge without any detriment: An essential item in any Hackett collection.

The Unauthorised Biography
Virgin Records CDVM 9014, 1992

Narnia / Hackett To Pieces / Don't Fall Away From Me / Spectral Mornings / The Steppes / The Virgin And The Gypsy / The Air-Conditioned Nightmare / Cell 151 / Slogans / Icarus Ascending / Prayers And Dreams / Star Of Sirius / Hammer In The Sand / Ace Of Wands / Hoping Love Will Last

The first compilation album of Hackett material to be released and a fine resume of Steve's time with Charisma/Virgin to boot! Rather than go for the usual "Greatest Hits" package however, this album showcased the various sides of his musical output from the established classics such as Spectral Mornings and Ace Of Wands alongside more underrated tracks such as the glorious Hoping Love Will Last and The Virgin & The Gypsy. Replete with two never before released tracks as well, this was a nice package for old and new fans alike.

Guitar Noir
Permanent Records PERMCD13, 1993

Take These Pearls / Dark As The Grave / Paint Your Picture / There Are Many Sides To The Night / Like An Arrow / Walking Away From Rainbows / Sierra Quemada / Lost In Your Eyes / Little America / In the Heart Of The City / A Vampyre With A Healthy Appetite / Cassandra** / Theatre Of Sleep* / Sierra Quemada (Demo)* / Take These Pearls (Rough Mix)* / In The Heart Of The City (Original Version)* / A Vampyre With A Healthy Appetite (Demo)*

* Bonus tracks on 1994 re-issue. ** Bonus track on US version.

If ever an album could be said to be truly pivotal in an artists' career, then Guitar Noir without doubt holds that position in the canon of Steve's work. His first rock album since 1983 and the one in which he truly found his "voice" where lyrics, vocals and music merged into one unified body. As usual, Steve covered a lot of ground with this album and began that process of self-examination, which has coloured the majority of his work since.
Never afraid to look the darker corners of the human psyche in the eye; he did so here with wonderfully observant portraits of the human condition such as There Are Many Sides To The Night and In The Heart Of The City as well as proving that the art of the searing instrumental was not dead either. Sierra Quemada lives up to its name (The Scorched Earth) in more ways than one, while the wistful Walking Away From Rainbows and Tristesse perpetuate Steve's dedication to melody and musical lyricism. With this album he drew a line under and closed the book on his earlier work and opened a new one which has been the ongoing wellspring ever since.

Blues With A Feeling
Permanent Records PERMCD27, 1994

Born In Chicago / The Stumble / Love Of Another Kind / Way Down South / A Blue Part of Town / Footloose / Tombstone Roller / Blues With A Feeling / Big Dallas Sky / The 13th Floor / So Many Roads / Solid Ground

If Guitar Noir was an album replete with explorations of the dark side then Blues With A Feeling dragged us back into the light with a wonderful celebration of the music that was Steve's first love. If any album exemplifies the fun aspect of making music it is this one. Back to basics but raw and energetic; Steve managed to mix established blues standards with new material without the "join" being obvious. And all the while giving the overwhelming feeling that it had been an enormous amount of fun into the bargain. Sadly, he never did manage to get the G clamp and oxygen cylinder necessary to tour with this album but bits from it have surfaced in several guises in live shows ever since.

There Are Many Sides To The Night
Kudos CD2, 1995

Horizons / Black Light / The Skye Boat Song / Time Lapse At Milton Keynes / Beja Flor / Kim/ Second Chance / Oh How I Love You / The Journey / Bacchus / Walking Away From Rainbows / Cavalcanti / Andante In C (Giuliani) / Concerto In D(Vivaldi) / A Blue Part Of Town / Ace Of Wands / Cinema Paradiso / End Of Day

Another brave step this one. Now secure in the possession of his own record company, Steve was able to begin to release albums, which would never have been dreamed of previously. Beginning with this one, perhaps the first complete acoustic live album to have been released by an established artist. The real "Unplugged" article if you like, capturing him in fine form during his 1994 acoustic tour of Italy. Old classics and new ones mingle here in the more intimate setting of acoustic guitar and keyboard, throwing new light on this material creating the benchmark for later efforts.

Genesis Revisited
Mercury Records PHCR 1454 (1996)/Snapper Records SRECD704 (1997)

Watcher Of The Skies / Your Own Special Way / Dance On A Volcano / Valley Of The Kings / Déjà vu / Riding The Colossus* / For Absent Friends / Fountain Of Salmacis / Waiting Room Only / I Know What I Like / Firth of Fifth / Los Endos**

* Appears on the Japanese edition.
** Appears on the European edition.

Another surprise was in store for fans when this album was released, initially in Japan in 1996, with a subsequent release in Europe and the US where it was titled: Watchers Of The Skies. Steve had always steered clear of his illustrious past with Genesis but at last he decided to exorcise those old ghosts by re-working some of his favourite Genesis tracks. Sometimes it works; such as the glorious Watcher Of The Skies and Firth Of Fifth complete with Brazilian style percussion. Sometimes it falls rather flat and the attempted humour of the new version of I Know What I Like left me cold. Sandwiched between these tracks however, are several intriguing glimpses into unseen areas; Déjà vu; a lovely hark-back to the days of Selling England By The Pound and Valley Of The Kings and Riding The Colossus; brand new compositions which demonstrated that Steve's musical descriptive gifts are still working extremely well. An album which fans will either like or loathe, I rather like it myself!

King Biscuit Flower Hour Presents - GTR Live
BMG Records 70710-88021-2, 1997

Jekyll And Hyde / Here I Wait / Prizefighters / Imagining / Hackett to Bits / Spectral Mornings / I Know What I Like / Sketches In the Sun / Pennants / Rounbdabout / The Hunter / You Can Still Get Through / Reach Out (Never Say No) / When The Heart Rules The Mind

Finally released from the KBFH archives, this album illustrated both the strengths and the weaknesses of the GTR line-up. The material from the GTR album itself comes across as extremely weak and insipid when matched to classics such as Spectral Mornings and Roundabout but it was a brave stab and some tracks such as Here I Wait and When The Heart Rules The Mind do certainly sound infinitely better in the live context than they do on the studio version. An album that will satisfy the curiosity of anyone such as I, who didn't see GTR live at the time, but otherwise little more than curiosity value here.

The Tokyo Tapes
Camino Records CAMCD15, 1997

Watcher Of The Skies / Riding The Colossus / Firth Of Fifth / Battlelines / Camino Royale / In the Court Of The Crimson King / Horizons / Walking Away From Rainbows / Heat Of The Moment / In That Quiet Earth / A Vampyre With A Healthy Appetite / I Talk To The Wind / Shadow Of The Hierophant / Los Endos / Black Light / The Steppes / I Know What I Like / Firewall* / The Dealer*

*Studio recordings.

The release of Genesis Revisited simply begged for a live show to accompany it and fortunately, in December 1996, Steve was asked to perform a handful of shows in Japan based around the album. The result is a stunning piece of work. As a showcase or even an aural CV for the musicians involved (Steve; John Wetton; Chester Thompson; Julian Colbeck and Ian MacDonald) it is hard to beat. Classic follows classic here with flawless performances of timeless music such as I Talk To The Wind; In That Quiet Earth and The Steppes to name but three. An album that re-invigorated Steve's urge to play live after a lengthy lay off and an album which old and new fans will love.

A Midsummer Night's Dream
EMI Classics 7243 5 56348 2 5, 1998

The Palace Of Theseus / A Form In Wax / By Paved Fountain / Titania / Set Your Heart At Rest / Oberon / Within This Wood / In the Beached Margent Of The Sea / Between The Cold Moon And The Earth / Puck / Helena / Peaseblossom, Cobweb; Moth And Mustardseed / Mountains Turned Into Clouds / The Lunatic, The Lover And The Poet / Starlight / Lysander And Demetrius / Celebration / All Is Mended

A masterpiece, pure and simple: Not a simple re-telling of the Shakespearean play but a thematic examination of some of the central characters and descriptions from it. Merging, on occasions; themes from some of Steve's earlier work with fresh compositions; the interplay between the "little orchestra" of the acoustic guitar and its big brother; the symphony orchestra is as enthralling as the play itself! Drawing his inspiration from some of the Bard's finest lines; Steve has illuminated the beauty of the written word in music as well as bringing some of Shakespeare's most famous characters to vivid musical life. This is really Steve Hackett's coming of age. Classical in form and style but nonetheless the work of a modern master; Steve's muse was extremely kind with this one and I adore it!

Darktown
Camino Records CAMCD17, 1999

Omega Metallicus / Darktown / Man Overboard / The Golden Age Of Steam / Days Of Long Ago / Dreaming With Open Eyes / Twice Around The Sun / Rise Again / Jane Austen's Door / Darktown Riot / In Memoriam / Coming Home To The Blues* / The Well At World's End*

*Bonus tracks on Japanese edition.

Guitar Noir begun the process of rehabilitation and this natural process continued with the dramatic themes displayed in Darktown. This is Steve Hackett at his most vulnerable and his most angry, as he finally exorcises some of the personal ghosts from his own life... school ground bullying (Darktown); drug addiction (Jane Austen's Door); cynicism and manipulation of children (The Golden Age Of Steam). There are occasional glimpses of light however; such as the glorious instrumental Twice Around The Sun and the hymn to life after death Rise Again - an enormous album and one which stands shoulder to shoulder with the best of his work.

Sketches Of Satie - John Hackett & Steve Hackett
Camino Records CAMCD20, 2000

Gnossienne No3 / Gnossienne No2 / Gnossienne No1 / Gymnopedie No3 / Gymnopedie No2 / Gymnopedie No1 / Pieces Froides No1 (Airs A Faire Fuir i) / Pieces Froides No1 (Airs A Faire Fuir ii) / Pieces Froides No2 (Danse De Travers) / Avant Dernieres Pensees (Idylle A Debussy) / Avant Dernieres Pensees (Aubade A Paul Dukas) / Avant Dernieres Pensees (Meditation Albert Roussell) / Gnossienne No4 / Gnossienne No5 / Gnossienne No6 / Nocturne No1 / Nocturne No2 / Nocturne No3 / Nocturne No4 / Nocturne No5

Steve has always worked in terms of light and shade and if Darktown was very much the shade, then this album is definitely the light! Working solely on acoustic guitar and accompanied by his flautist brother John, this album shimmers like the sun on rippling water. Taking a selection of music, which is so well known and adapting, it is always risky but what is surprising about this project was how much of the music you will already recognise without realising it. An album that fans of Steve's acoustic music will take to their hearts immediately.

Feedback 86
Camino Records CAMCD21, 2000

Cassandra / Prizefighters / Slot Machine / Stadiums Of The Damned / Don't Fall / Oh, How I Love You / Notre Dame Des Fleurs / The Gulf

An album with an inordinately long gestation period even by Steve's standards! This should have been the follow up to 1986's GTR project but never made it. Working with a stellar cast including Brian May and Bonnie Tyler this should have been a bona fide hit but there you go. Tracks such as Cassandra and Slot Machine are superb examples of Steve's rock playing and coupling that with acoustic tracks such as Notre Dame Des Fleurs you have a definite throwback to the early '80's style of Hackett album. One, which deserves to be listened to and relished - and an abject lesson in what happens when lawyers start interfering in the creative process!

Somewhere In South America
Camino Records CAMCD29, 2000

The Floating Seventh / Mechanical Bride / Medley / Serpentine Song / Watcher of The Skies / Hairless Heart / Firth Of Fifth / Riding The Colossus / Pollution B / The Steppes / Gnossienne No1 / Walking Away From Rainbows /Sierra Quemada / The Wall Of Knives / Vampyre With A Healthy Appetite / A Tower Struck Down / Lucridus / Darktown / Camino Royale / In Memoriam / Horizons / Los Endos

Steve had been bitten by the touring bug again after the Genesis Revisited album and his extensive tour of South America was documented by this warts and all live recording from that tour. The first in what is now a well-established series of official "bootlegs" here is Mr Hackett road testing new material again and presenting new versions of old favourites to bring the usual mixture of familiar faces and new friends to the evening. As rock shows go, Steve's have never relied on excessive lighting; lasers and smoke machines etc; it has always been the music that has mattered and that is still the case here and it speaks in volumes!

Hungarian Horizons
Camino Records CAMCD30, 2001

Horizons / Gnossienne No 1 / Bouree-Bacchus / Firth Of Fifth / Bay Of Kings / Syrinx / Imagining / Second Chance / Jacuzzi / Overnight Sleeper / The Barren Land / Black Light / Kim / Time Lapse At Milton Keynes / The Chinese Jam / Concerto In D / Hairless Heart / Cinema Paradiso / Mustard Seed / Gymnopedie No 1 / Jazz On A Summer's Night / Little Cloud / Cavalcanti / Walking Away

From Rainbows / Andante In C / Concert For Munich / The Journey / The Skye Boat Song / By Paved Fountain / Etude In A Minor / Blood On The Rooftops / Hands Of The Priestess / C Minor Triplets / End Of Day / Ace Of Wands / Idylle-Aubade-Meditation

The next in this series of live recordings captured Steve in fine form at one of his acoustic trio shows. It never ceases to amaze me how much variety there can be within this form! Classic tracks such as Firth Of Fifth; Jacuzzi and Hairless Heart take on an entirely new life and they rub shoulders with established acoustic favourites such as Horizons and Jazz On A Summer's Night to bring a perfect blend to the performance, and only Steve could write an evocative track to his own cat - Little Cloud! Another excellent recording.

Live Archive '70's, '80's, '90's
Camino Records CAMCD23, 2001

Discs 1 & 2: Hammersmith Odeon London 30th June 1979: Please Don't Touch / Tigermoth / Every Day / Narnia / The Red Flower Of Taichi Blooms Everywhere / Ace Of Wands / Carry On Up The Vicarage / Etude In A Minor / Blood On The Rooftops / Horizons / Kim / The Optigon / A Tower Stuck Down / Spectral Mornings / Star Of Sirius / Shadow Of The Hierophant / Clocks - The Angel Of mons / I Know What I Like / Wardrobe Boogie / Racing In A / Racing In A Coda*

Disc 3: Castel Sant'Angelo Rome 13th September 1981: The Air-Conditioned Nightmare / Jacuzzi / Funny Feeling / Ace Of Wands / Picture Postcard / The Steppes / Every Day / Overnight Sleeper / Hope I Don't Wake / Slogans / A Tower Struck Down / Spectral Mornings / The Show / Clocks - The Angel Of Mons.

Disc 4: Grand Theatre Clapham 8th June 1993: Medley (Myopia-Los Endos-Imaging - Ace Of Wands-Hackett To Pieces) / A Vampyre With A Healthy Appetite / Sierra Quemada / Take These Pearls / In The Heart Of The City / Walking Away From Rainbows / There Are Many Sides To The Night / Kim / Dark As The Grave / Always Somewhere Else / Lost In Your Eyes / Spectral Mornings / Firth of Fifth - Clocks / Cinema Paradiso / In That Quiet Earth

Otherwise titled "How to beat the bootleggers at their own game" this is a superb boxed set of four discs spanning the three awesome band line-ups that Steve had during this period. For fans such as myself, who were actually in attendance at some of the shows captured here, the memories are brought sharply into focus once more and for fans who were not lucky enough to catch any of these gigs, here is a wonderful example of the brilliant music and performances that you missed!
The Japanese edition of the Live Archive set was issued as two double CDs

comprising the recordings from Rome 1981, and London 1993 along with a previously unreleased recording from the second Spectral Mornings UK tour and the Japanese release of the Feedback 86 studio album. The 1979 recording was subsequently issued directly by Camino Records and the details are as follows...

Camino Records CAMCD23X, 2000

Newcastle City Hall 26th October 1979: Please Don't Touch / Tigermoth/Every Day / The Steppes / Narnia / The Red Flower Of Taichi Blooms Everywhere / Sentimental Institution / Star Of Sirius / Spectral Mornings / Clocks - The Angel Of Mons / Ace Of Wands* / Hands Of The Priestess* / Racing In A*

* Tracks from Hammersmith 30th June 1979.

Genesis Files
Snapper Records Snapper Music SMCD362, 2002

Firth Of Fifth / Watcher Of The Skies / Riding The Colossus / Rise Again / Valley Of The Kings / Time Lapse At Milton Keynes / Your Own Special Way / The Fountain Of Salmacis / For Absent Friends / Twice Around The Sun / Horizons / Prizefighters / Camino Royale / I Know What I Like / Déjà vu / Waiting Room Only / Dance On A Volcano / The Steppes / In That Quiet Earth / Los Endos

A further compilation album, this time drawn mainly from the Genesis Revisited and Tokio Tapes albums: An interesting resume for newer fans and a curio for existing ones.

Live Archive NEARfest
Camino Records CAMCD32, 2003

The Floating Seventh / Mechanical Bride / Medley / Serpentine Song / Watcher of The Skies / Hairless Heart / Firth Of Fifth / Riding The Colossus / Pollution B / The Steppes / Gnossienne No1 / Walking Away From Rainbows / In Memoriam / The Wall Of Knives / A Vampyre With A Healthy Appetite / Spectral Mornings / Lucridus / Darktown /Camino Royale / Every Day / Horizons / Los Endos

Next album in this expanding series, this recording captures one of the handful of US shows which Steve did in the run up to the release of his next studio album and the usual road testing of new material accompanies the expected mix of classics.

To Watch The Storms
Camino Records CAMCD 31/CAMCD31SE, 2003
Universal Records International UICE 1064, 2003

Strutton Ground / Circus Of Becoming / The Devil Is An Englishman / Frozen Statues / Mechanical Bride / Wind, Sand And Stars / Brand New / This World / Rebecca / The Silk Road / Come Away / The Moon Under Water / Serpentine Song / Fire Island* / Marijuana Assassin Of Youth* / If You Only Knew* / Flame **

* Bonus tracks on "Special " edition.
** Bonus track on Japanese edition.

If Darktown was the darker side of Steve's character, then To Watch The Storms is definitely the sunshine after the rain! Another biographical trip through some of Steve's personal reminiscences; the place-association of Strutton Ground; the wonderfully evocative description of his father's artistic endeavours in Serpentine Song. This is the album where Steve also finally finds his own true voice not only in terms of singing but also in terms of lyrics, and there are some wonderfully evocative examples here. His literary influences are once again on display here with superbly observed homages to St Exupery and DuMaurier in Wind, Sand And Stars and Rebecca, and a bona fide "World Music" classic in The Silk Road. As the author remarked at the time of first hearing this record it is a showcase for all of the various styles of music which Steve has performed... a musical resume of the lighter side of life!

Live Archive 03
Camino Records CAMCD 33, 2004

Mechanical Bride / Serpentine Song / Watcher Of The Skies / Hairless Heart / Darktown / Camino Royale / Pollution B / The Steppes / Acoustic Medley / Kim / Walking Away From Rainbows / Slogans / Every Day / Please Don't Touch / Firth of Fifth / The Wall Of Knives / A Vampyre With A Healthy Appetite / Spectral Mornings / Brand New / Los Endos/Clocks - The Angel Of Mons / In That Quiet Earth

Fundamentally a tour souvenir of the fantastic 2003 To Watch The Storms tour, his first performances in the UK for ten years, captured for the fans and an essential addition to any collection.

Guitar Wars
Universal Music UICE 1070 (Japanese only release)

Getting Betta / Viking Kong / I Like Rock (Paul Gilbert Set) / Tidal / Steel Away

/ Nobody's Fault But Mine (John Paul Jones Set) / Gravity / Get The Funk Out / More Than Words (Nuno Bettencourt Set) / Firth of Fifth / Mechanical Bride / Los Endos (Steve Hackett Set) / Rock And Roll (Encore)

An unlikely setting for the thirtieth anniversary of the Japanese "Hard Rock Café" chain: Events like this seldom bring out the best in the participants and this album is no exception. Worthwhile for its curiosity value more than any intrinsic worth to the performances themselves.

Live Archive 04
Camino Records CAMCD34, 2004

Valley Of The Kings / Mechanical Bride / Circus Of Becoming / Frozen Statues / Slogans / Serpentine Song / Ace of Wands / Hammer In The Sand / Blood On The Rooftops / Fly On A Windshield / Please Don't Touch / Firth of Fifth / If You Can't Find Heaven / Darktown / Brand New / The Air-Conditioned Nightmare / Every Day / Clocks - The Angel Of Mons / Spectral Mornings / Los Endos

Continuing the series, this recording captures the almost complete 2004 shows where Steve gave his audience a definitive live set. Drawing from almost every album in his impressive arsenal of recordings and with some delightful surprises to boot. This is the "must have" live album for Hackett fans old and new alike.

Metamorpheus
Camino Records CAMCD35, 2005

The Pool Of Memory And The Pool Of Forgetfulness / To Earth Like Rain / Song To Nature / One Real Flower / The Dancing Ground / That Vast Life / Eurydice Taken / Charon's Call / Cerberus At Peace / Under The World - Orpheus Looks Back / The Broken Lyre / Severance / Elegy / Return To The Realm Of Eternal Renewal / Lyra

Another classic. Steve's mastery of the classical style and form reaches new heights here. Based around the Greek myth of Orpheus & Eurydice the album evokes the spirit and form of the myths but also explores the fundamental questions of life and death in a stunning manner. Severe and austere in places, the emphasis of this album is firmly on melody and there is no doubt that Steve's reputation as a composer of modern orchestral music (I dislike the term "classical" in this context) already established by A Midsummer Night's Dream has been greatly enhanced by this album, one of his greatest works to date.

Live Archive 05
Camino Records CAMCD36, 2005

Japonica / Andante In C / Tribute To Segovia / Metamorpheus Excerpts / Bay Of Kings / Classical Jazz / Sapphires / Mexico City / Black Light / The Skye Boat Song / Peaseblossom / Horizons / Jacuzzi / Bacchus / Firth Of Fifth / Improvisation / The Red Flower of Taichi Blooms Everywhere / Hands Of The Priestess / After The Ordeal / Hairless Heart / M3 / Imagining / Second Chance / Jazz On A Summer's Night / Next Time Around / Kim / Idylle - Aubade - Meditation / The Journey / Ace Of Wands / Walking Away From Rainbows / Gnossienne No1

Latest in this line of live recordings, this time capturing his first acoustic tour of the UK in almost twenty years. A complete and unedited recording from the "family outing" at London's Queen Elizabeth Hall it brings the delights of the trio to the fans in a wonderful recording - another worthy addition.

Live Archive 83
Camino Records CAMCD37, 2006

Calmaria / Hands Of The Priestess / Jacuzzi / The Barren Land / Tales Of The Riverbank / Second Chance / Oriental Improvisation / Petropolis / Kim / The Water Wheel / Concert For Munich / The Journey / Ace Of Wands / A Cradle Of Swans / Jazz On A Summer's Night / Horizons / Time Lapse At Milton Keynes / Bay Of Kings

Another blast from the past. This album features Steve's first foray into the realms of solo acoustic performances back in 1983. Another brave step and one, which paid off enormously as his highly successful acoustic tours since, have shown. Here we have a "warts and all" recording taken from "ahem" unofficial sources - a true official bootleg capturing the spirit of these gigs - and giving fans (yours truly included) a chance to hear what we missed!

Wild Orchids
Camino Records CAMCD38/38SE, 2006
Wild Orchids WHD Entertainment IECP 10066 (Japan)

A Dark Night In Toytown / Waters Of The Wild / Set Your Compass / Down Street / A Girl Called Linda / To A Close / Ego And Id / The Man In The Long Black Coat / Wolfwork / Why / She Moves In Memories / The Fundamentals Of Brainwashing / Howl - (Standard Edition)

Transylvanian Express / Waters Of The Wild / Set Your Compass / Down Street /

A Girl Called Linda / Bluer Child / To A Close / Ego And Id / Man In The Long Black Coat /Cedars Of Lebanon / Wolfwork / Why / She Moves In Memories / The Fundamentals Of Brianwashing / Howl / A Dark Night In Toytown / Until The Last Butterfly - (Special Edition)

Transylvanian Express / Waters Of The Wild / Set Your Compass / Down Street / A Girl Called Linda / To A Close / Ego And Id / Man In The Long Black Coat / Cedars Of Lebanon / Wolfwork / Why / She Moves In Memories / The Fundamentals Of Brianwashing / Howl / A Dark Night In Toytown / Eruption / Reconditioned Nightmare - (Japanese Edition)

Another visit to the fun fair! Yes, all the characters, the thrills and spills are here again for our delectation. There are thrills: Transylvanian Express, Wolfwork which in fact harks back to Steve's earliest composition: "Bats In The Belfry". There are candyfloss moments of delicious sweetness; Set Your Compass and She Moves In Memories, both of which give further evidence to the depth of his literary influences, which on this album take in everything from Dickens and Dylan to 17th Century Scottish verse. Then of course, there is the ghost train and our very own resident maniacal host taking us to Down Street. Steve presents the whole gamut here in typically tongue-in-cheek Hackett style!

Tribute
Camino Records CAMCD39, 2008

Gavottes / Courante / Jesu Joy / The Fountain Suite / The Earle Of Salisbury / La Catedral / El Noy De La Mare / Cascada / Sapphires / Prelude In D / Prelude In C Minor / Chaconne / La Maja De Goya

Another acoustic album but with a twist. This, as its title suggests; is a loving homage to the music that gave Steve his original inspiration: the work of Baroque masters such as J S Bach and their interpreter: Andres Segovia. Steve has taken some of the finest music from that period and with compositions of his own in the same style, seamlessly merged them into a gloriously unified whole. Not only that, but he and producer/engineer Roger King have also managed to recreate the wonderful warmth of the recordings made by Segovia in the 1920's and '30's to boot!

Out Of The Tunnel's Mouth
Wolfwork Records WWCD001 (Standard Edition)
Inside Out 0505388 (Special Edition)
WHD Entertainment IECP 110622 (Japanese Edition), 2009

Fire On the Moon / Nomads / Emerald And Ash / Tubehead/(All The) Sleepers (Send Their Dreams) / Ghost In The Glass / Still Waters / Last Train To Istanbul / Blood On The Rooftops (Live)* / A Tower Struck Down (Live)* / Firth Of Fifth (Live)* / Fly On A Windshield (Live)* / Broadway Melody Of 1974 (Live)* / Every Star In The Night Sky (Studio)*. Every Day (Live at Club Citta)+/ Fast Flower +

* *Bonus tracks on second disc of the special edition. Live tracks recorded at Stazione Birra Rome March 2009.* + *Bonus tracks on Japanese edition.*

Hackett does it again! Despite all of the current legal difficulties he has managed to put together an album that very much continues the trend towards variety of his more recent work. Fire On The Moon a haunting lament has already become a live favourite while Nomads demonstrates Steve's love of Flamenco guitar merging with some out and out rock licks. The album covers a lot of ground, and there is a lot more rock guitar work here than of late no more so than on Tubehead - not a lament for the state of London's underground railway as you might expect, but a homage to the world of valve amplifiers, Marshall stacks etc! Steve lets his love of the Blues shine again with Still Waters, a ravenous beast of a number while the on going series of travelogues continues with Last Train To Istanbul where the East meets the West in a typically evocative piece of Hackett. The special edition gives Genesis fans a treat too, containing live renditions of some of Steve's classics almost a mini "Live Archive" album.

Live Rails
Wolfwork Records WWCD002, 2010

Intro /Every Day / Fire On The Moon / Emerald And Ash / Ghost In The Glass / Ace Of Wands / Pollution C / The Steppes / Slogans / Serpentine Song / Tubehead / Spectral Mornings / Firth of Fifth / Blood On The Rooftops / Fly On A Windshield / Broadway Melody Of 1974 / Sleepers / Still Waters / Los Endos / Clocks

The fans' demand for a live album from Steve has been well and truly whetted with this magnificent offering. A double disc compiled from a selection of shows on the recent Around The World In Eighty Trains tour. Old and new mix and merge here without any problem only serving to illustrate once again how strong Steve's writing and performing capabilities are. Augmented by his new-look band this one is a must for any Hackett fan.

Beyond The Shrouded Horizon
Inside Out 0505632 (Standard 1 disc edition), Inside Out 0505630 (Special 2 disc edition), Inside Out 0505631 (2 LP vinyl edition), 2011

Loch Lomond / The Phoenix Flown / Wanderlust / Til These Eyes / Prairie Angel / A Place Called Freedom / Between The Sunset And The Coconut Palms / Waking To Life / Two Faces Of Cairo / Looking For Fantasy / Summer's Breath / Catwalk / Turn This Island Earth (Standard Edition)

Four Winds : North / Four Winds: South / Four Winds: East / Four Winds: West / Pieds En L'Air / She Said Maybe /Enter The Night / Eruption: Tommy / Reconditioned Nightmare (Limited Special Edition)

Steve's purple patch continues here with this, the 22nd (not the 24th as mentioned in the press release) studio album from the irrepressible Hackett. Beyond The Shrouded Horizon - a superb title, and one which fully describes the album. Here we go from the mist - shrouded shores of Loch Lomond to the glories and poverty of the Two Faces of Cairo. Steve has always been a painter of pictures in sound and there are plenty here but in addition there are a couple of brilliantly observed pictures in words too. A Place Called Freedom, brilliantly evokes the sweeping grandeur of the American prairie in both music and lyrics. Looking For Fantasy, is a stunningly observed portrait of some of the ladies in Steve's life with some wonderfully wry observations along the way.

There is a welcome return to the blues as well and Satan's stomp boxes get their moment to shine on Catwalk before we disappear off the planet altogether as Steve takes his audience on a trip round the universe during Turn This Island Earth.

For those fans that invested in the special edition, there is an extra forty or so minutes of music in a bewildering variety of styles. Short acoustic interludes and orchestra driven pieces are interspersed with a few familiar oldies, which have been "revisited" here. Most delightful to my ears is the reworking of Riding The Colossus under its new title Enter The Night with lyrics at last - this will be a guaranteed hit in the new live show!

Once again, there is something for fans of any aspect of Steve's music here and this one is up there with the very best from his catalogue.

Author's Note: All record company and catalogue number details in this section refer to the original release of each album and not to any subsequent re-issue or re-packaged versions unless otherwise stated.

APPENDIX 3

Collecting Hackett

For fans of any musician; the fascination of collecting various trivia associated with their hero is an ongoing and frequently expensive business. Steve has been no exception in this department and his career has been blessed with many items of collectable value over the years.

His time with Genesis generated many rare and unusual items usually in the shape of singles with those elusive B sides on them which never made it to album. Tracking these down was a challenge in itself but trying to find the original versions of some of the Genesis albums would also prove to be a stern challenge for serious fans. The fascination with "first pressings" is every bit as strong in the field of record collecting as it is in the world of "First Edition" books. I remember the artist responsible for many of the classic early Genesis album covers, Paul Whitehead, getting very excited when I showed him a copy of Nursery Cryme, which I was auctioning for charity at the 2002 Genesis Convention. Apparently it was one of only a handful of copies made to show the printers what the artwork should look like - I had no idea that the item was such an unusual one myself! Even relatively later sleeves such as Wind & Wuthering can separate a first pressing from subsequent ones. For those of you interested, the secret is in the texture of the sleeve itself. If the sleeve is a smooth lacquered effort, then it is a later printing, the original one had a textured sleeve rather like canvas itself.

Some of the more recent releases of Genesis material have become collectable in their own right. The 1999 re-issue of the band's entire catalogue in Japan as miniature CDs replete with reproduction artwork replicas of the original artwork sleeves are highly sought after and were limited in numbers. The two archive box sets also threw up a handful of rarities not least being the two sampler discs which were used to promote the sets via radio stations etc. There was also a two disc interview recorded during the now famous (or should that be infamous?) Heathrow Airport reunion meeting. Any of these will set you back a fair few pounds these days. Without doubt, though the rarest item from this period, and the one of most interest to Steve's fans, is the two disc BBC Sessions set which was compiled during the lead up to the release of the second box set in 2000. Pressed up in only a handful of copies available to band members and record company staff, this item contained almost all the band's BBC session recordings from 1970 - 72 although the final session was taken from an inferior quality bootleg recording because the original master recording could not be found at the time! Fortunately for fans, it has since been re-broadcast by BBC Radio Six with extra tracks no less! This item has never been officially released although it has since been widely bootlegged.

One track originally mooted for inclusion in the first box set was the re-worked version of Carpet Crawlers, which all the incumbents had worked on, sparking numerous rumours of a grand in-studio reunion. Sadly, this was not the case but the track was eventually released as a one-track CD single in some territories to tie in with the release of the Turn It On Again - The Hits compilation, one of EMI/Virgin's more cynical decisions.

The more recent re-issue of the entire band's back catalogue as part of EMI's flagship 5.1 remastering work, has thrown up a couple of rarities although the Gabriel era box set of albums has as its most interesting item for collectors the legendary "Genesis Plays Jackson" tape from 1970. Nonetheless, the bonus discs does contain a couple of single B sides from Steve's tenure with the band as does the second box. All of which, were of course, issued on the first and second Genesis Archive box sets a few years previously. The box containing the live albums however does give us a genuinely collectable item, with the appearance of the band's legendary Rainbow gig from October 1973. This has long been available on inferior bootleg and so fans were delighted to get their mitts on the real McCoy. Sadly, a golden opportunity was missed here to reunite the band's BBC session recordings with their respective albums but current BBC leasing policy makes this unlikely in the foreseeable future.

Even Steve's album with Quiet World is a collector's item and has only been released on CD in Japan making it quite a collectable (and expensive album). Strangely enough, the CD release does not take the opportunity of rounding up the non-album tracks from the four singles, which were released from the album between 1969 and 1971 - yes, a Quiet World single was issued after Steve had joined Genesis! Not that that did it any good in terms of commercial success though and all four of these items are seldom seen for sale these days.

Material from Steve's solo career post-Genesis has increased in value over the last few years, especially with his current high profile and frequent touring. Sadly, the days of Steve as a singles artist are now long behind him which makes those singles from his earlier solo career infinitely more collectable these days, and a brief look at the discography elsewhere in this book will give you an idea of what material there is to be searched out in those record fairs and second hand record stores which many of us still frequent from time to time! It is safe to say that any of the singles mentioned in that discography are collector's items these days but what is not so widely realised is that so are some of Steve's vinyl albums. First pressings of his albums from 1975 - 79 including the triumvirate of Voyage Of The Acolyte, Please Don't Touch and Spectral Mornings were all initially issued on the famous Charisma "Mad Hatter" label and are the most collectable; especially the first pressing of Please Don't Touch which also contained an inner lyric sleeve. Later albums such as Defector and Highly Strung are also worth checking; the former was initially issued with a limited edition poster and lyric sleeve, and the latter also contained a lyric sleeve. Other rarities in the vinyl days include the debut GTR single which, apart from the usual 7 and 12 inch versions also appeared as a 7 inch picture disc shaped like a guitar plectrum and a limited edition 7 inch version which contained a fold-out "Family Tree". Steve's charitable effort; Sailing is also a collectable and not just to Hackett fans, but also to fans of the multitude of other artists who appeared on it.

The original CD edition of Spectral Mornings also threw up an unintentional rarity in the form of the spoof track "The Cleaner" which was on the run-out of Spectral Mornings itself. This was subsequently dropped from later pressings of the CD and has only recently been restored to the newly re-mastered edition of the album. More recently, Gramy Records in Hungary re-issued the Sketches Of Satie album as a limited vinyl edition. Made from 180 gram vinyl and housed in an artwork sleeve; this release was limited to a mere 500 copies and is now a highly sought after item. Even some of Steve's later CD releases are collectable. The initial pressing of the There Are Many Sides To The Night live acoustic album for example. Originally limited to 1500 copies on the Kudos imprint, this has subsequently been re-issued by Camino Records. In fact, all of Steve's albums have now been re-issued on CD at least once making the original pressings collectable to fans. The US version of Guitar Noir also sports a collectable item in the shape of the bonus track; Cassandra, another track from the then as yet unreleased Feedback album. This was not issued on the Camino re-issue of the album but at least now has a home on the Feedback 86 album itself which finally saw the light of day in 2000.

With the recent re-emergence of vinyl as a collectable media again, there have been a few nice items for Hackett collectors to get their hands on. In 2000, Camino Records and Gramy Records of Hungary, a noted vinyl specialist, released a limited edition of the Sketches Of Satie album on 180 gram vinyl. Limited to a mere 500 copies these are highly sought after by collectors. Steve's most recent studio albums, Out Of The Tunnel's Mouth and Beyond The Shrouded Horizon have received the same treatment, with a standard and/or coloured vinyl edition being available in very limited numbers.

Promotional materials are also highly sought after and white label versions of singles or DJ radio station versions often contain edited or re-mixed versions of tracks which are not available elsewhere. A classic case of this was the Narnia single which was pressed up in two formats; one using John Perry which was the standard release and promotional versions for the US market featuring Steve Walsh from Kansas which was withdrawn because of record company objections at the time. More recently still; CD singles and "sampler" CDs have become the norm and in many cases these too contain material not available elsewhere. Strangely enough, CD samplers do not seem to be as uncommon as their vinyl counterparts but even so, the two ten track samplers from the Genesis Archive 1 and 2 sets now command a reasonable price.

Demos and out-takes from studio recording sessions also form another avenue of interest for collectors although as yet, not much has appeared from the Hackett archives in this particular area apart from the recycling of some dubious GTR era material. The Feedback 86 album was also widely available as a bootleg release long before it was issued as a bona fide CD in 2000 mainly because so many promotional cassette copies were circulated at the time. Thankfully, on the recent re-issues of Steve's EMI catalogue albums there has been a gathering up of some interesting loose ends although much more remains in the archives, and even some material was recently rescued from Steve's father's garden shed! Whether any of this will be made available to the fans remains to be seen (or heard) but it is a tantalising prospect.

Collectors can also content themselves with chasing up the various albums on which Steve has guested over the years either as a player or producer. These range from contributions of guitar parts to one or more songs, to complete pieces of music. Many of these have only appeared on albums in territories as diverse as Brazil and Italy which can make finding them quite a daunting prospect but hey, that's what collecting is all about - the thrill of the chase! For those of you without the necessary funds to acquire such juicy tidbits as Steve's contribution to Eddie Hardin's Wind In The Willows album or the two bonus tracks on the Japanese CD edition of Steve's 1999 Darktown album, then a series of "Hackett Rarities" discs have been compiled by fans and are in wide circulation among fans. At last count this is up to six discs so there is a lot to get your teeth into!

Other forms of promotional material include the ubiquitous poster; usually made and distributed for record store window or shop display or concert hall advertising; these items are highly sought after because of their rarity. Once the initial advertising period for the album/single etc is gone; these items are usually destined for the refuse bin! The same is usually the fate of concert posters. This is a shame because many of these items are works of art in their own right as well as being historical documents and anyone possessing such items should look after them well.

Concerts also generate their own forms of collectables; T shirts; badges and tour programmes are all much sought after additions to any collection. There have been T shirts made for all of Steve's solo tours over the years but for collectors of tour programmes your Hackett collection begins with the 1981 Cured tour programme which featured the usual mix of information and photographs. This was followed in 1983 by another brochure for the Highly Strung tour and a bona fide rarity in the shape of the Bay Of Kings postergramme which is extremely difficult to find these days. Momentum too, generated a tour programme but no commemorative brochure was issued for the Guitar Noir album in 1993. Subsequent tours have seen programmes including another delightful rarity in the form of the mini brochure issued to commemorate Steve's acoustic shows in Malta in 2002 and more recently his tours in support of the To Watch The Storms and Metamorpheus albums have also generated well produced and informative brochures.

The whole word of unofficial or "bootleg" recordings has effectively been dealt with elsewhere in the text of this project as indeed has the growing area of official and unofficial video/DVD material too. All in all though, there is plenty of scope for a Hackett fan to explore the world of collecting and one word of warning - collecting is infectious and it can seriously damage your bank balance!

APPENDIX 4
Discography

All dates throughout the following appendices are listed in European format of day - month - year.

7" & 12" Vinyl Singles/EP's

With QUIET WORLD...

Miss Whittington / There Is A Mountain - Dawn Records DNS1002 1969 (7")
Children Of The World / Love Is Walking - Dawn Records DNS100 1970 (7")
Rest Comfortably / Gemima - Pye Records 7N45005 1970 (7")
The Visitor / Sam - Pye Records 7N45074 4.6.71 (7")

Note: The Heather brothers recorded a further single under the name "Greenwich Village" which was issued in 1970. The tracks were as follows: In Somebody's Memory / Take It From Me. This was issued on the Dawn Records imprint with the following catalogue number: 7N17948. Whether Steve played on these recordings is not known, but other members of Quiet World, most notably Phil Henderson, did.

With GENESIS...

Happy The Man / Seven Stones - Charisma Records CB181 12.5.72
Happy The Man / Seven Stones - Charisma Records CB181 ?.10.72 (7" PS)
Twilight Alehouse - Charisma Records ?.10.73 (7" FD)
(One-sided flexi disc issued with the October edition of Zig Zag Magazine and subsequently given to the first 1000 members of the newly formed Genesis fan club, Genesis Information in October 1976)

I Know What I Like / Twilight Alehouse - Charisma Records CB224 25.1.74 (7")
Counting Out Time / Riding The Scree - Charisma Records CB238 12.11.74 (7")
The Carpet Crawlers / The Waiting Room (Evil Jam Live) - Charisma Records CB251 21.4.75 (7")
A Trick Of The Tail / Ripples - Charisma Records CB277 ?.3.76 (7")
Your Own Special Way / It's Yourself - Charisma Records CB300 ?.2.77 (7")
Match of The Day / Pigeons / Inside & Out - Charisma Records GEN001 ?.5.77 (7"PS)
Match of The Day / Pigeons / Inside & Out - Charisma/Virgin Records CDT40 1989 (3"CD)

STEVE HACKETT solo recordings...

How Can I? / Kim - Charisma Records CB312 ?.6.78 (7")
Narnia (Remixed) / Please Don't Touch - Charisma Records CB318 ?.10.78 (7")

Everyday / Lost Time In Cordoba - Charisma Records CB334 ?. 6.79 (7")
Clocks -The Angel Of Mons / Acoustic Set (live) - Charisma Records CB341 ?.9.79 (7")
Clocks -The Angel Of Mons / Acoustic Set (live) / Tigermoth (live) - Charisma Records CB341 12 ?.9.79 (12"PS)
The Show / Hercules Unchained - Charisma Records CB357 ?.3.80 (7"PS)
Sentimental Institution / The Toast - Charisma Records CB368 ?.8.80 (7"PS)
Hope I Don't Wake / Tales Of The Riverbank - Charisma Records CB385 ?.8.81 (7"PS)
Picture Postcard / Theme From "Second Chance" - Charisma Records CB390 ?.10.81 (7"PS)
Cell 151 (Edited) / Time-Lapse At Milton Keynes - Charisma Records CELL 1 16.4.83 (7"PS)
Cell 151(extended version) / The Air-Conditioned Nightmare (Live) / Time- Lapse At Milton Keynes - Charisma Records CELL 12 16.4.83 (12"PS)
(This was also a limited edition with a bonus free "white label" copy of the "Clocks" 12" single)

A Doll That's Made In Japan (Edited) / A Doll That's Made In Japan (instrumental) - Lamborghini Records LMG16 28.7.84 (7"PS)
A Doll That's Made In Japan / Just The Bones - Lamborghini Records 12MHG16 28.7.84 (12"PS)
Sailing / Sailing (Instrumental) - Epic Records EIRS 139 ?.6.90 (7"PS)
(This was the charity recording made for the "Rock Against Repatriation" project and includes Steve and a host of other celebrities)

With GTR...

When The Heart Rules The Mind / Reach Out (Never Say No) - Arista Records GTR1 28.4.86 (7"PS)
(This edition also appeared as a limited edition with poster "Family Tree" sleeve)

When The Heart Rules The Mind / Reach Out (Never Say No) - Arista Records GTRSD1 28.4.86 (7"PD)
When The Heart Rules The Mind / Reach Out (Never Say No) / Sketches In The Sun / Hackett To Bits - Arista Records GTR121 28.4.86 (12"PS)

Promotional Compact Disc Singles/EP's/Albums

The Lamb Lies Down On Broadway (live) / It (live) / Counting Out Time (live) / The Carpet Crawlers (live) / Dancing With The Moonlit Knight (live) / I Know What I Like (live) / Happy The Man / Watcher Of The Skies / In The Wilderness / Shepherd / Twilight Alehouse / Supper's Ready (live) - Virgin Records GBOX98 Sept 1998 (PS)
(Promotional 10-track sampler for Genesis Archive 1967-75)

Genesis Archive 1967-75 The Interviews - Virgin Records IVCDJBOX6 Sept 1998 (PS)
(2 CD promotional interview set accompanying the Genesis Archive 1967-75 Box set)

You Might Recall / Evidence Of Autumn / Inside & Out / I Can't Dance 12" / Illegal Alien (live) / Deep In The Motherlode (live) / Ripples (live) / The Brazilian (live) / Entangled (live) / Vancouver / It's Yourself / Mama (work in progress) - Virgin Records CDBOXDJ7 June 2000 (PS)
(10 track promotional sampler CD for Genesis Archive 1976 - 1992 Box Set)

The Carpet Crawlers 1999 - Virgin Records CRAWLCDJ August 1999 (PS)
(Promotional 1 track single)

Genesis BBC Recordings

CD1: Fountain Of Salmacis / Musical Box / The Return Of The Giant Hogweed (In Concert 2.3.72) / Shepherd / Pacidy / Let Us Now Make Love / Stagnation / Looking For Someone (Night Ride 22.2.70) / Musical Box (Sounds Of The Seventies 10.5.71).

CD2: Stagnation (Sounds Of The Seventie10.5.71) / Watcher Of The Skies / Twilight Alehouse / Get 'Em Out By Friday (Sounds Of The Seventies 25.9.72) / Harold The Barrel / Harlequin / The Return Of The Giant Hogweed (BBC Transcription Service 9.1.72) - Virgin Records No Catalogue No. 2000
(Promotional 2CD set as yet unreleased)
[The session from 9.1.72 was re-broadcast by the BBC on 19th March 2008 and amazingly enough also included The Fountain Of Salmacis which had been believed lost along with a previously unheard second take of Harold The Barrel.   All of these studio session recordings have since been issued as bonus material on their respective 5.1 remastered Genesis albums]

Turn It On Again - The Tour
Tracks are: Behind The Lines / Entangled / Dodo-Lurker / One For The Vine / Your Own Special Way / Turn It On Again / Follow You Follow Me /Abacab / Many Too Many / Los Endos - Virgin/EMI Records 0946 3 82145 9 5/ 382 1459 Nov 2006 (PS)
(Promotional 10 track sampler)
[5.1 Surround Sound promotional disc given to attendees at the "Pan European Press Conference" on 6th November 2006 to announce the reformation of the Banks/Collins/Rutherford incarnation of Genesis and to promote the first of the 3 box sets of 5.1 album remasters. The version of Abacab on this disc is not the mix eventually used on the remastered album itself]

Lost In Your Eyes/Dark As The Grave/There Are Many Sides To The Night - Permanent Records CDS Perm 11 ?.5.93
(Promotional album sampler)

Your Own Special Way - Snapper Music SRECD100P ?.9.97 (PS)
(One track single)

Between The Cold Moon & The Earth (Excerpt) / By Paved Fountain (Excerpt) / Helena (Excerpt) / Starlight/ Celebration - EMI Classics HACK001 ?.8.98 (PS)
(Promotional album sampler)

Days Of Long Ago - Camino Records CAMCD17S ?.5.99 (PS)
(One track single)

Balfour Street - INKYTHINGS LTD 2006 (PS)
(One track promotional single featuring Steve and Annabel Lamb as a fundraiser for the Hope For Children charity)

Vinyl and Compact Disc Albums.

With CANTERBURY GLASS / QUIET WORLD...

Sacred Scenes And Characters - ORK Records ORK 005 2007 (CD)
(Album recorded in 1968 but never released at the time. Steve features on one track)

The Road - Dawn Records DNLS 3007 1970 (LP)
The Road - Dawn Records ESMCD 776 1999 (CD)

With GENESIS...
Nursery Cryme - Charisma Records CAS 1052 21.10.71 (LP & Cassette)
Nursery Cryme - Charisma Records CASCD1052 1989 (CD)

Nursery Cryme - Virgin Records CASCDX1052 ?.6.94 (CD Remaster)
Nursery Cryme - Toshiba EMI Records VJCP 68092 30.3.01 (Japan CD)
Nursery Cryme - EMI Records 60999 519547 2 7 10.11.08 (5.1 Remaster)
Foxtrot - Charisma Records CAS 1058 20.11.72 (LP & Cassette)
Foxtrot - Charisma Records CASCD105 1989 (CD)
Foxtrot - Virgin Records CASCDX1058 ?.6.94 (CD Remaster)
Foxtrot - Toshiba EMI Records VJCP 68093 30.3.01 (Japan CD)
Foxtrot - EMI Records 50999 519552 2 9 10.11.08 (5.1 Remaster)
Genesis Live - Charisma Records Class 1 ?.5.73 (LP & Cassette)
Genesis Live - Charisma Records CLACD1 1989 (CD)
Genesis Live - Virgin Records CLACDX1 ?.6.94 (CD Remaster)
Genesis Live - Toshiba EMI Records VJCP 68094 30.3.01 (Japan CD)
Selling England By The Pound - Charisma Records CAS1074 ?.11.73 (LP & Cassette)
Selling England By The Pound - Charisma Records CASCD1074 1984 (CD)
Selling England By The Pound - Virgin Records CASCDX1074 ?.6.94 (CD Remaster)
Selling England By The Pound - Toshiba EMI Records VJCP 68095 31.3.01 (Japan CD)
Selling England By The Pound - EMI Records 50999 519559 2 2 10.11.08 (5.1 Remaster)
The Lamb Lies Down On Broadway - Charisma Records CGS1 ?.11.74 (LP & Cassette)
The Lamb Lies Down On Broadway - Charisma Records CGSCD1 1984 (CD)
The Lamb Lies Down On Broadway - Virgin Records CGSCDX1 ?.6.94 (CD Remaster)
The Lamb Lies Down On Broadway - Toshiba EMI Records VJCP 68096-97 31.3.01(Japan CD)
The Lamb Lies Down On Broadway - EMI Records 509995 1956323/4/5 10.11.08 (5.1 Remaster)
A Trick of The Tail - Charisma Records CDS4001 13.2.76 (LP & Cassette)
A Trick Of The Tail - Charisma Records CDSCD4001 1984 (CD)
A Trick Of The Tail - Virgin Records CDSCDX4001 ?.11.94 (CD Remaster)
A Trick Of The Tail - Toshiba EMI Records VJCP 68096 31.3.01 (Japan CD)
A Trick Of The Tail - EMI Records 94638 50462 7 2.4.07 (5.1 Remaster)
Wind & Wuthering - Charisma Records CDS4005 23.12.76 (LP & Cassette)
Wind & Wuthering - Charisma Records CDSCD4005 1985 (CD)
Wind & Wuthering - Virgin Records CDSCDX4005 ?.11.94 (CD Remaster)
Wind & Wuthering - Toshiba EMI Records VJCP 68097 31.3.01 (Japan CD)
Wind & Wuthering - EMI Records 94638 50482 5 2.4.07 (5.1 Remaster)
Seconds Out - Charisma Records GEN2001 15.10.77 (LP & Cassette)
Seconds Out - Charisma Records GENCD2001 1986 (CD)
Seconds Out - Virgin Records GECDX2001 ?.11.94 (CD Remaster)
Seconds Out - Toshiba EMI Records VJCP 68098 31.3.01 (Japan CD)
Three Sides Live - Virgin/Charisma Records GEN2002 ?.6.82 (UK edition only) (LP & Cassette)
Three Sides Live - Virgin Records GECD2002 1984 (CD) (UK Edition only)
Three Sides Live - Virgin Records GECDX200 ?.11.94 (CD Remaster UK)
Three Sides Live - Toshiba EMI Records VJCP 68105-06 31.3.01 (Japan CD)
Genesis Archive 1967-75 -Virgin Records CD BOX6 22.9.98 (CD)
Turn It On Again: The Hits - Virgin Records GENCDX8 7243 8 48523 20 (CD)
Genesis Archive 1976-1992 - Virgin Records CDBOX 7 ?.6.00 (CD)
The Platinum Collection - EMI Records 7243 63730 2 1 4.11.04 (CD)
Turn It On Again: Tour Edition - EMI Records 94639 62352 5 ?.6.07 (CD)

STEVE HACKETT solo recordings...

Voyage Of The Acolyte - Charisma Records CAS111 ?.10.75 (LP & Cassette) (UK 26)
Voyage Of The Acolyte - Chrysalis Records CHR 1112 ?.10.75 (USA) (LP & Cassette) (USA 191)
Voyage Of The Acolyte - Virgin Records CASCD111 1988 (CD)
Voyage Of The Acolyte - Caroline Records CAROL 1863 1994 (USA) (CD)
Voyage Of The Acolyte - Virgin Records CASCDR111 19.9.05 (CD Remaster)☐
Voyage Of The Acolyte - WHD Entertainment VJCP -68773 2007 (Japan CD)
Please Don't Touch - Charisma Records CDS4012 31.3.78 (LP & Cassette) (UK 38)
(Initial copies contained lyric sleeve)

Please Don't Touch - Chrysalis Records CHR1174 31.3.78 (USA) (LP & Cassette) (USA 138)
Please Don't Touch - Virgin Records CDSCD4012 ?.9.89 (CD)
Please Don't Touch - Caroline Records CAROL 1861 1994 (USA) (CD)
Please Don't Touch - Virgin Records CDSCDR4012 19.9.05 (CD Remaster)☐
Please Don't Touch - WHD Entertainment VJCP-68774 2007 (Japan CD)
Spectral Mornings - Charisma Records CDS4017 15.5.79 (LP & Cassette) (UK 22)
Spectral Mornings - Chrysalis Records CHR1223 29.5.79 (USA) (LP & Cassette) (USA 138)
Spectral Mornings - Virgin Records CDSCD4017 ?.9.89 (CD)
(Initial copies of the compact disc of this CD album had a bonus spoof track "The Cleaner" as a run out at the end of the disc. This has been restored to the recent Virgin re-issued version of the album)

Spectral Mornings - Caroline Records CAROL 1862 1994 (USA) (CD)
Spectral Mornings - Virgin Records CDSCDR4017 19.9.05 (CD Remaster)☐
Spectral Mornings - WHD Entertainment VJCP-68775 2007 (Japan CD)
Defector - Charisma Records CDS4018 13.6.80 (LP & Cassette)
(Initial Copies contained lyric sleeve and first 20,000 contained poster of Steve at the 1979 Reading Festival)

Defector - Charisma Records CL-1-3103 21.7.80 (USA) (LP & Cassette)
Defector - Virgin Records CDSCD4018 ?.9.89 (CD) (UK 9)
Defector - Caroline Records CAROL 1859 1994 (USA) (CD) (USA 144)
Defector - Virgin Records CDSCDR4018 19.9.05 (CD Remaster)☐
Defector - WHD Entertainment VJCP-68776 2007 (Japan CD)
Cured - Charisma Records CDS4021 21.8.81 (LP & Cassette) (UK 15)
(Initial copies contained lyric sleeve)

Cured - Charisma/Epic Records ARE 37632 25.9.81 (USA) (LP & Cassette) (USA 169)
Cured - Virgin Records CDSCD4021 ?.9.89 (CD)
Cured - Caroline Records CAROL 1858 1994 (USA) (CD)
Cured - Virgin Records CASCDR4021 30.5.06 (CD Remaster)☐
Cured - WHD Entertainment VJCP-68800 2007 (Japan CD)
Highly Strung - Charisma Records HACK1 23.4.83 (LP & Cassette) (UK 16)
(Initial copies contained lyric sleeve)

Highly Strung - Charisma Records BFE-38515 8.5.84 (USA) (LP & Cassette)
(No, this is not a misprint! Due to contractual problems, the US release of Highly Strung was delayed for over a whole year!)

Highly Strung - Virgin Records HACKCD1 ?.4.89 (CD)
Highly Strung - Caroline Records CAROL 1860 1994 (USA) (CD)
Highly Strung - Virgin Records HACKCDR1 30.5.06 (CD Remaster)☐
Highly Strung - WHD Entertainment VJCP-68801 2007 (Japan CD)

Bay Of Kings - Lamborghini Records LMGLP3000 19.11.83 (LP & Cassette) (UK 70)
Bay Of Kings - Chrysalis Records PV 41572 25.10.83 (USA) (LP & Cassette)
(Japanese vinyl edition was released with different artwork on album sleeve due to Japanese sensibilities over the depiction of female nudity. Strangely enough, the US edition of this album appeared before its UK counterpart)

Bay Of Kings - Start Records SCD10 ?.5.87 (CD)
Bay Of Kings - Permanent Records PERMCDL20 ?.5.94 (CD)*
Bay Of Kings - Herald/Caroline Records11HER2 1994 (USA) (CD)
Bay Of Kings - WHD Entertainment IECP-10101 2007 (Japan CD)
Till We Have Faces - Lamborghini Records LMGLP4000 ?.7.84 (LP & Cassette) (UK 54)
(Initial copies contained lyric sleeve)

Till We Have Faces - Chrysalis Records FV 41571 ?.7.84 (USA) (LP & Cassette)
Till We Have Faces - Start Records SCD11 ?.5.87 (CD)
Till We Have Faces - Permanent Records PERMCDL19 ?.5.94 (CD)*
Till We Have Faces - Chrysalis Records VK 41571 ?.5.94 (USA) (CD)
Till We Have Faces - WHD Entertainment IECP-10102 2007 (Japan CD)
GTR - Arista Records 207716 17.4.86 (LP & Cassette) (UK 41)
GTR - Arista Records 257716 17.4.86 (CD)
GTR - Arista Records ARCD8400 24.4.86 (USA) (CD) (USA 41)
GTR - Arista Records AR8400 24.4.86 (USA) (CD)
Momentum - Start Records STLP15 28.3.88 (LP & Cassette)
Momentum - Start Records SCD15 28.3.88 (CD)
Momentum - Permanent Records PERMCDL21 ?.5.94 (CD)*
Momentum - Herald/Caroline Records 9HER2 1994 (USA) (CD)
Momentum - WHD Entertainment IECP-10103 2007 (Japan CD)
Timelapse: Steve Hackett Live - Crisis Records 500 001-2 ?.8.91 (CD)
(Initial Dutch release of this album)

Timelapse - Camino Records CAMCD11 1994 (CD)
Timelapse - Blue Plate Records CAROL 1839-2 1994 (USA) (CD)
Timelapse - WHD Entertainment IECP-10104 2007 (Japan CD)
The Unauthorised Biography - Virgin Records CDVM9014 ?.10.92 (CD)
Guitar Noir - Permanent Records PERMCD13 21.5.93 (CD)
Guitar Noir - Viceroy Music VIC8008-2 21.5.93 (USA) (CD)
Guitar Noir - Camino Records CAMCD12 ?.10.97 (CD)*
Guitar Noir - WHD Entertainment IECP-10105 2007 (Japan CD)
Blues With A Feeling - Permanent Records PERMCD27 19.9.94 (CD)
Blues With A Feeling - Herald/Caroline Records 13HER2 19.9.94 (USA) (CD)
Blues With A Feeling - WHD Entertainment IECP-10106 2007 (Japan CD)
There Are Many Sides To The Night - Kudos Records KUDOSCD2 ?.10.94 (CD)
There Are Many Sides To The Night -WHD Entertainment IECP-10107 2007 (Japan CD)
Genesis Revisited - Mercury Records PHCR -1454 ?.8.96 (CD)
A Midsummer Night's Dream - EMI Records 5 56348 2 24.3.97 (CD)
A Midsummer Night's Dream - Angel Records 7243 5 56348 2 5 24.3.97 (USA) (CD)
A Midsummer Night's Dream - WHD Entertainment IECP-10110 2007 (Japan CD)
GTR Live - King Biscuit Flower Hour 70710-88021-2 ?.7.98 (CD)
Genesis Revisited - Reef Records SRECD704 22.9.97 (CD)
Watcher Of The Skies - Guardian Records 7243 8 21943 2 3 22.9.97 (USA) (CD)
(This is the Genesis Revisited album re-titled for the American market)

Discography

The Tokyo Tapes - Camino Records CAMCD15 27.4.98 (CD)
The Tokyo Tapes - Snapper Music 5567 27.4.98 (USA) (CD)
Darktown - Camino Records CAMCD17 26.4.99 (CD)
Darktown - Mercury Records PHCW 1027 ?.6.99 (CD)
(Japanese edition contained two extra tracks)

Darktown - WHD Entertainment IECP-10108 2007 (Japan CD)
Sketches Of Satie - Camino Records CAMCD20 1.5.00 (CD)
Sketches Of Satie - WHD Entertainment IECP-10111 2007 (Japan CD)
Feedback '86 - Camino Records CAMCD21 9.10.00 (CD)
Feedback '86 - WHD Entertainment IECP-10109 2007 (Japan CD)
Steve Hackett Live Archive: 70's / 80's / 90's - Camino Records CAMCD23 12.11.01 (4CD)
(This release is a four disc live set comprising recordings from Steve's 1979, 1981 and 1993 live sets - an official bootleg series, as it has been called by several fans)

Steve Hackett Live Archive: Newcastle City Hall 26.10.79 - Camino Records CAMCD23X 12.11.01 (CD)
(This is the bonus disc from the archive set available only through Steve's record company)

Steve Hackett Live Recordings 70's / 80's - Victor Records VICP-61608~9 12.11.01 (2CD)
(The '70's disc in this case is the Newcastle '79 show, released as a bonus disc in other territories)

Steve Hackett Feedback 86 / Live 90's - Victor Records VICP-61610~11 12.11.01 (2CD)
(Both of the above are the Japanese editions of the Archive, released as two double CD sets. The latter contains the first release of Feedback 86 in Japan where it had previously been unavailable)

The Genesis Files - Snapper Music SMDCD382 ?.2.02 (2CD)
Guitare Classique - XXX-21 Productions XXI CD 2 1440 ?.7.02 (Canada) (CD)
(A Canada-only compilation release)

Somewhere In South America - Camino Records CAMCD30 9.12.02 (2CD)
To Watch The Storms - Camino Records CAMCD31 26.5.03 (CD)
To Watch The Storms - Camino Records CAMCDSE 31 26.5.03 (Special Edition CD)
(Special edition contained four extra recordings)

NEARfest - Camino Records CAMCD32 ?.7.03 (CD)
To Watch The Storms - Universal Records UICE 1064 ?.11.03 (CD) #
Live Archive 03 - Camino Records CAMCD33 8.1.04 (2CD)
Live Archive 04 - Camino Records CAMCD34 28.6.04 (2CD)
Guitar Wars - Universal Records UICE 1070 2004 (Japan) (CD)
Metamorpheus - Camino Records CAMCD35 28.3.05 (CD)
Metamorpheus - WHD Entertainment IECP-10112 2007 (Japan) (CD)
Sketches Of Satie - Gramy Records/Camino Records GR-055/CAMLP20 ?.4.05 (LP)
(This was a limited edition vinyl edition on 180 gram vinyl released by the Hungarian record label Gramy in association with Camino)

Live Archive 05 - Camino Records CAMCD36 6.6.05 (2CD)
Live Archive 83 - Camino Records CAMCD37 20.2.06 (CD)
Wild Orchids - Camino Records CAMCD38 11.9.06 (CD)
Wild Orchids - Camino Records CAMCDSE38 11.9.06 (Special Edition CD)
Wild Orchids - WHD Entertainment IECP10066 ?.9.06 (Japan) (CD)
Tribute - Camino Records CAMCD39 11.2.08 (CD)
Out Of The Tunnel's Mouth - Wolfwork Records WWCD001 27.10.09
Out Of The Tunnel's Mouth - Inside Out 0505388 4.5.10 (Special Edition CD)

Out Of The Tunnel's Mouth Wolfwork Records 2010
(Limited edition 180gm vinyl available in black (1,000), smokey (200) & white (300))

Out Of The Tunnel's Mouth - WHD Entertainment   IECP 110622 2010 (Japan)
(Contains two non-album tracks: Everyday live from Club Citta and a new studio track: Fast Flower)

Steve Hackett - Live Rails - Wolfwork Records WWCD002 15.11.10
Beyond The Shrouded Horizon (Standard edition)   Inside Out 0505632 26.9.11
Beyond The Shrouded Horizon (Special edition)   Inside Out 0505630 26.9.11
Beyond The Shrouded Horizon (Black vinyl edition)   Inside Out 0505631 26.9.11
Beyond The Shrouded Horizon (Transparent blue vinyl edition) Inside Out 0505631 11.11

* Albums marked thus were originally issued on the Lamborghini Records label and subsequent compact disc editions appeared on the Start Records label and later on, on Steve's (now former) label: Camino. These albums have also had additional tracks added to them and have been re-mastered.

\# This is the Japanese edition of the album, which features a revised running order, one track unavailable on the previous releases and different artwork design on the sleeve.

☐ These are the recently issued Virgin re-masters of Steve's Charisma solo albums each containing extra tracks and fully re-mastered by Steve himself and Ben Fenner at MAP Studios.

(Japan CD) = these were the Japanese editions of the 1994 Genesis "Definitive Remasters" series which in Japan were issued in replica artwork sleeves and were only available for a limited time making them very collectable).

The WHD Entertainment re-issues of Steve's solo albums were housed in a special boxed set, which was accompanied by a "bonus" disc of a DVD film of Steve's gig at the Bottom Line Club NY in 1992.

(UK 15) = highest chart position achieved by single/album on initial release in the UK and USA.

The latest album from Steve comes in a plethora of editions, a standard edition, limited edition 2CD set with media book, and a limited edition 180 gram vinyl edition. No doubt there will be a Japanese edition too, to tempt the more die hard Hackett collectors.

(PS) = Picture sleeve
(PD) = Picture disc
(FD) = Flexi disc

My thanks to Dick Driver, Billy Budis and Jonathan Dann for their help with the release dates and catalogue information for several of the overseas releases.

Associated Artists, Compilations and Session Work

Peter Banks: Two Sides Of Peter Banks - Sovereign Records SVNA 7256 1973
Ritchie: Vao De Coracao - Epic Records 14468 1983 (Brazil)
Kimmy: Paint It Black / Just For You And I - RCA Records 1010968 1984 (Brazil)
(7" Single performed by Steve's now ex-wife: Kim Poor. A Brazil-only release)
Night Wing: My Kingdom Come - Gull Records 1040 1984
Eddie Hardin / Zak Starkey: Wind In The Willows - President Records PTLS 1078 1985
Box Of Frogs: Strange Land - Epic Records 26375 1986
Ritchie: Loucura & Magica - Philips Records 832.263-1 1987 (Brazil)
David Palmer: We Know What We Like - RCA Records RCA RD 86242 1987
David Palmer: Object Of Fantasy - RCA Records 7960-2 RC 1989
Various Artists: Guitar Speak III - IRS Records X2-13111 1991 (USA)
(Contains the unreleased track: A Life In Movies)
Gandalf: Gallery Of Dreams - Columbia Records COL 471064-2 1992
Julian Colbeck: Back To Bach - EG Records EEG 2104-2 1992
Mae McKenna: Mirage & Reality - Virgin Records VJCP 57 1992
Cristiano Prunas: Cippo - Sugar/RTI 4427-2 1995 (Italy)
Max Bacon: The Higher You Climb - Now And Then Records NTHEN23 1996
John Wetton: Arkangel - Eagle Records EAGCD020 1998
Ian MacDonald: Drivers Eyes - Camino Records CAMCD18 19/7/99
Various Artists: Best Magazine - AG 6/00 2000
Ian Mosley / Ben Castle: Postmankind - Racket Records 10 2001
John Wetton: Sinister - Giant Electric Pea Records GEPCD1029 2001
Gordian Knot: Emergent - Sensory Records SR3016 2003
Various Artists: Progressive Times - Inside And Out Music SPV8000608 2003
(German Sampler CD for the record label including Brand New and Firth Of Fifth)
Djabe: Tancolnak A Kazlak - Gramy Records GR-039 2003
Various Artists: Guitar Wars - Universal Music UICE 1070 2004
Nick Magnus: Hexameron - Magick Nuns Records MNCD1001 ?/7/04
John Hackett: Checking Out Of London - Hacktrax Records HTRX002 7/2/05
Chris Squire: Chris Squire's Swiss Choir - Stone Ghost CV 009 2007
Simon Collins: U Catastrophe - Razor & Tie 82988 2008
John Hackett: Prelude To Summer - Hacktrax HTRX004 3/11/08
Djabe: Sipi Benefit Concert - Gramy Records GR-080 2009
Jim McCarthy: Sitting On The Top Of Time - Troubadour TRBCD010 2009
Algebra: J L - ? 2009 (Italy)
Nick Magnus: Children Of Another God - Magick Nuns Records MNCD 1002 2010
Gary Husband: Dirty And Beautiful Vol 1 - No Catalogue Number 2010
Marco Lo Muscio: The Book Of Bilbo And Gandalf - Drycastle Records DR-035 010
Cavalli Cocchi Lanzetti: Roversi CCLR - Esoteric Recordings ECLEC 2280 2011
Djabe: In The Footsteps Of Attila And Genghis- Gramy Records GR-094 2011
Steven Wilson: Grace For Drowning - K-Scope Records KSCOPE176 2011
John Wetton: Raised In Captivity - Frontiers Records FR CD 522 2011

APPENDIX 5

Filmography

Steve's fans have been lucky to have several wonderful visual, filmed documents, which have captured several important parts of his career. Although some of the footage listed below has now surfaced on the Genesis 5.1 box sets, not all of the items below have been officially sanctioned. They are all nonetheless important to the documentation of Steve's career. This is a brief list of the more important items in his visual archive both while he was a member of Genesis and his subsequent solo career.

"Pop Deux" Belgian TV studios 1972
First visual representation of the band with both Steve and Phil Collins. Tracks: *The Musical Box/ Fountain Of Salmacis/Twilight Alehouse/The Return Of The Giant Hogweed*. Now available as an official release on the DVD disc of Foxtrot on the 1970-75 box set.

Bataclan Club Paris 10th February 1973
ORTF "Canal Jimmy" French TV Broadcast. Tracks: *The Musical Box* (including Peter in the now famous Fox head and red dress); *The Return Of The Giant Hogweed/Supper's Ready/The Knife* plus interviews with band members. Now available as an official release on the DVD disc of Selling England By The Pound on the 1970-75 box set.

"Tony Stratton-Smith Presents... Genesis In Concert" 30th & 31st October 1973
Promotional film recorded for cinematic release at the Shepperton Film Studios but subsequently shelved. Now available as an official release on the DVD disc of Selling England By The Pound on the 1970-75 box set. Tracks: *Watcher Of The Skies/Dancing With The Moonlit Knight/I Know What I Like/Musical Box/Supper's Ready*. It was the footage of I Know What I Like from this recording that was to have been used as the promotional video for the single but was deemed unsuitable by the band.

"Midnight Special" Burbank Studios Hollywood 19th December 1973
Tracks: *The Musical Box/Watcher Of The Skies*. Interesting because the versions of both tracks differ slightly either musically or lyrically from the recorded versions. Now available as an official release on the bonus DVD disc on the 1970-75 box set.

"Melody" ORTF French TV Studios broadcast 12th January 1974
Tracks: *I Know What I Like/Supper's Ready*. Now available as an official release on the DVD disc of The Lamb Lies Down On Broadway on the 1970-75 box set.

"Trefpunkte" WDR German TV Broadcast 24th January 1975

The only officially available footage from The Lamb Lies Down On Broadway tour featuring interview with promoter Billy Graham and backstage and concert footage of the Shrine Auditorium gig including clips of *In The Cage* and *The Colony of Slippermen*.

"The Lamb Live Down On Broadway"

Compilation DVD created by long time Genesis fan, Chris West and containing all the known private Super 8mm footage of the band from this tour lovingly organised into its correct sequence and lasting almost 76 minutes in total.

Festhalle Bern 29th March 1975

Another recently surfaced item and an enjoyable one at that, comprising some superior quality audience footage from the gig including segments of: *The Lamb Lies Down On Broadway/Fly On A Windshield/Broadway Melody Of 74/In The Cage/Back In NYC/Counting Out Time/The Colony Of Slippermen/It/Musical Box*. No doubt its appearance caused Chris West to tear his hair out! 27 Minutes.

Video clips from all three of the above Lamb Lies Down items are now available as part of an official release in the 'Slideshow' on the DVD disc of The Lamb Lies Down On Broadway on the 1970-75 box set.

Patinoire Rheims 16th May 1975

Yet another reason for poor old Mr West to have a fit! Yes, a whole 2 minutes and 24 seconds of pro shot footage of Counting Out Time from this gig. Filmed from multiple angles and evidently including a pre-gig shot of the audience and road crew. This one begs the all important questions: where is the rest of it and who did the filming? French TV sources are silent on this one but surely there must be more of it available, somewhere?

"Genesis In Concert" 1976 Film

Cinematic release by Miramax featuring footage from the band's gigs at Stafford and Glasgow on the A Trick Of The Tail tour of 1976. Tracks: *Intro, I Know What I Like/Fly On A Windshield/Carpet Crawlers/Cinema Show (pt2)/Entangled/Supper's Ready Pt2/Los Endos*. Now available as an official release on the DVD disc of A Trick Of The Tail on the 1976-82 box set.

Rainbow Theatre London January 1977

Japanese TV broadcast of: *11th Earl Of Mar/One For The Vine/Firth Of Fifth*.

Some sections of the above show feature on the official box set release of Wind And Wuthering that is included in the 1976-82 box set.

Mike Douglas Show US TV March 1977

Tracks: *Your Own Special Way/Afterglow*. Now available as an official release on the DVD disc of Wind And Wuthering on the 1976-82 box set.

Moody Coliseum Dallas 21st March 1977

Tracks: *Firth Of Fifth//The Lamb Lies Down On Broadway/Musical Box (Closing Section)/Dance On A Volcano/Los Endos*.

There is reputed to be footage in the TV archives of gigs in Paris and Brazil from the 1977 tours in addition to an alleged pro-shot film of the show from Houston although exact details of all of the above are the subject of conjecture at present.

Isstadion Stockholm 4th June 1977

Another recent escapee from the vaults. This is a seven minute slice through several songs from this gig including Squonk, One For The Vine and Firth Of Fifth. Privately filmed but above average quality, this is another tantalising glimpse of the band at what for many fans view (me included) as their creative apogee.

Milton Keynes Concert Bowl 2nd October 1982
Complete onstage recording of the "Reunion" gig, which featured Steve for the last two songs. The existence of this film has been known for quite some time but its current location remains a mystery - although educated guesses may be made if you wish - the author could not possibly comment!

"Spectral Mornings"
The most recent official DVD is also the oldest. This TV broadcast released by ARD on 20th May 2005 comprises footage from Steve's first solo tour in support of the Please Don't Touch album and recorded on 8th November 1978, this DVD captures Steve as he set out on his first solo tour and includes classic performances from his first two solo albums, as well as the as yet unreleased third album: Spectral Mornings, making it an essential item for Hackett collectors. Track Listing: *Please Don't Touch/Racing in A/Ace Of Wands/Narnia/A Tower Struck Down/ Spectral Mornings/Kim/Acoustic Set (Including The Optigan)/Shadow Of The Hierophant/Clocks-The Angel Of Mons/Carry On Up The Vicarage(*)/Band Intros (*)/Star Of Sirius (*)* (*) = DVD bonus tracks. Radio Bremen ISBN 3-937308-57-1, 71 Minutes.

The Making Of GTR
The first video release to feature Steve filmed during the making of the GTR album with Steve Howe. Released domestically in the US, it is an interesting look at the making of the one and only GTR album and includes interviews with all the band members and rehearsal footage, making it a worthwhile addition to any collection of material by Steve.
RCA/Columbia Video 43396-60633. 30 Minutes.

GTR Live
An official release of the band's concert from the Alabamahalle in Munich on 22nd September 1986. Available only in Japan at present, this film features the following tracks: *Jekyll And Hyde/Here I Wait/The Hunter/When The Heart Rules The Mind/Prizefighters/Imagining/Hackett To Bits (Edit)/Roundabout/You Can Still Get Through/Reach Out (Never Say No)*. WHD Entertainment IEBP-10015. 45 Minutes.

Steve Hackett - Live
A long overdue live video from Steve appeared in 1991. Initially recorded on 13th September 1990 for the Central TV "Bedrock" series and screened on UK TV, this video was eventually released on Castle Music Pictures in 1991. The video contained the following tracks: *Camino Royale/Please Don't Touch/Everyday/In That Quiet Earth/Depth Charge/Wonderpatch/ In The Heart Of The City/Black Light/Horizons/Jacuzzi/Theatre Of Sleep/Jazz Jam/Spectral Mornings/Clocks.*
Castle Music Promotions CMP6064. 60 Minutes.

Horizons
This was a re-issue of the above by Classic Rock Productions released in 2003 and which featured an edited version of the above. CRL015.

The Tokyo Tapes
Steve's performances in Tokyo in December 1996 for the "Genesis Revisited album were captured on video and released by his own record company; Camino Records in 1997. This was Steve's first video to be released on DVD format. The video captures the entire show as performed by Steve and his band of intrepid musos and contains the following tracks:
Watcher Of The Skies/Riding The Colossus/Firth Of Fifth/Battle Lines/Camino Royale/In The Court Of The Crimson King/Horizons/Walking Away From Rainbows/Heat Of The Moment/In That Quiet Earth/A Vampyre With A Healthy Appetite/I Talk To The Wind/Shadow Of The

Hierophant/Los Endos/Black Light/The Steppes/I Know What I Like. The DVD version, released in 2001 contained a bonus eighteen minutes of rehearsal footage.
CAMVT15 104 Minutes CAMDV15 122 Minutes

Somewhere In South America
The next release from the Hackett camp captured another fine performance from Steve's South American rock tour in 2001 with a set list which comprised: *The Floating Seventh/Mechanical Bride/Medley/Serpentine Song/Watcher Of The Skies/Hairless Heart/ Firth Of Fifth/Riding The Colossus/Pollution B/The Steppes/Gnossienne #1/Walking Away From Rainbows/Sierra Quemada/The Wall Of Knives/A Vampyre With A Healthy Appetite/A Tower Struck Down/Lucridus/Darktown/Camino Royale/In Memoriam/Horizons/Los Endos.* The DVD version was released with bonus footage from Steve's Italian tour in 2000 and was packaged with the two CD audio soundtrack to the gig. CAMTV29. 90 Minutes CAMDV29 104 minutes.

Hungarian Horizons
Continued the trend for visually documenting Steve's tours. This was the first to be released solely as a DVD without an accompanying VHS version and once again it was packaged with the two CD audio soundtrack. Filmed at Steve's 2002 gig at the Petofi Csarnok in Budapest; this release captures the acoustic side of Hackett containing bonus rehearsal and backstage footage. Track listing: *Horizons/Gnossienne #1/Bourree/Bacchus/Firth Of Fifth/Bay Of Kings/Syrinx/Imagining/Second Chance/Jacuzzi/Overnight Sleeper/The Barren Land/Black Light/Kim/Time Lapse At Milton Keynes/The Chinese Jam/Concerto In D/Hairless Heart/Cinema Paradiso/Mustard Seed/Gymnopedie No1/Jazz On A Summer's Night/Little Cloud/ Cavalcanti/Walking Away From Rainbows/Andante In C/Concert For Munich/The Journey/The Skye Boat Song/By Paved Fountain/Etude In A Minor/Blood On The Rooftops/Hands Of The Priestess/C Minor Triplets/End Of Day/Ace Of Wands/Idylle-Aubade-Meditiation.*
CAMDV30 104 Minutes.

To Watch The Storms EPK
An interesting look behind the making of, and inspirations for the To Watch The Storms album.

Guitar Wars
An unlikely event staged where else but in Japan to celebrate the 20th anniversary of the Hard Rock Café chain, this guitar fest featured Steve in the company of such guitar "giants" as Paul Gilbert, Nuno Bettencourt and John Paul Jones. The DVD was recorded at the Akasaka Blitz on 28th and 29th August 2003. Steve's contribution came in the shape of a short set comprising: *Classical Gas/Firth Of Fifth/Mechanical Bride/Los Endos* as well as Steve's appearance in the grand finale; an all-star performance of the Led Zeppelin classic: Rock And Roll. Not perhaps the best way to see our hero but an interesting item nonetheless! So far this DVD has only been issued in Japan by Universal Music.

Once Above A Time
Brings the full spectacle of his 2004 tour to eager fans. Filmed once again at Hungary's Petofi Csarnok on 3rd April 2004 and released by Eagle Vision on 22nd November of that year; this is music without props. A genuine "live" video capturing the show with little gimmickry and containing the usual amusing bonus backstage and rehearsal footage and comprising the following tracks: *Valley Of The Kings/Mechanical Bride/Circus Of Becoming/Frozen Statues/Slogans/Serpentine Song/Ace Of Wands/Hammer In The Sand/Blood On The Rooftops/ Fly On A Windshield/Please Don't Touch/Firth Of Fifth/If You Can't Find Heaven/Darktown/ Brand*

New/The Air-Conditioned Nightmare/Every Day/Clocks/Spectral Mornings/Los Endos.
Eagle Vision EREDV451 104 Minutes.

Wild Orchids EPK
Another promotional DVD giving an interesting look at the making of Steve's latest rock album including interview and studio performance footage.

Steve Hackett In New York 1992
Another lovely item from Japan. This was the bonus disc in the Japanese boxed set of remastered Hackett albums issued in 2007 and as such it is a real gem. Strangely enough, this is not an official release, Steve had no knowledge of it until recently! Steve's evening gig from the same venue on 18th September had been broadcast by US/Japanese "pay-per-view" TV at the time in an edited hour-long format (see details elsewhere). What we have here, however, is the complete gig from the afternoon show at the Bottom Line on the same date and not from a subsequent gig at the same venue as stated on the packaging! As such it is another essential visual item. Track listing: *Opening Medley (inc: Myopia-Los Endos-Ace of Wands)/Camino Royale/Vampyre With A Healthy Appetite/Flight Of The Condor/Take These Pearls/Always Somewhere Else/In The Heart Of The City/Walking Away From Rainbows/There Are Many Sides To The Night/In That Quiet Earth/Depth Charge/Every Day/Blood On The Rooftops/Horizons/The Stumble.* WHD Entertainment IEZP-6 DVD 1 Disc 15.

Tribute EPK
The latest in this series of promotional DVDs for Steve's albums once again featuring studio performance and interviews.

Gandalf & Friends Live In Vienna
Another interesting item. This is the concert performed by Gandalf in 1992. Okay, so Steve only appears on one track; Face In The Mirror, which was issued as a promotional video. Nevertheless, completists will want this one for their collections. Prudence 398.6748.2 (CD and DVD)

Sipi Benefit Concert
A tribute to Sipos Andras, the recently deceased founder member of Djabe. Steve has been a contributor to several Djabe projects and was invited to take part in this concert and features on several tracks as well as performing a version of his acoustic set.
Gramy Records GR-081 (DVD)

Thoughts Of Hackett
Author's ninety minute interview filmed in Twickenham 18th April 2009 for inclusion as a DVD with the first edition hardback of 'Sketches Of Hackett'. Wymer WLY001

TV And Unofficial Video Recordings

Fortunately for Steve's fans; his career has also been well documented by TV broadcasts and more recently by private films made by fans at gigs with a variety of recording equipment and with varying degrees of success! In some cases, these are the only visual documents of a particular gig or tour and are vital additions to any collection and this is a brief look at some of these items.

Home Movies. Super 8mm footage compiled by a friend of Steve's in the summer of 1968 and recently transferred to DVD featuring Steve and friends with a variety of "props" and in various locations in and around the London area.

How Can I? (Promotional Video) 1978.

Shadow Of The Hierophant/Clocks (Circus Swedish TV Studio performance) 1978.

Every Day/Clocks (Promotional Videos) 1979.

Reading Festival 26.8.79 (Private Film) Track Listing: *If You Break It, It's Yours/Tigermoth/Every Day/The Optigon/A Tower Struck Down/Spectral Mornings/Clocks/I Know What I Like.*

The Show (Promotional Video) 1980.

Grand Casino Montreux (Japanese TV "WowWow" broadcast) Montreux Jazz Festival 13.7.80: *Slogans/Every Day/Spectral Mornings/Time To Get Out/The Steppes/Narnia/Acoustic Set/Jacuzzi/A Tower Struck Down/ Clocks.* 63 Minutes.

Grand Casino Montreux (Swiss TV "Canards Sauvages" broadcast) Montreux Jazz Festival 13.7.80: *Jacuzzi/A Tower Struck Down/Clocks (Complete Version)/Land Of A Thousand Autumns/Please Don't Touch/Spectral Mornings.*
Bottom Line Club New York City 30.9.80 (Japanese TV broadcast) *Slogans/Everyday/The Red Flower Of Taichi Blooms Everywhere/Tigermoth/Time To Get Out/The Steppes/Acoustic Set/Kim/Narnia/Jacuzzi/Sentimental Institution/Spectral Mornings/A Tower Struck Down(Inc: Overnight Sleeper instrumental section)/Clocks/ The Show/It's Now Or Never (Oh Sole Mio)/Please Don't Touch.*

Rock City Nottingham 27.8.81 (UK TV/WOT TV Video 81016)
The Air- Conditioned Nightmare/ Funny Feeling/Hope I Don't Wake/Jacuzzi/Slogans. 25 Mins.

Triangle Theatre Rochester NY 30.10.81 (Unreleased Pro Shot)
The Air Conditioned Nightmare/Jacuzzi/ Funny Feeling/Ace Of Wands/Picture Postcard/The Steppes/Everyday/The Red Flower Of Taichi Blooms Everywhere/Tigermoth/Hope I Don't Wake/Slogans/A Tower Struck Down/Spectral Mornings/Land Of A Thousand Autumns/Please Don't Touch/The Show/Clocks.

Elixii Festival Brest 15.7.82 (French TV): *Hope I Don't Wake/Funny Feeling.*

Interview with Steve and Kim (Private Film) Montreal 1982 .

Cell 151 (Promotional Video).

Highly Strung UK TV advertisements for album (x2) 1983 the latter also advertising Steve's gig at the Hammersmith Odeon in London.

Gas Tank (Channel 4 TV) 1982. Steve appeared on this show twice the first featured performances of My Baby/CC Rider with Suzi Quatro and the second featured *Camino Royale,* an interview with the show's host Rick Wakeman, and a performance of *Hackett's Boogie.* More recently still, a series of out-takes from this series has emerged and is now available on DVD comprising the following tracks: *Camino Royale* (Takes 1-6)/*Blues Jam* (Take 1-2)/*Blues Jam Reprise* (Take 1) as well as out-takes from Suzi Quatro's performance as well.

Chas & Dave's Happy Hour ITV 1982/83. An impromptu appearance by Steve on this short-lived TV show. Steve performed a ramshackle version of *Cell 151* and *Camino Royale.*

Plymouth Polytechnic 1.11.83 Backstage interview with Steve and performance of *Bay Of Kings.*

A Doll That's Made In Japan (Austrian TV performance) 1984.

When The Heart Rules The Mind (Promotional Video) 1986.
The Hunter (Promotional Video) 1986.

American Bandstand (US TV) Performance of: *When The Heart Rules The Mind/The Hunter* and interview with Hackett and Howe 1986.

First Run (US TV) Hackett and Howe as guest VJs 1986.

Munich Alabamahalle 22.9.86 (German TV) Live broadcast and interviews includes performances of *Jekyll And Hyde/Here I Wait/The Hunter/When The Heart Rules The Mind/Imagining/You Can Still Get Through/ Reach Out (Never Say No)*

Breakfast Time BBC TV 25.4.88 Interview and acoustic performance and demonstration of the Stepp DGI guitar synthesiser.

Teatro Orfeo Milan 22.5.88 (Edited Private Film)
Hands Of The Priestess/ Jacuzzi/Cavalcanti/Second Chance/Portrait Of A Brazilian Lady/Still Life/Jazz On A Summer's Night/Concert For Munich/Notre Dame Des Fleurs/Momentum/Guitar-Stepp DGI Improvisation/Kim/Cuckoo Cocoon/The Carrot That Killed My Sister.
"In Concert" RAI Italian TV 22.5.88 Three tracks from the Milan gig plus interview.

Paradiso Amsterdam 26.5.88 (Complete Private Film)
Horizons/Bay Of Kings/A Bed, A Chair & A Guitar/Time Lapse At Milton Keynes/Tales Of The Riverbank/Ace Of Wands/ Hands Of The Priestess/Overnight Sleeper/Cavalcanti/Second Chance/Portrait Of A Brazilian Lady/ Still Life/Silver/Munich/Notre Dame Des Fleurs/Momentum/Stepp DGI Improvisation/The Steppes/ Classical Improvisation (inc: Finlandia)/Kim/The Carrot That Killed My Sister/Blood On The Rooftops/Troubled Spirit.

Het Noordelight Tilburg 28.5.88 (Complete Private Film) Track Listing as above.

Zeche Bochum 17.9.88 (Complete Private Film)
Medley/Horizons/Bay Of kings/A Bed, A Chair & A Guitar/Time Lapse At Milton Keynes/Cavalcanti/Tales Of The Riverbank/Portrait Of A Brazilian Lady/Still Life/Harmonics/Notre Dame Des Fleurs/Momentum/Medley/The Barren Land/Chinese Jam/Silver/Troubled Spirit/The Vigil/Medley/End Of Day/Horizons/Medley.

Sailing (Promotional Video) 1990.

P.O.P. (German TV) 24.9.90

Face In The Mirror (Promotional Video for Gandalf single featuring Steve) 1992.

Bottom Line Club New York 18.9.92 (Satellite TV Broadcast).

Richmond Hill Hotel London TWR interview 23.4.93 (Private Film).

Villa Torlonia Frascati Italy 5.7.93 (Complete Private Film)
Myopia Medley/Camino Royale/A Vampyre With A Healthy Appetite/Sierra Quemada/Take These Pearls/ In The Heart Of The City/Walking Away From Rainbows/There Are Many Sides To The Night/Dark Is The Grave/Depth Charge/Bass-Drum Duet/Lost In Your Eyes/Everyday/Spectral Mornings/Clocks/Acoustic Set/Horizons/Cinema Paradiso/In That Quiet Earth.

Stadio del Plebiscito Selvazzano Padua 6.7.93 (Complete Private Film)
Track Listing as above.

Cabaret San Jose 12.11.93 (Complete Private Film)
Myopia Medley/Please Don't Touch/Camino Royale/A Vampyre With A Healthy Appetite/Shadow

Of The Hierophant/Take These Pearls/Sierra Quemada/Depth Charge/In The Heart Of The City/Walking Away From Rainbows/There Are Many Sides To The Night/Acoustic Set/Bass-Drum Duet/Air Conditioned Nightmare/Lost In Your Eyes/Everyday/Spectral Mornings/Clocks/Acoustic Reprise/Horizons/ Cinema Paradiso/In That Quiet Earth.

Golden Stag TV Festival Brasov 7.9.94 (Romanian TV).

Olgiate Comasco 26.11.94 (Complete Private Film)
Skye Boat Song/Black Light/Kim/ Second Chance/Oh, How I Love You/The Journey/Harmonics (The Baroque)/Walking Away From Rainbows/Cavalcanti/Tales Of The Riverbank/A Blue Part Of Town/There Are Many Sides To The Night/Ace Of Wands/Cinema Paradiso/Blues Jam/Jazz On A Summer's Night/Medley.

Sonny Boy Club Treviso 1.12.94 (Complete Private Film)
Skye Boat song/Horizons/ Black Light/Medley/Time Lapse At Milton Keynes/Beja Flor/Kim/Second Chance/Oh, How I Love You/The Journey/Momentum/Bacchus/Walking Away From Rainbows/Cavalcanti/Tales Of The Riverbank/Andante In C/A Blue Part Of Town/There Are Many Sides To The Night/Chinese Jam/Ace Of Wands/Cinema Paradiso/Blues Jam/Jazz On A Summer's Night/Medley/End Of Day.

(VH1) 23.4.97 Interview and acoustic performance: *All Is Mended/By Paved Fountain.*

(Superchannel TV) 24.2.98

Vivegano Festival 9.7.00 (Incomplete Private Film)
Pre-gig Q & A Session/Soundcheck/*Mechanical Bride/Watcher Of The Skies/Hairless Heart/Firth Of Fifth/The Steppes/Walking Away From Rainbows/Sierra Quemada/ Shadow Of The Hierophant/Darktown/Los Endos.*

Castello Malatestiana Cesena 11.7.00 (Incomplete Private Film)
Pre-gig Q & A Session/*Serpentine Song/Watcher Of The Skies/Hairless Heart/Firth Of Fifth* / After Gig footage

Sketches Of Satie (Hungarian TV) 2000. Interview and performances by Steve and John.

Outwitting Hitler (Show Time US TV Documentary) 2002.
Uses music from several of Steve's albums.

Poker D'Assisi Blues Jam 26.4.02 (Private Film)

Teatro Sociale Trento Italy 28.4.02 (Private footage of concert rehearsals).

Theatre Of Living Arts Philadelphia 1.7.02 (Incomplete Private Film)
Watcher Of The Skies/Hairless Heart/Firth of Fifth/Riding The Colossus/Pollution B/The Steppes/In Memoriam/ Slave Girls/A Vampyre With A Healthy Appetite/Spectral Mornings/Lucridus/Darktown/Camino Royale/Every Day/Los Endos Medley.

Borders Bookstore Columbus Ohio 10.8.02 (Complete Private Film)

Borders Bookstore Cleveland Heights 11.8.02 (Complete Private Film)
Intro Chat/*Smoke On the Water/Classical Jazz/Brand New-Blood On The Rooftops-Horizons/By Paved Fountain/The Journey/The Pool Of Memory And The Pool Of Forgetfulness/This Vast Life/Bay Of Kings.*

Borders Bookstore Bryn Mawr 11.8.02 (Complete Private Film)
Classical Jazz/Black Light/Cavalcanti/Tales Of The Riverbank/Brand New-Mexico City/Rebecca-Horizons/Bouree/Tribute To Segovia/Skye Boat Song/Pease Blossom/By Paved Fountain/Black

Light/The Pool Of Memory And The Pool Of Forgetfulness/Bay Of Kings.

Borders Bookstore Chicago 12.8.02 (Complete Private Film).
Live Music Hall Cologne 6.10.03 (Complete Private Film)
Mechanical Bride/Serpentine Song/Watcher Of The Skies/Hairless Heart/Darktown/Camino Royale / Pollution B/The Steppes/ Acoustic Medley/Kim/Walking Away From Rainbows / Slogans / Every Day/Please Don't Touch/Firth Of Fifth/The Wall Of Knives/A Vampyre With A Healthy Appetite/Spectral Mornings/Brand New/Los Endos/Clocks/In That Quiet Earth.

Kubo Cafe Leini (Turin) 25.3.04 (Complete Private Film)
Valley Of The Kings/Mechanical Bride/Circus Of Becoming/Frozen Statues/Slogans/Serpentine Song/Ace Of Wands/Hammer In The Sand/Acoustic Set/Horizons/Kim/Blood On The Rooftops/Fly On A Windshield/Please Don't Touch/A Dark Night In Toytown/Darktown/Brand New/The Air Conditioned Nightmare / Everyday/ Clocks/Spectral Mornings/Los Endos.

Stazione Birra Rome 28.3.04 (Complete Private Film)
Valley Of The Kings/Mechanical Bride/Circus Of Becoming/Frozen Statues/Slogans/Serpentine Song/Ace of Wands/Hammer In The Sand/Acoustic Set/Horizons/Kim/Blood On The Rooftops/Fly On A Windshield/Please Don't Touch/Firth Of Fifth/A Dark Night In Toytown/Darktown/Brand New/The Air-Conditioned Nightmare/Every Day/Clocks - The Angel Of Mons/Spectral Mornings/Los Endos.
Foro Italico Stadio Del Tennis Rome 26.7.04 (Incomplete Private Film)
Mechanical Bride/Circus of Becoming/Frozen Statues/ Slogans/Serpentine Song/Ace Of Wands / Hammer In The Sand / Blood On The Rooftops / Brand New / Every Day / Spectral Mornings / Los Endos.

Stadio Della Verdura Palermo 28.7.04 (Incomplete Private Film).

Metamorpheus Interview ?.2.05 (Promotional interview DVD) 15 Minutes.

Pacific Road Arts Centre Birkenhead 30.4.05 (Incomplete Private Film).

TVE 3 Madrid TV Studios 21.5.05.
Intro/Jam/Jacuzzi-Overnight Sleeper/Horizons/Walking Away From Rainbows/Bacchus-Firth Of Fifth-Bacchus/The Pool Of Memory And The Pool Of Forgetfulness/Bay Of Kings/After The Ordeal/Hairless Heart/Ace Of Wands.

Tower Ballroom Buffalo NY 14.10.05 (Incomplete Private Film)
Jaczzi/Bacchus/Firth Of Fifth/Improvisation/The Red Flower Of Taichi Blooms Everywhere / Hands Of The Priestess/After The Ordeal/Hairless Heart/M3/Imagining/Second Chance/Jazz On A Summer's Night/Next Time Around/Kim/The Journey/Ace Of Wands/Walking Away From Rainbows/Gnossienne #1.

Astoria London 28.5.06 (Private film) Steve's appearance at the 2006 Genesis Convention as guest to his brother John Hackett for two tracks: *A Tower Struck Down and Ego And Id.*

Vaillant Palace Genoa 12.3.09 (Complete Private Film)
Fire On The Moon/ Every Day/Ace Of Wands/Pollution B/The Steppes/Darktown/Slogans/ Serpentine Song/Firth Of Fifth/Acoustic Set/Walking Away From Rainbows/Blood On The Rooftops/Mechanical Bride/Spectral Mornings/Wall Of Knives/Fly On A Windshield/Please Don't Touch/A Tower Struck Down/In That Quiet Earth/Storm Chaser/Los Endos/Clocks.

Estival Jazz Festival Lugano Switzerland 4.7.09 (Swiss TV Broadcast)
Fire On The Moon/Everyday/Ace Of Wands/Pollution B/The Steppes/Firth of Fifth/Walking Away From Rainbows/Blood On The Rooftops / Mechanical Bride / Spectral Mornings / Los Endos / Clocks / Interview with Steve.

Fabrik Hamburg 30.10.09 (Private Recording)
Mechanical Bride/Fire On The Moon/Everyday/Emerald And Ash/Ghost In The Glass/Ace Of Wands/Pollution B/The Steppes/Slogans/Serpentine Song/Tubehead/Spectral Mornings/Firth Of Fifth/Acoustic Set/Blood On The Rooftops/ Fly On A Windshield-Broadway Melody Of '74/Sleepers/Still Waters/Los Endos/Clocks.

Paris Le Splendid 7.11.09 (Private Recording) As above.

Shepherds Bush Empire Theatre London 14.11.09 (Incomplete Private Recording).
Mechanical Bride/Ghost In The Glass/Ace Of Wands/Pollution B/The Steppes/ Slogans/Serpentine Song/Fly On A Windshield/Broadway Melody Of 1974/Sleepers/ Myopia/Los Endos/Clocks.

The Ferry Glasgow 19.11.09 (Private Recording) Set omitted Slogans and Fly On A Windshield. Steve duetted with Nick Beggs during his "Stick" solo and Walking Away From Rainbows was included as part of the acoustic set.

The Assembly Leamington Spa 1.12.09 (Private Recording) As for Hamburg plus Jacuzzi featuring John Hackett on flute.

Parkwest Chicago Il USA 29.6.10 (Private Recording): Intro/Every Day/Emeraldn And Ash/Fire On The Moon.

Performing Arts Centre South Milwaukee WI USA 30.6.10 (Private Recording)
Intro/ Every Day/Emerald And Ash/Fire On The Moon/Ace Of Wands/Serpentine Song/Spectral Mornings/Blood On The Rooftops/Fly On A Windshield/Broadway Melody Of 1974/Sleepers/Los Endos/Firth of Fifth.

The Ferry Glasgow 18.11.10. (Private Recording)
Every Day/Valley Of The Kings/ Emerald And Ash/The Golden Age Of Steam/Watcher Of The Skies/Carpet Crawlers/Fire On The Moon/Ace Of Wands/Shadow Of The Hierophant/Sierra Quemada/Acoustic Set (Inc; Horizons)/Blood On The Rooftops/Tubehead/ Sleepers/Tava/Still Waters/Prairie Angel/Los Endos/Firth Of Fifth/Clocks.

Picturedome Holmfirth 26.11.10. (Private Recording). Set List As above with *Valley Of The Kings* and *Every Day* switching places.

Pacific Road Arts Centre Birkenhead 27.11.10. (Private Recording). Set List: As above.

Estragon Club Bologna 12.5.11. (Private Recording).
Intro/Valley of The Kings/Every Day/Emerald And Ash/The Golden Age Of Steam/Watcher Of The Skies/Carpet Crawlers/Fire On The Moon/Still Waters/Firth Of Fifth/Clocks/Gary O'Toole Drum Solo.

Teatro Tendastrisce Rome 13.5.11 (Complete Private Recording): As for Birkenhead 2010.

Twickenham 13.8.11 (Author's filmed interview).

APPENDIX 6

Unofficial Recordings

Despite the best efforts of record companies and many artists themselves, the unofficial or "bootleg" recording has been around for a very long time and Steve's career has been well documented in this format. I am not going to delve into the rights and wrongs of this vexed issue only to say that it would not be right to ignore the presence of such material in this book. This is a list (not an exhaustive one, though!) of some of the better known and better quality recordings from Steve's solo career and a selection of the more interesting live documents from his time in Genesis.

GENESIS - 1971/73 Nursery Cryme and Foxtrot Tours

"Beside The Silent Mirror" La Ferme Woluwe St Lambert Belgium 7.3.71 A vitally important document; not only is it currently the earliest surviving live recording of a Genesis gig but it is also an unusual live set with two very rare performances. Track Listing: *Happy The Man/Stagnation/The Light/Twilight Alehouse/The Musical Box/The Knife/Going Out To Get You.* Source: Audience 1 CD.

"The Musical Fox" Salle Petite Arlon Belgium 15.1.72 Another early venture overseas for the band captured in this audience recording. Track Listing: *Happy The Man / Stagnation / The Fountain Of Salmacis/Twilight Alehouse/The Musical Box/The Return Of The Giant Hogweed.* Source: Audience 1 CD.

"Shade Of Dawning" Watford Technical College 4.3.72 An excellent live record of the band in fine form during the final part of the Nursery Cryme tour. Track Listing: *Harlequin/Stagnation/The Fountain Of Salmacis/Twilight Alehouse/The Musical Box/The Return of The Giant Hogweed/The Knife.* Source: Audience 1 CD.

Other recordings from this period include:

Palasport Pavia 14.4.72 Two recordings exist from the afternoon and evening shows at this venue one of which contains the extremely unusual rendering of *Can-Utility & The Coastliners* under the title of *"Bye, Bye Johnny".* Both afternoon and evening shows are available as audience recordings.

Lugo Di Ravenna 15.4.72
Happy The Man/Stagnation/The Fountain Of Salmacis/Twilight Alehouse/The Musical Box./The Return Of The Giant Hogweed/The Knife/Going Out To Get You. Source: Audience 1 CD.

Piper 2000 Club Rome 18.4.72 Track Listing: As above. Source: Audience 1 CD.

Watford Town Hall 28.6.72 Another excellent recording featuring an early rendition of Watcher of The Skies from the as yet unreleased Foxtrot album. Track Listing: *Watcher Of The Skies/Stagnation/The Fountain Of Salmacis/Happy The Man/Twilight Alehouse/The Return of The Giant Hogweed/The Knife.* Source: Audience 1 CD.

Reading Festival 11.8.72 Source: Audience 1 CD.

Piper 2000 Club Viareggio Italy 20.8.72 Source: Audience 1 CD.

Teatro Alcione Genoa 22.8.72 Source: Audience 1 CD.

National Stadium Dublin 28.9.72 Memorable gig for the first appearance of Peter's famous Fox head and red dress costumes. Source: Audience 1 CD.

St George's Hall Bradford 11.10.72 Source: Audience 1 CD.

"Dirty Uncle Henry" Imperial College London 18.11.72 Source: Audience 1 CD.

Philharmonic Hall New York City NY 17.12.72 Source: Audience 1 CD.

Stadthalle Heidelberg 15.1.73 Source: Audience 1 CD.

Jahrhunderthalle Frankfurt 17.1.73 Source: Audience 1 CD.

Green's Playhouse Glasgow 16.1.73 Source: Audience 1 CD.

Sheffield City Hall 17.2.73 Source: Audience 2 CDs.

GENESIS - 1973/74 Selling England By The Pound Tour

The band's profile reached another creative highpoint with the release of their fifth studio album: Selling England By The Pound and their shows have fortunately been documented by a fine series of recordings.

"Selling England By The Session" Island Studios Rehearsal Sessions August 1973.
A 2 CD selection of studio rehearsal and demo recordings from the album sessions.
Track Listing: *Improvisations 1 & 2/The Battle Of Epping Forest (#1-5)/ Cinema Show (Fast Take)/ Cinema Show (Slow takes #1-4)/Dancing With The Moonlit Knight (Fast takes #1-3)/The Battle Of Epping Forest/The Last Time/You Really Got Me/The Battle Of Epping Forest (various takes)/I Know What I Like (Instrumental 1& 2)/Cinema Show (instrumental)/Drum solo#1-2/Firth Of Fifth (slow)/Firth Of Fifth (Fast)/Cinema Show/After The Ordeal (Fast)/Dancing With The Moonlit Knight (Vocal & Piano #1-2)/Dancing With The Moonlit Knight (Band version #1-2)/The Battle Of Epping Forest (jams #1-4)/Cinema Show (Rehearsal)/Dancing With The Moonlit Knight (2nd version #1-2)/More Fool Me/After The Ordeal (Pts 1 & 2)/I Know What I Like.* Source: Studio recordings.

"Welcome To Epping Forest" Rainbow Theatre London 20.10.73
Watcher of The Skies/Dancing With The Moonlit Knight/I Know What I Like/Firth Of Fifth/More Fool Me/Supper's Ready. Source: Audience 1 CD.

Massey Hall Toronto 8.11.73
Watcher Of The Skies/Dancing With The Moonlit Knight/Cinema Show/I Know What I Like/Firth Of Fifth/Musical Box/More Fool Me/Supper's Ready. Source: Audience 2 CD set

Tufts University Medford 17.11.73 Source: Audience 1 CD.

"Romeo Show" Felt Forum New York NY 22.11.73
Watcher Of The Skies/Firth Of Fifth/Musical Box/Dancing With The Musical Box/Cinema Show/I Know What I Like/Horizons/More Fool Me/The Battle Of Epping Forest/The Knife/Supper's Ready. Source: Audience 2 CD set.

"Fantasia" Roxy Theatre Los Angeles 19.12.73
Watcher of The Skies/Dancing With The Moonlit Knight/Cinema Show/I Know What I Like/Firth Of Fifth/The Musical Box/Horizons/Supper's Ready. Source: Audience 2 CD set.

"Drury Lane '74" Theatre Royal Drury Lane London 20.1.74
Watcher Of The Skies/Dancing With The Moonlit Knight/Cinema Show/I Know What I Like/Firth Of Fifth/Harold The Barrel/The Musical Box/Horizons/More Fool Me/The Battle Of Epping Forest/Supper's Ready. Source: Audience 2 CD set.

Eulach Halle Winterthur 28.1.74 Track Listing: As above. Source: Audience 1 Cassette.

Stadthalle Offenbach 31.1.74 Track Listing: As above. Source: Audience 1 Cassette.

"Selling Dusseldorf By the Pound" Philipshalle Dusseldorf 30.1.74
Watcher Of The Skies/Dancing With The Moonlit Knight/The Cinema Show/I Know What I Like/Firth Of Fifth/Musical Box/More Fool Me/The Battle Of Epping Forest/Supper's Ready/Harold The Barrel. Source: Audience 2 CD set.

Palasport Reggio Emilia 4.2.74 Track Listing: As for Offenbach. Source: Audience 1 Cassette.

Palasport Rome 5.2.74 Track Listing: As above. Source: Audience 1 Cassette.

Sports Arena Fort Wayne 7.3.74 Track Listing: As above. Source: Audience 1 Cassette

"Live In Toledo '74" Student Union Auditorium Toledo 6.4.74 Source: Audience 2 CD set.

Ford Auditorium Detroit 16.4.74 Source: Audience 2 CD set.

"Live In Montreal" Montreal University Sports Arena 21.4.74
Watcher Of The Skies/Dancing With The Moonlit Knight/Cinema Show/I Know What I Like/Firth Of Fifth/Musical Box/Horizons/The Battle Of Epping Forest/Supper's Ready. Source: Radio broadcast 2 CD set.

"More Fool Me" Orpheum Theatre Boston 24.4.74 Source: Audience 2 CD set.

Allen Theatre Cleveland 29.4.74 Source: Audience 2 CD set.

"Voices In The Academy" Academy Of Music, New York NY 6.5.74 Source: Audience 2 CD set.

GENESIS - 1974/75 The Lamb Lies Down on Broadway Tour

Still without doubt the most controversial and talked about album in the band's career. "The Lamb" was once again well documented by live and studio recordings; of which the following are a small sample:

"The Demo Mix On Broadway" Headley Grange Studio 1974.
An excellent two CD set of rehearsal and studio recordings from the album. Track Listing: *The Lamb Lies Down On Broadway (Different Mix #1-2)/Fly On A Windshield (Rehearsal Take & Different Demo Mix)/Cuckoo Cocoon (Different Mix Demo #1-4)/In the Cage (Different Mix and instrumental rehearsal take)/The Grand Parade Of Lifeless Packaging (Different Mix #1, Incomplete demo mix #2,Different demo mix#3)/Back In NYC (Different Demo Mix #1, Endings To Demo Mixes #2-4)/Counting Out Time (Incomplete Different bass in demo)/The Carpet Crawlers (Different Demo Mix #1-2)/Lilywhite Lilith (Different Demo Mix)/The Waiting Room (Sound effects only demo, Different Mix Demo, Different Mix Final Demo)/ Anyway (Different Mix demo, Different Mix Final Demo)/Here Comes The Supernatural Anaesthetist (Different Mix final demo with Phil on vocals, Rehearsal Instrumentals #1-4)/The Lamia (Different Mix Demo #1-2)/The Colony Of Slippermen (Rehearsal Instrumentals Takes #1-3, Ending Rehearsal Instrumental take)/The Light Dies Down On Broadway (Different Vocal Rehearsal Take)/Riding The Scree (Different Mix Demo)/In The Rapids (Incomplete Different demo mixes #1-2, demo Mixes #1-2, Rehearsal Take)/It (Rehearsal Takes #1-2).* Source: Studio.

"Hedley Grange Spring 1974 Tape 17" A long witheld 2 CD recording of more of the band's rehearsals for the album comprising the following tracks: *Here Comes The Supernatural Anaesthetist (Takes 1& 2)/In the Cage (Instrumental solos 1-5)/Evil Jam 1/Evil Jam2/Evil Jam (Long version)/Flute Solo/Flute & Guitar/A Visit To The Doktor/Here Comes The Supernatural Anaesthetist (Jam)/Here Comes The Supernatural Anaesthetist ((Takes 3-5)/The Colony Of Slippermen (Flute Instrumental)/In The Rapids/It/The Light Dies Down On Broadway/Here Comes The Supernatural Anaesthetist (Take 6).* Source: Studio

Academy Of Music New York NY 6.12.74 Track Listing: Complete *"Lamb"* plus encore of *The Musical Box.* Source: Audience 2 Cassettes.

"Rael Imperial Aerosol Kid" Palace Theatre Providence RI 8.12.74 Track Listing: Complete *"Lamb"* plus encore of *The Musical Box.* Source: Audience 2 CD set.

"The Boston Lamb" Musical Hall Boston MA 9.12.74 Track Listing: Complete *"Lamb"* plus encore of *The Musical Box.* Source: Audience 2 CD set.

"The Lamb Descend On Waterbury" Palace Theatre Waterbury 12.12.74 Track Listing: Complete *"Lamb"* plus encore of *The Musical Box* and selection of studio demos/out-takes. Source: Audience/Studio 2 CD set.

Lakeland Arena Lakeland FL 11.1.75 Track Listing: As above (minus demos/out-takes) Source: Audience 2 CD set.

Carre Hotel Amsterdam 24.2.75 Track Listing: As above. Source: Audience 2 CD set.

Palais Des Grottes Cambrai 26.2.75 Track Listing: Complete *"Lamb"*... Source: Audience 2 Cassettes.

"The Real Last Time" Palasport Turin 29.3.75 Track Listing: As above plus *Watcher Of The Skies*. Source: Audience 2 CD set.

Jahrhunderthalle Frankfurt 3.4.75 Track Listing: As for Providence. Source: Audience 2 CD set.

"German Melody of '75" Westfalenhalle Dortmund 7.4.75 Track Listing: As above. Source: Audience 2 CD set.

Vorst Nationale Brussels 12.4.75 Track Listing: Complete *"Lamb"*... plus encores: *The Musical Box/The Knife*. Source: Audience 2 Cassettes.

Empire Pool Wembley 15.4.75 Released under various guises, this is the FM radio broadcast of the band's London gig available in several permutations.

Empire Theatre Liverpool 19.4.75 Incomplete soundboard recording 2CD set.

Palace Theatre Manchester 27.4.75 Track Listing: As for Dortmund. Source: Audience 2 CD set.

Birmingham Hippodrome Theatre 2.5.75 Track Listing: As above plus *The Knife*. Source: Audience 2 CD Set.

GENESIS - 1976 A Trick Of The Tail Tour

The final years of Steve's time with the band saw the release of two of the band's finest albums both of which have been well documented by live and studio recordings.

"A Trick Of The Takes" Trident Studios 1975.
A compilation of alleged "studio" demos from the A Trick Of The Tail album. Track Listing: *It's Yourself/Ripples (pt1 & 2)/Robbery, Assault & Battery/Los Endos (Pts 1 & 2)/Mad Man Moon/A Trick Of The Tail/Entangled (Take 1)/Entangled (Take 2)/Dance On A Volcano/Squonk*.. Source: Studio tape? 1 CD.

Civic Centre Kitchener Ontario 27.3.76
Dance On A Volcano/The Lamb Lies Down On Broadway/Fly On A Windshield/The Carpet Crawlers/Cinema Show/Robbery, Assault & Battery/White Mountain/Firth Of Fifth/Entangled/Squonk/I Know What I Like/Los Endos. Source: Open Mics 2 CD set.

Memorial Auditorium Buffalo NY 28.3.76 Track Listing: As above. Source: As above 2 CD set.

Both of the previous two listed recordings, recently emerged from the band's archives, and are unusual for the omission of Supper's Ready and It/Watcher Of The Skies which were only integrated into the set from the following gig at Toronto.

Maple Leaf Gardens Toronto 1.4.76
Dance On A Volcano/The Lamb Lies Down On Broadway/Fly On A Windshield/The Carpet Crawlers/The Cinema Show/Robbery, Assault & Battery/White Mountain/Firth Of Fifth/Entangled/Squonk/Supper's Ready/I Know What I Like/Los Endos/It-Watcher Of The Skies. Source: Audience 2 CD set.

The set for Toronto became the standard set for the remainder of the 1976 tour.

Tower Theatre Upper Darby 7.4.76 As above.

Orpheum Theatre Boston 10.4.76 Track Listing: As above. Source: As above 2 CD set.

"The Bubble Will Burst" Syria Mosque Pittsburgh 13.4.76 Track Listing: As above. Source: FM Radio broadcast 2 CD set.

Music Hall Cleveland 15.4.76. Track Listing: As above. Source: Audience 2 CD set.

"Just A Pool Of Tears" Ford Auditorium Detroit 20.4.76 Track Listing: As above. Source: Audience 2 CD set.

Ambassador Theatre St Louis 23.4.76 Track Listing: As above. Source: Audience 2 CD set.

Community Center Berkeley 29.4.76 Track Listing: As above. Source: Audience 2 CD set.

Starlight Bowl Burbank 1.5.76 As above.

Will Rogers Auditorium Fort Worth 7.5.76 As above.

Hammersmith Odeon London 10.6.76 Track Listing: As above. Source: Sound Board Recording 2CD set.

Hammersmith Odeon London 11.6.76 Track Listing: As above. Source: Audience 2 CD set.

Dusseldorf '76. Philipshalle Dusseldorf 18.6.76 Track Listing: As above. Source: Audience 2 CD set.

"We're Hot On Your Tail" St Goarhsausen Lorelei Freilichtbuhne 3.7.76 Track Listing: As above. Source: Audience 2 CD set.

GENESIS - 1977 Wind & Wuthering Tour

"Wot Gorilla Lilith?" Rainbow Theatre London 1.1.77
Eleventh Earl Of Mar/Carpet Crawlers/Firth Of Fifth/Your Own Special Way/Robbery, Assault & Battery/In That Quiet Earth/Afterglow/Lilywhite Lilith/The Waiting Room/Wot Gorilla?/One For The Vine/All In A Mouse's Night/Supper's Ready/I Know What I Like/Dance On A Volcano/The Lamb Lies Down On Broadway/Musical Box (Closing section). Source: Audience 2 CD set.

Rainbow Theatre London 3. 1. 77 Track Listing: As above minus *Lilywhite Lilith/The Waiting Room/Wot Gorilla?* Source: Mixing Desk Recording 2 CD set.

"Live In Liverpool" Empire Theatre Liverpool 9.1.77
Squonk/One For The Vine/Robbery, Assault & Battery/Your Own Special Way/In That Quiet Earth/Afterglow/I Know What I Like/Eleventh Earl Of Mar/Firth Of Fifth/Supper's Ready/Dance On A Volcano/Los Endos/The Lamb Lies Down On Broadway/Musical Box (Closing Section). Source: Audience 2 CD set.

Free Trade Hall Manchester 11.1.77 Track Listing: Same as Southampton. Source: Audience 2 Cassettes.

Gaumont Theatre Southampton 19.1.77 Source: Audience 2 Cassettes.

"In A House Of Dreams" Gaumont Theatre Southampton 20.1.77
Squonk/One For The Vine/Robbery, Assault & Battery/Your Own Special Way/Firth Of Fifth/In That Quiet Earth/Afterglow/I Know What I Like/Eleventh Earl Of Mar/Carpet Crawlers/All In A Mouse's Night/Supper's Ready/Dance On A Volcano/Drum Duet/Los Endos/The Lamb Lies Down On Broadway/Musical Box (Closing section). Source: Mixing Desk. 2 CD set.

Kiel Open House St Louis 6.2.77 Source: Audience 1 Cassette.

"On The Air" City Auditorium Chicago 16.2.77 Source: FM Radio broadcast 2 CD set.

Madison Square Garden New York NY 23.2.77 Source: Audience 2 Cassettes.

Bushnell Auditorium Hartford CT 25.2.77 Source: Audience 2 Cassettes

Memorial Auditorium Buffalo NY 28.2.77 Source: Audience 2 Cassettes.

Winterland San Francisco CA 25.3.77 Source: Soundboard Recording 2CD Set.

Ibirapuera Stadium SaoPaolo 15.5.77 Source: Mixing desk 2 CD set.

Isstadion Stockholm 4.6.77 Source: Audience 2 Cassettes.

"Before Riches" Earls Court Arena London 25.6.77
Squonk/One For The Vine/Robbery, Assault & Battery/Inside & Out/Firth Of Fifth/The Crawlers/In That Quiet Earth/Afterglow/I Know What I Like/Eleventh Earl Of Mar/Supper's Ready/Dance On A Volcano/Los Endos/The Lamb Lies Down On Broadway/Musical Box/The Knife. Source: FM Radio broadcast 2 CD set..

Hallenstadion Zurich 2.7.77 Source: Mix Desk 2 CD set.

"The Last Gig" Olympiahalle Munich 3.7.77 Track Listing: As above minus *The Knife*. Source: Audience 2 CD set.

"Six Of The Best" Milton Keynes Concert Bowl 2.10.82 The legendary "reunion" gig with Peter Gabriel also featured Steve for the encores.
Back In NYC/Dancing With The Moonlit Knight/Carpet Crawlers/Firth of Fifth/Musical

Box/Solsbury Hill/Turn It On Again/The Lamb Lies Down On Broadway/Fly On A Windshield/ Broadway Melody Of 74/In The Cage/Supper's Ready/I Know What I Like/The Knife.

FAde 003 (Fan Approved Definitive Edition) Source: Audience 2 CD set.

Recently a soundboard recording of one of the band's rehearsals at Hammersmith Odeon on 27th September 1982 has surfaced. Steve, however, took no part in that rehearsal and was still in Brazil at the time.

STEVE HACKETT Solo Live Recordings

Steve began his solo performing career a mere year after leaving Genesis in support of his second solo album Please Don't Touch. His live performances have been well documented by recordings ever since.

1978 Please Don't Touch Tour

"The First Gig" Chateau Neuf Oslo 4.10.78
Please Don't Touch/Racing In A/Carry On Up The Vicarage/Ace Of Wands/Hands Of The Priestess/Icarus Ascending/Acoustic Set/The Optigan/A Tower Struck Down/Spectral Mornings/Star Of Sirius/Shadow Of The Hierophant/Clocks/I Know What I Like. Source: Audience 1CD.

"Star Of Sirius" Gota Lejon Stockholm 5.10.78 Track Listing: As above. Source: Audience 2 CD set

Congresgebouow Den Haag 19.10.78 Track Listing: As above. Source: Audience Cassette.

"Hail The New Messiah" Cardiff University 23.10.78 Track Listing: As above. Source: Audience 2 CD set.

Apollo Theatre Manchester 24.10.78
Tigermoth/Please Don't Touch/Racing In A/Carry On Up The Vicarage/Ace Of Wands/Hands Of The Priestess/Icarus Ascending/Narnia/ Acoustic Set/Kim/The Optigan/A Tower Struck Down/Spectral Mornings/Shadow Of The Hierophant/Star Of Sirius/Clocks/I Know What I Like. Source: Audience 2 CD set.

Apollo Theatre Glasgow 26.10.78 Track Listing: As above plus *Acoustic medley reprise.* Source: Audience 2 CD set.

1979 Spectral Mornings Tour

Empire Theatre Liverpool 24.6.79
Please Don't Touch/Tigermoth/Everyday/Narnia/The Red Flower Of Taichi Blooms Everywhere/Ace Of Wands/Carry On Up The Vicarage/Acoustic Set/Kim/The Optigan/A Tower Struck Down/Spectral Mornings/Star Of Sirius/Shadow Of The Hierophant/Clocks/I Know What I Like/Racing In A/Ace Of Wands/Racing In A (Acoustic reprise). Source: Audience 2 CD set.

Guildhall Southampton 29.6.79 Track Listing: As above up to *I Know What I Like*. Source: Audience " CDs..

"Star Of Hammersmith" Hammersmith Odeon London 30.6.79 Track Listing: As for Liverpool minus *Racing In A (Acoustic reprise)*. Source: Audience 2 Cassettes.

"If You Break It, It's Yours" Reading Festival 25.8.79
Please Don't Touch/Tigermoth/Every Day/The Optigan/A Tower Struck Down/Spectral Mornings/Clocks/I Know What I Like. Source: FM Radio broadcast 1 CD.

Theatre Royal Drury Lane 11.11.79
Please Don't Touch/Tigermoth/Every Day/Jacuzzi/Ace of Wands/Sentimental Institution/The Red Flower Of Taichi Blooms Everywhere/Spectral Mornings/Clocks/Acoustic Set/Kim.
Source: Radio Broadcast 1 CD.

"A Poole Of Tears" Poole Arts Centre 12.11.79
Please Don't Touch/Tigermoth/Every Day/Narnia/Ace Of Wands/The Virgin & The Gypsy/The Steppes/Narnia/Sentimental Institution/The Red Flower Of Taichi Blooms Everywhere/The Lovers-Shadow Of The Hierpohant/Spectral Mornings/A Tower Struck Down/Clocks/Acoustic Set/Kim/The Ballad Of The Decomposing Man/Hercules Unchained Source: Audience 2 CD set.

1980 Defector Tour

Apollo Theatre Manchester 16.6.80
Slogans/Everyday/The Red Flower Of Taichi Blooms Everywhere/ Tigermoth/Kim/Time To Get Out/The Steppes/The Toast/Narnia/Acoustic set/Sentimental Institution/ Jacuzzi/ Spectral Mornings/A Tower Struck Down/Clocks/Please Don't Touch/The Show/Oh Sole Mio/Hercules Unchained. Source: Audience 2 Cassettes.

City Hall Sheffield 17.6.80 Track Listing: As above. Source: FM Radio broadcast 2 CD set.

Guildhall Preston 20.6.80 Track Listing: As above. Source: Audience 2 cassettes.

Grand Casino Montreux 13.7.80
Slogans/Everyday/Spectral Mornings/Time To Get Out/The Steppes/ Narnia/Acoustic Set/Jacuzzi/A Tower Struck Down/Clocks. Source: TV broadcast 1 CD.

ABC Theatre Canterbury 3.7.80 Track Listing: As Manchester. Source: Audience 1 Cassette.

Bottom Line Club New York NY 29.9.80 Track Listing: As Manchester. Source: Audience 1 Cassette.

Old Waldorf Theatre Washington DC 5.10.80 Track Listing: As above up to *Please Don't Touch*. Source: Audience 1 Cassette.

Park West Chicago 10.10.80
Slogans/Everyday/The Red Flower Of Taichi Blooms Everywhere/ Tigermoth/Time To Get Out/The Steppes/Blood On The Rooftops-Horizons/Kim/Narnia/Jacuzzi/Sentimental Institution/Spectral Mornings/A Tower Struck Down/Clocks. Source: Radio Broadcast 1 CD.

Rijnhal Nijmegen 14.11.80 Track Listing: As Manchester. Source: Audience 1 Cassette.

Salle Des Fetes De Thonex Geneva 19.11.80 Track Listing: As for Manchester. Source: Audience 2 CD set.

Palasport Rome 26.11.80 Track Listing: As Manchester. Source: Audience 1 Cassette.

Palasport Pianella Cantu 29.11.80 Track Listing: As for Manchester. Source: Audience 2 CD set.

1981 Cured Tour

Reading Festival 28.8.81
The Air- Conditioned Nightmare/Every Day/Ace Of Wands/Funny Feeling/The Steppes/Overnight Sleeper/Slogans/A Tower Struck Down/Spectral Mornings/The Show/Clocks.
Source: FM Radio Broadcast 1 CD.

Carre Rocktempel Amsterdam 31.8.81
Jacuzzi/Funny Feeling/Picture Postcard/The Steppes/ Kim/ Overnight Sleeper/The Red Flower Of Taichi Blooms Everywhere/Every Day/Slogans/Hope I Don't Wake/A Tower Struck Down/Spectral Mornings. Source: FM Radio Broadcast 1 CD.

L'Ancienne Belgique Brussels 1.9.81
Jacuzzi/Funny Feeling/Picture Postcard/The Steppes/Kim/ Overnight Sleeper/The Red Flower Of Taichi Blooms Everywhere/Every Day/Slogans/Hope I Don't Wake/A Tower Struck Down/Spectral Mornings/Acoustic Set. Source: Audience 1 CD.

Milan Rolling Stone Theatre 8.9.81
The Air- Conditioned Nightmare/Jacuzzi/Slogans/Funny Feeling/Ace of Wands/Picture postcard/The Steppes/Every Day/The Red Flower Of Taichi Blooms Everywhere/Please Don't Touch/Acoustic Set/Overnight Sleeper/Hope I Don't Wake/A Tower Struck Down/Spectral Mornings/The Show/Clocks/I Know What I Like. Source: Audience 1 Cassette.

Palasport Rome 13.9.81 Track Listing: As above. Source: Audience 1 Cassette.

Parco Virgiliano Naples 14.9.81 Track Listing: As above. Source: Audience 2 Cassettes.

Casino Den Bosch Hertogenbosch 26.9.81 Track Listing: As above. Source: Audience 1 CD.

"Kill Or Cure" Empire Theatre Liverpool 3.10.81 Track Listing: As above minus *I Know What I Like*. Source: Audience 2 CD set.

Hammersmith Odeon London 11.10.81 Track Listing: As for Liverpool. Source: Audience 2 Cassettes.

The Agora Cleveland 26.10.81 Track Listing: As above. Source: Audience 2 CD set.

"Poland Aid" S.U.N.Y. Oswego 8.11.81 Track Listing: As above.
Source: Audience 2 Cassettes.

1982/83 Highly Strung Tour

Elixii Festival Brest 15.7.82 Exact details of live set are not known at present but two tracks: *Hope I Don't Wake* and *Funny Feeling* were broadcast live on French TV.

Venue Club London 13.12.82
The Steppes/Funny Feeling/Can't let Go/Hackett To Pieces/A Tower Struck Down/Spectral Mornings/Acoustic Set/Overnight Sleeper/Slogans/Please Don't Touch/The Show/Clocks/The Air-Conditioned Nightmare/Hackett's Boogie/Radio 2 interview. Source: Audience/Radio 1 CD.

Guildford Civic Hall 29.1.83
The Steppes/Picture Postcard/Jacuzzi/Hackett To Pieces/Every Day/A Tower Struck Down/Horizons/Kim./Overnight Sleeper/The Show/Clocks/Here Comes The Flood*/Solsbury Hill*/Reach Out (I'll Be There)*/I Know What I Like*/Slogans.
* = Tracks with Peter Gabriel/Mike Rutherford.   Source: Audience 1 CD.

"Rocking The Apollo To Pieces" Manchester Apollo Theatre 23.4.83
The Steppes/Camino Royale/Funny Feeling/Weightless/Always Somewhere Else/Hackett To Pieces/Slogans/Give It Away/Spectral Mornings/ Acoustic Set/Kim/Overnight Sleeper/Cell 151/Please Don't Touch/Everyday/Walking Through Walls/The Show/ Clocks/Hackett's Boogie.
Source: Audience 2 CD set.

Bradford University 25.4.83 Track Listing: As above. Source: Audience 2 Cassettes.

Empire Theatre Liverpool 26.4.83 Track Listing: As above. Source: Audience 2 CD set.

Hammersmith Odeon London 1.5.83
The Steppes/Camino Royale/Give It Away/Spectral Mornings/ Acoustic set/Kim/Overnight Sleeper/Please Don't Touch/The Air- Conditioned Nightmare/Hackett's Boogie.
Source: Audience 1 CD.

University Of East Anglia Norwich 9.5.83 Track Listing: As Liverpool. Source: Audience 2 CDs.

1983 Bay Of Kings Tour

Warwick University 26.10.83
Horizons/Time-Lapse At Milton Keynes / Bay Of Kings / Calmaria / Hands of The Priestess / Jacuzzi / Medley / Tales Of the Riverbank / Second Chance / Chinese Improvisation / Petropolis / Kim / The Water Wheel (also known as: Butterfly) / The Journey / Ace Of Wands / Cradle Of Swans/ Jazz On A Summer's Night. Source: Audience 1 CD.

"The Acoustic King" Mountford Hall Liverpool University 27.10.83 Track Listing: As above plus Horizons (extra encore). Source: Audience 1 CD.

Leeds University 28.10.83 Track Listing: As above plus Friday Rock Show Session tracks: *Cell151/Hackett To Pieces/Please Don't Touch/Walking Thru Walls.* Source: Audience/Radio 1 CD.

Keele University Great Hall 2.11.83 Track Listing: As above plus Signal Radio interview. Source: Audience/Radio 2 CD Set.

Queens Hall Edinburgh 4.11.83 Track Listing: As above. Source: Audience 1 CD.

Barbican Centre London 7.11.83
Horizons/Blood On The Rooftops/Time-Lapse At Milton Keynes/Bay Of Kings/Calmaria/Hands Of The Priestess/Jacuzzi/Overnight Sleeper/Hairless Heart/The Barren Land/Black Light/Second Chance/Chinese Improvisation/Petropolis/Kim/Untitled Piece/Concert For Munich/The Journey/Ace Of Wands/Cradle Of Swans/Jazz On A Summer's Night/Horizons/Ace Of Wands.
Source: Audience 1 CD.

Vanbrugh Dining Hall York University 14.11.83
Horizons/Blood On The Rooftops Medley/Bay Of Kings/Calmaria/Hands Of The Priestess/Jacuzzi/Hairless Heart/Medley/Tales Of The Riverbank/Second Chance/ Chinese Improvisation/Petropolis/Kim/Untitled Piece/Concert For Munich/The Journey/Ace Of Wands/Cradle Of Swans/Jazz On A Summer's Night/Horizons(Reprise)/Kim (Reprise)
Source: Audience 1 CD.

1986 GTR Tour

Tower Theatre Upper Darby PA USA 28.6.86
Steve Hackett Acoustic Set/Steve Howe Acoustic Set/From A Place Where Time Runs Slow/Jekyll And Hyde/Here I Wait/Prize Fighters/Imagining/ Hackett To Bits/Spectral Mornings/In That Quiet Earth/I Know What I Like/Toe The Line/Sketches In The Sun/Pennants/Roundabout/The Hunter/Reach Out (Never Say No)/You Can Still Get Through/When the Heart Rules The Mind.
Source: Audience 2 Discs.

Birmingham Odeon Theatre 12.9.86
Steve Hackett Acoustic Set/Steve Howe Acoustic Set/Jekyll And Hyde/Here I Wait/Prize Fighters/Imagining/Hackett To Bits/Spectral Mornings/I Know What I Like/Toe The Line/Sketches In The Sun/Pennants/Roundabout/The Hunter/You Can Still Get Through/Reach Out(Never Say No)/When The Heart Rules The Mind. Source: Audience 2 Cassettes.

1988 Momentum UK/European Tour

Manchester Opera House 1.5.88
The Journey/Horizons/Bay Of Kings/A Bed, A Chair And A Guitar/ Time-Lapse At Milton Keynes/Tales Of The Riverbank/Ace of Wands/Hands Of The Priestess/Jauzzi/Overnight Sleeper/Cavalcanti/Second Chance/Portrait Of A Brazilian Lady/Still Life/Jazz On A Summer's Night/Concert For Munich/Notre Dame Des Fleurs/Momentum/Guitar Synthesiser Improvisation/Silver/The Carrot That Killed My Sister. Source: Audience 1 CD.

Cliffs Pavilion Southend 8.5.88 Track Listing: As above. Source: Audience 1 Disc.

Royal Concert Hall Nottingham 14.5.88 Track Listing: As above. Source: Audience 1 Disc.

Teatro Colosseo Turin 19.5.88 Track Listing: As above. Source: Audience 1 Disc.

Teatro Verdi Genoa 21.5.88 Track Listing: As above. Source: Audience 1 Disc.

Teatro Tenda A Strisce Rome 22.5.88 Track Listing: As above. Source: Audience 1 Disc

New Morning Paris 19.9.88
Horizons/Bay Of Kings/A Bed, A Chair And A Guitar/Time-Lapse At Milton Keynes/Cavalcanti/Portrait Of A Brazilian Lady/Still Life/Harmonics/Notre Dame Des Fleurs/Momentum/ Blood On The Rooftops-Unquiet Slumbers-Hairless Heart Medley/Chinese Improvisation/Silver/Troubled Spirit/The Carrot That Killed My Sister/Harry Lime Theme/Bouree/The Journey. Source: Audience 2 Discs.

"Cutting Through The Bedrock" Central TV Studios Nottingham 13.9.90
Camino Royale/Please Don't Touch/Everyday/In That Quiet Earth/Depth Charge/Wonderpatch/In The Heart of The City/Black Light/ Horizons/Jacuzzi/Overnight Sleeper/Theatre Of Sleep/Jazz Jam/Spectral Mornings/Clocks. Source: Laserdisc 1 Disc.

1992 Tour Noir US Tour

The Strand Redondo Beach Los Angeles 8.9.92
Myopia Medley/Camino Royale/A Vampyre With A Healthy Appetite/Flight Of The Condor (Sierra Quemada)/Take These Pearls/Always Somewhere Else/In The Heart Of The City/Walking Away From Rainbows/There Are Many Sides To The Night/In That Quiet Earth/Dark As The Grave/Etruscan Serenade/Depth Charge/Every Day/Acoustic Set-Horizons/The Stumble.
Source: Audience 2 Discs.

Max's On Broadway Baltimore 23.9.92
Myopia Medley/Camino Royale/A Vampyre With A Healthy Appetite/Flight Of The Condor(Sierra Quemada)/Take These Pearls/Always Somewhere Else/In The Heart Of The City/There Are Many Sides To The Night/Dark As the Grave/Etruscan Serenade/The Air-Conditioned Nightmare/Lost In Your Eyes/Everyday/Spectral Mornings/Firth of Fifth/Clocks/The Stumble.
Source: Audience 2 Discs.

23 East Cabaret Philadelphia 24.9.92 Track Listing: As above 2 discs. Source: Audience.

1993 Guitar Noir UK Tour

"The Spectral King Returns" Neptune Theatre Liverpool 21.5.93
Medley/Camino Royale/A Vampyre With A Healthy Appetite/Sierra Quemada/Take These Pearls/In The Heart Of The City/Walking Away From Rainbows/There Are Many Sides To The Night/Dark As The Grave/Depth Charge/In That Quiet Earth/Bass-Drum Duet/Always Somewhere Else/Lost In Your Eyes/Everyday/Blood On The Rooftops/Horizons/Cinema Paradiso/Spectral Mornings/Firth Of Fifth/Clocks. Source: Audience 2 Discs.

Hop & Grape Manchester University 25.5.93 Track Listing: As above 2 Discs. Source: Audience.

Wulfrun Hall Wolverhampton 28.5.93 Track Listing: As above plus extra encore of opening medley. Source: Audience 2 Discs.

De Montfort Hall Leicester 29.5.93 Track Listing: As Liverpool. Source: Audience 2 Cassettes.

Lead Mill Sheffield 31.5.93 Track Listing: As above. Source: Audience 2 Discs.
Bierkeller Bristol 7.6.93 Track Listing: As above. Source: Audience 2 Discs.

Grand Theatre Clapham London 8.6.93 Track Listing: As above plus *Kim* with John Hackett on flute. Source: Audience 2 Discs

Brewery Arts Centre Kendal 11.6.93 Track Listing: As Liverpool. Source: Audience 2 Discs.

Woughton Centre Milton Keynes 12.6.93 Track Listing: As above. Source: Audience 2 Discs.

Villa Torlonia Frascati nr Rome 5.7.93 Track Listing: As above. Source: Audience 2 Cassettes.

Stadio Plebiscito Selvazzano nr Padua 6.7.93 Track Listing: As above. Source: Audience 2 Cassettes.

Castello Brescia 7.7.93 Track Listing: As above. Source: Audience 2 Cassettes.

Charity's Irving Plaza NY 26.10.93 Track Listing: As above. Source: Audience 2 CD set.

"Classical Gas" Ancienne Belgique Brussels 3.5.94
Turn It On Again/Turn It On Again/Whole Lotta Love/Money/Los Jigos/Living In The Past/Rock Piece/Tub Thumping/Black Light/Blood On The Rooftops/Cuckoo Cocoon/Chinese Improvisation/Unquiet Slumbers For The Sleepers/Horizons/Cavalcanti/Tales From The Riverbank/Classical Piece/The Journey/Notre Dame Des Fleurs/Run Like Hell/Owner Of A Lonely Heart/Roundabout. Source: Audience: 2 CD set. (This gig was one of the Orchestral gigs by David Palmer and the LSO at which Steve was a guest.)

1994 Italian Acoustic Tour

Sonny Boy Club Treviso 24.11.94
Kim/Black Light/Second Chance/Oh How I Love You/Blood On The Rooftops-Horizons/The Journey/Bacchus/Walking Away From Rainbows/Cavalcanti/Andante In C/Concerto In D/A Blue Part Of Town/There Are Many Sides To The Night/Ace Of Wands/Cinema Paradiso/Cuckoo Cocoon/Chinese Improvisation/Jazz On A Summer's Night/End of Day. Source: Audience 1 Disc.

Olgiate Comasco 26.11.94
Beja Flor/Kim/Second Chance/Oh How I Love You/The Journey/Baroque/ Walking Away From Rainbows/Concerto In D/A Blue Part Of Town/There Are Many Sides To The Night/Ace Of Wands/Cinema Paradiso/Blues Coda/Jazz On A Summer's Night. Source: Audience 1 Disc.

The Standard Barcelona 10.11.94 Track Listing: As for Treviso. Source: Audience 1 CD.

1996 "Tokyo Tapes" Tour

Kosei Nenkin Hall Tokyo 16.12.96 Track Listing: As for "Tokyo Tapes" album. Source: Audience 1 Cassette.

Kosei Nenkin Hall Tokyo 17.12.96 Track Listing: As for "Tokyo Tapes" album. Source: Audience 1 Cassette.
Both of the above have also recently been re-packaged as a four CD set under the title "A Friendly Fold" by the good people at The Steve Hackett Remastering Project.

Castle Hall Osaka 19.12.96 Track Listing: As for "Tokyo Tapes" album. Source: Audience 2CD set.

Rainbow Hall Nagoya 20.12.96 Track Listing: As for "Tokyo Tapes" album. Source; Audience 2CD set.

The Multi Track Sessions BBC World Service 20.8.98
Black Light/Horizons/The Skye Boat Song/The Journey / Peaseblossom / Cobweb / Moth / Mustardseed. Source: Radio Broadcast Cassette.

2000 Italian Tour

Castello Vivegano 9.7.00
The Floating Seventh/Mechanical Bride/Serpentine Song/Lucridus/ Watcher Of The Skies/Hairless Heart/Firth Of Fifth/Riding The Colossus/The Steppes/Walking Away From Rainbows/Sierra Quemada/A Vampyre With A Healthy Appetite/Gnossienne #1/A Tower Struck Down/Darktown/Camino Royale/In Memoriam/Los Endos. Source: Audience 1 Cassette.

Castello Malatestiana Cesena 11.7.00
The Floating Seventh/MechanicalBride/Serpentine Song/Watcher Of The Skies/Hairless Heart/Firth Of Fifth/Riding The Colossus/The Steppes/Walking Away From Rainbows/Sierra Quemada/A Vampyre With A Healthy Appetite/Gnossienne #3/A Tower Struck Down/Darktown/Camino Royale/In Memoriam/Los Endos. Source: Audience 1 CD

Teatro Della Ciminiera Catania 13.7.00 Track Listing: As above. Source: Audience 1 Disc.

Piazza Duomo Vecchio Molfetta (Bari) 14.7.00. Track Listing: As above. Source: Audience 1 Cassette.

2001 South American Tour

Teatro Coliseo Buenos Aires 1.7.01
Mechanical Bride/Hackett To Bits/Serpentine Song/Watcher Of The Skies/Hairless Heart/Firth Of Fifth/Riding The Colossus/Pollution/The Steppes/Gnossienne #3/Walking Away From Rainbows/Sierra Quemada/A Vampyre With A Healthy Appetite/A Tower Struck Down/Lucridus/Darktown/In Memoriam/Acoustic Set-Black Light-Horizons/Los Endos/In That Quiet Earth. Source: Mixing Desk 2 CD set.

Santa Rosa Las Condes Santiago Chile 3.7.01
Mechanical Bride/Hackett To Bits/Serpentine Song/Watcher Of The Skies/Hairless Heart/Firth Of Fifth/Riding The Colossus/Pollution/The Steppes/Gnossienne #3/Walking Away From Rainbows/Sierra Quemada/A Vampyre With A Healthy Appetite/A Tower Struck

Down/Lucridus/Darktown/In Memoriam/Acoustic Set-Black Light-Horizons/Los Endos/In That Quiet Earth. Source: Mixing desk 2 CD.

2002 Japanese Acoustic Shows

Odaiba Aqua City Tokyo 12.1.02
Horizons/Gnossienne #1/Bacchus/Firth Of Fifth/Bay Of Kings/ Syrinx/Imagining/Second Chance/Jacuzzi/Overnight Sleeper/The Barren Land/Time Lapse At Milton Keynes/ Improvisation/Concerto In D/Hairless Heart/Cinema Paradiso/Mustardseed/Gymnopedie#1/Jazz On A Summer's Night/Little Cloud/Cavalcanti/Walking Away From Rainbows/Tales Of The Riverbank/The Journey/Skye Boat Song/By Paved Fountain/Blood On The Rooftops/Hands Of The Priestess/All Is Mended/Ace Of Wands/Idylle-Aubade-Meditation/Bacchus/Firth Of Fifth. Source: Mixing Desk 2 Disc set.

Odaiba Aqua City Tokyo 13.1.02   Track Listing: As above plus *Jacuzzi (Reprise)*.   Source: Mixing Desk 2 Disc set.

Odaiba Aqua City Tokyo 14.1.02   Track Listing: As above plus *Jazz On A Summer's Night (Reprise)*. Source: Mixing Desk 2 Disc set.

2002 Italian Tour

Teatro Solva Rosignano nr Pisa 23.4.02
Horizons/Gnossienne #1/Bacchus/Firth Of Fifth/Bay Of Kings/Syinx/Imagining/Second Chance/Jacuzzi/Overnight Sleeper/The Barren Land/Kim/Time Lapse At Milton Keynes/Blood On The Rooftops/Improvisation/Concerto In D/Hairless Heart/Cinema Paradiso/Mustardseed/ Gymnopedie No1/Jazz On A Summer's Night/Cavalcanti/Walking Away From Rainbows/Tales Of The Riverbank/Concert For Munich/The Journey/Sky Boat Song-By Paved Fountain/Hands Of The Priestess/Ace Of Wands/Idylle-Aubade-Meditation/Hairless Heart (Reprise).
Source: Audience 2 Disc set.

Teatro Sociale Trento 28.4.02   Track Listing: As above minus reprise. Source: Audience 2 Disc set.

2002 US Tour

The Birchmere Music Hall Alexandria VA 27.6.02
The Floating Seventh/Mechanical Bride/Myopia Medley/Serpentine Song/Watcher Of The Skies/Hairless Heart/Firth Of Fifth/Riding The Colossus/Pollution/The Steppes/Gnossienne #1/Walking Away From Rainbows/In Memoriam/A Vampyre With A Healthy Appetite/Spectral Mornings/Darktown/Camino Royale/Everyday/Shadow Of The Hierophant/Los Endos/Dancing With The Moonlit Knight. Source: Audience 2 Disc set.

BB Kings' Blues Club New York NY 28.6.02   Track Listing: As above. Source: Audience 2 Disc set.

Patriots Theatre Trenton NJ 30.6.02   Track Listing: As above. Source: Mixing Desk 2 CD set.

2002 Italian Acoustic Tour

Club Naima Forli 1.11.02
Horizons/Gnossienne #1/Medley: Bouree-Bacchus-Improvisation-Firth of Fifth/Bay Of Kings/Medley: Syrinx-Imagining-Second Chance-Jacuzzi-Overnight Sleeper/The Barren Land/Kim/Medley: Cuckoo Cocoon-Dancing With The Moonlit Knight-Blood On The Rooftops/Time Lapse At Milton Keynes/ Improvisation/Hairless Heart/Cinema Paradiso/Gymnopedie #1/Jazz On A Summer's Night/Cavalcanti/Walking Away From Rainbows/Tales Of The Riverbank/Concert For Munich/The Journey/Skye Boat Song/By Paved Fountain/Hands Of The Priestess/Ace Of Wands/Idylle-Aubade-Meditation. Source: Audience 2 Disc set.

2003 To Watch The Storms Tour

PR3 Studios Warsaw ?.6.03
Horizons/Gnossienne#1/Bacchus-Firth Of Fifth/Bay Of Kings/Cinema Paradiso/Skye Boat Song-By Paved Fountain/Hairless Heart/The Barren Land/Black Light/Imagining-Second Chance/Walking Away From Rainbows/Ace Of Wands. Source: Radio Broadcast 1 Disc.

Festival Hall London 21.7.03 Track Listing: Performance of *City In The Sea* by Evelyn Glennie. Source: Audience 1 Disc.

Levinson Arts Studio/Borders Bookstore Cleveland Heights Cleveland 11.8.03
Brand New (Studio)/Interview/Classical Gas Medley/Interview/Blood On The Rooftops-Horizons/Interview/The Journey/Medley/Improvisation/Horizons/Blood On The Rooftops/Skye Boat Song/The Barren Land. Source: Radio/Audience 1 Disc.

Het Noorderlight Tilburg 27.9.03
Mechanical Bride/Serpentine Song/Watcher of The Skies/Hairless heart/Darktown/Camino Royale/The Steppes/Acoustic Set/Walking Away From Rainbows/Slogans/Everyday/Please Don't Touch/Firth Of Fifth/A Vampyre With A Healthy Appetite/Clocks/Spectral Mornings/Brand New/Los Endos/In That Quiet Earth. Source: Audience 2 Disc set.

Zoetemeer Boerderij 28.9.03 Track Listing: As above 2 CD set. Source: Audience.

The Stables Milton Keynes 3.10.03 Track Listing: As above 2 CD set.. Source: Audience.

The Stables Milton Keynes 4.10.03 Track Listing: As above 2 CD set.. Source: Audience

Wulfrun Hall Wolverhampton 5.10.03 Track Listing: As above 2 CD set.. Source: Audience.

City Varieties Leeds 6.10.03 Track Listing: As above 2 CD set. Source: Audience.

Palace Theatre Newark 7.10.03 Track Listing: As above 2 CD set. Source: Audience.

Huntingdon Hall Worcester 9.10.03 Track Listing: As above 2 CD set.. Source: Audience

Coal Exchange Cardiff 10.10.03 Track Listing: As above 2 CD set. Source: Audience

Oakwood Centre Rotherham 11.10.03 Track Listing: As above plus *Jacuzzi* (with John Hackett) Source: Audience 2 CD set.

Renfrew Ferry Glasgow 12.10.03 Track Listing: As for Cardiff. Source: Audience 2 CD set.

Neptune Theatre Liverpool 13.10.03 Track Listing: As above. Source: Audience 2 CD set.

Newcastle Opera House 18.10.03 Track Listin: As above. Source: Audience 2 CD set.

Academy 2 Manchester 19.10.03 Track Listing: As above. Source: Audience 2 CD set.

De Montfort Hall Leicester 20.10.03 Track Listing: As above plus Jacuzzi (with John Hackett) Source: Audience 2 CD set.

High Wycombe Town Hall 21.10.03 Track Listing: As for Liverpool. Source: Audience 2 CD set.

Queen Elizabeth Hall London 28.10.03 Track Listing: As for Leicester. Source: Audience 2 CD set.

Fairfield Hall Croydon 29.10.03 Track Listing as Liverpool plus *Kim* (with John Hackett) Source: Audience 2 CD set.

Meier Music Hall Braunschweig 8.11.03 Track Listing: As for Liverpool plus *In Memoriam.* Source: Audience 2 CD set.

Villa Berg Stuttgart 9.11.03
Intro/Everyday/Watcher Of The Skies/Pollution B/The Steppes/Please Don't Touch/Firth Of Fifth/A Vampyre With A Healthy Appetite/Spectral Mornings/In Memoriam.
Source: FM Radio Broadcast 1 Disc.

Mannheim Capitol 10.11.03 Track Listing: As for Braunschweig. Source: Audience 2 CD set.

2004 To Watch The Storms/Live Archive 04 Tour

Mick Jagger Centre Dartford 4.3.04
Valley of The Kings/Mechanical Bride/Circus Of Becoming/Frozen Statues/Slogans/Serpentine Song/Ace Of Wands/Hammer In The Sand/Acoustic Set/Blood On The Rooftops/Fly On A Windshield/Please Don't Touch/Firth Of Fifth/A Dark Night In Toytown/Darktown/Brand New/The Air-Conditioned Nightmare/Every Day/Clocks/Spectral Mornings/Los Endos.
Source: Audience 2 CD set.

Derngate Theatre Northampton 5.3.04 Track Listing: As above plus *Kim* (with John Hackett) Source: Audience 2 CD set.

Pacific Arts Centre Birkenhead 6.3.04 Track Listing: As for Dartford.
Source: Audience 2 CD set.

Windsor Rooms St George's Hall Blackburn 7.3.04 Track Listing: As for Northampton. Source: Audience 3 CD set. Including soundcheck.

Corn Exchange Cambridge 12.3.04 Track Listing; As for Dartford. Source: Audience 2 CD set.

London Shepherds Bush Empire 13.3.04 Track Listing: As above. Source: Audience 2 CD set.
Colston Hall Bristol 14.3.04 Track Listing: As above. Source: Audience 2 CD set.

Alexandra Theatre Birmingham 15.3.04 Track Listing: As above. Source: Audience 2 CD set.

Rock City Nottingham 16.3.04 Track Listing: As above. Source: Audience 2 CD set.

Middlesbrough Town Hall Crypt 18.3.04 Track Listing: As above. Source: Audience 2 CD set.

Oxford New Theatre 19.3.04 Track Listing: As above. Source: Audience 2 CD set.

Southampton Guildhall 20.3.04 Track Listing: As above. Source: Audience 2 CD set.

Kubo Turin 25.3.04 Track Listing: As above. Source: Audience 2 CD set.

O41 Marghera Venice 26.3.04 Track Listing: As above. Source: Audience 2 CD set.

Stazione Birra Rome 27.3.04 Track Listing: As above. Source: Audience 2 CD set.

Musiktheater Rex Lorsch 30.3.04 Track Listing: As above. Source: Audience 2 CD set.

Gewerkschafthaus Erfurt 31.3.04 Track Listing: As above. Source: Audience 2 CD set.

Dietrich-Keuning-Haus Dortmund 1.4.04 Track Listing: As above. Source: Audience 2 CD set.

2005 Acoustic Trio Tour

Pacific Arts Centre Birkenhead 30.3.05

Quays Theatre Lowry Centre Manchester 31.3.05
Medley/Andante In C/Tribute To Segovia/Metamorpheus Excerpts/Bay Of Kings/Classical Jazz (inc: Classical Gas-Cuckoo Cocoon-Brand New) Sapphires/Mexico City/Black Light-The Barren Land/Skye Boat Song/Mustard Seed/Horizons/Jacuzzi-Overnight Sleeper/Bacchus-Firth Of Fifth/Whole-Tone Jam-The Red Flower Of Taichi Blooms Everywhere-Hands Of The Priestess/After The Ordeal/ Hairless Heart/M3/Imagining/Second Chance/Jazz On A Summer's Night/Next Time Around/Kim/Idylle-Aubade-Meditation/The Journey/Ace Of Wands/Walking Away From Rainbows/Gnossienne #1. Source: Audience 2 CD set.

The Platform Morecambe 1.4.05 Track Listing: As above. Source: Audience 2 CD set.

Darwin Suite Assembly Rooms Derby 2.4.05 Track Listing: As above. Source: Audience 2 CD set.

The Rum Store Carnglaze Caverns Liskeard 8.4.05 Track Listing: As above. Source: Audience 2 CD set.

Wulfrun Hall Wolverhampton 10.4.05. Track Listing: As above. Source: Audience 2 CD set.

Maddermarket Theatre Norwich 11.4.05 Track Listing: As above. Source: Audience 2 CD set.

The Stables Milton Keynes 13/14.4.05 Track Listing: As above. Source: Audience 2 CD set (Both nights).

The Broadway Barking 16.4.05 Track Listing: as above. Source: Audience 2 CD set.

Ashcroft Theatre Croydon 17.4.05
Classical Jazz/Japonica/Mexico City/Cavalcanti/Skye Boat Song/Horizons/Jacuzzi/Bacchus/Whole Tone Jam-The Red Flower Of Taichi Blooms Everywhere-Hands Of The Priestess/After The Ordeal/Hairless Heart/M3/ Imagining/Second Chance/Jazz On A Summer's Night/Next Time Around/Kim/Idylle-Aubade-Meditation/The Journey/Ace Of Wands/Walking Away From Rainbows/Gnossienne #1. Source: Audience 2 CD set.

Saschall Florence 26.4.05 Track Listing: As above. Source: Audience 2 CD set.

Harmonie Bonn 16.6.05 Track Listing: As above. Source: Audience 2 CD set.

St Maximin Trier 17.6.05 Track Listing: As above. Source: Audience 2 CD set.

Waldbuhne Hardt Wuppertal 18.6.05
Horizons/Jacuzzi/Bacchus/Firth Of Fifth/Whole Tone Jam-The Red Flower Of Taichi Blooms Everywhere/Hands Of The Priestess/After The Ordeal/Hairless Heart/Classical Jazz/Imagining-Second Chance/Mexico City/Black Light/Kim/The Barren Land/Ace Of Wands.
Source: Audience 1 CD.

Freilichtbuhne den Loreley St Goarshausen 19.6.05
Horizons/Jacuzzi/Bacchus/Whole Tone Jam-The Red Flower Of Taichi Blooms Everywhere-Hands Of The Priestess/After The Ordeal/Hairless Heart/Imagining-Second Chance/Classical Gas/Mexico City/Black Light/Kim/The Journey/Jazz On A Summer's Night/Walking Away From Rainbows/Ace Of Wands. Source: Audience 1 CD.

Le Medley Montreal QC Canada 29.9.05
Medley/Horizons/ Japonica/Tales Of The Riverbank/Segovia/The Pool Of Memory, The Pool Of Forgetfulness/Bay Of Kings/Classical Jazz/Mexico City/Skye Boat Song/Jacuzzi/Bacchus/Whole Tone Jam-The Red Flower Of Taichi Blooms Everywhere-Hands Of The Priestess/After The Ordeal/Hairless Heart/M3/\Imagining/Second Chance/Jazz On A Summer's Night/Next Time Around/Kim/Idylle-Aubade-Meditation. 2 CD Set. Source: Audience.

Hamilton Place Theatre -The Studio Hamilton ON Canada 2.10.05 Source: Audience 2 CD

Summerville Theatre Boston MA USA 9.10.05 Source: Audience 2 CD.

Music Hall Troy NY 10.10.05 Source: Audience 2 CD.

Town Hall Ballroom (The Sphere) Buffalo NY 14.10.05. Source: Audience 2 CD.

XM Radio Studios Washington DC October 2005.
Horizons/Classical Jazz/Jacuzzi/Bacchus/Segovia/Jazz On A Summer's Night/Mexico City/Ace Of Wands/Hands Of The Priestess/The Journey/Interview. Source: FM Radio broadcast. 1CD.

The Swedish American Music Hall San Francisco CA USA 27.10.05 Source: Audience 2 CD

Quartier Modo Berlin 1.10.06
Classical Jazz Medley (Inc: Classical Gas-Cuckoo Cocoon)/Sapphires/Blood On The Rooftops- Tales Of The Riverbank-The Fountain Suite-Black Light-The Journey/The Pool Of Memory, The Pool Of Forgetfulness-Bay Of Kings/Mexico City/Skye Boat Song/End Of Day/Horizons/The Barren Land/Jacuzzi/Roger King Improvisation/Apocalypse in 9/8/After The Ordeal/ Hairless Heart/M3/Next Time Around/Jazz On A Summer's Night/Imagining/Second Chance/Walking Away From Rainbows/Whole Tone Jam-The Red Flower Of Taichi Blooms Everywhere-Hands Of The Priestess/Kim/The Hermit-Ace Of Wands/Bacchus/Ace Of Wands (Reprise).
Source: Audience 2CD Set.

Teatro Chiabrera Savona 24.3.07
Classical Jazz/ Japonica/Andante In C/Tales Of The Riverbank/Segovia/Metamorpheus Medley/ Bay of Kings/Sapphires/Mexico City/The Barren Land/Black Light/the Skye Boat Song/Peaseblossom/Horizons/All Is Mended/Time-Lapse At Milton Keynes/ Fountain Of Salamis (excerpt)/The Journey/Jacuzzi/Apocalypse In 9-8/After The Ordeal/Hairless Heart/M3/Next Time Around/Jazz On A Summer's Night/ Imagining/Second Chance/Walking Away From Rainbows/Whole Tone Jam/The Red Flower Of Taichi Blooms Everywhere/Hands Of The Priestess/Kim/The Hermit/Ace of Wands/Gnossienne #1/Bacchus.
Source: Audience 2 CD Set.

2009 Tour

Vaillant Palace Genoa 12.3.09
Fire On The Moon / Every Day / Ace Of Wands / Pollution B / The Steppes / Darktown / Slogans / Serpentine Song / Firth Of Fifth/Acoustic Set/Walking Away From Rainbows/Blood On The Rooftops/ Mechanical Bride/Spectral Mornings/Wall Of Knives/Fly On A Windshield/Please Don't Touch/A Tower Struck Down/In That Quiet Earth/Storm Chaser/Los Endos/Clocks.
Source: Audience 2 CD Set.

Deposito Giordano Pordenone 14.3.09   Track Listing: As above. Source: Audience 2 CD Set.

Estival Jazz Festival Piazza Dei Riforma Lugano Switzerland 4.7.09
Fire On The Moon/Every Day/Ace Of Wands/Pollution B/ The Steppes/Firth Of Fifth/Walking Away From Rainbows/Blood On The Rooftops/Mechanical Bride/Spectral Mornings/Los Endos/Clocks/ Interview with Steve. Source: FM Radio Broadcast 2 CD Set.

Night Of The Prog Festival Freiluftbuhne St Goarshausen 11.7.09
Mechanical Bride/Everyday/Fire On The Moon/Ace Of Wands/Pollution B/The Steppes/Slogans/Serpentine Song/Firth of Fifth/Walking Away From Rainbows/Acoustic Set (Inc: The Barren Land-Horizons)/Blood On The Rooftops/Spectral Mornings/The Wall Of Knives/Fly On A Windshield/Please Don't Touch/A Tower Struck Down/In That Quiet Earth/Los Endos/Clocks. Source: Audience Recording 2 CD Set.

Ino-Rock Festival Teatr Letni Inowroclaw 12.9.09
Mechanical Bride/Fire On The Moon/Every Day/Ace Of Wands/Pollution B/The Steppes/Serpentine Song/Firth of Fifth/Walking away From Rainbows/Horizons/ Blood On The Rooftops/Spectral Mornings/Fly On A Windhsield-Broadway Melody Of 74/Slogans/ A Tower Struck Down/In That Quiet Earth/Los Endos/Clocks.

Boerderij Zoetermeer 28.10.09
Mechanical Bride/Fire On The Moon/Everyday/Emerald And Ash/Ghost In The Glass/Ace Of Wands/Pollution B/ The Steppes/Slogans/Serpentine Song/Tubehead/Spectral Mornings/Firth Of Fifth/Acoustic Set- Horizons/Blood On The Rooftops/Fly On A Windshield-Broadway Melody Of '74/Sleepers/Still Waters/Los Endos/Clocks.

Boerderij Zoetermeer 29.10.09. Track Listing: As above.

Fabrik Hamburg 30.10.09. Track Listing: As above.

Zeche Bochum 31.10.09. Track Listing: As above.

Salle la Kursaal Dolhain (Limbourg) 1.11.09. Track Listing: As above.

Alhambra Paris 7.11.09. Track Listing: As above.

Shepherds Bush Empire Theatre London 14.11.09. Track Listing: As above, plus Jacuzzi, played as part of the acoustic set.

University of East Anglia Norwich 15.11.09. Track Listing: As for Paris.

The Stables Milton Keynes 16.11.09
Mechanical Bride (Take 1)/Blues Improvisation/Mechanical Bride (Take 2)/Fire On The Moon/Every Day/Emerald And Ash/Ghost In The Glass/Ace Of Wands/Pollution B/The Steppes/Slogans/Serpentine Song/Tubehead/Spectral Mornings/Firth Of Fifth/Jacuzzi (with John Hackett)/Acoustic Set/Horizons/Blood On The Rooftops/Fly On A Windshield/Broadway Melody Of '74/Sleepers/Tava/Still Waters/Los Endos/Clocks.

Opera House Buxton 17.11.09. Track Listing: As for Zoetermeer.

Wulfrun Hall Wolverhampton 18.11.09. Track Listing: As for Zoetermeer.

Renfrew Ferry Glasgow 19.11.09. Track Listing: As above apart from omission of Slogans and Fly On A Windshield and the inclusion of Walking Away From Rainbows as part of the acoustic set.

Quays Theatre Salford 21.11.09. Track Listing: As for London.

Picturedome Holmfirth 22.11.09. Track Listing: As for Shepherds Bush.

The Brook Southampton 29.11.09. Track Listing: As for Zoetermeer.

The Assembly Leamington Spa 1.12.09. Track Listing: As for Holmfirth.

2010 Tour

Savoy Theatre Helsinki 6.2.10
Mechanical Bride/Fire On The Moon/Every Day/Emerald And Ash/Serpentine Song / Tubehead / Spectral Mornings/ Firth Of Fifth/Walking Away From Rainbows/Horizons/Blood On The Rooftops/Fly On A Windshield/Broadway Melody Of 1974/Sleepers/Tava/Still Waters/Los Endos/Clocks.

The Boerderij Zoetermeer 2.5.10
Mechanical Bride/Fire On The Moon/Every Day/Emerald And Ash/Carpet Crawlers/Ace Of Wands/Serpentine Song/ Spectral Mornings/Firth Of Fifth/Walking Away From Rainbows/Acoustic Set/Horizons/ Blood On The Rooftops/Fly On A Windshield/Broadway Melody Of 1974/Sleepers/ The Darkness In Man's Heart/Still Waters/Myopia-Los Endos/Clocks.

La Gare Werentzhouse 22.5.10
Intro/Classical Jazz/Black Light/ Andante In C/Bay Of Kings/Improvisation/Horizons/Jacuzzi/The Journey/Supper's Ready (Excerpt)/After The Ordeal/Hairless Heart/M3/Next Time Around/Jazz On A Summer's Night/Imagining/Second Chance/Walking Away From Rainbows/ Improvisation/Hands Of The Priestess/The Hermit/Ace Of Wands/Bacchus/Firth Of Fifth.
(Acoustic Trio Gig)

La Gare Werentzhouse 23.5.10. Set List: As for Zoetermeer.

Dommelsch Zaal Mezz, Breda 24.5.10. Set List: As above.

Music Hall Tarrytown NY 16.6.10
Intro/Classical Jazz/Jacuzzi/The Journey/Genesis Medley: Supper's Ready-After The Ordeal-Hairless Heart)/Jazz On A Summer's Night/Imagining/Second Chance/Walking Away From Rainbows/The Red Flower Of Tai Chi Blooms Everywhere/Hands Of The Priestess/Ace Of Wands/Bacchus/Firth Of Fifth. (Acoustic Trio Show).

Regent Theatre Arlington MA 22.6.10
Mechanical Bride/Fire On The Moon /Every Day/Emerald And Ash/Ace Of Wands/The Steppes/Slogans/ Serpentine Song/Blood On The Rooftops/Fly On A Windshield/Broadway Melody Of 1974/Sleepers/Still Waters/In That Quiet Earth/Firth Of Fifth/Clocks.

"River To River Festival" Rockerfeller Park New York NY 23.6.10
Every Day/Fire On The Moon/Ace Of Wands/Sleepers/Still Waters/Los Endos/Clocks.

Park West Chicago IL 29.6.10
Every Day/Emerald And Ash/ Fire On The Moon/Ace Of Wands/Spectral Mornings/Sleepers/Still Waters/Los Endos/Firth Of Fifth.

South Milwaukee Performing Arts Centre South Milwaukee WI 30.6.10
Every Day/Emerald And Ash/Fire On The Moon/Ace Of Wands/ Serpentine Song/Spectral Mornings/Acoustic Medley/Blood On The Rooftops/Fly On A Windshield/Sleepers/Still Waters/Los Endos/Firth of Fifth.

House Of Blues Cleveland OH 1.7.010. As above minus acoustic set.

"High Voltage Festival" Victoria Park London 25.7.10
Every Day/Fire On The Moon/Ace Of Wands/Sleepers/Los Endos.

Hibiya Open Air Theatre Tokyo 22.8.10
Everyday/Fire On The Moon/Ace Of Wands/Serpentine Song/Fly On A Windshield/Broadway Melody Of 1974/Sleepers/Still Waters/Los Endos/Firth of Fifth/Clocks.

Renfrew Ferry Glasgow 18.11.10
Every Day/Valley Of The Kings/Emerald And Ash/The Golden Age Of Steam/Watcher of The Skies/Carpet Crawlers/Fire On The Moon/Ace Of Wands/Shadow Of The Hierophant/Sierra Quemada/Acoustic Set (Inc: Horizons)/Blood On The Rooftops/Tubehead/Sleepers/ The Darkness In Men's Hearts (Nick Beggs Stick solo)/Still Waters/Prairie Angel/Los Endos/Firth Of Fifth/Clocks.

Academy 3 Manchester 19.11.10. Track Listing: As above with Valley Of The Kings and Every Day switching places.

Arts Centre Pontardawe 20.11.10. Track Listing: As above.

The Assembly Leamington Spa 21.11.10. Track Listing: As above.

Komedia Bath 25.11.10. Track Listing: As above.

Holmfirth Picturedome 26.11.10. Track Listing: As above.

Pacific Road Arts Centre Birkenhead 27.11.10. Track Listing: As above.

Shepherds Bush Empire Theatre London 30.11.10. Track Listing: As above plus performance of All Along The Watchtower featuring John Wetton.

The Junction Cambridge 2.12.10. Track Listing: As for Birkenhead.

The Stables Milton Keynes 3.12.10. Track Listing: As above.

The Maltings Farnham 16.12.10. Track Listing As above.

2011 Tour

Lazienki Park Warsaw 14.5.11
Improvisation/Jacuzzi/ Overnight Sleeper/Apocalypse In 9-8/After The Ordeal/Hairless Heart/Jazz On A Summer's Night/Imagining/Second Chance/Walking Away From Rainbows/Hands of The Priestess/Ace Of Wands/Bacchus-Firth of Fifth-Bacchus/Voodoo Child.

La Cigale Paris 9.10.11. Track Listing: As for Farnham above.

APPENDIX 7
Genesis Gigs 1971-77

Steve had seen Genesis at their Lyceum gigs in late December 1970, and he officially joined them at the beginning of 1971. From then on it was full steam ahead for him and the band.

Trespass/Nursery Cryme Tours 1971

University College	London	England	14.1.71
Technical College	High Wycombe	England	15.1.71
Tower Theatre	Blackpool	England	17.1.71
Assembly Rooms	Derby	England	19.1.71
City University	London	England	22.1.71
Lyceum Theatre	London	England	24.1.71 *
Town Hall	Birmingham	England	25.1.71 *
Colston Hall (Aft)	Bristol	England	26.1.71 *
Town Hall (Eve)	Watford	England	26.1.71
City Hall	Sheffield	England	27.1.71 *
St George's Hall	Bradford	England	28.1.71 *
Free Trade Hall	Manchester	England	30.1.71 *
City Hall	Newcastle	England	31.1.71 *
?	Hattton	England	5.2.71 *
Friars Club	Aylesbury	England	6.2.71
Rainbow Theatre	London	England	9.2.71
The Dome	Brighton	England	11.2.71 *
Winter Gardens	Bournemouth	England	13.2.71 *

(*These shows were part of the first Charisma "Package Tour" which featured Genesis with label mates: Van Der Graaf Generator and Lindisfarne)

City Hall	Hull	England	19.2.71
University	Southampton	England	20.2.71
Colston Hall	Bristol	England	22.2.71
Blaises Club	London	England	23.2.71
Mountford Hall LSU	Liverpool	England	25.2.71
University Great Hall	Durham	England	28.2.71
Tower Theatre	Blackpool	England	4.3.71

Venue	City	Country	Date
University Great Hall	York	England	5.3.71
Lyceum Theatre	Birmingham	England	6.3.71
La Ferme	Woluwe St Lambert	Belgium	7.3.71

(This was Genesis' first overseas gig)

Venue	City	Country	Date
TV Studios	Brussels	Belgium	8-9.3.71

(Session performances for "Pop Shop" Genesis's first overseas TV appearances and one which sadly appears to have been erased from the TV Company's archives)

Venue	City	Country	Date	
University Great Hall	Essex	England	13.3.71	
East Street Hall	London	England	14.3.71	
Sophia Gardens	Cardiff	Wales	16.3.71	
Dacorum College	Hemel Hempstead	England	2.4.71	
Technical College	Farnborough	England	3.4.71	
Angel Hotel	Godalming	England	4.4.71	
Lyceum Theatre	London	England	9.4.71	
Fairfield Hall	Croydon	England	11.4.71	**
Guildhall	Portsmouth	England	13.4.71	**
Civic Hall	Guildford	England	15.4.71	**
Floral Hall	Southport	England	22.4.71	**
Green's Playhouse	Glasgow	Scotland	23.4.71	**
Caird Hall	Dundee	Scotland	24.4.71	**
Caley Cinema	Edinburgh	Scotland	25.4.71	**
Free Trade Hall	Manchester	England	26.4.71	**

(** Further gigs with Van Der Graaf Generator and Lindisfarne)

Venue	City	Country	Date
Arts College	Kingston	England	30.4.71
Resurrection Club	Hitchin	England	1.5.71
Guildhall	Portsmouth	England	4.5.71
Marquee Club	London	England	6.5.71
University Of East Anglia	Norwich	England	7.5.71
Clarence's	Halifax	England	8.5.71
BBC Studios	Shepherds Bush	England	10.5.71

("Sounds Of The Seventies" session: Musical Box/Stagnation)

Venue	City	Country	Date
Youth Centre	Bletchley	England	21.5.71
Kingston Hall	Watford	England	22.5.71
TV Studios	Brussels	Belgium	4-6.6.71

(Possible recording session for "Pop Shop" TV Show Exact details of the broadcast are not currently known)

Venue	City	Country	Date
Lyceum Theatre	London	England	8.6.71
Queen Margaret College	Edinburgh	Scotland	12.6.71
Cheltenham Girls College	Cheltenham	England	18.6.71
Friars Club	Aylesbury	England	19.6.71
Festival	Reading	England	26.6.71
Addison Centre (Friars Club)	Bedford	England	2.7.71
Farx Club	Southall	England	3.7.71
Marquee Club	London	England	9.7.71
Lyceum Theatre	London	England	14.7.71
?	Brussels	Belgium	7-8.8.71

(Possible recording session for "Pop Shop"/"Rock Of The Seventies" programmes)

Weeley Festival	Clacton	England	28.8.71

(Festival line up also included: Van Der Graaf Generator and King Crimson)

Pavilion	Hemel Hempstead	England	5.9.71
Civic Centre	Gravesend	England	16.9.71
The Temple	London	England	18.9.71
Surrey Rooms	Kennington	England	22.9.71
Town Hall	Kensington	England	23.9.71
Sevens, The Leas	Letchworth	England	25.9.71
Kingham Hall	Watford	England	9.10.71
William Street Club	Windsor	England	12.10.71
Lyceum Theatre	London	England	14.10.71 □
Guildhall	Preston	England	16.10.71 □
The Halls	Dorking	England	19.10.71 □
Town Hall	Oxford	England	21.10.71 □

(□gigs featured Van Der Graaf Generator)

University	Essex	England	23.10.71
Guildhall	Southampton	England	26.10.71
Town Hall	Birmingham	England	27.10.71
City Hall	Newcastle	England	28.10.71
Lake Hall	Birmingham	England	29.10.71
Guildhall	Plymouth	England	31.1.0.71
The Dome	Brighton	England	1.11.71
Starlight Club	Crawley	England	2.11.71
Kings Hall	Derby	England	3.11.71
Tower Theatre	Blackpool	England	4.11.71
College Of Technology	Slough	England	6.11.71
City Hall	Salisbury	England	7.11.71
Community Centre	Slough	England	19.11.71
Sevens, The Leas	Letchworth	England	20.11.71
Surrey Rooms	Kennington	England	22.11.71
Lyceum Theatre	London	England	24.11.71
Corn Exchange	Cambridge	England	25.11.71
Eton College	Windsor	England	26.11.71
City Hall	Newcastle	England	28.11.71
City Hall	Sheffield	England	30.11.71
Lyceum Theatre	London	England	2.12.71
Red Lion	Leytonstone	England	3.12.71
Lawkins Centre	Cottingham	England	4.12.71
Hobbit's Garden	Wimbeldon	England	7.12.71
Technical College	Kings Lynn	England	8.12.71
Teeside Polytechnic	Middlesborough	England	9.12.71
Culham College	Abingdon	England	10.12.71
Cranbrook School	High Wycombe	England	11.12.71
Windrush Twilight Club	High Wycombe	England	12.12.71
Big Brother Club	Greenford	England	15.12.71
Grammar School	Weymouth	England	16.12.71
South Parade Pier	Portsmouth	England	21.12.71
Kingham Hall	Watford	England	23.12.71

1971 was to be a pivotal year for Genesis with the arrival of Phil Collins and Steve and a dramatic upturn in the number of gigs that the band were now performing up and down the country and their first tentative forays overseas as well. Their live set increased in length too and now included; *Happy The Man / Fountain Of Salmacis / Seven Stones / Twilight Alehouse / The Light / White Mountain / Musical Box / Harlequin / The Knife / Going Out To Get You / The Return Of The Giant Hogweed.*

The Roundhouse	Dagenham	England	1.1.72
Maltings	Farnham (Rehearsals)	England	4-6.1.72
Technical College	Bradford	England	7.1.72
Baths Hall	Epsom	England	8.1.72
BBC Studios	Shepherds Bush	England	9.1.72

(Recordings made for both "Sounds Of The Seventies" and "Top Gear" programmes: Harold The Barrel/Harlequin/Fountain Of Salmacis/The Return Of The Giant Hogweed. The Top Gear programme referred to here was a radio show hosted by John Peel and not the current TV show of the same name!)

Maltings	Farnham (Rehearsals)	England	11-13.1.72
?	Brussels (Rehearsal)	Belgium	14.1.72
Salle Petite	Arlon	Belgium	15.1.72
Festival	Charleroi	Belgium	16.1.72
Maltings	Farnham (Rehearsal)	England	17.1.72
Island	Ilford (Rehearsal)	England	18.1.72

(The band also recorded another "Top Gear" performance for the BBC on this date)

College Of Education	Coventry	England	19.1.72
St John's College	Manchester	England	20.1.72
Woluwe St Pierre	Brussels	Belgium	22.1.72

(Possibly a performance for either "Pop Shop" or "Rock Of The Seventies" exact details are unknown and the footage appears to have been erased from the TV company archives)

Palais Des Beaux Arts	Charleroi	Belgium	23.1.72
TV Studios	Brussels	Belgium	24.1.72

(Possibly a performance for either "Pop Shop" or "Rock Of The Seventies" exact details are unknown and the footage has not been seen on TV since 1972/3)

Trocadero	Liege	Belgium	24.1.72
Toby Jug	Tolworth	England	27.1.72
Town Hall	High Wycombe	England	28.1.72
University Of Surrey	Guildford	England	29.1.72
Black Prince	Bexley Heath	England	30.1.72
Maltings	Farnham (Rehearsals)	England	1-3.2.72
Queen Elizabeth Hall	London	England	4.2.72
College Of Technology	Luton	England	5.2.72
Lancing College	Sussex	England	6.2.72
Maltings	Farnham (Rehearsal)	England	8.2.72
Rainbow Theatre	London	England	9.2.72
The Dome	Brighton	England	10.2.72
Winter Gardens	Penzance	England	11.2.72
Van Dyke Club	Plymouth	England	12.2.72
University College Of Wales	Aberystwyth	Wales	14.2.72

Green's Playhouse	Glasgow	Scotland	16.2.72
City Hall	Sheffield	England	17.2.72
Medway Technology College	Maidstone	England	18.2.72

(This gig was cancelled due to a power cut in the locality)

Alex Disco	Salisbury	England	19.2.72
The Greyhound	Croydon	England	20.2.72
Winter Gardens	Cleethorpes	England	21.2.72
City Hall	Newcastle	England	22.2.72
Polytechnic	Leicester	England	23.2.72
Town Hall	High Wycombe	England	24.2.72
Locarno Ballrooms	Sunderland	England	25.2.72
Sports Centre	Bracknell	England	26.2.72
Civic Centre	Chelmsford	England	28.2.72

(This gig was cancelled and the band undertook a day's rehearsal instead)

Rehearsals	West Hampstead	England	29.2.72
Civic Centre	Chelmsford	England	1.3.72
BBC Paris Studios	London	England	2.3.72

("In Concert" live radio session: Fountain Of Salmacis/Musical Box/The Return of The Giant Hogweed)

Island Studios	London (Recording)	England	3.3.72
Technical College	Watford	England	4.3.72
Rehearsals	West Hampstead	England	7-9.3.72
South Parade Pier	Portsmouth	England	10.3.72
Friars Club	Aylesbury	England	11.3.72
The Tram Shed	Woolwich (Rehearsals)	England	13-15.3.72
Princes Theatre	Hull	England	16.3.72
Aston University	Birmingham	England	17.3.72

(Harlequin from the 9.1.72 BBC session was finally broadcast by the BBC as part of the John Peel Sessions on this date)

Fete Saint Gratien	Troyes	France	18-19.3.72
TV Studios	Brussels	Belgium	20-21.3.72

(Earliest surviving visual document of the band featuring: Fountain Of Salmacis/Musical Box/Twilight Alehouse/The Return Of The Giant Hogweed performed for the "Pop Shop" programme)

?	Essex	England	24.3.72
Carshalton College	Essex	England	25.3.72
The Manor	Essex (Recording)	England	26.3.72
Rehearsals	Blackheath	England	29-31.3.72
Trident Studios	London (Mixing)	England	4.4.72
Heathrow Airport	London	England	5.4.72

(Band set off for their first Italian tour)

Palasport	Beluno	Italy	6.4.72
Apollo 2000	Godega di S Urbano Treviso	Italy	7.4.72
Dancing Paradiso	Trieste	Italy	8.4.72

(This gig was cancelled by the police due to political unrest in the area and Peter dedicates the following night's gig to the people of Trieste)

Lem (2 shows)	Verona	Italy	9.4.72
Palasport	Pesaro	Italy	11.4.72
Palasport	Reggio Emilia	Italy	12.4.72
Le Rotonde	Cuorgne Turin	Italy	13.4.72

Palasport (2 shows)	Pavia	Italy	14.4.72
Hit Parade (2 shows)	Lugo di Romagna Ravenna	Italy	15.4.72
Supertivoli	Travagliato Brescia	Italy	16.4.72
Palasport	Siena	Italy	17.4.72
Piper Club (2 shows)	Rome	Italy	18.4.72
Teatro Mediterraneo	Naples	Italy	19.4.72
Petite Salle	Arlon	Belgium	22.4.72
Zoom Club	Frankfurt	Germany	23.4.72
The Greyhound	Croydon	England	25.4.72
Van Dyke Club	Plymouth	England	26.4.72
Branton (?)	Essex (Rehearsal)	England	27.4.72
Polytechnic	Kingston	England	28.4.72
Polytechnic	Isleworth	England	29.4.72
Civic Hall	Guildford	England	3 0.4.72
Red Lion	Leytonstone	England	5.5.72
University College	Bangor	Wales	6.5.72
University Of Essex	High Wycombe	England	8.5.72
Town Hall	Oxford	England	9.5.72
Cleopatra's	Derby	England	11.5.72
Mecca Ballrooms	Newcastle	England	19.5.72
City Hall	St Albans	England	20.5.72
Youth Centre	Bletchley	England	21.5.72
Winter Gardens	Penzance	England	25.5.72
Van Dyke Club	Plymouth	England	26.5.72
Technical College	Farnborough	England	27.5.72

Foxtrot Tour 1972/73

Great Western Festival	Lincoln	England	28.5.72

(Line up included: Joe Cocker/Status Quo/Monty Python/The Beach Boys/Van der Graaf Generator)

The Pier	Hastings	England	2.6.72
Technical College	Luton	England	3.6.72
Lyceum Theatre	London	England	4.6.72
Olympia Theatre	Paris	France	5.6.72
The Rock Club	Wellingborough	England	6.6.72
Polytechnic	Leeds	England	9.6.72
Argus	Peterlee	England	11.6.72
Corn Exchange	Cambridge	England	12.6.72
Rehearsals	Blackheath	England	13-15.6.72
Corn Exchange (Friars Club)	Bedford	England	16.6.72
The Rock	Wellingborough	England	17.6.72
Top Rank	Swansea	Wales	19.6.72
Rehearsals	Blackheath	England	20-22.6.72
Castle	Durham	England	23.6.72
Pier Pavilion	Felixstowe	England	24.6.72
Town Hall	Watford	England	25.6.72
Olympia Theatre	Paris	France	26.6.72

(Show also featured Van Der Graaf Generator and Lindisfarne)

Town Hall	Watford	England	28.6.72

Town Hall	Shoreditch	England	29.6.72
Community Centre	Slough	England	30.6.72
The Greyhound	Croydon	England	2.7.72
Rehearsals	Blackheath	England	3-5.7.72
Marquee Club	London	England	7.7.72
Carre Hotel	Amsterdam	Holland	8.7.72
Island Studios	London (Recording)	England	10-12.7.72
Uppingham School	Uppingham	England	13.7.72

(This was a rehearsal for the band's gig at the Lyceum the following night)

Lyceum Theatre	London	England	14.7.72
Coatham Hotel	Redcar	England	16.7.72
Rehearsals	Blackheath	England	17-20.7.72
Red Lion	Leytonstone	England	21.7.72
Alex Disco	Salisbury	England	22.7.72
The Wake Arms	Epping	England	23.7.72
Civic Hall	Solihull	England	25.7.72
Winter Gardens	Cleethorpes	England	27.7.72
Archer Hall	Bilericay	England	28.7.72
Rehearsals	Blackheath	England	31.7.72
Rehearsals	Blackheath	England	4.8.72
Island Studios	London (Recording)	England	6.8.72
Carre Hotel	Amsterdam	Holland	7.8.72
Festival	Bilsen	Belgium	8.8.72
Island Studios	London (Recording)	England	9-10.8.72
Festival	Reading	England	11.8.72
Island Studios	London (Recording)	England	11.8.72
Palasport	Reggio Emilia	Italy	15.8.72
Corte Malatestana	Fano	Italy	16.8.72 *
Dancing Lago delle Rose	Monselice	Italy	18.8.72 *
Jolly Club (2 shows)	Ravenna	Italy	19.8.72 *
Piper 2000 Club (2 shows)	Viareggio	Italy	20.8.72 *
Palasport	Albegna	Italy	21.8.72 *
Teatro Alcione	Genoa	Italy	22.8.72 *
La Locanda del Lupo	Rimini (2 Shows)	Italy	23.8.72 *

(*Shows performed with Jumbo/Osanna)

Island Studios	London (Mixing)	England	25-27.8.72
Civic Hall	Merton	England	1.9.72
Friars Club	Aylesbury	England	2.9.72
Chelsea Village	Bournemouth	England	3.9.72
Halle Polyvalente	Montbeliard	France	9.9.72
Big Brother Club	Greenford	England	13-15.9.72
Sports Centre	Bracknell	England	16.9.72
The Greyhound	Croydon	England	17.9.72
Marquee Club	London	England	19.9.72
Friars Club	Aylesbury	England	22.9.72
Tait Hall	Kelso	Scotland	23.9.72
BBC Studios	London	England	25.9.72

("Sounds Of The Seventies" recording session: Watcher Of The Skies/Twilight Alehouse/Get 'Em Out By Friday)

National Stadium	Dublin	Rep Of Ireland	28.9.72

(Peter Gabriel wore the red dress and fox's head for the very first time at this gig)

Friars Club	Aylesbury	England	29.9.72
Oval	Kennington	England	30.9.72

(Melody Maker "Poll Winner's Party" festival: ELP/Wishbone Ash/Argent/Focus/Fudd)

City Hall	Newcastle	England	1.10.72 *
City Hall	Sheffield	England	3.10.72 *
Music Hall	Aberdeen	Scotland	4.10.72 *
Green's Playhouse	Glasgow	Scotland	6.10.72 *
Empire Theatre	Edinburgh	Scotland	7.10.72 *
Free Trade Hall	Manchester	England	10.10.72 *
St George's Hall	Bradford	England	11.10.72 *
De Montfort Hall	Leicester	England	12.10.72 *
Winter Gardens	Bournemouth	England	13.10.72 *
Polytechnic	Kingston	England	14.10.72 *
Coliseum	London	England	15.10.72 *
Top Rank Club	Liverpool	England	16.10.72 *
City Hall	Hull	England	17.10.72 *
Top Rank Club	Watford	England	18.10.72 *
Trentham Gardens	Stoke On Trent	England	19.10.72 *
Top Rank Club	Bristol	England	20.10.72 *
New Theatre	Oxford	England	21.10.72 *
Guildhall	Preston	England	22.10.72 *
Guildhall	Portsmouth	England	24.10.72 *
Odeon Theatre	Birmingham	England	25.10.72 *
Top Rank Club	Cardiff	Wales	26.10.72 *
Top Rank Club	Brighton	England	27.10.72 *
Odeon Theatre	Lewisham	England	29.10.72 *

(*These gigs were another Charisma package tour featuring Genesis with either Lindisfarne or Rab Noakes)

Cooksferry Inn	Edmonton	England	30.10.72
Hard Rock Concert Theatre	Stretford	England	2.11.72
Ciciv College	Ipswich	England	3.11.72
University	Leeds	England	4.11.72
The Wake Arms	Epping	England	5.11.72
Winter Gardens	Cleethorpes	England	6.11.72
Sundown Club	Mile End Brixton (Rehearsals)	England	8-9.11.72
Brunel University	Uxbridge	England	10.11.72

(This gig featured the first live performance of Supper's Ready)

Marquee Club (Afternoon)	London	England	11.11.72
Alex Disco (Evening)	Salisbury	England	11.11.72
Fairfield Hall	Croydon	England	12.11.72
Lyceum Theatre	London (Rehearsals)	England	13-14.11.72
Polytechnic	Kingston	England	15-16.11.72
Essex University	Chelmsford	England	17.11.72
Imperial College	London	England	18.11.72
Town Hall	Cheltenham	England	19.11.72
Corn Exchange	Kings Lynn	England	24.11.72
The Belfry Hotel	Sutton Coldfield	England	25.11.72
Lords Club Civic Hall	Gravesend	England	26.11.72

Sundown Club	Mile End Brixton	England	6.12.72
University	Southampton	England	7.12.72
Guildhall	Plymouth	England	8.12.72
Brandeis University	Boston MA	USA	16.12.72 **
Carnegie Hall	New York City NY	USA	17.12.72 **
Salle D'Expositions	Mulhouse	France	19.12.72 (?)
Salle Penfield	Strasbourg	France	20.12.72 (?)

(**These were Genesis's first US gigs, the following two gigs in France are still subject to some debate but advertising documentation for them does exist although in view of the US dates, it is likely that they were cancelled and they are included here for the sake of completeness only).

The band's continuous gigging was finally beginning to pay dividends and their live show expanded considerably during this period to include: *Watcher Of The Skies / Fountain Of Salmacis / The Musical Box / Get 'Em Out By Friday / Can-Utility & The Coastliners / Supper's Ready / Twilight Alehouse / The Knife / Going Out To Get You / The Return Of The Giant Hogweed.*

The Greyhound	Croydon	England	7.1.73
Place D'Hiver	Marseilles	France	9.1.73
Bataclan Club	Paris	France	10.1.73

(Recorded for the TV show "Pop Deux" and recently re-broadcast on French TV)

Congresshalle	Hamburg	Germany	13.1.73
Statdtahlle	Heidelberg	Germany	15.1.73
Statdtahlle	Offenbach	Germany	16.1.73
Jahrhunderthalle	Frankfurt	Germany	17.1.73

(Recorded for the "Best Of British Festival" the footage is still extant but unbroadcast)

Palasport	Rome	Italy	19.1.73 *
Palasport	Reggio Emilia	Italy	20.1.73 *
Palasport	Rome	Italy	21-22.1.73 *

(*Gigs performed with Lindisfarne/Capability Brown and Balletto di Bronzo)

Sundown Club	Mile End Brixton (Rehearsals)	England	30.1.73 - 1.2.73
Arts Festival	Lanchester	England	2.2.73
Hippodrome	Bristol	England	4.2.73 **
Rainbow Theatre	London (Rehearsal)	England	8.2.73 **
Rainbow Theatre	London	England	9.2.73 **

(First gig Peter appeared on stage with full costumes)

The Dome	Brighton	England	10.2.73 **
Guildhall	Plymouth	England	12.2.73 **
University Great Hall	Exeter	England	14.2.73 **
Green's Playhouse	Glasgow	Scotland	16.2.73 **
City Hall	Sheffield	England	17.2.73 **
Town Hall	Birmingham	England	18.2.73 **
New Theatre	Oxford	England	19.2.73 **
University Great Hall	York	England	21.2.73 **
City Hall	Newcastle	England	22.2.73 **
University Great Hall	Lancaster	England	23.2.73 **
Free Trade Hall	Manchester	England	24.2.73 **
De Montfort Hall	Leicester	England	25.2.73 **

Civic Hall	Dunstable	England	26.2.73 **

(**Another Charisma "Package Tour" featuring Genesis and String Driven Thing. The gigs at Manchester and Leicester were recorded by US radio and emerged later as the basis of the "Genesis Live" album)

"Bob Harris Show"	New York NY	USA	1.3.73
Carnegie Hall	New York NY	USA	2.3.73
Grand Theatre	Quebec City QC	Canada	3.3.73
Forum	Montreal QC	Canada	4.3.73
Gusman Hall	Miami FL	USA	5.3.73 (?)
Carnegie Hall	New York NY	USA	8.3.73
Tower Theatre	Upper Darby PA	USA	10.3.73
Alpine Theatre	Pittsburgh PA	USA	13.3.73
Alexander Hall	Princeton NJ	USA	28.3.73
Seton Hall University	East Orange NJ	USA	31.3.73
Philharmonic Hall	New York NY	USA	2-3.4.73
Grand Theatre	Quebec QC	Canada	6.4.73
MapleLeaf Gardens	Toronto ON	Canada	7.4.73
Boston University (Cancelled)	Boston MA	USA	10.4.73
War Memorial Auditorium	Rochester NY	USA	11.4.73
Case Western University	Cleveland OH	USA	15.4.73
Henry Levitt Arena	Wichita KS	USA	17.4.73
Aragon Ballroom	Chicago IL	USA	20.4.73
University	Princeton NJ	USA	22.4.73
Brandeis University	Waltham MA	USA	23.4.73
Music Hall	Boston MA	USA	24.4.73
Olympia Theatre	Paris	France	7.5.73

(This was a performance for the French "Musicorama" Radio Show)

L'Ancienne Belgique	Brussels	Belgium	8.5.73
ORTF TV Sessions	Paris	France	6.7.73
Olympia Theatre	Paris	France	7.7.73
Festival	Reading	England	26.8.73
Olympia Theatre	Paris	France	19.9.73
Munsterhalle	Munster	Germany	25.9.73
Congresshalle	Hamburg	Germany	26.9.73
Stadthalle	Darmsdorff	Germany	27.9.73
Palais De Beaulieu	Lausanne	Switzerland	29.9.73
Festhalle	Frankfurt	Germany	30.9.73

Selling England By The Pound Tour 1973/74

Apollo Theatre	Glasgow	Scotland	5.10.73

(Gig cancelled due to electrical problems and re-scheduled for 9th October)

Opera House	Manchester	England	6.10.73
New Theatre	Oxford	England	7.10.73
Apollo Theatre	Glasgow	Scotland	9.10.73
Gaumont Theatre	Southampton	England	11.10.73
Winter Gardens	Bournemouth	England	12.10.73
The Dome	Brighton	England	15.10.73
Colston Hall	Bristol	England	16.10.73

De Montfort Hall	Leicester	England	18.10.73
Rainbow Theatre	London	England	19-20.10.73
Empire Theatre	Liverpool	England	23.10.73
City Hall	Sheffield	England	25.10.73
City Hall	Newcastle	England	26.10.73
Hippodrome	Birmingham	England	28.10.73
Shepperton Film Studios	Borehamwood	England	30-31.10.73

(Filming for the "Tony Stratton-Smith Presents - Genesis In Concert" film.)

Massey Hall	Toronto ON	Canada	8.11.73
Queens University	Kingston ON	Canada	9.11.73
University Sports Arena	Montreal QC	Canada	10.11.73
State University Auditorium	Buffalo NY	USA	11.11.73
Kosh Auditorium	Lawrence NY	USA	13.11.73
Tower Theatre	Upper Darby PA	USA	15.11.73
Tufts University	Medford MA	USA	17.11.73
Bergen Community College	Paramus NJ	USA	18.11.73
Felt Forum	New York NY	USA	22.11.73
Princeton University	Princeton NJ	USA	24.11.73
Gusman Hall	Miami FL	USA	26.11.73
Institute Of Technology	Rochester NY	USA	27.11.73
The Agora	Columbus OH	USA	29.11.73
Allen Theatre	Cleveland OH	USA	30.11.73
State University New Gym	Buffalo NY	USA	1.12.73
North Western University	Chicago IL	USA	3.12.73
Perdue Regional Ballroom	Fort Wayne IN	USA	7.12.73
Peace Auditorium	Ypsilpanti MI	USA	8.12.73
Hara Theatre	Toledo OH	USA	9.12.73
Ford Auditorium	Detroit MI	USA	13.12.73
Roxy Theatre (2 shows)	Hollywood CA	USA	17.12.73
Roxy Theatre (2 shows)	Hollywood CA	USA	18.12.73
Roxy Theatre (2 shows)	Hollywood CA	USA	19.12.73
NBC Studios	Burbank CA	USA	20.12.73

("Midnight Special" TV broadcast: Musical Box/Watcher Of The Skies both of which were slightly different to the album versions)

Hippodrome	Bristol	England	13.1.74
Theatre Royal	London	England	15-16.1.74
Theatre Royal	London	England	18-20.1.74
Vorst Nationale	Brussels	Belgium	26.1.74
Congresshalle	Hamburg	Germany	27.1.74
Eulach Halle	Winterthur	Switzerland	28.1.74
Victoria Conzertshalle	Geneva	Switzerland	29.1.74
Philipshalle	Dusseldorf	Germany	30.1.74
Statdthalle	Offenbach	Germany	31.1.74
Palasport	Turin	Italy	3.2.74
Palasport	Reggio Emilia	Italy	4.2.74
Palasport	Rome	Italy	5.2.74
Teatro Mediterraneo	Naples	Italy	6.2.74
Salle Vaubier	Winterthur	Switzewrland	8.2.74
Palais Des Sports	Marseilles	France	9.2.74
Place D'Hiver	Lyon	France	10.2.74

ORTF TV Studios	Paris	France	12.2.74
(Recording for "Melody" TV show: I Know What I Like/Supper's Ready)			
Capitol Theatre	Passaic	USA	1.3.74
Tower Theatre	Upper Darby PA	USA	2-3.3.74
East Wind Ballroom	Baltimore MD	USA	4.3.74
T P Warner Theatre	Washington DC	USA	5.3.74
Sports Arena	Fort Wayne IN	USA	7.3.74
Fox Theatre	Atlanta GA	USA	8.3.74
Gusman Hall	Miami FL	USA	9.3.74
Muthers	Nashville TN	USA	12.3.74
North Hall	Memphis TN	USA	13.3.74
Armadillo World HQ	Austin TX	USA	17.3.74
Civic Plaza Assembly Hall	Phoenix AZ	USA	20.3.74
Civic Reunion Center	Santa Monica CA	USA	21-22.3.74
Winterland Arena	San Francisco CA	USA	24.3.74
Arena	Seattle WA	USA	26.3.74
Garden Auditorium	Vancouver ON	Canada	27.3.74
Philharmonic Hall	New York NY	USA	2.4.74
Orpheum Theatre	Davenport IO	USA	3.4.74
Embassy Theatre	Fort Wayne IN	USA	5.4.74
Student Union Auditorium	Toledo OH	USA	6.4.74
The Agora	Columbus OH	USA	7.4.74
Centre Culturel Grande Salle	Sherbrooke QC	Canada	8.4.74
Guthrie Theatre	Minneapolis IN	USA	9.4.74
(Cancelled)			
Spectrum	Philadelphia PA	USA	10.4.74
Auditorium Theatre	Chicago IL	USA	11.4.74
Convention Centre	Indianapolis IN	USA	12.4.74
Kiel Theatre	St Louis MO	USA	13.4.74
Memorial Hall	Kansas City MO	USA	14.4.74
Ford Auditorium	Detroit OH	USA	16.4.74
McGaw Hall	Evanston IL	USA	17.4.74
Centre de Congres	Quebec QC	Canada	18.4.74
Civic Centre	Ottawa ON	Canada	19.4.74
Sports Arena	Montreal QC	Canada	20-21.4.74
Auditorium Theatre	Rochester NY	USA	22.4.74
Music Hall	Boston MA	USA	24.4.74
A G Hall	Allentown PA	USA	25.4.74
Century Theatre	Buffalo NY	USA	27.4.74
Allen Theatre	Cleveland OH	USA	28-29.4.74
Massey Hall (2 shows)	Toronto ON	Canada	2.5.74
Syria Mosque	Pittsburgh PA	USA	3.5.74
Academy Of Music	New York NY	USA	4 & 6.5.74

1973 and 1974 were to be still more busy times. The band consolidated their success at home and on the Continent with relentless tours in between which they still managed to find time to write and record their new album, Selling England By The Pound, which gave them their first minor "hit" with the Steve Hackett driven riff of *I Know What I Like*. The band's shows expanded commensurately and were essentially a "Greatest Hits" package featuring: *Watcher Of The Skies/ Dancing With The Moonlit Knight/Cinema Show/I Know What I Like/Firth Of Fifth/Musical Box/ More Fool Me/The Battle Of Epping Forest/Horizons/Supper's Ready* and occasional outings for *Harold The Barrel*.

1974 was also to see the band's most controversial project: The Lamb Lies Down On Broadway which took them on an enormous jaunt around the UK, Europe and the USA and Canada throughout the winter of 1974 and spring of 1975. This project was a massive technical undertaking for which the entire album was presented live with encores consisting of either *The Musical Box, Watcher Of The Skies* and very seldom; *The Knife*. Peter Gabriel's decision to leave at the end of the tour was also the spur which prompted Steve to record his own first solo album: Voyage Of The Acolyte which was released in the summer of 1975 to widespread acclaim before he rejoined the remaining members of Genesis for work on their next album.

The Lamb Lies Down On Broadway Tour 1974/75

City Hall (Fan Club show?)	Newcastle	England	29.10.74 *
City Hall	Newcastle	England	30.10.74 *
Palace Theatre	Manchester	England	1-2.11.74 *
Empire Pool	Wembley	England	4.11.74 *
Usher Hall	Edinburgh	Scotland	6-7.11.74 *
Hippodrome	Bristol	England	8-9.11.74 *
Hippodrome	Birmingham	England	1-12.11.74 *

(*Original UK dates cancelled as a result of Steve's hand injury)

Auditorium Theatre	Chicago IL	USA	20-21.11.74
Indiana Convention Center	Indianapolis IN	USA	22.11.74
Ambassador Theatre	St Louis MO	USA	23.11.74
Music Hall	Cleveland OH	USA	25-26.11.74
Veterans Memorial		USA	27.11.74
Masonic Temple	Detroit MI	USA	28.11.74
National Guard Armory	Fort Wayne IN	USA	29.11.74
Syria Mosque	Pittsburgh PA	USA	30.11.74
Lyric Theatre	Baltimore MD	USA	1.12.74
Warner Theatre	Washington DC	USA	2 (or) 3.12.74

(Originally 2-3 November are days off from the tour schedule)

Mosque	Richmond VA	USA	4.12.74
Philadlephia Civic Center	Philadelphia PA	USA	5.12.74
Academy Of Music	New York NY	USA	6-7.12.74
Palace Theatre	Providence RI	USA	8.12.74
Music Hall	Boston MA	USA	9.12.74
Palace Theatre	Albany CT	USA	11.12.74
Palace Theatre	Waterbury CT	USA	12.12.74
Capitol Theatre	Passaic NJ	USA	13.12.74
Market Square Arena	Indianpolis IN	USA	14.12.74

(This date was not on the original tour schedule)
Forum	Montreal QC	Canada	15.12.74
Maple leaf Gardens	Toronto ON	Canada	16.12.74
The Dome	Rochester NY	USA	17.12.74
Century Theatre	Buffalo NY	USA	18.12.74
Gusman Hall	Miami FL	USA	9-10.1.75
Civic Centre Concert Hall	Lakeland FL	USA	11.1.75
Fox Theatre	Atlanta GA	USA	12.1.75
Music Hall	New Orleans MO	USA	15.1.75
Music Hall	Houston TX	USA	17.1.75
McFarland Auditorium	Dallas TX	USA	18.1.75

(Cancelled)

Civic Centre Music Hall	Oklahoma City OK	USA	19.1.75
Civic Centre	Phoenix AZ	USA	20.1.75

(This date was not on the original tour schedule)

University Of Colorado	Boulder Boulder CO	USA	21.1.75
Community Center	Berkeley CA	USA	22.1.75
Old Waldorf Astoria	San Francisco CA	USA	23.1.75

(22 and 23 January shows not on original tour schedule)

Shrine Auditorium	Los Angeles CA	USA	24.1.75
Golden Hall	San Diego CA	USA	25.1.75
Community Centre	Berkeley CA	USA	26.1.75
Civic Centre	Phoenix AZ	USA	27.1.75
Queen Elizabeth Theatre	Vancouver BC	Canada	28.1.75
Kansas Memorial Hall	Kansas City MO	USA	1.2.75
Grand Valley State College	Grand Rapids MI	USA	2.2.75
MemorialColiseum	Fort Wayne IN	USA	3.2.75
Arie Crown Theatre McCormick Place	Chicago IL	USA	4.2.75

(Last five dates are not included on original tour schedules)

Ekeberghallen	Oslo	Norway	19.2.75
Falkoner Theatrit	Copenhagen	Denmark	21.2.75
Niedersachsenhalle	Hanover	Germany	22.2.75
Eishalle (Deutschlandhalle)	Berlin	Germany	23.2.75
Theatre Carre	Amsterdam	Holland	24-25.2.75
Palais Des Grottes	Cambrai	France	26.2.75
Parc D'Expositions	Colmar	France	28.2.75
Parc D'Expositions	Dijon	France	1.3.75
Palais Des Sports	St Etienne	France	2.3.75
Palais Des Sports	Paris	France	3.3.75
Pavilhao Dos Desportos Cascais	nr Lisbon	Portugal	6-7.3.75
Nuevo Pabellon Club Juventud	Barcelona	Spain	9-10.3.75
Pabellon Real Madrid	Madrid	Spain	11.3.75
Porte de Versailles	Paris	France	17.3.75
Salle D'Expositions	Annecy	France	22.3.75
Palasport Parco Rufino	Turin	Italy	24.3.75
Messezentrum Halle A	Nuremberg	Germany	27.3.75
Festhalle	Berne	Switzerland	29.3.75

Saarlandhalle	Saarbrucken	Germany	30.3.75
Fredrich Ebert Halle	Ludwigshafen	Germany	1.4.75
Killesberghalle 14	Stuttgart	Germany	2.4.75
Jahrhunderthalle	Frankfurt	Germany	3.4.75
Zirkus Krone	Munich	Germany	4.4.75
Statdhalle	Heidelberg	Germany	5.4.75
Philipshalle	Dusseldorf	Germany	6.4.75
Westfalenhalle 3	Dortmund	Germany	7.4.75
Congress Centrum	Hamburg	Germany	8.4.75
Martinihal-Centrum	Groningen	Holland	10.4.75
Ahoy Sportpaleis	Rotterdam	Holland	11.4.75
Vorst Nationale	Brussels	Belgium	12.4.75
Empire Pool	Wembley	England	14-15.4.75
Gaumont Theatre	Southampton	England	16.4.75
Empire Theatre	Liverpool	England	17-19.4.75
Usher Hall	Edinburgh	Scotland	22-23.4.75
City Hall	Newcastle	England	24-25.4.75
Palace Theatre	Manchester	England	27-28.4.75
Colston Hall	Bristol	England	29-30.4.75
Hippodrome	Birmingham	England	1-2.5.75
Ostseehalle	Kiel	Germany	10.5.75
Grugahalle	Essen	Germany	11.5.75
Rhein Am Main Halle	Wiesbaden	Germany	12.5.75
Statdhalle	Bremen	Germany	13.5.75
Patinoire	Rheims	France	15-16.5.75
Velodromo Anoeta	San Sebastian	Spain	18.5.75
Porte De Versailles	Paris	France	20.5.75
Palais Des Grottes	Cambrai	France	21.5.75
Parc D'Expositions	Colmar	France	23.5.75
Palais Des Sports	Dijon	France	25.5.75
Palais Des Sports	Besancon	France	27.5.75

A Trick Of The Tail Tour 1976

Reunion Centre (Rehearsals)	Las Colinas TX	USA	18-24.3.76
Civic Centre	London ON	Canada	25.3.76
Auditorium	Kitchener ON	Canada	27.3.76
Century Theatre	Buffalo NY	USA	28.3.76
Hamilton Place Great Hall	Hamilton ON	Canada	29.3.76
Maple Leaf Gardens	Toronto ON	Canada	31.3.76
Forum	Montreal QC	Canada	2.4.76
Civic Centre	Ottawa ON	Canada	3.4.76
Colisee De Jeunesse	Quebec QC	Canada	4.4.76
Tower Theatre (2 shows)	Upper Darby PA	USA	7.4.76
Beacon Theatre	New York NY	USA	8.4.76
Beacon Theatre (2 shows)	New York NY	USA	9.4.76
Orpheum Theatre	Boston MA	USA	10.4.76
Lyric Theatre	Baltimore MD	USA	12.4.76

Syria Mosque	Pittsburgh PA	USA	13.4.76
Music Hall	Cleveland OH	USA	14.4.76
Ohio Theatre (Cancelled)	Columbus OH	USA	15.4.76
Music Hall (Replacing the show at Columbus)	Detroit	USA	15.4.76
Auditorium Theatre	Chicago IL	USA	16-17.4.76
Ohio Theatre (Rescheduled from 15th)	Columbus OH	USA	19.4.76
Ford Auditorium	Detroit MI	USA	20.4.76
Riverside Theatre	Milwaukee WI	USA	21.4.76
Civic Centre	Grand Rapids MI	USA	22.4.76
Ambassador Theatre	St Louis MO	USA	23.4.76
Memorial Hall	Kansas City MO	USA	25.4.76
Community Centre	Berkeley CA	USA	29.4.76
Warner Theatre	Fresno CA	USA	30.4.76
Starlight Bowl	Burbank CA	USA	1.5.76
Sports Arena	San Diego CA	USA	3.5.76
Memorial Auditorium	Austin TX	USA	5.5.76
Music Hall	Houston TX	USA	6.5.76
Will Rogers Auditorium	Fort Worth TX	USA	7.5.76
Hammersmith Odeon	London	England	9-14.6.76
New Bingley Hall	Stafford	England	15.6.76
Ahoy Sportpaleis	Rotterdam	Holland	16.6.76
Philipshalle	Dortmund	Germany	18.6.76
Deutschlandhalle	Berlin	Germany	19.6.76
Vorst Nationale	Brussels	Belgium	22.6.76
Pavilion De Paris	Paris	France	23.6.76
Palais Des Sports	Lyon	France	24.6.76
Festhalle	Berne	Switzerland	26.6.76
Olympiahalle	Munich	Germany	27.6.76
Festhalle	Berne	Switzerland	28.6.76
Congresshalle	Hamburg	Germany	29.6.76
Scandinavium	Gothenburg	Sweden	30.6.76
Philipshalle	Dusseldorf	Germany	2.7.76
Freilichtbuhne	St Goarshausen	Germany	3.7.76
Rhein Neckar Halle	Heidelberg	Germany	4.7.76
Apollo Theatre (2 shows)	Glasgow	Scotland	8-9.7.76
New Bingley Hall	Stafford	England	10-11.7.76

Wind & Wuthering Tour 1977

Rainbow Theatre (Dress Rehearsal)	London	England	31.12.76
Rainbow Theatre	London	England	1-3.1.77
Odeon Theatre	Birmingham	England	7-8.1.77
Empire Theatre (2 shows)	Liverpool	England	9.1.77
Free Trade Hall	Manchester	England	10-11.1.77
Playhouse Theatre (2 shows)	Edinburgh	Scotland	14.1.77

Venue	City	Country	Date
Caird Hall	Dundee	Scotland	15.1.77
City Hall	Newcastle	England	16-17.1.77
Gaumont Theatre	Southampton	England	19-20.1.77
De Montfort Hall (2 shows)	Leicester	England	21.1.77
De Montfort Hall	Leicester	England	22.1.77
Hippodrome (2 shows)	Bristol	England	23.1.77
Mackey Auditorium	Boulder CO	USA	2.2.77
Municipal Theatre	Tulsa OK	USA	4.2.77
Municipal Auditorium	Kansas City MO	USA	5.2.77
Kiel Auditorium	St Louis MO	USA	6.2.77
Orpheum Theatre	Minneapolis MN	USA	8.2.77
Dane County Memorial Coliseum	Madison WI	USA	9.2.77
Auditorium	Milwaukee WI	USA	10.2.77
Ballrooms	Nashville TN	USA	11.2.77
Masonic Auditorium	Detroit OH	USA	12.2.77
Wings Stadium	Kalamazoo MI	USA	13.2.77
Auditorium Theatre	Chicago IL	USA	15-17.2.77
Winnipeg Auditorium	Winnipeg MN	Canada	19.2.77
Memorial Auditorium	Kitchener ON	Canada	21.2.77
Madison Square Garden	New York NY	USA	23.2.77
Bushnell Auditorium	Hartford CT	USA	25.2.77
Onondaga County War Memorial	Syracuse NY	USA	26.2.77
Richfield Coliseum	Cleveland OH	USA	27.2.77
Memorial Auditorium	Buffalo NY	USA	28.2.77
Forum	Montreal QC	Canada	2.3.77
Colisee De Quebec	Quebec QC	Canada	3.3.77
Maple Leaf Gardens	Toronto ON	Canada	4.3.77
Civic Centre	Ottawa ON	Canada	5.3.77
Maple leaf Gardens	Toronto ON	Canada	6.3.77
The Spectrum	Phildelphia PA	USA	8.3.77
Civic Centre	Baltimore MD	USA	9.3.77
Civic Arena	Pittsburgh PA	USA	10.3.77
Vanderbilt University	Nashville TN	USA	12.3.77
Fox Theatre	Atlanta GA	USA	13-14.3.77
Municipal Auditorium	New Orleans MO	USA	16.3.77
Sam Houston Coliseum	Houston TX	USA	17.3.77
Texas Hall (Cancelled)	Arlington TX	USA	18.3.77
Moody Coliseum	Dallas TX	USA	19.3.77
Municipal Auditorium	Austin TX	USA	21.3.77
Forum	Los Angeles CA	USA	24.3.77
Winterland Arena	San Francisco CA	USA	25-26.3.77
Sports Centre	San Diego CA	USA	27.3.77
Civic Centre	Phoenix AZ	USA	29.3.77
Paramount Theatre	Portland OR	USA	1.4.77
Coliseum	Vancouver BC	Canada	2.4.77
Paramount Northwest	Seattle WA	USA	3.4.77
Starlight Bowl	Burbank CA	USA	1.5.77
Maracananzinho Stadium	Rio De Janeiro (2 shows)	Brazil	14.5.77
Maracananzinho Stadium	Rio De Janeiro (2 shows)	Brazil	15.5.77

Anhembi Stadium	Sao Paolo	Brazil	18-19.5.77
Ibirapuera Stadium	Sao Paolo (2 shows)	Brazil	21.5.77
Ibirapuera Stadium	Sao Paolo (2 shows)	Brazil	22.5.77
Olympiapark Olympiahalle	Munich	Germany	2.6.77
Isstadion	Stockholm	Sweden	4.6.77
EisSporthalle	Berlin	Germany	6.6.77
Isstadion	Stockholm	Sweden	7.6.77
Palais Des Sports (2 shows)	Paris	France	11.6.77
Palais Des Sports (2 shows)	Paris	France	12.6.77
Palais Des Sports	Paris	France	13-14.6.77
Muengersdorfer Sportstadion	Cologne	Germany	17.6.77
Stadion Bieberer Berg	Offenbach	Germany	19.6.77

(Open Air Festival also featuring: Manfred Mann's Earth Band/Lake/Gentle Giant)

Earls Court Arena	London	England	23-25.6.77
Vorst Nationale (2 shows)	Brussels	Belgium	28.6.77
Ahoy Sportpaleis	Rotterdam	Holland	29.6.77
Parc Des Expositions	Colmar	France	1.7.77
Hallenstadion	Zurich	Switzerland	2.7.77
Olympiahalle	Munich	Germany	3.7.77

1976 and 1977 were years of consolidation and triumph over the odds and cynicism of the critics. Both A Trick Of The Tail and Wind & Wuthering brought further success to the band but Steve's desire to work outside the parameters of Genesis eventually brought about his decision to leave and he quit the band in late July 1977.

APPENDIX 8
Solo Gigs 1978-2012

Please Don't Touch Tour 1978

Chateau Neuf	Oslo	Norway	4.10.78 *
Gota Lejon	Stockholm	Sweden	5.10.78 *
Konserthuset	Gothenburg	Sweden	14.10.78
Olympia Theatre	Paris	France	16.10.78
Palais Des Fleurs	Aix-Les-Bains	France	17.10.78
Beat Club	Bremen	Germany	18.10.78 *
Congresshal	Den Haag	Holland	19.10.78
University	Cardiff	Wales	23.10.78 *
Apollo Theatre	Manchester	England	24.10.78 *
Apollo Theatre	Glasgow	Scotland	26.10.78 *
Friars Club	Aylesbury	England	28.10.78
Odeon Theatre	Birmingham	England	29.10.78
Hammersmith Odeon	London	England	30.10.78 *
WDR TV Studios	Baden Baden	Germany	8.11.78 *

1978 and Steve's first solo outing, which follows on the back of his second highly successful solo album Please Don't Touch. This tour finally gives Steve the opportunity to prove exactly what Genesis were missing from his contribution to the band's sound, and indeed 1978 was a rich year all round for Genesis fans, with extensive tours by Genesis and Peter Gabriel in addition to Steve.

Set List: *Please Don't Touch/Racing In A/Carry On Up The Vicarage/Ace Of Wands/Hands Of The Priestess (pt1)/Icarus Ascending/Narnia/Guitar Solo-Horizons-Kim/A Tower Struck Down/Spectral Mornings/Star Of Sirius/Shadow Of The Hierophant/Clocks- The Angel Of Mons/I Know What I Like.*

Tour Personnel: Steve (Guitar/backing vocals), Nick Magnus (Keyboards), Peter Hicks (Vocals), John Hackett (Flute/Bass Pedals), Dik Cadbury (Bass/ backing vocals), John Shearer (Drums/Percussion).

Spectral Mornings Summer Tour 1979

Concerthaus	Gothenburg	Sweden	25.5.79
Chateau Neuf	Oslo	Norway	29.5.79
Liederhalle	Stuttgart	Germany	2.6.79
Hosschulekuenste	Berlin	Germany	3.6.79
Alte Oper	Frankfurt	Germany	4.6.79
Zirkus Krone	Munich	Germany	5.6.79
Hugenottenhalle	Neu Isenburg	Germany	6.6.79
Sartory Saal	Cologne	Germany	8.6.79
Audimax	Hamburg	Germany	9.6.79
L'Ancienne Belgique	Brussels	Belgium	10.6.79 *
Pavilion De Paris	Paris	France	11.6.79
Theatre Sebastapol	Lille	France	12.6.79
La Bourse Du Travail	Lyon	France	14.6.79
Theatre De Verdune	Nice	France	15.6.79
Musik Centrum	Utrecht	Holland	17.6.79
Odeon Theatre	Edinburgh	Scotland	21.6.79
City Hall	Sheffield	England	22.6.79
University	Leicester	England	23.6.79
Empire Theatre	Liverpool	England	24.6.79 *
The Dome	Brighton	England	25.6.79
Pavilion	Hemel Hempstead	England	27.6.79
Civic Hall	Wolverhampton	England	28.6.79
Gaumont Theatre	Southampton	England	29.6.79 *
Hammersmith Odeon	London	England	30.6.79 *
New Theatre	Oxford	England	1.7.79
Festival	Reading	England	26.8.79 *

Spectral Mornings Autumn Tour 1979

Capitol Theatre	Aberdeen	Scotland	22.10.79
Apollo Theatre	Glasgow	Scotland	23.10.79
Apollo Theatre	Manchester	England	24.10.79 *
Royal Court Theatre	Liverpool	England	25.10.79
Victoria Halls	Hanley (Stoke-On-Trent)	England	26.10.79
City Hall	Newcastle	England	27.10.79
Town Hall	Middlesbrough	England	28.10.79
Maxwell Hall (Friars)	Aylesbury	England	28.10.79

(This gig appears in press advertisements for the tour. The Middlesbrough gig is listed in the UK tour itinerary)

St George's Hall	Bradford	England	29.10.79 *
Odeon Theatre	Birmingham	England	31.10.79
Colston Hall	Bristol	England	1.11.79
Odeon Theatre	Chelmsford	England	3.11.79
Gaumont Theatre	Ipswich	England	4.11.79
Assembly Rooms	Derby	England	5.11.79
West Runton Pavilion	Cromer	England	6.11.79
Polytechnic	Plymouth	England	8.11.79
Brunel University	Uxbridge	England	9.11.79

Theatre Royal Drury Lane London		England	11.11.79 *
Arts Centre	Poole	England	12.11.79 *

(According to press reports this gig was cancelled in favour of the gig at Drury Lane the night before but a bootleg recording from Poole is in general circulation. The Drury Lane show was also broadcast by the BBC).

Spectral Mornings was to become a massive success and Steve undertook two separate tours in support of the album in Europe and the UK throughout the summer and autumn months of 1979.

Set List (Summer): *Please Don't Touch/Tigermoth/Everyday/Narnia/The Red Flower Of Taichi Blooms Everywhere/Ace Of Wands/Carry On Up The Vicarage/Acoustic Set/Horizons/The Optigon/A Tower Struck Down/Spectral Mornings/Star Of Sirius/Shadow Of The Hierophant/Racing In A/Ace Of Wands/Clocks - The Angel Of Mons/I Know What I Like.*

Set List (Autumn): *Please Don't Touch/Tigermoth/Everyday/Ace Of Wands/The Virgin & The Gypsy/The Steppes/Sentimental Institiution/The Red Flower Of Taichi Blooms Everywhere/Star Of Sirius/Spectral Mornings/A Tower Struck Down/Clocks - The Angel Of Mons/Acoustic Set/ Horizons/The Ballad Of The Decomposing Man/Hercules Unchained/Racing In A.*

Tour Personnel: SH (Guitar/ backing vocals), John Hackett (Flute/Bass pedals), Nick Magnus (Keyboards), Peter Hicks (Vocals). Dik Cadbury (Bass/ backing vocals), John Shearer (Drums/Percussion).

Defector Tour 1980

Assembly Rooms	Derby	England	11.6.80
Odean Theatre	Edinburgh	Scotland	13.6.80
Apollo Theatre	Glasgow	Scotland	14.6.80
City Hall	Newcastle	England	15.6.80
Apollo Theatre	Manchester	England	16.6.80 *
City Hall	Sheffield	England	17.6.80 *
City Hall	Hull	England	19.6.80
Guildhall	Preston	England	20.6.80 *
Odeon Theatre	Birmingham	England	21.6.80
New Theatre	Oxford	England	22.6.80
De Montfort Hall	Leicester	England	23.6.80
Davenport Arts Centre	Coventry	England	24.6.80
Civic Centre	Guildford	England	26.6.80
Gaumont Theatre	Southampton	England	27.6.80 *
Arts Centre	Poole	England	28.6.80
Top Rank Club	Cardiff	Wales	29.6.80
Royal Court Theatre	Liverpool	England	1.7.80
Odeon Theatre	Hammersmith	England	4-5.7.80 *
Odeon Theatre	Canterbury	England	6-7.7.80 *
Grand Casino	Montreux	Switzerland	13.7.80 *
Palais Montcalm	Quebec QC	Canada	19.9.80

O'Keefe Centre	Toronto ON	Canada	21.9.80
Club Montreal Theatre	Montreal QC	Canada	22.9.80
Paradise Theatre	Boston MA	USA	24.9.80
Toad's Place	Newhaven CT	USA	25.9.80
Uncle Sam's	Syracuse NY	USA	26.9.80
Auditorium Theatre	Rochester NY	USA	27.9.80
Uncle Sam's	Buffalo NY	USA	28.9.80
Bottom Line Club	New York NY	USA	29-30.9.80 *

(The gig on the 30th was filmed and has recently appeared on an unofficial DVD)

Hillwood Hall	Long Island	USA	1.10.80
Bergen County College	Bergen NJ	USA	3.10.80
Tower Theatre	Upper Darby PA	USA	4.10.80
Bayou Club	Washington DC	USA	5.10.80
The Agora	Cleveland OH	USA	?.10.80 *
Harpo's	Detroit OH	USA	9.10.80
The Parkwest	Chicago IL	USA	10.10.80 *
Uptown Theatre	Milwaukee WI	USA	11.10.80
Dooley's	Phoenix AZ	USA	14.10.80
Old Waldorf Theatre	San Francisco CA	USA	15-16.10.80 *
Civic	San Jose CA	USA	19.10.80
Paramount Theatre	Seattle WA	USA	22.10.80
Commodore	Vancouver	USA	23.10.80
Chateau Neuf	Oslo	Norway	11.11.80
Gota Lejon	Stockholm	Sweden	12.11.80
Rijnhal	Arnhem	Holland	14.11.80
Musik Centrum	Utrecht	Holland	15.11.80 *
Palasport	Turin	Italy	24.11.80 *
Palasport	Bologna	Italy	25.11.80 *
Palasport	Rome	Italy	26.11.80 *
Palasport	Turin	Italy	27.11.80
Palasport Cavernaghi	Mestre-Venice	Italy	28.11.80 *
Palasport Pianella	Cantu	Italy	29.11.80 *
Palasport E.I.B	Brescia	Italy	30.11.80
Palasport	Genoa	Italy	1.12.80

1980 and Steve consolidated his success with a UK top ten album, Defector. Touring duties took in most of Europe and the UK and Europe again with a prestigious appearance at the Montreux Festival. Steve also visited the USA for the first time as a solo performer during the year.

Set List: *Slogans/Everyday/The Red Flower Of Taichi Blooms Everywhere/Tigermoth/Kim/Time To Get Out/The Steppes/Acoustic Set/Horizons/Sentimental Institution/Jacuzzi/Spectral Mornings/A Tower Struck Down/Clocks - The Angel Of Mons/Please Don't Touch/The Show/It's Now Or Never/Hercules Unchained.*

Tour Personnel: S H (Guitar/ backing vocals), John Hackett (Flute/Bass Pedals), Nick Magnus (Keyboards), Dik Cadbury (Bass/ backing vocals), Peter Hicks (Vocals), John Shearer (Drums/Percussion).

Cured Tour 1981

Lees Cliff Pavilion	Folkestone	England	22.8.81
Arts Centre	Poole	England	23.8.81
Coliseum	St Austell	England	24.8.81
Gaumont Theatre	Ipswich	England	26.8.81
Rock City	Nottingham	England	27.8.81 *
Festival	Reading	England	28.8.81 *
Carre Theatre	Amsterdam	Holland	31.8.81 *
Vorst Nationale	Brussels	Belgium	1.9.81 *
Hallenstadion	Zurich	Switzerland	3.9.81
Palasport	Milan	Italy	4.9.81 *
Festival	San Remo	Italy	5.9.81
Palasport	Trento	Italy	6.9.81
Palasport	Bolzano	Italy	7.9.81
Rolling Stone Theatre	Milan	Italy	8-9.9.81 *
Palasport	Reggio Emilia	Italy	10.9.81
Palasport	Viareggio	Italy	11.9.81
Castel Sant' Angelo	Rome	Italy	13.9.81 *

(Original venue for this gig was in Udine Italy according to details in the Cured tour programme)

Parco Virgiliano	Naples	Italy	14.9.81 *

(Original venue for this gig was in Ljubjana in the Yugoslav Republic according to details in the Cured tour programme)

Sporthall	Zagreb	Yugoslavia	15.9.81

(Apparently this gig was also a non-starter although why this was the case and whether an alternative gig was played elsewhere remains unknown)

Zirkus Krone	Munich	Germany	17.9.81
Festhalle	Mannheim	Germany	18.9.81
Salle D'Expositions	Colmar	France	19.9.81
Congreshalle	Hamburg	Germany	20.9.81
Ostseehalle	Kiel	Germany	21.9.81
Metropol	Berlin	Germany	22.9.81
Grugahalle	Essen	Germany	23.9.81
Festhalle	Frankfurt	Germany	24.9.81
Concerthal	Den Haag	Holland	25.9.81
Casino Den Bosch (2 shows)	Hertogenbosch	Holland	26.9.81 *
L'Hippodrome Pantin	Paris	France	27.9.81
Guildhall	Portsmouth	England	29.9.81
Colston Hall	Bristol	England	30.9.81
Leisure Centre	Gloucester	England	1.10.81
Victoria Hall	Hanley (Stoke-On-Trent)	England	2.10.81
Empire Theatre	Liverpool	England	3.10.81 *
City Hall	Newcastle	England	4.10.81
Playhouse	Edinburgh	Scotland	5.10.81 *
City Hall	Sheffield	England	6.10.81
Odeon Theatre	Birmingham	England	7.10.81
Apollo Theatre	Manchester	England	8.10.81 *
University Great Hall	York	England	9.10.81
Hammersmith Odeon	London	England	11-12.10.81 *

The Agora	Cleveland OH	USA	26.10.81
Parkwest	Chicago IL	USA	27.10.81
Toad's Place	Newhaven CT	USA	29.10.81
Triangle Theatre	Rochester NY	USA	30.10.81*

(A complete film recording of this gig exists)

Uncle Sam's	Buffalo NY	USA	1.11.81
Massey Hall	Toronto ON	Canada	2.11.81
Pavilion De La Jeunesse	Quebec QC	Canada	4.11.81
Le Club	Montreal QC	Canada	5-7.11.81
State University Of New York	Oswego NY	USA	8.11.81 *

("Poland Aid" gig organised as fundraiser after the declaration of Martial Law in Poland)

Savoy Theatre	New York NY	USA	10-11.11.81

(Part of this gig was subsequently used for the Timelapse live album)

Paradise Theatre	Boston MA	USA	12.11.81
Tower Theatre	Upper Darby PA	USA	13.11.81
North Stage Theatre	Glencove LI	USA	15.11.81
The Bayou	Washington DC	USA	16.11.81
The Agora	Atlanta GA	USA	18.11.81
McAllister Auditorium	New Orleans MO	USA	19.11.81
Agora	Dallas TX	USA	22.11.81
Dooley's	Phoenix AZ	USA	24.11.81
Bachanale	San Diego CA	USA	25.11.81
The Roxy	Hollywood CA	USA	26-28.11.81
Perkins Palace	Pasadena WI	USA	29.11.81
The Old Waldorf	San Francisco CA	USA	23.12.81
Civic	San Jose CA	USA	4.12.81
University Of Washington	Seattle WA	USA	6.12.81
Commodore	Vancouver BC	Canada	7.12.81
Royal Theatre	Victoria ON	Canada	8.12.81

Another year of change for Steve with a stripped down sound and the decision to sing for himself, touring was as extensive as usual even taking in several territories previously untouched by major Western rock bands.

Set List: *The Air Conditioned Nightmare/Jacuzzi/Funny Feeling/Ace Of Wands/Picture Postcard/ The Steppes/Everyday/The Red Flower Of Taichi Blooms Everywhere/Tigermoth/Horizons/Kim/ Overnight Sleeper/Hope I Don't Wake/Slogans/A Tower Struck Down/Spectral Mornings/Please Don't Touch/The Show/Clocks - The Angel Of Mons.*

Tour Personnel: SH (Guitar/Vocals), John Hackett (Bass Pedals/Flute) Nick Magnus (Keyboards), Chas Cronk (Bass), Ian Mosley (Drums/Percussion).

Chapiteau "Elixii Festival"	Brest	France	15.7.82 *
Venue Club	London	England	18.12.82 *

(Another fundraising gig for Poland medical charities after the imposition of Martial Law in that country)

Civic Centre	Guildford	England	29.1.83 *

(Fundraising gig for the Tadworth Children's hospital featuring special guests: Mike Rutherford and Peter Gabriel)

Set List (Venue): *The Steppes/Funny Feeling/Can't Let Go/Hackett To Pieces/A Tower Struck Down/Spectral Mornings/Acoustic Set/Horizons/Overnight Sleeper/Slogans/Please Don't Touch/The Show/Clocks - The Angel Of Mons/Air Conditioned Nightmare/Hackett's Boogie.*

Set List (Guildford): *The Steppes/Funny Feeling/Jacuzzi/Hackett To Pieces/Everyday/A Tower Struck Down/Horizons/Kim/Overnight Sleeper/Slogans/The Show/Clocks - The Angel Of Mons/Here Comes The Flood/Solsbury Hill/Reach Out (I'll Be There)/I Know What I Like.*

Highly Strung Tour 1983

Pavilion	Worthing	England	19.4.83
Odeon Theatre	Birmingham	England	20.4.83
City Hall	Newcastle	England	21.4.83
Apollo Theatre	Manchester	England	22.4.83 *
Playhouse	Edinburgh	Scotland	23.4.83 *
Leisure Centre (Coatham Bowl) Redcar		England	24.4.83

(A complete privately shot film of this gig is reputed to exist)

University	Bradford	England	25.4.83 *
Empire Theatre	Liverpool	England	26.4.83 *
Colston Hall	Bristol	England	27.4.83
Queensway Hall	Dunstable	England	28.4.83
Gaumont Theatre	Southampton	England	29.4.83
Hammersmith Odeon	London	England	30.4-1.5.83 *
Apollo Theatre	Oxford	England	2.5.83

(This gig appears in press advertisements for the tour but not in the tour programme)

Cliffs Pavilion	Southend	England	3.5.83

(This gig appears in press advertisements for the tour but not in the tour programme)

Derngate Centre	Northampton	England	4.5.83
City Hall	Sheffield	England	5.5.83
Royal Centre	Nottingham	England	6.5.83
Winter Gardens	Margate	England	7.5.83
Arts Centre	Poole	England	8.5.83
University Of East Anglia	Norwich	England	9.5.83 *

Another extremely busy year for Steve; Highly Strung brought him a "hit" single in the shape of Cell151 and further extensive touring duties in the UK. Set List: *The Steppes/Camino Royale/Funny Feeling/Weightless/Always Somewhere Else/Hackett To Pieces/Slogans/Give It Away/Spectral Mornings/Acoustic Set/Kim/Overnight Sleeper/Cell 151/ Please Don't Touch/Everyday/Walking Through Walls/The Show/Clocks - The Angel Of Mons/ Hackett's Boogie.*

Tour Personnel: SH (Guitars/Vocals), John Hackett (Bass Pedals/Flute), Nick Magnus (Keyboards), Chas Cronk (Bass), Ian Mosley (Drums/Percussion).

Bay Of Kings Tour 1983

University	Warwick	England	26.10.83 *
Mountford Hall LSU	Liverpool	England	27.10.83 *
University	Leeds	England	28.10.83 *
University	Loughborough	England	29.10.83
Ashton Metro (Cancelled)	Ashton-Under-Lyne	England	30.10.83
Polytechnic	Plymouth	England	1.11.83 *
University	Keele	England	2.11.83 *
University	Newcastle	England	3.11.83 *
Queens Hall	Edinburgh	Scotland	4.11.83 *
University	Dundee	Scotland	5.11.83
Barbican Centre	London	England	7.11.83 *
Festival Hall	Corby	England	8.11.83
Leas Cliff Hall	Folkestone	England	9.11.83
Polytechnic	Oxford	England	11.11.83
Surrey University	Guildford	England	12.11.83
Leisure Centre	Mansfield	England	13.11.83
Vanbrugh Dining Hall	York	England	14.11.83 *
Town Hall	Birmingham	England	15.11.83
University	Cardiff	England	16.11.83 *
Taliesin Theatre	Swansea	Wales	17.11.83 *

An unexpected autumn tour in support of Steve's first acoustic album. The audience reaction to this one was mixed mainly due to appallingly bad advertising. However, Steve let the "small orchestra" weave its magic and the set for these shows was as follows:

Horizons/Time Lapse At Milton Keynes/Bay Of Kings/Calmaria/Hands Of The Priestess/ Jacuzzi/Overnight Sleeper/The Barren Land/Blood On The Rooftops/Tales Of The Riverbank/ Second Chance/Chinese Improvisation**/Petropolis/Kim/Butterfly** (Also known as: The Water Wheel)/Munich/ The Journey/Ace Of Wands/ Cradle Of Swans/Jazz On A Summer's Night**/Horizons.

(** Unreleased at the time of the tour and in the case of The Water Wheel/Butterfly, remain unreleased on a studio album by Steve although they do appear on the Live Archive '83 CD)

Tour Personnel: SH (Acoustic Guitars), John Hackett (Flute)

Hammersmith Odeon	London	England	6.2.86

(Steve was special guest of Marillion at this gig, appearing for the encore: I Know What I Like)

G T R Tour 1986

Lyric Theatre	Baltimore MD	USA	20.6.86
Stanley Theatre	Utica NY	USA	21.6.86
Ulster Performing Arts Centre	New York NY	USA	22.6.86
Orpheum Theatre	Boston MA	USA	23.6.86
Beacon Theatre	New York NY	USA	25.6.86

Palace Theatre	Newhaven CT	USA	27.6.86
Tower Theatre	Upper Darby PA	USA	28.6.86
Constitution Hall	Washington DC	USA	29.6.86
Convention Centre	Quebec QC	Canada	2.7.86
Congress Centre	Ottawa ON	Canada	3.7.86
Verdune	Montreal QC	Canada	4.7.86
Massey Hall	Toronto ON	Canada	5.7.86
Music Hall	Cleveland OH	USA	6.7.86
Syria Mosque	Pittsburgh PA	USA	8.7.86
State Theatre	Detroit OH	USA	9.7.86
Riviera Theatre	Chicago IL	USA	10.7.86
Performing Arts Centre	Milwaukee WI	USA	11.7.86
The Orpheum	Minneapolis IN	USA	12.7.86
Music Hall	Omaha NB	USA	13.7.86
McNicholls Centre	Denver CO	USA	15.7.86
Warfield Theatre	San Francisco CA	USA	18.7.86
Wiltern Theatre	Los Angeles CA	USA	19.7.86
California Theatre	San Diego CA	USA	21.7.86
Arizona State University	Mesa CA	USA	22.7.86
Coliseum	Austin TX	USA	24.7.86
Bronco Bowl	Dallas TX	USA	25.7.86
Music Hall	Houston TX	USA	26.7.86
Sam Gore Theatre	New Orleans LO	USA	27.7.86
Bayfront Theatre	St Petersburg FL	USA	30.7.86
Arena	Miami FL	USA	31.7.86
Apollo Theatre	Manchester	England	8.9.86
Odeon Theatre	Birmingham	England	10.9.86 *
Hammersmith Odeon	London	England	12.9.86
Apollo Theatre	Glasgow	Scotland	14.9.86
Alabamahalle	Munich	Germany	22.9.86 *
Hammersmith Odeon	London	England	29.9.86

Steve must have temporarily taken leave of his senses to embark on the adventures of another "Super Group". GTR took the American charts by storm and the single from the album: When The Heart Rules The Mind even grazed the bottom end of the UK top thirty. Surprisingly enough for such a combination of talents, there were only a handful of UK shows in support of the album and the band were destined to fold shortly afterwards among acrimony and legal disputes.

Set List: *Hackett Acoustic Set (Including; Horizons, Blood On The Rooftops)/Howe Acoustic Set (Including: Clap, Mood For A Day)/From A Place Where Time Runs Slow/Jekyll & Hyde/Here I Wait/Prize Fighters/Imagining/Hackett To Pieces/Hackett-Genesis Medley/Tow The Line/Sketches In The Sun/Pennants/Roundabout/The Hunter/You Can Still Get Through/Reach Out (Never Say No)/When The Heart Rules The Mind.*

Tour Personnel: SH (Electric/Acoustic Guitar), Steve Howe (Electric/Acoustic Guitar), Max Bacon (Vocals), Phil Spalding (Bass), Jonathan Mover (Drums/Percussion), Matt Clifford (Keyboards).

Momentum Tour 1988

Venue	City	Country	Date
Ritz Studios (Rehearsals)	Putney	England	23.4.88
Town Hall	Cheltenham	England	25.4.88
Leas Cliff Pavilion	Folkestone	England	26.4.88
University	Warwick	England	27.4.88
University Of East Anglia	Norwich	England	28.4.88
The Dome	Brighton	England	29.4.88
Essex University	Colchester	England	30.4.88
Opera House	Manchester	England	1.5.88 *
Derngate Arena	Northampton	England	2.5.88 *
Colston Hall	Bristol	England	3.5.88
Polytechnic	Leicester	England	4.5.88
Wessex Hall	Poole	England	5.5.88
The Forum	Hatfield	England	6.5.88
Sadlers Wells Opera House	London	England	7.5.88
Cliffs Pavilion	Southend	England	8.5.88 *
Corn Exchange	Cambridge	England	10.5.88
Civic Hall	Guildford	England	11.5.88
St David's Hall	Cardiff	Wales	12.5.88
Concert Hall	Lewisham	England	13.5.88
Royal Centre	Nottingham	England	14.5.88 *
Alexandra Theatre	Birmingham	England	15.5.88
The Orchard Theatre	Dartford	England	16.5.88
Hexagon Theatre	Reading	England	17.5.88
Teatro Colosseo	Turin	Italy	19.5.88 *
Teatro Orfeo	Milan	Italy	20.5.88 *
Teatro Verdi	Genoa	Italy	21.5.88 *
Teatro Tenda A Strisce	Rome	Italy	22.5.88 *
Osterpoort	Groningen	Holland	24.5.88
Music Centrum	Utrecht	Holland	25.5.88
Paradiso	Amsterdam	Holland	26.5.88 *
De Doelen	Rotterdam	Holland	27.5.88
Het Noorderlight	Tilburg	Holland	28.5.88 *
L'Ancienne Belgique	Brussels	Belgium	29.5.88
"Fife Aid" Craigtoun Park	St Andrews	Scotland	24.7.88
"Rock Glasnost" Festival	Tallinn	Estonia	26.8.88
Central Tejo	Lisbon	Portugal	3.9.88
Teatro Rivoli	Opporto	Portugal	4.9.88
Festa Della Unita	Modena	Italy	5.9.88
Sardines	Oslo	Norway	8.9.88
Gota Lejon	Stockholm	Sweden	9.9.88
Saga Theatre	Copenhagen	Denmark	11.9.88
Quartier Latin	Berlin	Germany	12.9.88
Markthalle	Hamburg	Germany	15.9.88
Zeche	Bochum	Germany	16.9.88 *
Scala	Ludwigsburg	Germany	17.9.88
New Morning	Paris	France	19.9.88 *

(Steve had Mae McKenna as his special guest at all of the UK shows apart from Sadlers Wells where the guests were The Panic Brothers)

Still recovering from the Rock 'n' Roll excess of GTR, Steve returned to his acoustic work for 1988's Momentum. An album of Classical austerity and excellence, which garnered plaudits from Sir Yehudi Menuhin no less! Steve toured extensively in the UK and Europe in support of the album, which was well received by critics and fans alike.

Set List: *Horizons/Bay Of Kings/A Bed, A Chair & A Guitar/Time Lapse At Milton Keynes/Tales Of The Riverbank/Ace Of Wands/Hands Of The Priestess/Overnight Sleeper/Cavalcanti/Second Chance/Portrait Of A Brazilian Lady/Still Life/Jazz On A Summer's Night (Previously known as: Butterfly)/Munich/Notre Dame Des Fleurs/Stepp DGI Guitar Synth Improvisation (including: Sabre Dance or Finlandia)/Kim/The Vigil/The Carrot That Killed My Sister.*

Tour Personnel: SH (Acoustic Guitar), John Hackett (Flute).

| Central TV Studios | Nottingham | England | 13.9.90 * |

Show Personnel: SH (Electric/Acoustic Guitar), Fudge Smith (Drums/Percussion), Julian Colbeck (Keyboards),

Tour Noir US Tour 1992

Le Spectrum	Montreal QC	Canada	14.8.92
El Mocambo	Toronto ON	Canada	15.8.92
D'Auteuil	Quebec QC	Canada	16.8.92
Bottom Line Club (2 Shows)	New York NY	USA	18.8.92 *
Birchmere Auditorium	Alexandria NY	USA	19.8.92
The Penguin	Ottawa ON	Canada	22.8.92
Impaxx Concert Theatre	Buffalo NY	USA	23.8.92
Shank Hall	Milwaukee WI	USA	25.8.92
The Agora	Cleveland OH	USA	27.8.92
The Marquee	Detroit MI	USA	28.8.92
City Limits	Dallas TX	USA	2.9.92
Concert Theatre	Ventura AZ	USA	5.9.92
The Cave	Las Vegas NV	USA	7.9.92
The Strand	Redondo Beach CA	USA	8.9.92
Coach House	San Juan Capistrano CA	USA	9.9.92
Mason Jar	Tempe CA	USA	10.9.92
Cabaret	San Jose CA	USA	12.9.92
Club Soda	Montreal QC	Canada	19.9.92
Bottom Line Club	New York NY	USA	20.9.92 *
Max's On Broadway	Baltimore MD	USA	23.9.92 *
23 East Cabaret	Philadelphia PA	USA	24.9.92 *
Club Bene	South Amboy NJ	USA	27.9.92

Tour Personnel: SH (Vocals/Acoustic/Electric Guitar), Hugo Degenhardt (Drums/Percussion), Dave Ball (Bass), Julian Colbeck (Keyboards)

Guitar Noir Tour 1993

Venue	City	Country	Date
Grand Rex Theatre	Buenos Aires	Brazil	16-17.4.93
Canocao	Rio De Janeiro	Brazil	20.4.93
Palace Theatre	Sao Paolo	Brazil	22.4.93
Town Hall (Rehearsals)	Whitchurch	England	21.5.93
Neptune Theatre	Liverpool	England	22.5.93 *
Renfrew Ferry	Glasgow	Scotland	22.5.93 *
Coatham Bowl	Redcar	England	23.5.93
Spring Street Theatre	Hull	England	24.5.93
Hop & Grape	Manchester	England	25.5.93 *
The Old Bourbon (Cancelled)	Harrogate	England	26.5.93
Wulfrun Hall	Wolverhampton	England	27.5.93 *
De Montfort Hall	Leicester	England	28.5.93 *
University Of East Anglia	Norwich	England	29.5.93
Lead Mill	Sheffield	England	31.5.93 *
Assembly Halls	Worthing	England	1.6.88
Princess Hall	Aldershot	England	2.6.93
Leas Cliff Pavilion	Folkestone	England	3.6.93
Polygon	Southampton	England	4.6.93
Wedgewood Rooms	Portsmouth	England	5.6.93
The Swan Theatre	High Wycombe	England	6.6.93
Bierkeller	Bristol	England	7.6.93 *
The Grand Theatre	London	England	8.6.93 *
Arts Centre	Kendal	England	11.6.93 *
Woughton Centre	Milton Keynes	England	12.6.93 *
St George's Hall (Cancelled)	Bradford	England	13.6.93
Villa Torlonia	Frascati	Italy	5.7.93 *
Centro Sportivo	Selvazzano nr Padua	Italy	6.7.93 *
Castello	Brescia	Italy	7.7.93
Stadio del Pini	Sassari	Italy	9.7.93
Stadietto San Gaviro	Ozieri	Italy	10.7.93
Teatro Tenda	Cagliari	Italy	11.7.93
Irving Plaza	New York NY	USA	26.10.93 *
Charity's	Clifton Park NY	USA	28.10.93 *
The Icon	Buffalo NY	USA	29.10.93
El Mocambo	Toronto ON	Canada	30.10.93
Café Du Palais	Sherbrooke ON	Canada	1.11.93
D'Auteuil (2 shows per night)	Quebec QC	Canada	23.11.93
Club Soda	Montreal QC	Canada	4.5.11.93
The Penguin	Ottawa ON	Canada	6.11.93
The Town Pump	Vancouver BC	Canada	8.11.93
Chillers	San Diego CA	USA	10.11.93
The Coach House	San Juan Capistrano CA	USA	11.11.93
Cabaret	San Jose CA	USA	12.11.93 *
The Strand	Redondo Beach CA	USA	13.11.93
Ventura Theatre	Ventura CA	USA	14.11.93 *

After disappearing off the radar for almost four years, Steve roared back to life with his first rock album since 1994's Till We Have Faces. 1993's Guitar

Noir was his most personal album yet and most of it had been road tested with his new band during the previous year's shows in the USA and Canada.

Set List (Tour Noir 92): *Myopia Medley/A Vampyre With A Healthy Appetite/Flight Of The Condor (Sierra Quemada)/Take These Pearls/Always Somewhere Else/In The Heart Of The City/Walking Away From Rainbows/There Are Many Sides To The Night/In That Quiet Earth/Dark As The Grave/Etruscan Serenade (Omega Metallicus ?)/Depth Charge/Everyday/Cuckoo Cocoon/Blood On The Rooftops/Horizons/The Stumble.*

Set List (Guitar Noir 93): *Myopia Medley/Camino Royale/A Vampyre With A Healthy Appetite/Sierra Quemada/Take These Pearls/In The Heart Of The City/Walking Away From Rainbows/There Are Many Sides To The Night/Dark As The Grave/Depth Charge/In That Quiet Earth/Bass-Drum Duet/Always Somewhere Else/Lost In Your Eyes/Every Day/Blood On the Rooftops/Horizons/Cinema Paradiso/Spectral Mornings/Firth Of Fifth/Clocks - The Angel Of Mons.*

Tour Personnel: SH (Vocals/Acoustic/Electric Guitar), Hugo Degenhardt (Drums/Percussion), Julian Colbeck (Keyboards), Doug Sinclair (Bass)

There Are Many Sides To The Night Tour 1994

Venue	City	Country	Date
Vorst Nationale	Brussels	Belgium	3.5.94 □ *
Teatro Teresa Carrenas	Caracas	Venezuela	7-8.5.94 □
Planet Pul Festival	Uden	Holland	4.6.94 *
Statdhalle	Vienna	Austria	8.6.94 □
Tanzbrunnen	Cologne	Germany	12.6.94 □

(□ Shows were as part of the orchestral tour by David Palmer and the LSO)

Venue	City	Country	Date
Rock Summer Festival	Tallinn	Estonia	17.6.94
Golden Stag TV Festival	Brasov	Romania	7.9.94
Standard	Barcelona	Spain	12.11.94
Sonny Boy	Treviso	Italy	24.11.94 *
Teatro CTM	Brescia	Italy	25.11.94
Teatro Aurora	Como	Italy	26.11.94
Teatro Michetti	Pescara	Italy	28.11.94
Teatro Palladium	Rome	Italy	29.11.94
Teatro Metropolitan	Palermo	Italy	1.12.94 *
Teatro Nuovo	Catania	Italy	2.12.94

1994 saw Steve continuing to tour with both a brand new acoustic duo show featuring him and Julian Colbeck on keyboards as well as performing several shows under the auspices of David Palmer's orchestral interpretations of the music of Genesis, Yes and Pink Floyd.

Set List (Palmer shows): *Turn It On Again/Whole Lotta Love/Money/Los Jigos/Living In The Past/Drum Solo/Black Light/Blood On The Rooftops/Cuckoo*

Cocoon/Chinese Improvisation - Unquiet Slumbers For The Sleepers/Horizons/Cavalcanti/Tales Of The Riverbank/Classical Piece/ The Journey/Notre Dame Des Fleurs/Silence/Run Like Hell/Owner Of A Lonely Heart/ Roundabout.

Set List (Acoustic gigs): *Horizons/Black Light/The Skye Boat Song/Time Lapse At Mi;ypm Keynes/ Beja Flor/Kim/Second Chance/Oh How I Love You/The Journey/Baroque/Walking Away From Rainbows/Cavalcanti/Andante In C/Concerto In D (largo)/A Blue Part Of Town/There Are Many Sides To The Night/Ace Of Wands/Cinema Paradiso/Blues Coda/Jazz On A Summer's Night/End Of Day.*

Tour Personnel: SH: (Acoustic Guitar), Julian Colbeck (Keyboards).

Genesis Revisited/Tokyo Tapes Tour 1996

Koseinenkin Hall	Tokio	Japan	16-17.12.96 *
Koseinenkin Hall	Osaka	Japan	19.12.96 *
Koseinenkin Hall	Nagoya	Japan	20.12.96 *

Steve took everyone by surprise in 1996 by releasing the Genesis revisited album. Taking a fresh look at some of the classic Genesis tracks he had been involved with. The resulting album generated mixed opinions among fans but the resulting live shows in Japan certainly were classic Hackett performances.

Set List: Available on CD, VHS and DVD.

Tour Personnel: SH (Electric/Acoustic Guitar/Vocals/Harmonica), Ian MacDonald (Flute/Saxophone/Guitar/Keyboards/Vocals), John Wetton (Bass/Guitar/Vocals), Julian Colbeck (Keyboards/Vocals), Chester Thompson (Drums).

"The Italian Job" Italian Tour 2000

Ritz Studios (Rehearsals)	Putney	England	1-6.7.00
Festival	Vivegano	Italy	9.7.00 *
Castello Malatestiana	Cesena	Italy	11.7.00 *
Teatro De La Ciminiera	Catania	Italy	13.7.00 *
Piazza Duomo Vecchio	Molfetta	Italy	14.7.00 *
Arena Stella Maris	Pescara	Italy	15.7.00
(Cancelled)			

The turn of the new Millennium saw Steve return to full-scale touring with this short tour of Italy during which he revamped his live set to accommodate material of his more recent projects including the recently released Darktown album. A brand new live show and a new look band brought fresh vitality to the Hackett "Experience"

Set List: *Mechanical Bride/Serpentine Song/Watcher Of The Skies/Hairless Heart/Firth Of Fifth/ Riding The Colossus/Pollution B/The Steppes/Gnossienne #3/Walking Away From Rainbows/ Sierra Quemada/Slavegirls/A Vampyre With A Healthy Appetite/A Tower Struck Down/Lucridus/ Darktown/Camino Royale/In Memoriam/Horizons/Los Endos/In That Quiet Earth.*

Tour Personnel: SH (Electric/Acoustic Guitar/Harmonica/Vocals), Ben Castle (Saxophone), Roger King (Keyboards), Gary O'Toole (Drums/Vocals), Terry Gregory (Bass/Vocals)

"Gira Latino Americana" - Somewhere In South America Tour 2001

Auditorio La Fundacion	Rosario	Argentina	28.6.01
Teatro Real	Cordoba	Argentina	29.6.01
Bristol Martinez	Buenos Aires	Argentina	30.6.01
Teatro Coliseo	Buenos Aires	Argentina	1.7.01 *
Gimnasio	Santiago	Chile	3.7.01*
Canal De La Musica	Curitiba	Brazil	5.7.01
Teatro Carlos Gomez	Blumenau	Brazil	6.7.01
Teatro CIC	Florianopolis	Brazil	7.7.01
Teatro Opiniao	Porto Alegre	Brazil	8.7.01
Canecao	Rio De Janeiro	Brazil	9.7.01
Funchal	Sao Paolo	Brazil	10.7.01
Casa Hacienda Moreyra	Lima	Peru	12.7.01
Santa Rosa De Lima	Caracas	Venezuela	14-15.7.01
Frogs	Panama	Panama	16.7.01
Melico Salazar	Costa Rica	Costa Rica	18.7.01
Premiere	Mexico City	Mexico	20-22.7.01

Steve's first full-scale tour of the South American continent including hijacked gear and rapturously received gigs, all captured for posterity on the subsequent live CD and DVD!

Set List: *Mechanical Bride/Hackett To Bits/Serpentine Song/Watcher Of The Skies/Hairless Heart/ Firth Of Fifth/Riding The Colossus/Pollution B/The Steppes/Gnossienne #3/Walking Away From Rainbows/Sierra Quemada/A Vampyre With A Healthy Appetite/A Tower Struck Down/Lucridus/ Darktown/Camino Royale/In Memoriam/Acoustic Set: Black Light/Horizons/Los Endos/In That Quiet Earth.*

Tour Personnel: SH (Vocals/Harmonica/Electric/Acoustic Guitar), Roger King (Keyboards), Gary O'Toole (Drums/Vocals), Terry Gregory (Bass/Vocals), Rob Townsend (Saxophone/Flute).

Acoustic Horizons Tour 2002

Daiba Aqua City	Tokio	Japan	12-14.1.02 *
Petofi Csarnok	Budapest	Hungary	26.1.02
Teatro Solva	Rosignano nr Pisa	Italy	23.4.02 *
Teatro Mediterraneo	Naples	Italy	24.4.02
Auditorio San Domenico	Foligno	Italy	25.4.02
Blues Jam	Assisi	Italy	26.4.02 *
Barfly	Ancona	Italy	27.4.02
Teatro Sociale	Trento	Italy	28.4.02 *

Tour Personnel: SH (Acoustic Guitar), Roger King (Keyboards), John Hackett (Flute).

US Rock Shows 2002

The Birchmere	Alexandria VA	USA	27.6.02 *
BB Kings	New York NY	USA	28.6.02 *
War Memorial "NEARfest"	Trenton NJ	USA	30.6.02 *
Theatre Of Living Arts	Philadelphia PA	USA	1.7.02
L'International	Trois Rivieres QC	Canada	3.7.02
City Festival	Quebec City QC	Canada	4.7.02

Once again, Steve continued the trend of road-testing new material but also gave his US fans a treat with several classics as well in a revised new set:

The Floating Seventh/Mechanical Bride/Medley (Inc: Myopia-Los Endos-Ace Of Wands-Please Don't Touch)/Serpentine Song/Watcher Of The Skies/Hairless Heart/Firth Of Fifth/Riding The Colossus/Pollution B/The Steppes/In Memoriam/Slave Girls/Vampyre With A Healthy Appetite/Spectral Mornings/Lucridus/Darktown/Camino Royale/Every Day/Medley (Inc: Los Endos-Dancing With The Moonlit Knight)/Los Endos.

Tour Personnel: SH (Electric/Acoustic Guitar/Vocals), Roger King (Keyboards), Rob Townsend (Saxophone/Flute), Terry Gregory (Bass/Vocals), Gary O'Toole (Drums/Vocals).

Acoustic and Orchestral Shows 2002

Bridgewater Hall	Manchester	England	19.7.02
Queen Elizabeth Hall	London	England	21.7.02

(Both of these shows were with Evelyn Glennie's "Rhythm Sticks" Ensemble)

Piazza Del Popolo	Todi	Italy	25.7.02
Corte Del Castello	Falconara	Italy	26.7.02
Cortile Teresiano	Pavia	Italy	27.7.02
Waterfront Hall	Belfast	Northern Ireland	22.8.02

(Show with Evelyn Glennie)

Teatro Sala Tripovich	Trieste	Italy	20.10.02
Manoel Theatre	St Julians	Malta	28-29.10.02
Naima	Forli	Italy	1.11.02 *
Teatro Toniodei	Lanusei (NU)	Italy	2.11.02

Once again revisiting the acoustic side of his career, Steve undertook further acoustic gigs in Japan, Hungary and Italy gigs with Classical percussionist Evelyn Glennie and her "Rhythm Sticks" Ensemble, and even managed to cram in a short series of Rock gigs in the US and Canada - where does he get his energy from?

Set List (Early 2002 Acoustic gigs): *Horizons/Gnossienne #1/Bacchus/Firth Of Fifth/Bay Of Kings/Syrinx/ Imagining (Intro)/Second Chance/Jacuzzi/Overnight Sleeper/The Barren Land/Kim/Time Lapse At Milton Keynes/Blood On The Rooftops/Improvisation/Concerto In D/Hairless Heart/ Mustardseed/Gymnopedie #1/Jazz On A Summer's Night/Cavalcanti/Walking Away From Rainbows/Tales Of The Riverbank/Concert For Munich/The Journey/Medley: Skye Boat Song-By Paved Fountain/Hands Of The Priestess/Ace Of Wands/Idylle- Aubade-Meditation (By: Erik Satie)/ Hairless Heart (Reprise).*

Set List (Rock gigs): *The Floating Seventh/Mechanical Bride/Myopia Medley: Imagining-Los Endos-Imagining/Ace Of Wands/Hackett To Pieces/Serpentine Song/Watcher Of The Skies/Hairless Heart/Firth Of Fifth/Riding The Colossus/Pollution B/The Steppes/Gnossienne #1/Walking Away From Rainbows/In Memoriam/Slave Girls/A Vampyre With A Healthy Appetite/Spectral Mornings/Lucridus/Darktown/Camino Royale/Everyday/Horizons/Fire Hydrant/Los Endos/Sierra Quemada.*

Set List (Late 2002 Acoustic gigs): *Horizons/Bay Of Kings/Colony Of Slippermen/Cuckoo Cocoon/Unquiet Slumbers For The Sleepers/Blood On The Rooftops/The Journey/The Barren Land/Cavalcanti/ Black Light/Tales Of The Riverbank/Time Lapse At Milton Keynes/Skye Boat Song/By Paved Fountain/End Of Day/Mustardseed.*

Tour Personnel: SH (Acoustic Guitar), Roger King (Keyboards), John Hackett (Flute).

To Watch The Storms Tour 2003

PR3 Radio Studios	Warsaw	Poland	?.6.03 *
Guilfest Acoustic Stage	Stone Park Guildford	England	5.7.03
Borders Bookstore	New York NY	USA	5.8.03
Borders Bookstore	White Plains NY	USA	6.8.03
Borders Bookstore	Philadlephia PA	USA	8.8.03 *
Borders Bookstore	Bryn Mawr PA	USA	8.8.03 *
Borders Bookstore	Monroeville PA	USA	9.8.03
Borders Bookstore	Columbus OH	USA	10.8.03
Borders Bookstore	Cleveland Heights OH	USA	11.8.03 *
Borders Bookstore	Chicago IL	USA	12.8.03 *
Borders Bookstore	Minneapolis MN	USA	13.8.03

Tour Personnel: SH (Acoustic Guitar)

| Akasaka Blitz | Tokio | Japan | 29.8.03 * |
| Nanba Hatch | Osaka | Japan | 1.9.03 * |

Tour Personnel: SH: (Electric Guitar/Acoustic Guitar/Vocals/Harmonica), John Paul Jones (Bass/Lap Steel Guitar/Mandolin), Paul Gilbert (Guitars/Vocals), Nuno Bettencourt (Guitars/Vocals/Drums), Pat Mast lotto (Drums), Roger King (Keyboards), Gary Cherone (Vocals).

Borderij	Zoetermeer	Holland	28.9.03 *
Het Noorderlight	Tilburg	Holland	29.9.03 *
The Stables	Milton Keynes	England	3-4.10.03
Wulfrun Hall	Wolverhampton	England	5.10.03 *
City Varieties	Leeds	England	6.10.03 *
Palace Theatre	Newark	England	7.10.03 *
Huntingdon Hall	Worcester	England	9.10.03 *
Coal Exchange	Cardiff	Wales	10.10.03 *
Oakwood Centre	Rotherham	England	11.10.03 *
Renfrew Ferry	Glasgow	Scotland	12.10.03 *
Neptune Theatre	Liverpool	England	13.10.03 *
Whelans	Dublin	Rep of Ireland	15.10.03
Waterfront Hall	Belfast	N Ireland	16.10.03
Opera House	Newcastle	England	18.10.03
Academy 2	Manchester	England	19.10.03 *
De Montfort Hall	Leicester	England	20.10.03 *
Town Hall	High Wycombe	England	21.10.03
Astor Theatre	Deal	England	25.10.03
Queen Elizabeth Hall	London	England	28.10.03 *
Fairfield Hall	Croydon	England	29.10.03 *
Nalen	Stockholm	Sweden	31.10;03
KB	Malmo	Sweden	2.11.03
Tradgarn	Gothenburg	Denmark	3.11.03
Fabrik	Hamburg	Germany	5.11.03
Live Music Hall	Cologne	Germany	6.11.03
Colos-saal	Aschaffenburg	Germany	7.11.03
Meier Music Hall	Braunschweig	Germany	8.11.03 *
Villa Berg	Stuttgart	Germany	9.11.03 *
Capitol	Mannheim	Germany	10.11.03
Centre De Culture	Limbourg	Belgium	11.11.03
Wisla Hall	Krakow	Poland	14.11.03

Steve's first full-scale UK rock tour since 1993 and in support of the highly acclaimed To Watch The Storms saw Steve give his fans a potted history of his solo career with most albums getting a look in in the new live set. Preceding this tour was an unusual series of "master class" solo acoustic gigs sponsored by the Borders Bookstore chain in the US.

Set List (Borders Bookstores gigs): *Classical Gas / Black Light / Medley / By Paved Fountain / Cavalcanti / A Bed, A Chair & A Guitar / Medley / Skye Boat Song / Bay Of Kings*

(Note: The above is a combination of two of the sets played on these shows to give an idea of the differing sets played during each short acoustic performance).

Set List (UK/Europe): *Mechanical Bride/Serpentine Song/Watcher Of The Skies/Hairless Heart / Darktown/Camino Royale/The Steppes/Acoustic Set/Walking Away From Rainbows/Slogans/ Everyday/Please Don't Touch/Firth Of Fifth/A Vampyre With A Healthy Appetite/Clocks/Spectral Mornings/Brand New/Los Endos/In That Quiet Earth/In Memoriam (*)*

(*) Played at handful of German gigs as extra encore.
(The shows at Rotherham and Leicester also saw the guest appearance of John Hackett for a performance of Jacuzzi, and one of Kim at the show in Croydon)

Tour Personnel: SH (Acoustic/Electric Guitars/Harmonica/Vocals), Roger King (Keyboards), Rob Townsend (Saxophone/Flute/Percussion/Vocals), Terry Gregory (Bass/Vocals), Gary O'Toole (Drums/Percussion/Vocals).

To Watch The Storms/Live Archive Tour 2004

Mick Jagger Centre	Dartford	England	4.3.04 *
Derngate Theatre	Northampton	England	5.3.04 *
Pacific Arts Centre	Birkenhead	England	6.3.04 *
St George's Hall	Blackburn	England	7.3.04 *
Lead Mill (Cancelled)	Sheffield	England	11.3.04
Corn Exchange	Cambridge	England	12.3.04 *
Shepherds Bush Empire	London	England	13.3.04 *
Colston Hall	Bristol	England	14.3.04 *
Alexandra Theatre	Birmingham	England	15.3.04 *
Rock City	Nottingham	England	16.3.04 *
Town Hall "The Crypt"	Middlesbrough	England	18.3.04 *
New Theatre	Oxford	England	19.3.04 *
Guildhall	Southampton	England	20.3.04
Phoenix	Exeter	England	21.3.04
Spirit Of 66	Verviers	Belgium	23.3.04
Kubo	Turin	Italy	25.3.04 *
Marghera	Venice	Italy	26.3.04
Stazione Birra	Rome	Italy	28.3.04 *
Musictheatre Rex	Lorsch	Germany	30.3.04
Gewerkshafthaus	Erfurt	Germany	31.3.04
Dietrich-Keuning-Haus	Dortmund	Germany	1.4.04
Petofi Csarnok	Budapest	Hungary	3.4.04
Laiterie (Cancelled)	Strasbourg	France	7.4.04
Stadio Centrale Del Tennis Foro Italico	Rome	Italy	26.7.04 *
Teatro Di Verdura	Palermo	Italy	28.7.04
Fort Manoel Manoel Island	Valetta	Malta	1.8.04

Yet another full-scale tour with perhaps the most representative live set that Steve has ever played. Unexpected and previously unheard classics such as a complete performance of *Blood On The Rooftops* and *Hammer In The Sand* made this tour another superb outing for old and new fans.

Set List (UK/Europe): *Valley Of The Kings/Mechanical Bride/Circus Of Becoming/Frozen Statues/ Slogans/Serpentine Song/Ace Of Wands/Hammer In The Sand/Acoustic Set: Classical Gas-Black Light-Horizons-Imagining-Second Chance/Blood On The Rooftops/Fly On A Windshield/Please Don't Touch/Firth Of Fifth/A Dark Night In Toytown/Darktown/Brand New/Air Conditioned Nightmare/Clocks - The Angel Of Mons/Spectral Mornings/Every Day/Los Endos.*

Set List (Italy): *Mechanical Bride/Circus Of Becoming/Frozen Statues/Slogans/Serpentine Song/Ace Of Wands/Hammer In The Sand/Acoustic Set/Horizions/Blood On The Rooftops/Fly On A Windshield/Please Don't Touch/Firth Of Fifth/Darktown/Brand New/Air Conditioned Nightmare/ Every Day/Clocks - The Angel Of Mons/Spectral Mornings/Los Endos.*

Tour Personnel: SH (Electric/Acoustic/Electric Guitar/Vocals), Roger King (Keyboards), Terry Gregory (Bass/Vocals), Rob Townsend (Saxophone/Flute/Percussion/Vocals), Gary O'Toole (Drums/Percussion/ Vocals).

Acoustic Trio Tour 2005

Grand Theatre (Spirit Of 66)	Verviers	Belgium	13.3.05
Oakwood Centre	Rotherham	England	26.3.05
Pacific Arts Centre	Birkenhead	England	30.4.05 *
The Lowry Centre	Salford Quays	England	1.4.05 *
The Platform	Morecambe	England	2.4.05 *
Darwin Suite (Assembly Rooms) Derby		England	3.4.05 *
Queen Elizabeth Hall	London	England	3.4.05 *
Komedia	Brighton	England	4.4.05 *
Huntingdon Hall	Worcester	England	5.4.05 *
St George's Hall	Bristol	England	7.4.05 *
Carnglaze Caverns	Liskeard	England	8.4.05 *
Wulfrun Hall	Wolverhampton	England	10.4.05 *
Maddermarket Theatre	Norwich	England	11.4.05 *
The Stables	Milton Keynes	England	13-14.4.05 *
The Broadway	Barking	England	16.4.05 *
Ashcroft Theatre	Croydon	England	17.4.05 *
Luz De Gas	Barcelona	Spain	19.4.05
Clamores	Madrid	Spain	21.4.05 *
TVE 3 TV Studios	Madrid	Spain	21.4.05 *
Saschall	Florence	Italy	26.4.05
Teatro Metropolitan	Catania	Italy	27.4.05
Teatro Elena	Sesto San Giovanni (MI)	Italy	28.4.05
Teatro Astra	Schio (VI)	Italy	29.4.05
Staatstheater	Oldenburg	Germany	13.6.05
Haus der Jugend	Osnarbruck	Germany	14.6.05

St Jakobi Kirche	Braunschweig	Germany	15.6.05
Harmonie	Bonn	Germany	16.6.05 *
St Maximin	Trier	Germany	17.6.05 *
Waldbuhne Den Hardt	Wuppertal	Germany	18.6.05 *
Freilichtbuhne	St Goarshausen	Germany	19.6.05 *
Imperial De Quebec	Quebec QC	Canada	28.9.05
Le Medley	Montreal QC	Canada	29.9.05 *
Markham Theatre	Toronto ON	Canada	30.9.05
Capital Music Hall	Ottawa ON	Canada	1.10.05
Hamilton Place Theatre	Hamilton ON	Canada	2.10.05 *
IMAC Theatre	Huntington NY	USA	7.10.05
Society For Ethnic Culture	New York NY	USA	8.10.05
Summerville Theater	Boston MA	USA	9.10.05 *
Troy Savings Bank Music Hall	Troy NY	USA	10.10.05 *
The State Theatre	Falls Church VA	USA	12.10.05
XM Radio Performance Theatre	Washington DC	USA	12.10.05 *
Keswick Theatre Glenside	Pasadena PA	USA	13.10.05
The Sphere	Buffalo NY	USA	14.10.05 *
The Kent Stage	Kent OH	USA	15.10.05
Royal Oak Music Theater	Detroit MI	USA	16.10.05
Shank Hall	Milwaukee WI	USA	18.10.05
The Abbey	Chicago IL	USA	19.10.05
Springfield Center For The Arts	Springfield IL	USA	20.10.05
Rosses Blue Star Room	Minneapolis MN	USA	22.10.05
The Triple Door	Seattle OR	USA	25.10.05
Aladdin Theatre	Portland OR	USA	26.10.05
The Swedish American Music Hall	San Francisco CA	USA	27.10.05 *
Galaxy Concert Theatre	Santa Ana CA	USA	28.10.05
Centro Cultural Ollin Yoliztli Col Isidro Fabela Del Tlalpan	Mexico City	Mexico	30.10.05

Another busy year. Steve's latest studio album; the orchestral Metamorpheus was issued in February and Steve has undertaken extensive tours of the UK, Italy; Germany and the USA and Canada with an acoustic show comprising the best of his solo material alone with some more unexpected surprises. For these shows, Steve was accompanied by his brother John on flute and Roger King on keyboards.

Set List (UK/Europe/USA/Canada): *Japonica/Andante In C/Tribute To Segovia/Metamorpheus Medley/Bay Of Kings/Classical Jazz/Sapphires/Mexico City/Skye Boat Song/Pease Blossom/Horizons/Jacuzzi-Overnight Sleeper/Bacchus/Firth Of Fifth/Whole Tone Jam-The Red Flower Of Taichi Blooms Everywhere-Hands Of The Priestess/After The Ordeal/Hairless Heart/M3/Imagining/Second Chance/Jazz On A Summer's Night/Next Time Around/Kim/Aubade-Meditation-Idylle/The Journey/Ace Of Wands/Walking Away From Rainbows/Gnossienne #1.*

(On at least one occasion (Liskeard) Steve also managed to squeeze in a few bars of Inside & Out during one of the medleys)

Set List (German Festivals): *Horizons/Jacuzzi/Bacchus/Whole Tone Jam-The Red Flower Of Taichi Blooms Everywhere-Hands Of The Priestess/After The Ordeal/Hairless Heart/Imagining-Second Chance/Classical Jazz/Mexico City/Black Light/Kim/The Journey/Jazz On A Summer's Night/Walking Away From Rainbows/ Ace Of Wands.*

Tour Personnel: SH (Acoustic Guitar), Roger King (Keyboards), John Hackett (Flute).

Soundstage Studios (Warm-up)	Acton	England	23.4.06
Charterhouse Public School	Godalming	England	1.5.06
The Boardwalk	Sheffield	England	20.5.06
The Borderline (Cancelled)	London	England	21.5.06
The Astoria	London	England	28.5.06

These gigs were the first shows by Steve's brother John, and Steve was in the unusual position of being "guest" at each of them. The set for these gigs comprised a mix of material from John's albums, albums by Nick Magnus and some Steve Hackett classics.... *Ace Of Wands/Whispers/Late Trains/Fantasy/Another Life/DNA/Brother Son, Sister Moon/Double Helix/Dream Town/Let It Rain Down/Winter/Jacuzzi/Hands Of The Priestess/A Tower Struck Down/Ego And Id/More.*

Tour Personnel: John Hackett (Guitar/Vocals), Tony Patterson (Vocals), Nick Magnus (Keyboards), Andy Gray (Guitar), S H (Guitar), Nigel Appleton (Drums/Percussion).

Acoustic Trio Tour 2006/07

Kulturhset	Bodo	Norway	28.9.06

(A gig at The Tivoli in Utrecht in Holland was originally scheduled for this date and subsequently cancelled)

Kulturhuset	Tromso	Norway	29.9.06
Quartier Modo	Berlin	Germany	1.10.06 *
Peter Paul Kirche	Reichenbach	Germany	2.10.06
Abbaye De Neu Munster	Luxembourg	Luxembourg	4.10.06
Karlstadt Kulturcafe	Nurnburg	Germany	5.10.06
Christuskirche	Bochum	Germany	6.10.06
Alte Stadthalle	Melle	Germany	7.10.06
Blue Note	Nagoya	Japan	24.11.06
STB 139	Tokyo	Japan	25-26.11.06
Blue Note	Osaka	Japan	27.11.06
Teatro Communale	Belluno	Italy	21.3.07
Teatro Verdi	Pisa	Italy	22.3.07
Stazione Birra	Rome	Italy	23.3.07
Teatro Chiabrera	Savona	Italy	24.3.07

The set list for the 2007 acoustic gigs was fundamentally the same as it had been on the 2005 tour although one notable inclusion this time around was an acoustic treatment of part of Supper's Ready!

Take Five	Budapest	Hungary	18.7.08
Jazz Festival	Garana	Romania	19.7.08
Teatro Mancinelli	Orvieto (TR)	Italy	20.9.08
(Acoustic gig by Steve and John as part of the Italian Genesis fan magazine Dusk's "Dusk Day #4")			
Festival		Malaysia	5.12.08

Set List (Budapest): *Said Solo/Reflections Of Thierache/Winter Forest/Firth Of Fifth/Angklung-Sipi/Bass Solo/Distant Dance (1st Set). Flying/Butterfly/Clouds Dance/First Step/Witchi Tai To/In That Quiet Earth (2nd set)*

Set List (Garana): *Flying/Butterfly/Reflections Of Thierache/Firth of Fifth/Winter Forest/Clouds Dance/Angklung-Sipi/First Step/Witchi Tai To/In That Quiet Earth*

Tour Personnel: SH (Acoustic Guitar), John Hackett (Flute), Roger King (Keyboards).

Train On The Road Tour 2009

Vaillantpalace	Genoa	Italy	12.3.09
Teatro Astra	Schio (VI)	Italy	13.3.09
Deposito Giordano	Pordenone	Italy	14.3.09 *
Stazione Birra	Rome	Italy	15.3.09
Auditorio Alfredo Kraus	Las Palmas	Spain	19.6.09
Lugano Estival Jazz	Lugano	Switzerland	4.7.09
Night of the Prog Festival	Loreley	Germany	11.7.09
Summer Festival	Slovenj Gradec	Slovenia	17.7.09
(Steve Hackett and Djabe)			
Jazz Sommer	Graz	Austria	18.7.09
(Steve Hackett and Djabe)			
Asti, Piazza	Cattedrale	Italy	23.7.09
Rock Blues Festival	Casalmaggiore	Italy	24.7.09
Afraka Rock Festival	Afragola	Italy	25.7.09
Tivoli Rock Anfiteatro Bleso	Tivoli	Italy	26.7.09
Ino-Rock Festival Teatr Letni	Wroclaw	Poland	12.9.09
Summers End Festival	Lydney	England	9.10.09
Boerderij	Zoetermeer	Holland	28.10.09
Live Music Hall	Koln	Germany	29.10.09
Fabrik	Hamburg	Germany	30.10.09
Zeche	Bochum	Germany	31.10.09
Le Forum	Limbourg	Belgium	1.11.09
Colos Saal	Aschaffenburg	Germany	3.11.09
Longhom	Stuttgart	Germany	4.11.09
	Pratteln	Switzerland	5.11.09

Mühle Hunziken	Berne	Switzerland	6.11.09
Alhambra	Paris	France	7.11.09
Princess Pavilion	Falmouth	England	11.11.09
Phoenix	Exeter	England	12.11.09
Shepherds Bush Empire	London	England	14.11.09
UEA	Norwich	England	15.11.09
Opera House	Buxton	England	17.11.09
The Robin 2	Wolverhampton	England	18.11.09
The Renfrew Ferry	Glasgow	Scotland	19.11.09
Pacific Road Arts Centre	Birkenhead	England	20.11.09
Lowry Theatre	Salford	England	21.11.09
Picturedome	Holmfirth	England	22.11.09
The Brook	Southampton	England	29.11.09 *
The Assembly	Leamington Spa	England	1.12.09 *

Set List (Summer's End): Mechanical Bride/Fire On The Moon/Everyday/Ace Of Wands/Pollution B/ The Steppes/Darktown/Slogans/Serpentine Song/Firth of Fifth/Walking Away From Rainbows/Acoustic Set - Horizons/Blood On The Rooftops/Spectral Mornings/Fly On A Windshield/Broadway Melody Of '74/Please Don't Touch/A Tower Struck Down/In That Quiet Earth/Los Endos/Clocks.

Set List (Zoetermeer): Intro Music (Last Train To Istanbul)/ Mechanical Bride/Fire On The Moon/Everyday/Emerald And Ash/Ghost In The Glass/Ace Of Wands/Pollution B/The Steppes/Slogans/Serpentine Song/Tubehead/Spectral Mornings/ Firth Of Fifth/Acoustic Set/Horizons/Blood On The Rooftops/Fly On A Windshield-Broadway Melody Of 74/Sleepers/Still Waters/Los Endos/Clocks.

Note: Myopia was also played as part of the Los Endos medley at at least one show in Europe. Jacuzzi was performed as part of the acoustic medley at the gigs in London, Holmfirth and Leamington Spa gigs where John Hackett joined Steve and the band.

The Glasgow set omitted both Slogans and Fly On A Windhsield. Steve duetted with Nick Beggs during his "Stick" solo and Walking Away From Rainbows was performed as part of the acoustic set.

Tour Personnel (Summer 2009 shows): SH (Acoustic/Electric Guitar/Vocals), Roger King (Keyboards), Nick Beggs (Bass/Stick/Backing Vocals), Rob Townsend Saxophone/Flute/Percussion/Vocals), Gary O'Toole (Drums/Percussion/Vocals). Dik Cadbury appeared at several of the summer gigs on bass due to Nick Beggs' other commitments.

Tour Personnel (Train On The Road Tour): SH (Acoustic/Electric Guitar/Vocals), Roger King (Keyboards), Nick Beggs (Bass/Stick/Backing Vocals), Rob Townsend (Flute/Saxophone/Percussion/Backing Vocals), Gary O'Toole (Drums/Vocals), Amanda Lehmann (Backing Vocals).

Around The World In Eighty Trains Tour 2010

Savoy Theatre	Helsinki	Finland	6.2.10
Avenida Alfonso Molina S/N	Coruna	Spain	1.4.10

Teatro-Cine de Gouveia	Gouveia	Portugal	18.4.10
Erdei Ferenc Muvelodesi Kozpont Kecskemet		Hungary	20.4.10 ~
Kolcsey Kozpont	Debrecen	Hungary	21.4.10 ~
Palace Of Arts	Budapest	Hungary	17.5.10 ~
Agora Szombathelyi Kulturalis Kozpont Szomathely		Hungary	18.5.10 ~
Ziquodome	Compiegne	France	21.5.10
La Gare Salle Polyvalente Grand Rue Werentzhouse Alsace		France	22.5.10 #
La Gare Salle Polyvalente Grand Rue Werentzhouse Alsace		France	23.5.10
Mezz	Breda	Holland	24.5.10 *
Boerderij	Zoetermeer	Holland	25.5.10
Spirit Of 66	Verviers	Belgium	26.5.10
NEARFest Zoellner Arts Center Bethlehem PA		USA	18.6.10
Performing Arts Centre	Westhampton Beach	USA	20.6.10 x
Regent Theatre	Arlington TX	USA	22.6.10 * x
"River To River Festival"	Rockerfeller Park New York	USA	23.6.10 *
State Theatre	Falls Church	USA	24.6.10 x
Palace Theatre	Greensburg	USA	25.6.10 x
Park West	Chicago IL	USA	29.6.10 * x
Performing Arts Centre	Milwaukee WI	USA	30.6.10 x *
House Of Blues	Cleveland OH	USA	1.7.10 * x
Water Street Music Hall	Rochester NY	USA	2.7.10 x
Hart Theatre	Albany NY	USA	3.7.10 x
Queen Elizabeth Theatre	Toronto ON	Canada	7.7.10
Cisco Ottawa Blues Festival	Ottawa ON	Canada	8.7.10
Place Des Arts Theatre Maisonneuve Montreal QC		Canada	9.7.10
Theatre Granada	Sherbrooke QC	Canada	10.7.10
International Summer Festival Quebec QC		Canada	12.7.10
City Winery	New York NY	USA	13.7.10
Sellersville Theatre 1894	Sellersville	?	14.7.10 #
Tarrytown Music Hall	Tarrytown NY	USA	16.7.10 #
High Voltage Festival	London	England	25.7.10
Incontra Il Mondo	Rome	Italy	28.7.10
Fortezza Priamar	Savona	Italy	29.7.10
Piazza Del Popolo	Todi	Italy	31.7.10
Summer Rock Festival	Trieste	Italy	1.8.10
Don Chento Jazz Festival	Kaliningrad	Russia	7.8.10 ~
International Jazz Festival	Bansko	Bulgaria	12.8.10 ~
Nisville Jazz Festival	Nis	Serbia	14.8.10 ~
?	Belgrade	Serbia	15.8.10 ~
Hibiya Open Air Theatre	Tokyo	Japan	22.8.10
Kawasaki Club Citta	Tokio	Japan	28.8.10
Spacio Piscina Parco Monte Verita Ticino		Switzerland	17.9.10 #
Aula Magna	Lisbon	Portugal	22.10.10
The Brook	Southampton	England	16.11.10
Renfrew Ferry	Glasgow	Scotland	18.11.10
University	Manchester	England	19.11.10
Arts Centre	Pontardarwe	Wales	20.11.10
The Assembly	Leamington Spa	England	21.11.10
Komedia	Brighton	England	23.11.10

Komedia	Bath	England	25.11.10
Picturedome	Holmfirth	England	26.11.10
Pacific Road Arts Centre	Birkenhead	England	27.11.10
The Sage	Gateshead	England	28.11.10
Robin 2	Bilston	England	29.11.10
Shepherds Bush Empire Theatre	London	England	30.11.10
The Junction	Cambridge	England	2.12.10
The Stables	Milton Keynes	England	3.12.10
The Maltings	Farnham	England	16.12.10

Tour Personnel: S H: (Guitar/Vocals), Roger King: (Keyboards), Nick Beggs: (Bass/Stick/B Vox), Rob Townsend: (Flute/Saxophone), Gary O'Toole: (Drums/Percussion/Vocals), Amanda Lehmann: (Guitar/B Vox).

Set List (Helsinki): Intro/Mechanical Bride/Fire On The Moon/Every Day/Emerald And Ash/Serpentine Song/Tubehead/Spectral Mornings/Firth Of Fifth/Walking Away From Rainbows/Horizons/Blood On The Rooftops/Fly On A Windshield-Broadway Melody Of 1974/Sleepers/Tava/Still Waters/Los Endos/ Clocks.

Set List (Breda): Mechanical Bride/Fire On The Moon/Every Day/Emerald And Ash/Carpet Crawlers/Ace Of Wands/Serpentine Song/Spectral Mornings/Firth Of Fifth/Walking Away From Rainbows/Acoustic Set/Horizons/Blood On The Rooftops/Fly On A Windshield/Broadway Melody Of 1974/Sleepers/The Darkness In Man's Heart/Still Waters/Myopia-Los Endos/Clocks.

Set List (Arlington MA): Mechanical Bride/Fire On The Moon/Every Day/Emerald And Ash/Ace Of Wands/The Steppes/Slogans/Serpentine Song/Blood On The Rooftops/Fly On A Windshield/ Broadway Melody Of 1974/Sleepers/Still Waters/In That Quiet Earth/Firth Of Fifth/Clocks.

Set List (Glasgow UK): Every Day/Valley Of The Kings/Emerald And Ash/The Golden Age Of Steam/Watcher Of The Skies/Carpet Crawlers/Fire On The Moon/Ace Of Wands/Shadow Of The Hierophant/Sierra Quemada/Acoustic Set (inc Horizons)/Blood On The Rooftops/Tubehead/ Sleepers/Tava/Still Waters/Prairie Angel/Los Endos/Firth Of Fifth/Clocks.

From the Manchester show onwards, Valley Of The Kings and Every Day swapped places in the running order.

Tour personnel: SH (Gtr/Vox), Rob Townsend (Saxophone/Flute), Roger King (Keyboards), Gary O'Toole (Drums/Percussion/Vox), Amanda Lehmann (Gtr/B Vox), Nick Beggs (Bass/Stick/ B Vox).

Lee Pomeroy from It Bites fulfilled bass duties for the Japanese gigs due to Nick Beggs having other commitments.

John Wetton and Steven Wilson were special guests at the band's London gig. At this gig the acoustic set was dropped in favour of a performance of All Along The Watchtower.

Concerts marked by an asterisk are documented by official/unofficial live audio and/or video footage. See relevant section for further details.

Orbita Hall	Wroclaw	Poland	29.4.11 #
Teatro Ciak	Milan	Italy	11.5.11

Estragon Club	Bologna	Italy	12.5.11
Teatro Tendastrisce	Rome	Italy	13.5.11
Lazienki Park	Warsaw	Poland	14.5.11
Teatro Kennedy	Fasano	Italy	8.6.11
Columbus Ship	Budapest	Hungary	13.7.11 ~
MMC Club	Bratislava	Slovakia	14.7.11 ~
Hegyalija Festztival	Rakmaz Tokaj	Hungary	15.7.11 ~
Civic Korzo	Debrecen	Hungary	16.7.11 ~
Cera Sol Rock Parco di Sierra	San Bartolo Vittoria	Italy	28.7.11
Piazza Castello	Mantova	Italy	30.7.11
Piazza Duomo	Spilimbergo	Italy	1.8.11
Ziquodome	Compeigne	France	8.10.11
La Cigale	Paris	France	9.10.11

This gig was the last one of the Around The World In Eighty Trains shows, at time of writing a new set was being put through its paces in a rehearsal room somewhere in deepest darkest Twickenham for what will shortly be the Breaking Waves Tour which should see Steve and the band continue to bring their unique brand of music to audiences in the UK and further afield.

Tour Personnel: SH (GTR/Vox), Roger King (Keyboards), Amanda Lehmann (GTR/Vox), Rob Townsend (Flute/Saxophone), Phil Mulford (Bass), Gary O'Toole (Drums/Percussion/Vox).

Phil Mulford who performed with Steve during his shows in Italy back in 2000 steps into the breach left by Nick Beggs who has other touring/recording commitments at present.

~ = Concerts by Djabe at which Steve is a guest.
\# = Concert by Acoustic Trio (Steve, John Hackett, Roger King)
x = Steve and Renaissance

Breaking Waves Tour 2011

The Wharf	Tavistock	England	10.11.11
Guildhall	Gloucester	England	11.11.11
Royal Northern College Of Music	Manchester	England	12.11.11
O2 Academy	London	England	13.11.11
Die Rohre	Stuttgart	Germany	20.11.11
Live Music Hall	Cologne	Germany	21.11.11
Airport Casino	Basel	Switzerland	22.11.11
Colos-Saal	Aschaffenburg	Germany	23.11.11
Salle Le Kursaal	Verviers	Belgium	25.11.11
Borderij	Zoetermeer	Holland	26.11.11

Breaking Waves Tour 2012

The Maltings	Farnham	England	10.2.12
Lemon Tree	Aberdeen	Scotland	16.2.12

Queens Hall	Edinburgh	Scotland	17.2.12
Picturedome	Holmfirth	England	18.2.12
Opera House	Buxton	England	19.2.12
Floral Pavilion	New Brighton	England	20.2.12
The Brook	Southampton	England	22.2.12
Komedia	Bath	England	23.2.12
The Assembly	Leamington Spa	England	24.2.12
Robin 2	Bilston	England	25.2.12
The Stables	Milton Keynes	England	26.2.12

* Throughout this Steve Hackett Solo gig-guide, concerts that are marked by an asterisk are documented by official/unofficial live audio and/or video footage. See relevant section for further details.

This Gig Guide has been compiled by Alan Hewitt with the assistance of: Nick Magnus; Vernon Parker; Pam Bay and Phil Morris and the kind contributions of Peter Gozzard, Joanna Lehmann, Billy Budis and Paul Gibbon. The Genesis section of the Gig Guide has been compiled with the kind assistance of: Phil Collins, Annie Callingham; David Lawrence; Jonathan Dann and the late Mal Lord. Previously published as part of the author's book, "Genesis Revisited" and updated exclusively for this book.

APPENDIX 9

Chronology

Not exactly a be all and end all of events in Steve's life, but a reference guide to some of the more important and influential ones perhaps...

12th February 1950: Stephen Richard Hackett born at University Hospital London.
13th March 1955: John Hackett born.
1962: Steve begins serious composition of music.
1966: Steve leaves school and commences series of jobs, also starts placing advertisements in back pages of Melody Maker looking for like-minded musicians.
1968: Steve appears on the Canterbury Glass album; Sacred Scenes And Characters, his first recorded effort. Gigs with the band also take place during this year exact details of which are not known.
1969: Steve joins Quiet World who record The Road album, released in 1970.
29th December 1970: Steve sees Genesis for the first time at a gig at the Lyceum Ballroom London.
January 1971: Steve joins Genesis.
14th January 1971: Steve's first gig with Genesis at University College London.
24th January - 13th February 1971: First Charisma "Six Bob Tour" in the UK.
7th March 1971: First overseas gig by Genesis at La Ferme Woluwe St Lambert Belgium.
11th April - 26th April 1971: Second Charisma "Six Bob Tour" in the UK.
10th May 1971: "Sounds Of The Seventies" BBC Radio session.
20th November 1971: Nursery Cryme album released.
20th-21st March 1972: Pop Deux TV Session for Belgian/French TV earliest surviving TV performance by the band.
6th April - 19th April 1972: First tour of Italy.
16th August - 23rd August 1972: Second tour of Italy.
September 1972: Steve marries Helen Busse his first wife at Kensington Registry Office. His son Oliver is born the following year.
1st October 29th October 1972: Third and final Charisma "Six Bob Tour" in UK.
20th October 1972: Foxtrot album released.
16th December 1972: First US gig by Genesis at Brandeis University Boston MA.
17th December 1972: Second US gig by Genesis at Carnegie Hall New York NY.
4th - 26th February 1973: First full-scale headlining tour of UK supported by String Driven Thing.

1st March -24th April 1973: First full-scale US tour by Genesis.
October 1973: Selling England By The Pound album released.
30th -31st October 1973: Tony Smith Presents Genesis In Concert film shot at Bray Film Studios Windsor.
20th November 1974: The Lamb Lies Down On Broadway tour starts in Chicago IL.
November 1974: The Lamb Lies Down On Broadway album released.
6th December 1974: Steve meets future wife Kim Poor for first time after Genesis gig in New York.
25th May 1975: Final gig of The Lamb... tour at the Palais Des Sports Besancon.
18th August 1975: Peter Gabriel announces his departure from Genesis.
October 1975: Steve's first solo album; Voyage Of The Acolyte released.
13th February 1976: A Trick Of The Tail album released.
27th March 1976: First gig of the Trick.. Tour takes place in London Ontario Canada.
23rd December 1976: Wind & Wuthering album released.
31st January 1976: Full dress rehearsal for the Wind & Wuthering world tour takes place at The Rainbow.
1st January 1977: Wind & Wuthering world tour commences at the Rainbow Theatre London.
3rd July 1977: Final gig of the Wind & Wuthering tour takes place at the Olympiahalle Munich.
8th October 1977: Steve officially announces his departure from Genesis in the music press.
15th October 1977: Seconds Out album released.
31st March 1978: Please Don't Touch album released.
June 1978: How Can I? Released as the first solo single by Steve.
4th October 1978: Steve's first solo gig takes place at Chateau Neuf Oslo Norway.
23rd October 1978: Steve's first UK solo gig takes place at Cardiff University.
15th May 1979: Spectral Mornings album released.
23rd May 1979: Steve commences touring for the Spectral Mornings album.
23rd August 1979: Steve plays the Reading Festival for the first time.
September 1979: Spectral Mornings album released.
11th June 1980: Defector Tour starts in Derby.
13th June 1980: Defector album released.
August 1981: Cured album released.
14th August 1981: Steve marries Kim Poor at Chelsea Town Hall.
21st August 1981; Cured album released.
22nd August 1981: Cured Tour starts in Folkestone.
2nd October 1982: Six Of The Best reunion concert at Milton Keynes Concert Bowl.
16th April 1983: Cell 151 single released.
19th April 1983: Highly Strung UK tour starts in Worthing.
23rd April 1983: Highly Strung album released.
26th October 1983: Bay Of Kings album released UK tour for same starts in Warwick.
August 1984: Till We Have Faces album released.
March 1986: When The Heart Rules The Mind single released.
March 1986: GTR debut album released.
20th June 1986: GTR US tour starts in Baltimore MD.
18th April 1988: Momentum album released.
25th April 1988: Momentum UK tour starts in Cheltenham.
1990: Sailing single released in aid of the "Rock Against Repatriation" charity.
13th September 1990: Central TV Studios concert for the "Bedrock" TV series.
January 1992: Timelapse live album released.
14th August 1992: Tour Noir US tour starts in Montreal Canada.

October 1992: The Unauthorised Biography album released.
21st May 1993: Guitar Noir album released. UK tour for same starts in Liverpool.
19th September 1994: Blues With A Feeling album released.
June 1995: There Are Many Sides To The Night album released.
June 1996: GTR King Biscuit Flower Hour live album released.
October 1996: Genesis Revisited album released in Japan.
16th -20th December 1996: Steve's first gigs in Japan.
March 1997: A Midsummer Night's Dream album released.
22nd September 1997: Genesis Revisited album released in UK.
April 1998: Tokio Tapes album and live video released.
11th May 1998: Steve is briefly reunited with his former Genesis band mates for release of the first Genesis Archive 1967 -75 box set promotional get together at Heathrow Airport London.
26th April 1999: Darktown album released.
1st May 2000: Sketches Of Satie album released.
9th October 2000: Feedback 86 album released.
28th June 2001: "Gira Latinoamericana" South American Tour begins in Rosario Argentina.
12th November 2001: Live Archive '70's, '80's, '90's box set released.
January 2002: Acoustic gigs performed in Japan and Hungary, the latter is filmed for release.
March 2002: Genesis Files album released.
27th June - 4th July 2002: First US rock gigs by Steve in almost ten years.
9th December 2002: Somewhere In South America live album/video released.
17th February 2003: Somewhere In South America live DVD released.
9th June 2003: To Watch The Storms album released.
July 2003: NEARfest live album released. Hungarian Horizon live album/DVD also released.
5th - 13th August 2003: Acoustic tour of Borders Bookstores in USA.
29th August and 1st September 2003: Gigs in Osaka and Tokio as part of the celebrations for the 20th Anniversary of the Hard Rock Café in Japan. Gigs filmed and subsequently released as the Guitar Wars album/DVD.
27th September 2003: To Watch The Storms tour commences in Zoetermeer Holland.
December 2003: to Watch The Storms album issued in Japan.
28th January 2004: Live Archive '03 album released.
March 1st 2004: John Hackett releases his first solo album: Velvet Afternoon.
4th March 2004: Live Archive '04 tour commences in Dartford.
28th June 2004: Live Archive '04 album released.
July 2004: Nick Magnus releases the Hexameron album featuring both John and Steve Hackett.
22nd November 2004: Once Above A Time live DVD released.
March 2005: Gramy Records in Hungary release limited edition vinyl edition of Sketches Of Satie.
13th March 2005: Acoustic Trio tour commences in Verviers Belgium.
28th March 2005: Metamorpheus album released.
20th May 2005: Spectral Mornings DVD released.
6th June 2005: Live Archive '05 album released.
13th June 2005: Acoustic Trio German tour commences in Oldenburg.
18th June 2005: Acoustic Trio German tour finishes in St Goarshausen.
19th September 2005: Virgin Records issue their remastered versions of Steve's Charisma albums; Voyage Of The Acolyte through to Defector.
28th September 2005: Acoustic Trio US tour commences in Quebec Canada.
30th October 2005: Acoustic Trio US tour ends in Mexico City.

20th February 2006: Live Archive '83 album released.
30th June 2006: Virgin Records issue their remastered versions of Steve's final Charisma albums: Cured and Highly Strung.
11th September 2006: Wild Orchids album released.
June 2007: Steve and Kim divorce.
11th February 2008: Tribute album released.
18th July 2008: Steve plays a show with Hungarian group Djabe in Budapest.
19th July 2008: Steve plays at the Garana Jazz Festival in Romania.
20th September 2008: Steve and John perform at Orvieto in Italy as part of the Italian Genesis fan magazine; Dusk's 4th "Dusk Day".
5th-6th December 2008: Steve appears as part of a music festival in Malaysia.
12th March 2009: Steve commences short Italian tour.
September 2009: Out Of The Tunnel's Mouth, the new Hackett album is released.
27th October 2009: Out Of The Tunnel's Mouth, Steve's 19th studio album is released on his new record label: Wolfwork.
28th October 2009: The "Train On The Road" 2009 Tour commences at Zoetermeer, Holland.
1st December 2009: The "Train On The Road" 2009 Tour ends at The Assembly Leamington Spa England.
6th February 2010: First show of 2010 Around the World In Eighty Trains Tour at the Savoy Theatre, Helsinki Finland.
18th June - 16th July 2010: Steve's first rock tour in the USA since 2003 sharing the billing with vintage Prog band Renaissance.
25th July 2010: Appearance at the High Voltage Festival London.
15th November 2010: Steve Hackett - Live Rails live album released.
16th November - 16th December 2010: UK tour.
14th February 2011: Steve announces his engagement to Joanna Lehmann.
11th - 14th May 2011: Italian tour.
4th June 2011: Steve marries Joanna Lehmann at St Albans Register Office.
26th September 2011: Beyond The Shrouded Horizon, Steve's 22nd studio album is released.
9th October 2011: Out Of The Tunnel's Mouth Tour concludes in Paris France.
10th November 2011: Breaking Waves tour commences in Tavistock England
21st November 2011: Fire & Ice live DVD released..
10th February 2012: Breaking Waves tour recommences in Farnham England.

APPENDIX 10

Bibliography And Other Source Material

These include all of the sources referred to in the text of this project and my thanks once again to everyone who provided them for the archive.

"The New Face Of Gabriel" Melody Maker interview with Chris Welch 26th October 1974.
"Hackett Relieves Himself" Interview in Sounds with Barbara Charone October 1975.
"Are You Ready For A Concept LP About The Tarot?" Sounds 1975
"Steve Hackett's Solo Voyage" US Radio interview 1975
"Mystic Voyage From Genesis" Sounds review 1975
WNEW interview 9/4/76
Los Angeles telephone interview 30/3/77
German Radio interview 1978
"Steve Hackett Solos In Style" Circus Magazine June 1978.
"Good Times" Magazine April 1978.
"Beat Instrumental" Magazine June 1978.
"While My Guitar Gently Goes On And On And On…" Spectral Mornings album review Sounds 1979.
Hallam Rock Radio interview 1979.
Capital Radio interview 1979.
Friday Rock Show interview 1979.
L'Ancienne Belgique Brussels, Hammersmith Odeon and Newcastle City Hall concert reviews 1979
"Hackett No Boots Shock" Sounds 5/7/80
New Haven Connecticut interview 25.9.80
WAQX Radio interview 26.9.80
Mercury Records promotional interview 16.11.80
"Hackett Sings Shock" Sounds 1981
Sands Hotel San Diego interview 25.4.81
"When In Rome" Melody Maker 26.9.81
"Steve Hackett - His Five Year Exodus From Genesis" Guitar Player Magazine April 1982
Montreal interview 1982.
"Steve's Dreams (Are Made Of This" Kerrang! Magazine April 1983
"Walking Through Walls" Sounds 14/5/83
Signal Radio interview 2.11.83

Till We Have Faces reviews 1984
"Guitar" Magazine August 1986
"Howe To Hackett" GTR album review Which Compact Disc? Magazine August 1986
GTR Beacon Theatre New York concert review Kerrang! Magazine July 1986.
GTR Hammersmith Odeon concert review Sounds 1986
"Music To His Ears" Birmingham Evening Mail 25/4/88
BBC Radio 2 interview 27.4.88
"Struggles Of A Supergroup" Birmingham Daily News 12/5/88
"Guitar Happiness" Alexandra Theatre Birmingham concert review Birmingham Evening Mail 16/5/88
"I Think It Is Silly To Pretend You Are 19 For Ever And A Day" St Albans Observer 19/5/88
"You can't go wrong if you buy an album by Segovia or Steve Hackett" TWR Magazine interview with Steve at the Royal Concert Hall Nottingham 14.5.88. Interview conducted by: Alan Hewitt and Ted Sayers.
"Rocker's Reprieve" Daily Mail 1991
"Strong Favourite As The Baroque Rocker" The Mail On Sunday 1/12/91
"Spectrally Speaking" Interview with Steve by Bill Brink for TWR Magazine 22.8.92
Philadelphia interview 20.9.92
"Pearls Of Wisdom" TWR Magazine interview with Steve at Manchester University Refectory 25.5.93 Interview conducted by Alan Hewitt.
"The Defector Speaks Out" TWR Magazine interview with Steve. Richmond Hill Hotel London 25.9.93. Interview Conducted by Alan Hewitt and Jonathan Dann.
Virgin Reissues review Q Magazine 1994
"I owe it all to the Richmond Hill tuna sandwiches!" TWR Magazine interview with Steve. Richmond Hill Hotel London 28.5.95. Interview conducted by Alan Hewitt, Richard and Andrew Nagy.
"Genesis Revelations" TWR Magazine interview with Steve. Richmond Hill Hotel London 1996. Interview conducted by: Alan Hewitt.
"Widening The Landscape" TWR Magazine interview with Steve. Richmond Hill Hotel London 1996. Interview conducted by: Alan Hewitt.
"Between The Tape Deck And The Tea Cup" TWR Magazine interview with Steve. Crown Studios London 21.8.97. Interview conducted by: Alan Hewitt.
"Box Set Blues" TWR Magazine interview with Steve. Crown Studios London 22.7.98. Interview conducted by: Alan Hewitt and Martin Dean.
Genesis Archive 1967-75: The Interviews 2 CD promotional set Virgin Records.
GTR King Biscuit Flower Hour Live CD review
"Illuminating Darktown" TWR Magazine interview with Steve. Crown Studios London 20.3.99. Interview conducted by: Alan Hewitt and Martin Dean.
"The Eternal Space Cadet" TWR interview with Nick Magnus. 25.8.99. Interview conducted by: Alan Hewitt and Manir Donaghue.
"Dark Matter - Recording Darktown" Sound On Sound August 1999
"Sketches Of Hackett" TWR Magazine interview with Steve and John Hackett. Richmond Hill Hotel London 19.2.00. Interview conducted by: Alan Hewitt and David Beaven.
Virtue TV. Com webcast interview with Steve and John 10.5.00
Live Archive '70's, '80's, '90's review
"Talking About Feedback" TWR Magazine interview with Steve. Crown Studios London 12.9.00. Interview conducted by: Alan Hewitt.
"In The Line Of Fire" TWR E- Mail interview with Chris Ward 2001.
"Notes From the Frontline" TWR Magazine interview with Steve. MAP Studios 28th

October 2001. Interview conducted by Alan Hewitt and Tony Burton.
"Delicious Agony" Cybercast 2002
"A Tale of thirteen bungalows" TWR interview MAP Studios London 3.5.03. Interview conducted by: Alan Hewitt.
To Watch The Storms album review Classic Rock Magazine
"Bradford Rocks" Radio interview City Varieties Leeds 6.10.03
Interview with John Hackett at John's home by Alan Hewitt and Richard Nagy 12.10.03
WCPN Radio interview 8.11.03
Author's Interview with Steve Hackett MAP Studios London 5.12.03
Spectral Mornings live DVD review
Bob Harris Show BBC Radio 17.2.04
Radio Caroline interview 21.2.04
TWR interview Crown/MAP Studios London 9.2.05. Interview conducted by: Alan Hewitt.
"Night Of Relaxed Fun And Banter" Liverpool Echo 18/3/05
Saga Radio interview 4.4.05
BBC Radio Hereford interview ?.4.05
EMI Remasters review Mojo Magazine 2005
Radio Cornwall interview 5.4.05
TWR Interview with Steve, John Hackett and Roger King. The Stables Milton Keynes 15.4.05. Interview conducted by: Alan Hewitt.
TWR "Let's Get Technical" Interview by Stuart Barnes with Steve Hackett and Roger King at MAP Studios 21.3.06
"Memoirs Of An Inveterate Dreamer" TWR interview with Steve Hackett. MAP Studios Twickenham 2nd April 2006. Interview conducted by: Alan Hewitt and Kevin Fearn.
"Movers And Shakers" Jonathan Mover E-mail interview for TWR.
"In Conversation" TWR interview with Steve Hackett MAP Studios Twickenham 3rd June 2007. Interview conducted by Alan Hewitt and Stuart Barnes.
"Paying Tribute" TWR interview with Steve Hackett at Steve's home 22nd February 2008. Interview conducted by: Alan Hewitt and Anthony Hobkinson.
Author's interview with June Leaney at Steve's home 2nd May 2008.
Author's interview with Joanna Lehmann at Steve's home 2nd May 2008.
Author's interview with Brian Gibbon at his home 18th July 2008.
"About Time" TWR intevriew with Dik Cadbury January 2009.
"Encounters With A Kilted Maniac - I Mean, Bass Player!" TWR interview with Nick Beggs April 2009.
"Catching The Last Train To Twickenham" TWR interview with Steve 13th June 2009.
7 WavesFM Radio interview with Steve 12.10.09
"Saxes With Wolves And Other Tales Of Madness" TWR interview with Rob Townsend and Gary O'Toole October 2009.
7 Waves FM interview 25th October 2009.
TWR Interview with Anthony Phillips Saturday 14th November 2009.
TWR interview with Dick Driver April 2010.
"Hack Attack" Classic Rock Presents Prog Magazine July 2010.
GRTR Radio interview 13th November 2010.
"Squackett and other mythical creatures" TWR interview with Steve 8th January 2011.
Facebook Interview 8th January 2011.
"Exploring The Shrouded Horizon" TWR interview with Steve 13th August 2011.

Bibliography

Armando Gallo: Genesis The Evolution Of Rock Band Sidgwick & Jackson 1978.
Armando Gallo: Genesis I Know What I Like Sidgwick & Jackson 1980 and reprint 1998.
Phil Kamin/Peter Goddard: Genesis, Peter Gabriel, Phil Collins And Beyond Sidgwick & Jackson 1984.
Hugh Fielder: The Book Of Genesis Sidgwick & Jackson 1984.
Dave Bowler/Bryan Dray: Genesis - A Biography Sedgwick & Jackson 1991.
Max Demont: Counting Out Time - The Worldwide Singles Discography Volume 1 Private Imprint.
Alan Hewitt: Opening The Musical Box - A Genesis Chronicle SAF Publishing 1999.
Alan Hewitt: Genesis Revisited Willow Farm Press 2007.
Alan Hewitt: Genesis Turn It On Again - A Live Guide 1976 - 2007 (Work In Progress)
Robin Platts: Genesis Inside & Out Collector's Guide Publishing Inc 2001
Robin Platts: Genesis Behind The Lines 1967-2007 Collector's Guide Publishing 2007.
Paul Russell: Genesis: Play Me My Song A Live Guide 1969 To 1975 SAF Publishing 2004.
Bob Carruthers: Genesis - The Gabriel Era Angry Penguin Publishing Ltd 2004
Dave Thompson: Turn It On Again: Peter Gabriel, Phil Collins And Genesis Backbeat Books 2005.
The Waiting Room Magazine (1987 - 2002)
The Waiting Room Online Internet magazine (2002 -)
Dusk Magazine (1991 -)
Ripples Magazine (1987 - 1991)
World Of Genesis website: www.worldofgenesis.com

ACKNOWLEDGEMENTS

The list of individuals who should be thanked for their assistance in making this possible would probably fill several pages so I hope those individuals will not mind if I have forgotten their names here (you know who you are!) There are however certain people whose contributions cannot go unrecognised and so I would like to extend my thanks to…

First of all to Mr Stephen Richard Hackett himself for being the inspiration for this book and for his kindness; friendship and encouragement both during the writing of both this, and also my previous efforts. Always approachable and amenable for those lengthy off-topic discussions, Steve has always been the perfect interview subject!

My thanks also to Steve's mum Mrs June Leaney and to his father Peter Hackett; his brother John, and his good lady Katrin for being generous with their time and their memories, and for welcoming me into their "family" with such warmness. Grateful thanks also to Steve's partner Joanna Lehmann for all her help, enthusiasm and encouragement with this project.

To that other "family"- Jake Locke; John Wood and Andy Lodge. Grateful thanks also to Brian and Paul Gibbon whose support and assistance has been incredible. To the road crews who have helped Steve present the amazing shows seen over the years, and of course to the musicians who have assisted in that creative process: Tony Banks; Phil Collins; Peter Gabriel; Mike Rutherford; Nick Magnus, Peter Hicks, Dik Cadbury, John Shearer, Chas Cronk, Ian Mosley, Fudge Smith, Dave Ball, Doug Sinclair, Hugo Degenhardt, Julian Colbeck, Roger King; Terry Gregory, Gary O' Toole and Rob Townsend; Nick Beggs - thank you for the gigs and the memories!

Oh… I nearly forgot (as if I would!) the larger "family": the fans. Over the years and in particular over the last few years during my stints on the "merch" stall at Steve's gigs; I have had the opportunity to meet some of the best and craziest fans in the rock world. Hackett fans - "Hacketteers" are a special

Acknowledgements

breed apart from your obvious rock fan. They will absorb any project that Steve cares to throw at them and he has thrown us some real curved balls in our time, hasn't he folks? Their dedication to and appreciation of his music is second to none. This project has been written for those fans that I hope will enjoy it, and a few in particular, whom have been especially helpful.

So, in no particular order, my thanks to: Ted Sayers and Peter Morton for persuading (read: nagging) me to join in the creation of TWR - without which, none of this would have been thinkable, much less possible! Pam Bay, Mike Ainscoe, Alan Perry and Andy Wilkinson; Albert Gouder; Andy Brailsford; Nick Glover, Roger Salem and Graeme Stewart for providing so much background material and resources. To Richard and Andrew Nagy for sharing the passion and to Richard for his superb graphics skills. To Sarah Dean for sharing the proofreading and the occasional glass of real ale! Kevin, Shirley and Rachel Powell for all the hospitality and the best Shepherds Pie in the Cosmos! To Peter Gozzard for his consistent "when are you going to write a book about Steve?" pestering. Mike Carzo, Mike Jackson, Richard Coppola and David Dunnington for the audio and other materials donated to this and other projects. To Messrs Hughes and Fearn for their chauffeuring skills. To Stuart Waby, Stephanie Kennedy, Phil and Richard Morris; Phil Eames and the elusive J R Hartley just for being... and to Jeremy Brown and his wonderful mother Carol, and to anyone else whose name doesn't appear here. I hope that you enjoy the end result although, if not: I am sure you won't hesitate to tell me, will you?

Thanks also to the inspiration of Messrs Bliss, Vaughan Williams, Holst and Sibelius when the going got tough!

This book is dedicated to the memories of Alan Davidson and Peter Vickers, good friends, long time Genesis fans, Hacketteers and dedicated music fans, and Tomi Inkinen all of whom are sadly missed - this one's for you, guys!

Photographic Sources...

The author would like to extend his grateful thanks to the following people for their kind permission to use their photographic and/or other materials in this project either in the book itself or the accompanying DVD. There remain several photographers whose identities remain unknown to the author or the publishers and we would be grateful if these individuals could make themselves known to us so that they can be properly credited for their efforts.

Charisma Records
Atco Records
Atlantic Records
Chrysalis Records
Epic Records
Columbia Records
EMI Records
Arista Records
Hackettsongs.com
Mrs J Leaney
Steve Hackett
Robert Ellis (Repfoto)
Alan Perry (www.concertphotos.uk.com)
Yuki Kuroyanagi
Paul Cox (Caroline Records)
Roger Salem
Mike Ainscoe
Stuart Barnes
Ted Sayers
Richard Nagy
Bill Brink
Andy Banks
Carlos X Noriega
Helmut Janisch
Kurt Lambert-Newgord
David Beaven
Anthony Hobkinson
Andy Wilkinson
Brian Gibbon
John Wilkinson
Nick Brailsford
Jack Beerman

Acknowledgements

David Negrin
Graeme Stuart
Jonanthan Guntrip
Albert Gouder
Richard Mills
Peter Blight
Nick Glover
David Roberts

All memorabilia, ticket stubs etc, contained within this book and its accompanying DVD are taken from the author's own personal collection unless otherwise stated. All rights are reserved by the above photographers and their kind permission to use their photographs within this book is gratefully acknowledged.

For further information on Steve Hackett please check the official website: www.hackettsongs.com or simply email to: info@hackettsongs.com

ABOUT THE AUTHOR

Alan Hewitt is a long-standing fan of Genesis and Steve Hackett for some thirty-plus years. His fascination with the subject has already been demonstrated in his previous two books; 1999's 'Opening The Musical Box' and 2007's 'Genesis Revisited'.

He is also the editor of 'The Waiting Room' fanzine / website which is now in its 25th year. His expertise has also been called upon for several TV projects including the BBC Mastermind series and the Genesis Songbook documentary.

In between indulging his passion for all things "Genesis", the author finds time for his interest in many other kinds of music and is a regular concert goer. He also enjoys gardening, history, and many other sedentary occupations.

INDEX

The index does not include references to appendices. Album titles are in italics; song titles in quotation marks.

3 *(group)* 107
10CC 74
'21st Century Schizoid Man' 15
'A Dark Night In Toytown' 149, 159
'A Doll That's Made In Japan' 98
A Midsummer Night's Dream 113, 128, 129, 137, 152, 164
'A Tower Struck Down' 69, 73
A Trick Of The Tail 48, 49, 52
'A Vampyre With A Healthy Appetite' 117
Abacab 87, 91
'Ace Of Wands' 43
Acock, John 42, 73, 75
'After The Ordeal' 27, 31, 154
Ager, John 13
'All In A Mouse's Night' 54
'All Quiet On The Western Front' 77
'Always Somewhere Else' 93
'Anarchy In The UK' 75
Angus, Mick 82
'Another Brick In The Wall (Pt2)' 131
Around The World In Eighty Trains Tour 176
'A Place Called Freedom' 181
Arista Records 102, 104, 107
Asia 101-103, 105, 106
B & C Records 38
Bach, Johann Sebastian 20, 76, 110, 153, 158, 162, 167
'Toccata and Fugue in D Minor' 20
Bacon, Max 103, 107, 108
Banks, Tony 1, 17, 18, 20, 22, 24, 27, 31, 32, 47, 49-51, 53-55, 58, 59, 123, 125-127, 148
Barrett, Syd 12
'Bats In The Belfry' 14
'Battle Lines'126
Bay Of Kings 96, 97, 109, 121, 127, 164
Beck, Jeff 107
Beggs, Nick 49, 169, 171
Ben Hur 32
Berry, Robert 107
Bettencourt, Nuno 147
Beyond The Shrouded Horizon 180
Blackmore, Ritchie vii
'Blood On The Rooftops' 53, 149
Blues With A Feeling 119, 120
Blunstone, Colin 125
Blyth, Nick 36
Bolland, John 9
Bonamassa, Joe 183
Bonham, Jason 183
Borodin, Alexander 153
'Bouree' 110
'Brand New' 145
Brand X 40, 41, 47, 49, 54, 56, 57, 96
Brezhnev, Leonid 79
Bronz 103
Bruce, Jack 171
Bruford, Bill 48, 51, 86, 87, 113, 144, 160
Budis, Billy 78, 112, 114, 118, 122, 132, 133

Busby Babes 110
Busse, Hellen 34
Byron, Lord George 145
Cadbury, Dik 69, 73, 74, 76, 82, 83, 86, 87, 148
Callaghan, James 75
Calling All Stations 138
Camino Records 96, 112, 114, 127, 130, 141, 157, 161, 175
'Camino Royale' 91, 94
Canterbury Glass: Sacred Scenes And Characters 14, 15
'Can-Utility And The Coastliners' 24
Captain Kirk 9
Carlisle, Belinda 169
'Carnival In Trinidad' 76
Caroline Records 116
'Carpet Crawlers' 138
Carrack, Paul 122, 125
'Carry On Up The Vicarage' 62
'Cassandra' 131, 139
Castaneda, Carlos 94
Castle, Ben 138, 150
Castle, Roy 138
'Catwalk' 181
'Cavalcanti' 109
Cecil "Titch" 2
'Cedars Of Lebanon' 162
'Cell 151' 93, 94, 103
'Chaconne' 158
Charisma Records 16, 19, 21, 22, 26, 27, 37, 38, 43, 56, 61, 66, 75, 79, 81, 82, 84, 90, 91, 92, 94-96, 110, 117
Charone, Barbara 46
'Checking Out Of London' 150
Chris Squire's Swiss Choir 171, 177
Christie, Agatha 62
Chrysalis Records 38, 66, 95
Churchill, Winston 159
'Cinema Show' 27
Clabburn, Nick 150
Clapton, Eric 42
Clarke, Steve 64, 67
'Cleopatra's Needle' 71
Clifford, Matt 103
'Clocks- The Angel Of Mons' 71, 74, 76, 77
Colbeck, Julian 117, 124
Collins, Andi 62
Collins, Phil 1, 7, 17, 19, 22-25, 28, 30, 35, 40-43, 47-49, 51-54, 56, 62, 63, 82, 87, 101, 138
Collins, Simon 168
Colson, Gail 38
'Come Away' 146
Cook, Peter 160
Court, Ritchie 85
Crawford, Randy 63, 64, 66, 114
Cronk, Chas 89
Crosby, Stills And Nash 74
Crowley, Aleister 31
Cured 85-89, 157
Curved Air 19
'Dance On A Volcano' 49
'Dancing With The Moonlit Knight' 28
Darktown 131-133, 137, 138, 142-144, 169, 171

Index

Davis, Nick 66, 151, 168
Davis, Rose "Saxon" 2
Dawson, Charles 9
'Days Of Long Ago' 137
Debij, Louis 76
Debussy, Claude 135, 136
Decameron 73, 74, 76
Defector 79-82, 84, 137, 147, 156
Degenhardt, Hugo 117
Delius, Frederick 135
'Depth Charge' 182
Derek & Clive 160
Diamond, Jim 137
Dickens, Charles 9, 159
Dire Straits 73
Dirty & Beautiful 178
Disney 28
Dixon Of Dock Green 8
Dolby, Thomas 145
'Don't Fall Away From Me' 114
'Down Street' 159, 162, 169
Downes, Geoff 103, 106
Downey Jr., Robert 131
Driver, Dick 150, 170
Du Maurier, Daphne 145
'Duel' 98
Dylan, Bob 158
'Eleventh Earl Of Mar' 53, 54
ELP 31
'Emeralds And Ash' 172
'Emergent' 144
Emerson, Keith 107, 171
EMI Records 38, 128, 129, 151, 169
'Entangled' 49
'Enter The Night' 182
'Everyday' 71, 77
'Evil Jam' 32
'Face In The Mirror' 115
'Fast Forward To The Future' 168
Feedback 107, 108, 112, 114, 127, 131, 139, 141, 167
'Feel A Whole Lot Better' 12
Fenner, Ben 132, 141, 152, 156, 157
Fire & Ice 183
'Fire Island' 147
'Fire On The Moon' 170, 171
'Firth Of Fifth' 27, 31, 123, 169
Fitzpatrick, Gerard 'Ged' 70, 71, 78
Fleetwood Mac 11
'Fly On A Windshield' 32
Fog On The Tyne 21
'For Absent Friends' 122
Formby, George 77
'Fountain Of Salmacis' 20, 21, 25
'Four Winds Suite' 182
Foxhall, Betty 6
Foxhall, Peter 6
Foxtrot 22, 25, 26, 29, 43, 53, 124
Friday Rock Show 89
Friedkin, William 37
Friedman, Aron 118, 148
Friedman, Jeanne 148
From Genesis To Revelation 16
'Frozen Statues' 145

Fungus 76
Gabriel, Peter 1, 7, 16-18, 22, 23, 25-28, 30, 32-34, 36, 37, 40, 41, 46-51, 54, 57-59, 64, 81, 91, 93, 123, 127, 141, 145, 162, 173
Gallery Of Dreams 115
Gallo, Armando 40
Gandalf 115, 168
Garber-Schieb, Dagmar 156
Gas Tank 91, 92
Geffen Records 102
Genesis vii, 4, 15-19, 21-31, 33-35, 38, 40-47, 49, 51-59, 61, 62, 64-66, 68-70, 75, 76, 79, 81, 86, 87, 89, 91, 96-98, 101, 102, 105, 106, 108, 110, 111, 116, 118-127, 129, 130, 132, 133, 137-138, 140, 141, 145, 149, 151, 156, 160, 162, 163, 165, 167, 168, 170, 172, 173, 179
Genesis Archive 1967-75 123, 127, 138
Genesis Live 27, 124
Genesis Revisited 122, 123, 126, 133, 138, 144, 149
Genet, Jean 140
'Get 'Em Out By Friday' 22
Gibbon, Brian 37, 56-58, 61, 84, 86, 94-96, 101, 102
Gibson, Mel 131
Gilbert and Sullivan 21
Gilbert, Paul 147
'Give It Away' 93, 94
Glam Rock 29
Glennie, Evelyn 143, 145
'God Save The Queen' 3, 7
Gordian Knot 144
Gothic 145
Grace For Drowning 183
Gramy Records 157
Green, Peter 12
GTR 101-109, 116, 127, 139, 154, 176, 180
Guitar Noir 117, 119, 120, 127, 130, 131, 144, 148
Guitar Wars 147
Hackett, John 5-7, 9, 14-17, 24, 42-44, 47, 56, 66, 68, 70, 73, 74, 78, 80, 89, 96, 97, 109, 110, 121, 129, 135-137, 142, 147, 148, 150, 151, 154, 155, 157, 164, 168, 170
Hackett (Leaney), June 1-9, 15, 17, 26, 68, 142
Hackett, Oliver 34, 156
Hackett, Peter 1, 2, 5-8, 142, 157, 164
'Hairless Heart' 123, 148
Hamlet 162
Hammer House Of Horrors 25, 159
'Hammer In The Sand' 81, 149
Hampshire, Susan 26
Handmade Films 110
'Hands Of The Priestess' 43, 44, 155
'Harold The Barrel'
Harrison, George 110
Havens, Richie 65, 162, 168
'Heat Of The Moment' 126
Heather Brothers 14, 15
Hentschel, Dave 53
'Hercules Unchained' 81
'Here I Wait' 103
Hexameron 150
Hicks, Peter 69, 76, 77, 81, 82, 148, 150
'Hideaway' 42
Highly Strung 90, 91, 93, 99, 112, 157
'Hope I Don't Wake' 87, 89
'Hoping Love Will Last' 62, 63, 66, 114

321

'Horizons' 24, 110
Horizons 113
'How Can I' 63
Howe, Steve 101-108, 113
Hull, Alan 19
Hurst, Mike 95
Husband, Gary 168, 177, 183
'I Know What I Like' 27, 31, 69, 91, 123
'I Know Where I Am Going' 153
'I Talk To The Wind' 15, 126
'I Wanna Be Your Man' 167
Icarus Ascending 63, 65
'If You Can't Find Heaven' 149
'I'm Not In Love' 74
'Imagining' 103
'Insanity Lane' 81
'In That Quiet Earth' 118, 169
'In the Beached Margent Of The Sea' 129
'In The Court Of The Crimson King' 126
'India Rubber Man' 94
'Inside & Out' 54
Island Records 38
'It's Now Or Never' 82, 83
'It's Yourself' 51
'Jacuzzi' 80, 81
'Jane Austen's Door' 131, 133
'Janowska' 137
'Jekyll And Hyde' 103
Jethro Tull 31, 110, 121, 168
John, Elton 51
Jon Anderson 50, 51
Jones, Brian 167
Jones, John Paul 147, 170
Judges, Barbara (*first girlfriend*) 12, 13, 71, 133, 182
Kansas 74, 202
Kerouac, Jack 177
'Kim' 136
King Biscuit Flower Hour 26, 27, 105, 127
King Crimson 15-17, 51, 125, 126, 130, 178
King, Lauren 170
King, Roger 27, 132, 133, 138, 146, 147, 152, 154, 155, 160, 161, 169, 170, 172, 174, 177, 181
Koothume 14
Kovacs, Ferenc 170
Lamborghini Records 95, 96
'Land Of A Thousand Autumns' 65, 69, 113
Lane, Brian 101, 102, 105
'Last Train To Istanbul' 170, 171
Lawrence, D H 72
Lawrence, David 35, 36
'Leaving' 81
LeBoult, Dave 63
Led Zeppelin 32, 147, 168
Lehmann, Amanda 170
Lehmann-Hackett, Joanna 114, 132, 153, 164, 170, 178, 181
Lennon, John 29
'Let Me Count The Ways' 98
Level 42 168, 177
Levin, Tony 125
Lewis, C S 97
Life Of Brian 110
Lindisfarne 19, 21, 38
'Little America' 117

Little Feat 73
'Loch Lomond' 180
London Chamber Orchestra 165, 166
'Looking For Fantasy' 182
'Los Endos' 49, 51, 125, 126
Lost In Space 182
'Loving Cup' 12
'Lyra' 152
MacDonald, Ian 15, 126, 130
MacPhail, Richard 18
Magenta 178, 183
Magnus, Nick 67, 70-72, 74, 75, 80, 81, 87-89, 109, 148, 150
Manchester United 110
'Man In The Long Black Coat' 158
Manuka 148
'Marijuana Assassin Of Youth' 147
Marillion 89, 103, 139, 150
Mario Lanza 2
Marshall Jaruzelski 93
Martin, Sir George 181
'Match Of The Day' 54
'Matilda Smith-Williams Home For The Aged' 98
May, Brian107, 109, 114, 139
Mayall, John 11, 120
McGuinn, Roger 12
McIvor, Rob 98
Mclaughlin, John 168, 177
'Mechanical Bride' 145, 161
Menuhin, Sir Yehudi 97
Mercury Records 125
Metamorpheus 151-154, 157, 164, 170
Mickey Mouse 30
Miller, Robin 45
Milligan, Spike 180
Mitchell, Joni 63
Momentum 108, 109, 111, 127, 140, 164
Mona Lisa 124
Monty Python's Flying Circus 110, 160
Moon Records 92
Mooncrest Records 38
Moore, Dudley 160
Morrison, Jim 98
Mosley, Ian 89, 109, 139, 150
Mother's Finest 156
'Mountains Turned Into Clouds' 129
Mover, Jonathan 103, 106
'Mr Tambourine Man' 12
Music Week 79
Music Weekly 133
'Narnia' 69, 97
'Needles And Pins' 12
'Night Of Mystery' 103
'Nights In White Satin' 12
Nightwing 103
'Nomads' 170, 171
'Notre Dame Des Fleurs' 140
Nursery Cryme 20-22, 29
'O Sole Mio' 83
Oberstein, Maurice 37
O'Brien, Denis 110
'Oh Susannah' 3
Oldfield, Mike 103
Olivier, Lawrence 145, 159

Index

'On The Transylvanian Express' 159, 162
Once Above A Time 150
O'Toole, Gary 148, 149, 169
Our Dark Twin 114
Out Of The Tunnel's Mouth 171, 179
Outwitting Hitler 137, 154
'Overnight Sleeper' 89
Pack, Terry 70
Palladino, Pino 125
Palmer, Carl 107
Palmer, David 107, 121, 124, 168
Pastorius, Jaco 63
Paul Butterfield Blues Band 11, 147
Peal, Jerry 132
Pendragon 113
'Pharaoh's 32
Phillips, Anthony 1, 17, 20, 22, 28, 47, 49, 91, 108, 127, 170, 172
Phillips, Simon 107, 171, 181
'Picture Postcard' 87, 89
'Pigeons' 54
Pink Floyd 3, 11, 12, 121, 131, 168
Pinocchio 159
Platinum Collection 151
Please Don't Touch 56, 62, 64, 65, 67, 71, 85, 113, 147, 156, 168
'Please Don't Touch' 53
PolyGram Records 62, 75
Poor, Kim 85
Pop Deux 25
Porcupine Tree 177
Portrait Of A Young Forger 137
Postmankind 150
Potter, Dennis 131
'Prairie Angel' 177, 181
'Prayers And Dreams' 114
Prelude To Summer 168
Presley, Elvis vi, 12, 83
Pretzel, Marian 137
'Prize Fighters' 138
Queen 121, 139
Quiet World 14, 15, 126, 152
Quintessence 16
Rachmaninov, Sergei 129, 153
'Racing In A' 69
Racket Records 150
RAK Records 95
'Reach Out (Never Say No)' 103, 105
Reagan, Ronald 79
Real Madrid Football Club 57
'Rebecca' 145
Record Collector 151
Reed, Lou 29
Reed, Rob 178, 183
Remarque, Erich Maria 77
Renaissance 15
Rhythm Sticks Ensemble 143
Richard Tauber 2
'Riding The Colossus' 123, 182
'Riding The Scree' 123
'Ripples' 49
Rock 'N' Roll Prophet 92
Ronaldo, Cristiano 57

Rooney, Wayne 95
Royal Philharmonic Orchestra 123, 169
Russell, Ken 145
Rutherford, Mike 1, 17, 18, 22, 23, 25, 26, 41-43, 47, 49, 50, 54, 56, 58, 93, 108
Sachs, Leonard 145
'Sailing' 112
Saint Exupery, Anton 32, 145
Sarabande 13
Satie, Erik 135-138
Schertz, Craig 36
'Scotland The Brave' 3, 4
Seconds Out 59
Segovia, Andres 158, 165
Selling England By The Pound 29, 30, 40, 123
Sensational Alex Harvey Band 34
'Sentimental Institution' 81, 82, 159
Sergeant Pepper's Lonely Hearts Club Band 33
'Serpentine Song' 146
'Set Your Compass' 162, 169
Seven 31
Shah of Iran 79
Shakespeare, William 128
Shearer, John 86
Sketches Of Satie 138, 157
'Slot Machine' 108, 139
Smith, Fudge 113
Smith, Tony 37, 56, 91
Sonja Kristina 19
Sounds 46, 64, 98
Sounds Of The Seventies 21
Spalding, Phil 103, 106, 107
Spectral Mornings 67, 71, 72, 75, 77, 79, 111, 119, 147, 151, 156, 180
Spinal Tap 30
'Spoonful' 11
Squackett 176, 183
Squire, Chris 170, 171, 176, 177, 179, 181, 183
'Squonk' 50
'Stadiums Of The Damned' 139
'Stagnation' 16, 18, 21
'Starlight' 129
Start Records 96, 112
Steel Pier 13
Stewart, Rod 112
'Still Waters' 171
'Storm Chaser' 171
Stratton-Smith, Tony 30, 37, 3, 43, 50, 64, 79, 81, 85, 90 92, 94, 109, 110
Strauss, Johann 122
String Driven Thing 26, 38
Strong, Andrew 115
'Strutton Ground' 144
Sugar, Alan 13
'Supper's Ready' 22-24, 28, 35, 52, 110, 119
'Taking The Easy Way Out' 98
Tavener, Roger 115
'Tchaikovskys Piano Concerto in B Flat Minor' 4, 5, 152
Tears For Fears 176
'That Vast Life' 154
Thatcher, Margaret 79
'The Air Conditioned Nightmare' 89
'The Ballad Of The Decomposing Man' 77

'The Battle Of Epping Forest' 28
The Beach Boys 11
The Beatles vi, 9, 11, 51
The Byrds 11, 12
'The Carrot That Killed My Sister' 110
'The City In The Sea' 143
The Commitments 115
'The Devil Is An Englishman' 145, 159
The Diary Of Anne Frank 132
The Enid 70
'The Fundamentals Of Brainwashing' 161
The Geese & The Ghost 47, 49, 108
The Genesis Songbook 138
'The Golden Age Of Steam' 131, 132, 169
'The Gulf' 139
'The Hermit' 17, 42, 43, 46
'The Hunter' 105, 107, 108
'The Janitor' 76, 77
'The Knife' 91, 110
The Lamb Lies Down On Broadway 32, 33, 34, 40, 49, 145, 151, 162, 179, 180
'The Lamb Lies Down On Broadway' 123
The Lamb Lies Down On Broadway Tour 35
The Little Prince 32, 145
'The Lover's 43
'The Moon Under Water' 146
'The Musical Box' 20, 24, 34, 139
'The Office Party' 76
'The Red Flower Of Taichi Blooms Everywhere' 72, 155
'The Red Priest' 115
The Road 14
The Rolling Stones 11
The Royal Academy of Dramatic Art 161
The Sex Pistols 15
The Shadows 9, 167
'The Show' 80, 81
'The Silk Road' 145
The Singing Detective 131
The Springfields 95
'The Steppes' 68, 80, 169
The Strawbs 89
'The Stumble' 118
The Texas Chain Saw Massacre 25
'The Toast' 81
The Unauthorised Biography 114
'The Virgin And The Gypsy' 72
'The Waiting Room' 32, 35, 123
The Waiting Room magazine 122
The Wizard Of Oz 159
Then There Were Three 79
There Are Many Sides To The Night 121, 141
'There Are Many Sides To The Night' 117
This Island Earth 182
'This World' 145
Thomas, Dylan 72
Thompson, Chester 55, 63, 82, 125, 130
Thompson, Chris 107, 109, 139
Thompson, Dave 12
Three Sides Live 91
Till We Have Faces 97-101, 121, 145
Time Lapse 114
'Time Lapse At Milton Keynes' 110
'Time To Get Out' 80, 81

To Watch The Storms 144, 146, 147, 149
Townsend, Christine 170
Townsend, Rob 49, 169, 170
Trevor (childhood friend) 152
Trespass 16, 18, 20
Tribute 165, 167
'Turn Back Time' 88
Turn It On Again: The Hits 138
Turn It On Again Tour 162
'Turn This Island Earth' 180, 182
'Two Faces Of Cairo' 180, 181
Tyler, Bonnie 107, 109, 139
U-Catastrophe 168
Uncle Ron 2
Underworld 132
Underworld Orchestra 170
'Unquiet Slumbers For The Sleepers' 53
'Valley Of The Kings' 149
Van Der Graaf Generator 19, 21
Van Gogh, Vincent 65
Vari*lite 68
Velvet Afternoon 150
Video Sounds 89
Virgin Records 56, 77, 90, 112, 114, 127, 138
Vivaldi, Antonio 115, 165
'Voo do Coracao' 85
Voyage Of The Acolyte 17, 33, 45-48, 52, 58, 63, 112, 156
Wakeman, Rick 89, 91, 92, 113, 160
'Walking Away From Rainbows' 137
'Walking Through Walls' 93, 94
Walsh, Steve 65
Ward, Chris 137
Warren-Green, Nigel 45
'Watcher Of The Skies' 23, 26, 124, 182
Weather Report 55, 63, 125
Webb, Jim 66
Welch, Chris 44, 92
Wetton, John 125, 126, 177
'What's My Name' 98
'When The Heart Rules The Mind' 104, 108
Whicker, Alan 30
Wild Orchids 14, 161, 169
Williams, John 111
Wilson, Ray 138
Wilson, Steven 177, 178, 183
Wind & Wuthering 52, 54, 76, 163, 182
'Wind, Sand And Stars' 145
'Wolf Work' 14
World Of Music Arts And Dance (WOMAD) 91
'Wot Gorilla' 53
Wright, Ian 67
Yes 31, 51, 101, 103-106, 108, 171, 176
'You Can Still Get Through' 103, 105
'Your Own Special Way' 54, 122
Zappa, Frank 55, 125
Zomba Music 114
Zox And The Radar Boys 47

Also available from Wymer Publishing

WP
WYMER
PUBLISHING

BOOKS

The More Black than Purple Interviews (compiled and edited by Jerry Bloom)
For over ten years the Ritchie Blackmore magazine, More Black than Purple has featured many interviews within its pages. Wymer Publishing has collected the best and most riveting of these in to one book. There are also previously unpublished interviews, and additional, previously unpublished parts to some of the others.
Each interview also includes background information and some amusing tales surrounding the stories behind them. The book is bolstered further by a selection of b/w photos, many of which have never been published before.
• Includes interviews with: Don Airey° • Ritchie Blackmore (x3) • Graham Bonnet • Tony Carey* • Mark Clarke • Bob Daisley* • Glenn Hughes* • John McCoy° • Steve Morse • Cozy Powell.
° Part, previously unpublished * Previously unpublished
ISBN 978-0-9557542-0-3
Paperback 149x210mm, 180pp, 33 b/w images. **£14.99**

Rock Landmark's: Rainbow's Long Live Rock 'n' Roll (Jerry Bloom)
This book, the first in a series on landmark albums is an in-depth look at the classic Rainbow album 'Long Live Rock 'n' Roll'. The full story behind the making of the album; track by track analysis, recollections by the band and crew, all combined in a full colour CD size book designed to sit on your CD shelf alongside the album as its perfect companion.
ISBN 978-0-9557542-2-7
Paperback 125x140mm, 64pp (8 x colour). **£7.99**

Sketches Of Hackett - The authorised Steve Hackett biography (Alan Hewitt)
The first full and authorised biography of former Genesis guitarist Steve Hackett. Written by Alan Hewitt, a recognised authority on Genesis, whose previous writings include the critically acclaimed Genesis Revisited. Hewitt is also editor of the Genesis web fanzine The Waiting Room. First edition hardback plus 90 min DVD.
ISBN: 978-0-9557542-3-4
Hardback, 234 x 156 mm, 320pp (16 b/w, 43 colour images). **£24.95**

Rock Landmark's: Judas Priest's British Steel (Neil Daniels)
The second in our series of landmark albums looks at the sixth album by the British heavy metal band Judas Priest, recorded at Tittenhurst Park, home of former Beatle John Lennon. It is arguably the album that really defined heavy metal and is regarded as the band's seminal recording.
Written and researched by respected Judas Priest authority Neil Daniels, author of the first full Judas Priest biography, Defenders Of The Faith.
Foreword by Ron "Bumblefoot" Thal
ISBN 978-0-9557542-6-5
Paperback, 125x140mm, 72pp, including 17 b/w images. **£4.99**

A Hart Life- Deep Purple & Rainbow's tour manager's Life Story (Colin Hart)
Hart devoted over thirty years of his life to these great rock musicians. This is his story and indeed theirs. A tale of excess in terms of greed, petulance, anger and devotion. It is counter balanced by extremes of pure talent, showmanship and, of course musicianship. He was the constant 'man in the middle' through all of the break ups, make-ups and revolving door line-up changes. A story of two of the most innovative, often copied, rock bands; seen through the eyes, ears and emotions of their 'mother hen' as Jon Lord described him. He was their minder, chauffeur, carer, provider, protector, father confessor & confidant. In truth he is the only one who can tell this tale of both bands as he was the only one there on the road throughout the life of, not one, but both gigantic bands.
ISBN: 978-0-9557542-7-2
Hardback, 234 x 156 mm, 288pp (15 b/w, 73 colour images). **£19.95**

Hart's Life- 1971-2001 (Colin Hart)
Limited edition, deluxe slipcase version of 'A Hart Life' with bonus book, 'Hart's Life 1971-2001'; 80 pages of photos and memorabilia from Colin's collection including reproductions of tour itineraries, faxes and letters. Also includes a facsimile of the 'Burn' 1974 tour programme.
ISBN: 978-0-9557542-8-9 (plus ISBN: 978-0-9557542-7-2)
Paperback, 240 x 160 mm, 80pp (plus A Hart Life, 288pp). **£35.00**

Zermattitis: A Musician's Guide To Going Downhill Fast (Tony Ashton)
Written in 1991, Tony Ashton's incredible tales of his career with Ashton Gardner & Dyke, Paice Ashton & Lord, bankruptcy, skiing in Zermatt, Switzerland and many other adventures within the heady world of the music business are documented in this hilarious roller coaster of a ride. His writings have laid unpublished for twenty years, but in conjunction with Tony's wife this wonderful and unbelievably amusing story will now finally see the light of day. With a delightful and moving foreword from his dear friend Jon Lord, this is truly the last word from a man who sadly died in 2001, but whose life enriched so many. Although Tony wasn't a household name, within the entertainment world his numerous friends read like a who's who, including Dave Gilmour, John Entwistle, Eric Clapton and George Harrison.
Foreword by Jon Lord (endorsed by Billy Connolly and Ewan McGregor)
ISBN: 978-0-9557542-9-6
Hardback, 234 x 156 mm, 192pp (Limited edition with DVD)* **£24.95**
*The DVD contains previously unreleased Ashton Gardner & Dyke material including a live performance from the Gala Rose of Montreux in 1970; a rare promo film, and a performance of their biggest hit 'Resurrection Shuffle'. The DVD also includes Tony's song 'Big Freedom Dance' written about John Lennon and filmed at Air Studios by TV presenter Chris Evans.

Zappa The Hard Way (Andrew Greenaway)
With a foreword by Zappa's sister Candy, this book documents Zappa's last tour, which was full of bitterness, skulduggery and band mutiny on a scale that no one could imagine. Greenaway has interviewed the surviving band members and others associated with the tour to unravel the goings on behind the scenes that drove Zappa to call a halt to proceedings, despite the huge personal financial losses.
ISBN: 978-1-908724-00-7
Paperback, 234 x 156 mm, 250pp (37 b/w images). **£14.95**

Norfolk Rebels: Fire In The Veins (Joanna Lehmann-Hackett)
Stories of Norfolk's rebels, from Boudicea to the modern day. Many of them linked and weaved into the vibrant tapestry of rebellion that is our inheritance. With a foreword by one of Norfolk's most well-known modern day rebels Keith Skipper, and an introduction, beautifully written by Joanna's husband, former Genesis guitarist Steve Hackett, *this book depicts the many fine men and women of Norfolk who through the centuries have defended their ways, as only Norfolk people can.*
ISBN: 978-1-908724-02-1
Paperback, 275 x 191 mm, 100pp **£9.99**

All titles can be ordered online at our webstore- www.wymeruk.co.uk/Store
or from any decent retailer by quoting the relevant ISBN.

MAGAZINES

More Black than Purple
Established in 1996 this is the leading Ritchie Blackmore magazine, documenting the Man In Black's exploits with Rainbow, Deep Purple & Blackmore's Night.
ISSN 1478-2499
More info at: www.moreblackthanpurple.co.uk

Autumn Leaves
The official magazine of Mostly Autumn, established in 2000. This A4 magazine published twice a year is the official spokespiece for York's finest band, and arguably one of the greatest British bands to have emerged over the past decade.
ISSN: 1473-7817
More info at: www.autumn-leaves.co.uk

Available from Wymer Records

WR
Wymer Records

The Good Old Boys - Live At The Deep Purple Convention
Catalogue No: TSA1001. Released 13th July 2009
The Good Old Boys is: Nick Simper (Deep Purple); Richard Hudson (The Strawbs); Pete Parks (Warhorse); Simon Bishop (Renaissance) & Alan Barratt (Jo Jo Gunne).
Recorded live 3rd May 2008 at the Deep Purple Convention to celebrate the 40th Anniversary of the formation of Deep Purple. A unique performance that showcases their rock 'n' roll roots and musicianship. This 13-track CD includes a blistering version of Hush, the song that launched Deep Purple all those years ago. It also comes with a 12-page booklet with full band history, behind the scenes stories and previously unpublished photos from the actual performance and soundcheck.
Tracks: I'm Ready / A Fool For Your Stockings / My Way / Shakey Ground / Sleepwalk / Twenty Flight Rock / Somebody To Love / Don't Worry Baby / C'mon Everybody / Shakin' All Over / Oh Well / Hush / All My Rowdy Friends Are Comin' Over Tonight //

Nick Simper & Nasty Habits - The Deep Purple MKI Songbook
Catalogue No: TSA1002. Released: 16th August 2010
The Deep Purple MKI Songbook is up to date re-workings of Deep Purple songs from the first three albums performed by original Purple bassist Nick Simper with Austrian band, Nasty Habits. Powerful and hard-hitting arrangements of Deep Purple songs that have largely been over-looked since Deep Purple first had success in America with these songs. This initial release is a special limited edition (1,000 copies only) enhanced CD with bonus video footage including a Nick Simper interview.
Reissued as standard CD without video, 19th September 2011 (TSA1004)
Tracks: And The Address / The Painter / Mandrake Root / Emmaretta / Chasing Shadows / Lalena / Wring That Neck / The Bird Has Flown / Why Didn't Rosemary / Kentucky Woman / Hush //

Nick Simper & Nasty Habits - Roadhouse Blues
Catalogue No: NOR500. Released: 16th August 2010
Three track single with storming version of the Doors' Roadhouse Blues, plus The Painter and alternative version of Hush (unavailable elsewhere).

Liam Davison - A Treasure Of Well-Set Jewels
Catalogue No: TSA1003. Released: 21st March 2011
The debut solo album by Mostly Autumn guitarist Liam Davison is a cornucopia of aural delights. Guests include fellow Mostly Autumn band mates, Heather Findlay, Anne-Marie Helder, Iain Jennings and Gavin Griffiths plus Paul Teasdale (Breathing Space) and Simon Waggott. The first edition strictly limited to 1,000 copies, is an enhanced CD with bonus tracks and video footage.
Tracks: Ride The Seventh Wave / The Way We Were / Emerald Eternity / Eternally Yours / In To The Setting Sun / Once In A Lifetime / Heading Home / Picture Postcard / Bonus tracks: A Moment Of Silence / Immortalized // Bonus video: Liam's Treasure //

Amy Leeder - Fisticuffs With Cupid
Catalogue No: TSA1005. To be released: Late 2011
With this album we have broken with our own policy of only releasing works by established artists. Just 18, Amy has been writing songs since she was 14 and we believe she is destined for stardom. The maturity in her songs belie her age. Songs such as Chavs Of 2023 and Rough Around The Edges will resonate with people of all ages.

All titles can be ordered online at our webstore- www.wymeruk.co.uk/Store or from any decent retailer. Also visit Wymer Records at http://records.wymeruk.co.uk

Lightning Source UK Ltd.
Milton Keynes UK
UKOW06f0214220316

270627UK00001B/35/P